A QUEST FOR SOULS

*Comprising all the Sermons Preached and Prayers
Offered in a Series of Gospel Meetings,
Held in Fort Worth, Texas.*

BY

GEORGE W. TRUETT, D.D.

PASTOR, FIRST BAPTIST CHURCH, DALLAS, TEXAS

Schmul Publishers
Rare Reprint Specialists
Salem, Ohio 44460
1981

Printed by
Old Paths Tract Society, Inc.
Shoals, Indiana 47581

TABLE OF CONTENTS.

FOREWORD.

Ever since the appearance of the first book of sermons by Dr. Geo. W. Truett I have been urging him to permit the publication of other volumes, with the result that I am now able to present to the public this new and much larger book. His first book with the title, "We Would See Jesus, and Other Sermons," has passed into its twelfth edition, and is selling now very rapidly. That volume contained sermons he had preached in his own pulpit in Dallas, and a brief sketch of his life and labors. The present volume is unique in that it is made up of a series of revival sermons preached in Fort Worth, Texas, to which are added the prayers offered by the author of the sermons during the meeting. The setting of each sermon shows forth in the sermon itself. These meetings were held under the auspices of the Broadway and College Avenue Baptist Churches, of which Drs. Forrest Smith and C. V. Edwards are the respective and nobly useful pastors.

It is proper to say that these sermons were stenographically reported by Mr. J. A. Lord, and that they appear practically without revision. I have gone carefully over them every one, but I was not willing that any substantial changes should be made in any of them. While I have not been privileged to examine all the sermon books extant that have been printed in the English language, I can truthfully say that there has never to my knowledge been a book of sermons published that carried messages more vital and winsome than are herein found. In their strength, their earnestness, their eloquence, their pathos, and their compelling heart appeals, they carry a pungency and power far beyond any other sermonic classics it has been my privilege to read. These sermons do truly justify the title of this book—"A Quest For Souls."

The great preacher whose sermons here appear is so shrinking in his modesty, which ofttimes reaches the point of timidity concerning any work of his own, that it has been a Herculean task to secure his consent to the publication of the sermons that are here given. The reader will rejoice, I know, when I say that I have in hand sufficient material for several other books of sermons by Dr. Truett, but I am having trouble all along to secure his consent and co-operation in their publication. It is only when I have pressed upon his great heart the insistent appeal that he allow his sermons to be published for the good they will accomplish in "A Quest For Souls" that my pleadings have been crowned with success.

And now it is with joy unspeakable that these sermons are sent out to the world. That they will accomplish untold good I have not the slightest doubt; that they will be a guide and help to many a preacher as he projects his revival services I am absolutely sure; that they will lead countless souls to Christ throughout the coming years I confidently hope. As I have perused them one by one I have been more deeply impressed than I have ever been impressed by the reading of any sermonic literature. It seems to me that no soul can resist the power and tenderness of their touching appeal. May God bless these sermons as He blessed the great preacher in their delivery, and may His enduring grace abound to everyone who shall read them throughout all the coming years!

J. B. CRANFILL.

Dallas, Texas.

Introduction

A Quest for Souls by Dr. George W. Truett is one of the most significant books of evangelistic sermons ever printed. The volume comprises all the sermons preached and prayers offered in a series of Gospel meetings in Ft. Worth, Texas, 1917. The title of the book is precisely descriptive of the life-passion of the author who was pastor of the First Baptist Church of Dallas, Texas, for 47 years. The phrase most often employed to describe and explain Dr. Truett was "heart-power." It is compellingly evident in *A Quest for Souls* where earnestness, eloquence, pathos, and heart-moving appeals are combined in a burning focus to win people to Jesus Christ. One of Dr. Truett's contemporaries, Joseph Fort Newton, stated frankly, "as an example of evangelistic preaching at its highest it has no volume to surpass it."

Shortly after my conversion and call to the ministry I read this book. Outside the Bible, it was the most influential book in my ministry as a young preacher. Dr. Truett's use of Holy Scripture, for example, greatly impressed me. With the aid of a concordance, I traced the source of references and wrote them in the margins of the book, marked them in my Bible, and undertook to memorize most of them. Often I knelt in prayer with the Scriptures open before me and read one or more of Dr. Truett's prayers before an evangelistic service as an exercise in heart-preparation. My personal debt to this man of God is very great. I commend the volume to every preacher, and especially to young men who are in preparation for the ministry.

Dr. William M. Arnett
Frank Paul Morris Professor of Christian Doctrine
Asbury Theological Seminary
Wilmore, Kentucky

I

OPENING SERVICE, MONDAY EVENING, JUNE 11, 1917.*

UNOFFERED AND UNANSWERED PRAYER.

Text: "Ye have not, because ye ask not. Ye ask, and receive not, because ye ask amiss, that ye may consume it upon your lusts."—James 4: 2, 3.

Before the reading of the Scriptures, I would be allowed a moment in which to express my grateful joy for the privilege of spending several days, the Lord willing, in daily special meetings in this city. I am glad thus to be the guest of the two noble churches, the Broadway and College Avenue Churches, and to be associated with their cherished and nobly capable pastors, Drs. Smith and Edwards. Their generous words of welcome very deeply touch my heart.

Just one concern have I in coming for this brief visit—if I know my own heart—and that is to help the people, if I may and as I may, and so to witness for our great, good Master as shall be pleasing in His sight. I am not an evangelist, as these honored fellow-pastors have already explained to you, but a busy pastor, in a modern city like yours, dealing with the same problems as those with which your pastors and churches are constantly dealing. Right at the beginning of these services, I would cast myself upon your most prayerful sympathy. I would appeal to

---

* All of the evening services of this series of meetings were held in a tent provided by the Broadway and College Avenue Baptist Churches, and all of the noon services were held in the Auditorium of the Chamber of Commerce.

you in the beseeching words of the apostle: "I beseech
you, brethren, for the Lord Jesus Christ's sake, and for
the love of the Spirit, that ye strive together with me, in
your prayers to God for me." Together, let us continually
look to God for His guidance and blessing, in everything
that is to be said and done in these proposed meetings.
What do we here without God's light and leading? Oh,
may the Divine Spirit teach us and empower us, at every
step, as we address ourselves to these services! And He
will, if only our hearts, our motives, our attitude shall
be right in God's sight — if we shall be humble before
Him, and shall eschew every evil way, and shall desire
above all else to know and to do Christ's holy will.

> Assembled here with one accord,
> Calmly we wait thy promised grace,
> The purchased of our dying Lord,
> Come, Holy Ghost, and fill this place.

Let us deeply ponder these sayings: "Ye shall receive
power, after that the Holy Ghost is come upon you: and
ye shall be witnesses unto me, both in Jerusalem, and in
all Judea, and in Samaria, and unto the uttermost part of
the earth." "Not by might, nor by power, but by my
Spirit, saith the Lord of Hosts." "If ye then, being evil,
know how to give good gifts unto your children, how much
more shall your Heavenly Father give the Holy Spirit to
them that ask Him." Above all else, and without ceasing,
let us seek the guidance and power of the Holy Spirit,
both in the public services and in the private efforts that
are to be had, in everything pertaining to these meetings.

You are now ready, I trust, to give reverent heed to
the reading of two passages from the Holy Scriptures.
The first is from the eleventh chapter of Luke. I read
from the first to the fourteenth verse:

And it came to pass, that, as He was praying in a certain place, when He
ceased, one of His disciples said unto Him, Lord, teach us to pray, as John
also taught his disciples. And He said unto them, When ye pray, say, Our
Father which art in heaven, hallowed be thy name. Thy kingdom come. Thy
will be done, as in heaven, so in earth. Give us day by day our daily bread.
And forgive us our sins; for we also forgive every one that is indebted to us.
And lead us not into temptation, but deliver us from evil. And He said unto
them, Which of you shall have a friend, and shall go unto him at midnight, and
say unto him, Friend, lend me three loaves; for a friend of mine in his journey
is come to me and I have nothing to set before him? And he from within shall
answer and say, Trouble me not: the door is now shut, and my children are with
me in bed; I cannot rise and give thee. I say unto you, though he will not rise
and give him, because he is his friend, yet because of his importunity he
will rise and give him as many as he needeth. And I say unto you, Ask, and

it shall be given you; seek, and ye shall find; knock, and it shall be opened unto you; for every one that asketh receiveth; and he that seeketh findeth, and to him that knocketh it shall be opened. If a son shall ask bread of any of you that is a father, will he give him a stone? or if he ask a fish, will he for a fish give him a serpent? Or if he shall ask an egg, will he offer him a scorpion? If ye, then, being evil, know how to give good gifts unto your children: how much more shall your Heavenly Father give the Holy Spirit to them that ask Him?

The second passage is from the fifth chapter of James, from the sixteenth verse to the end of the chapter:

Confess your faults one to another, and pray one for another, that ye may be healed. The effectual fervent prayer of a righteous man availeth much. Elias was a man subject to like passions as we are, and he prayed earnestly that it might not rain: and it rained not on the earth by the space of three years and six months. And he prayed again, and the heaven gave rain, and the earth brought forth her fruit. Brethren, if any of you do err from the truth and one convert him; let him know, that he which converteth the sinner from the error of his way shall save a soul from death, and shall hide a multitude of sins.

In casting about for a suitable word to speak at the beginning of these meetings, it has seemed to me that I could bring no more appropriate and important word than to direct your attention to the vital subject of prayer. The text for the message this evening is in the fourth chapter of James, and these are its two statements: "Ye have not, because ye ask not. Ye ask and receive not, because ye ask amiss, that ye may consume it upon your lusts." The text says two things very pungently. The first is that we do not pray enough: "Ye have not, because ye ask not." The second is an explanation for unanswered prayer: "Ye ask and receive not, because ye ask amiss, that ye may consume it upon your lusts." The two sentences challenge our attention to unoffered prayer and unanswered prayer. Let us for a little while consider the teaching of the two sentences.

And first, we do not pray enough: "Ye have not, because ye ask not." There is no mistaking the meaning of this sentence. It plainly tells us: "Ye have not, because ye ask not." We talk much about "unanswered" prayer. This sentence reminds us of unoffered prayer. It tells us that blessings are denied us, just because we do not ask for them.

Let me ask you the pointed, personal question: How much do you pray? What must your answer be? How much have you prayed to-day? How much time and thought do you give to prayer? How real and vital is prayer in your daily life? Do you know what it is, like Daniel, to have fixed times and places for prayer? Do you know what it is to live in the atmosphere of prayer, that is, to carry out the Bible injunction to us, to "pray without ceasing?" Is it not just at this point that we fail, and fail more hurtfully than at any other point? I make bold to say that just at this point, preachers are prone to fail, as perhaps at no other point. A little while ago, I was with a group of preachers one day, as they discussed the perils and problems of the preacher. This man and that suggested this peril and that, concerning which the preacher needs ever to be on his guard. When it came my time to question the group of fellow-preachers, this was my question: "How much do you pray?" I may add that every man of us in that group felt conscience-stricken, as we searched our hearts on that question. We saw that we were busy here and there, finding texts, making sermons, arranging for funerals, for committees, for visits, for interviews, for exacting and endless tasks, but not a man of us had made enough of prayer. What is your answer, oh, fellow-Christian, to the question: "How much do you pray?" Think again and deeply of these words of Jesus: "But thou, when thou prayest, enter into thy closet, and when thou hast shut thy door, pray to thy Father which is in secret; and thy Father which seeth in secret shall reward thee openly." Do you have the daily habit of secret prayer? You cannot afford to neglect such habit. Such neglect cannot be atoned for, whatever else you may say or do. I press the question upon every Christian before me—has "the closet with the closed door" been neglected? That closet with the closed door is the trysting place of power. The men and women who go in there come out with faces that shine, with visions that inspire, and with power that shakes the world. Keep the path worn to that closet with the closed door, I pray you. It will give you to know that you are not alone, but that a Divine Presence goes before you and with you.

In view of the mighty significance of prayer, everywhere set out in the Bible, is it not indeed amazing that we do not pray more? Like a golden thread, the efficacy of prayer may be seen all through God's blessed Book. God's cry to mankind is for them to call unto Him, and He will answer them, and He will show them great and mighty things which they do not know. Listen to this exhortation from the Apostle James: "If any of you lack wisdom"—surely that is what we all do sorely lack—"let him ask of God, that giveth to all men liberally, and upbraideth not, and it shall be given him. But let him ask in faith, nothing wavering. For he that wavereth is like a wave of the sea, driven with the wind and tossed." And listen to this exhortation from Jesus: "And I say unto you, Ask, and it shall be given you; seek, and ye shall find; knock, and it shall be opened unto you. For every one that asketh, receiveth; and he that seeketh, findeth; and to him that knocketh, it shall be opened." Then, Jesus goes on to make an argument for prayer that is irresistibly appealing. Note His words: "If a son shall ask bread of any of you that is a father, will he give him a stone? Or if he ask a fish, will he for a fish give him a serpent? Or if he shall ask an egg, will he offer him a scorpion? If ye then, being evil, know how to give good gifts unto your children, how much more shall your Heavenly Father give the Holy Spirit to them that ask Him?"

It is needful for us to remember that prayer is far more than a privilege. To be sure, it is that—a privilege priceless, a privilege incomparable, one of the highest privileges that shall ever be allowed us. But it is far more than a privilege—it is a bounden obligation, it is an inescapable duty. See how Jesus puts it: "Men ought always to pray, and not to faint." Mark that word "ought." That means duty, that means obligation. Neglect of prayer is neglect of duty—a duty of measureless importance. Prayer brings results. Prayer wins victories. Prayer achieves. Thus does Paul put it: "Ye also helping together by prayer for us." A way whereby we may help everybody, and perhaps the best way, is to pray for them. Thus may we help people at any time and at all times. It is no wonder therefore that Paul said: "I exhort therefore, that, first of all, supplications, prayers, intercessions, and giving of thanks, be made for all men." It is, indeed, a culpable matter if we neglect to pray for the people, for all of them, for any of them. And therefore, are the words of the old prophet Samuel always pertinent: "Moreover, as for me, God forbid that I should sin against the Lord in ceasing to pray for you." Do not, I pray you, deal with this great question of prayer as wicked men dealt with it in Job's day. They asked contemptuously: "What profit should we have if we pray unto Him?" If such question is yours, face it frankly, probe it deeply; stop not your questioning until you are assured as to the efficacy that there is in prayer. There is profit in prayer. It is worth while to call on God. If some one suggests to you that prayer is irrational, in that it suggests interference with law, it is enough to know that God is above law, that law is His tool, that God's reserves of wisdom and power and mercy and love are utterly beyond our measuring. Prayer is not only to the last degree reasonable, but our very nature demands it. It was not strange that a very wicked man said to me, when his child lay ill at death's door: "Oh, man, if you know how to pray, for God's sake, pray for my child!" Yes, prayer is reasonable and necessary, and it is both a privilege and a duty of measureless moment in the earthly life.

Much is heard these days on the subject of conservation. The doctrine of waste is being everywhere reprobated. The doctrine of conservation is being everywhere emphasized. We are being told, and properly so, that our waters must be preserved against the times of drouth. We are properly exhorted to remember that not one tree or bush should be cut down without a good reason. It is urged that even the by-products everywhere shall be saved. And just now the whole land rings with the doctrine of the conservation of all foods, that the world crisis through which we are passing may be worthily met by all the people. Let this doctrine of conservation be applied in the realm of prayer. "Ye have not, because ye ask not." How different things might have been if we had prayed more! Take this incident: A young man in a certain city committed a crime that broke his parents' hearts and will give them sorrow to their grave. A pastor in that community went at once to see the parents, when he knew of their poignant sorrow. As best he could, he counselled and comforted them. At last the sorrowing mother said: "Oh, sir, if I had prayed as I ought, this tragedy would not have been!" The pastor begged her not thus to upbraid herself, for her sorrow was deep enough without such added self-reproaches. But the mother protested: "I used to pray every morning, noon and night, for this boy, but that was in the other years. In recent years, my feet have been caught in the meshes of worldliness, and the things of religion have been given no practical place in my life. I have forsaken the church and neglected to pray. Oh, sir, I am to blame for my boy's downfall! It would not have come if I had remembered to be faithful in prayer." Will you say that she did not speak the truth? Oh, how different things might have been if we had prayed as we ought! "One of my keenest regrets," said one of our noblest preachers as he lay dying, "is that I have not prayed more." And when another of our mightiest preachers was told that he had but one remaining hour on earth to live, he said: "Let me spend that hour in prayer." Oh, let us pray more! Let us pray more! "The effectual, fervent prayer of a righteous man availeth much." Trace that truth in the case of Elijah. Prayer is probably the highest, creative function in a human life. Tennyson was right when he said that more things are wrought by prayer than this world ever dreams. Let us pray more! Prayer is the first agency we are to employ for the promotion of any spiritual undertaking. Prayer links us with God. "Without me, ye can do nothing." "I can do all things through Christ who strengtheneth me." Prayer breaks down difficulties. It opens fast-closed doors. It calls forth workers: "Pray ye, therefore, the Lord of the harvest, that He will send forth laborers into His harvest." It releases energies for the spread of Christ's kingdom and truth, beyond anything any of us can ever measure. It brings victory in hours of crisis. It gives power to the preached gospel. All this was illustrated in the lives of Abraham, and Elijah, and Hezekiah, and Samuel, and David, and Paul, and Livingstone, and Luther, and a host of other heroes of faith, all of them overcoming by believing prayer. Oh, let us pray more!

The world is in supreme need of intercessory prayer.
Surely, that is awfully true in this hour of world crisis.
Every hour now is big with destiny. On every side the
people are trembling as they think of what shall be on
the morrow, and their hearts are failing and ready to
faint. Let us pray more! There is no voice to satisfy,
but the voice of God. That noble prophet of God, Dr.
Charles E. Jefferson, spoke faithfully, a little while ago,
when he called attention to the fact that in America, "we
have suffered a heart-breaking disillusionment. We ex-
pected great things from liberty and education, and have
found they are broken reeds. Neither our wealth nor our
science has given us either peace or joy. The four wiz-
ards—liberty and education and wealth and science—have
performed their mightiest miracles under our flag; but
they cannot do the one thing essential; they cannot keep
the conscience quick, or the soul alive to God. Our sins
are as scarlet and our vices are red like crimson, and we
need prophets to turn the nation to the God who will
abundantly pardon." Oh, let us pray more! Let us seek
to-day, and every day, to help all the people by prayer.
"Ye have not, because ye ask not."

Your earnest attention is now directed to the second
sentence in the text: "Ye ask and do not receive, because
ye ask amiss, that ye may consume it upon your lusts,"
or pleasures. In that one sentence is one clear explanation
why prayer is often unanswered. It proceeds from a wrong
motive. "Ye ask and receive not, because ye ask amiss,
that ye may consume it upon your pleasures." The point
is plain—the motive is wrong. God looks ever for the
motive, in all our thoughts and prayers and deeds. He
does not see as man sees. Man looks on the outward appearance. God looks on the heart. The motive oxygen-
izes everything in life. If the motive in prayer be wrong,
then the reason why the prayer is not answered is at once
explained. What is your motive when you ask God for
this or that? I press that question upon every life before
me.

A wrong spirit toward others is also an explanation for
unanswered prayer. I pause a moment, to press this point

upon your every conscience. I have come to the end of
twenty-four years as a pastor, and through all these years
I have increasingly seen how men and women are hindered in their religious lives, in their praying, in every
good way, by a wrong spirit toward others. In that model
prayer which Jesus gives for the guidance of His disciples,
that same point of our relations toward our fellows is mag-
nified: "Forgive us our sins, as we forgive—as we have
already forgiven—those who have sinned against us." Are
you wrong in your spirit toward others? Do you have
malice, ill will, resentment, unforgiveness in your heart
toward others? If so, your unanswered prayers are at
once explained. One said to me, after an extended conversation: "Why cannot I get right with God?" He had once
been a joyful, victorious Christian, but now he was un-
happy, and shorn of his spiritual power, and prayer was
no longer a blessed experience with him. "Why cannot
I get right with God?" he plaintively asked. Before the
conversation was ended, he dropped one sentence that indicated the depth of his ill will toward another. The
reason why he was not right with God was at once made
plain. Our lives are most intimately bound up with the
lives of our fellows. Our relations to our fellows cannot
be escaped, cannot be ignored. When we pray for our
daily bread, we are to include our fellows: "Give us this
day our daily bread." If we are wrong in our hearts toward our fellows, we need not expect an answer to our
prayers. How searching are these words of Jesus: "And
when ye stand praying, forgive, if ye have aught against
any: that your Father also who is in heaven may forgive
you your trespasses. But if ye do not forgive, neither will
your Father who is in heaven forgive your trespasses."

Still again, unanswered prayer may be explained by a
wrong life. The psalmist said: "If I regard iniquity in
my heart, the Lord will not hear me." Indeed, He cannot
afford to answer our prayers if we willingly harbor sin
in our lives, if we regard it, if we coddle and pamper it.
That would be to compromise God. The one thing that
separates between God and us is sin. He himself so tells
us. The one thing which God hates is sin. Our attitude

toward sin must be in harmony with His attitude. It is
the prayer of a righteous man—not an unrighteous man—
that avails much. The Bible teaches us that we may expect Him to hear and answer our prayers when we keep
His commandments and do those things that are pleasing
in His sight. Is your life right in God's sight? Are you
right before Him in the secrecy of your own heart? If
you are pampering some wrong thing in your life, although
others may not know of it, yet in such fact you have the
explanation for your unanswered prayers. Listen to these
words of the psalmist: "Delight thyself also in the Lord;
and He shall give thee the desires of thine heart." You
will not miss the point—your delight is to be in the Lord.
Listen to these words from Jesus: "If ye abide in me,
and my words abide in you, ye shall ask what ye will,
and it shall be done unto you." Face faithfully the question asked in the simple song, "Is thy heart right with
God?" and know, if it is not, you have at hand an explanation for unanswered prayer.

Lack of earnestness may be the explanation for unanswered prayer. If we dawdle and sleep and dream over
our prayers, certainly we may not hope that they shall be
answered. The men of the Bible who prayed acceptably
and victoriously were earnest men. Listen to Moses, the
valiant leader of Israel, as he prayed for that neglecting,
backslidden, disobedient people: "Oh, this people have
sinned a great sin, and have made them gods of gold. Yet
now, if thou wilt forgive their sin—; and if not, blot me,
I pray thee, out of thy book which thou hast written." O
how terribly in earnest was Moses, as thus he prayed. He
was, indeed, a very Hercules in prayer. And take the case
of Paul. Listen to his pleadings: "I say the truth in
Christ, I lie not, my conscience also bearing me witness
in the Holy Ghost, that I have great heaviness and continual sorrow in my heart, for I could wish that myself
were accursed from Christ, for my brethren, my kinsmen
according to the flesh." When a man feels like that, is
willing to be accursed from Christ, that the people about
him may be saved, is it any wonder that such man scaled
the heavenlies when he prayed? Listen to Jacob at the

brook Jabbok, as he pleads: "I will not let thee go, except thou bless me." It is not at all surprising that a little later, Jacob is told: "Thy name shall be called no more Jacob, but Israel: for as a prince hast thou power with God and with men, and hast prevailed." Listen to John Knox, as he prays for Scotland: "Oh, God, give me Scotland, or I die!" Is it any wonder that hapless Queen Mary said: "I fear the prayers of John Knox more than I fear an army of ten thousand men." Oh, my fellow-Christians, let us be deeply in earnest when we come to the throne of grace to make known our requests unto God.

Once again, our prayers are often not answered, because we do not expect them to be—because of a lack of faith. Faith is just taking God at His word. Often we do not take Him at His word. We halt and higgle over His word, and we refuse to accept it and to act upon it. Jesus pointedly says to us: "According to your faith, so be it unto you." And again: "If thou canst believe, all things are possible to him that believeth." And again: "If two of you shall agree on earth, as touching anything that they shall ask, it shall be done for them of my Father who is in heaven." What a marvelous statement that is! How it challenges us to be united in prayer! Do we believe this great promise? Will we plead it in prayer, and claim it?

Years ago, when I was preaching for several days in a Southern city, I preached one morning on the text: "But without faith, it is impossible to please Him: for he that cometh to God must believe that He is, and that He is a rewarder of them that diligently seek Him." At the close of the service, an elderly woman—I should say she was three score and ten years of age — rose up and said: "Preacher, do you believe what you have preached today?" And I replied: "Indeed, I do, for I have proclaimed God's Word, which Word I surely believe." "Very well," she said, "I am so glad that you believe it. I am looking for some one who believes it. You quoted in your sermon, just now, that glorious promise from Jesus: 'If two of you shall agree on earth, as touching anything that they shall ask, it shall be done for them of my Father who is

in heaven'—do you believe that promise, and will you
plead it with me?" Before I answered, she spoke again:
"It is like this: My husband is, and has long been, a
captain on the boat that sails the river. He never goes
to church, and is exceedingly wicked, and now he is growing old. If you will join me in pleading that promise about
two agreeing, we will claim him for God and salvation and
heaven—will you join me?" And there I stood, thinking,
wondering, searching my heart. Did I really believe that
promise? Was I willing to plead it then and there, in the
case just named? And while I stood thus thinking and
hesitating, a plainly dressed man, a blacksmith, rose up
and said: "Auntie, I will join you in pleading that promise." And there, before us all, he walked over to her and
humbly said: "Let us plead it now." They knelt in prayer, and he began to pray. It was as simple as a little child
talking to its mother. He reminded the good Savior of
the promise He had made, and insisted that they twain,
there kneeling, accepted that promise, claimed it, pleaded
it as they asked Him to save the aged, sinful sailor. It
was all over in a few moments. The simplicity and the
pathos of it were indescribable. The people were dismissed. The day passed and the people gathered for the
evening service. The preacher stood up to preach, and
there before him came the old lady just described, and
with her came a white-haired old man. At the close of
the sermon, the preacher asked those who desired to be
Christians to come to the front pews for counsel and
prayer, while the people sang. The old man was on his
feet immediately, and was coming toward the front. He
was talked with and prayed for that night, but all seemed
utter darkness to him. Over there, to the right and the
left, sat the aged wife and the middle-aged blacksmith,
with faces shining like the morning. They had a secret
the rest of us did not have. They had pleaded and were
claiming the promise of Jesus, and their hearts knew that
all was well. The night service was ended, and the people
went their ways. The old man shambled out into the darkness of the night, his soul darker even than the night. The
next morning came, and the people were gathering for the

service. The preacher was alone in the study, behind the
pulpit, trying to make ready for the service. There was
a knock on the outer door of the study. The door was
opened, and there stood the old man. And thus he began:
"Sir, I can't wait for your sermon this morning. Tell me
now, if you know, how I can be saved." And there in that
study, before the service, he accepted the Lord Jesus
Christ as his Savior, and at the morning service, an hour
later, gave a testimony for Christ, the sweetness and glory
of which will outlast the stars. What is there remarkable
about this? Nothing at all, when you remember that two
friends of Jesus, honestly and actually pleaded and claimed
the promise of Jesus.

Oh, why is that we halt in the acceptance of the sure
promises of our dear Savior? Why are we so fearful and
the possessors of such feeble faith? May God forgive us,
even to-night and now, for our pitiful, miserable unbelief!

This other word, I would briefly say, in explantion of
unanswered prayer—and that is, our prayers are often unanswered because they lack submission to the will of God.
"Thy will be done," must be in every acceptable, victorious prayer. His will is always righteous and best, and
we are to be in harmony with that will. Above all else,
let us seek to know God's will, and ever let us pray: "Nevertheless, not my will, but thine be done."

Long enough have I spoken to you. Let us take the
two thoughts of the text, and hide them in our hearts.
Let us pray more, oh, let us pray more! To the last degree possible, let us be worthy intercessors, seeking thus
to help continually our needy, sinning, suffering world.
Let us pray more! "Ye have not, because ye ask not." And
let us seek ever to pray in that way, and with that motive
and spirit, that shall be well pleasing in God's sight. Lord,
teach us to pray! And may all the services of this proposed series of meetings be enveloped in humble, consistent, believing, victorious prayer. Let me give you a promise that tells us how this meeting may be made glorious.
It is from the seventh chapter of II Chronicles: "If my
people, who are called by my name, shall humble themselves, and pray, and seek my face, and turn from their

wicked ways; then will I hear from heaven, and will forgive their sin, and will heal their land." Again and again,
let us cry, "Lord, teach us to pray!"

THE CLOSING PRAYER.

Our holy, Heavenly Father, teach us to pray. Little do we know of this
blessed, glorious privilege and duty, and poor has been our behavior with reference to prayer. Forgive us, we pray thee, for our neglect, our ignorance, and
our disobedience. Summon us to prayer, O our God, and let us refuse to be dis-
mayed, whatever our difficulties and experiences, since God delights to hear and
answer prayer. Give us much of thy grace and light, that we may know how
to pray as we should. And in all the services of these proposed meetings, go
thou with us, we humbly pray thee, and so give us thy counsel and power, that
we shall wholly do thy will in all the important days that are just before us.
We ask it in Jesus' name. Amen.

II

NOON SERVICE, JUNE 12, 1917.

WHAT TO DO WITH LIFE'S BURDENS.

Text: "For every man shall bear his own burden." * * * "Bear ye one another's burdens, and so fulfill the law of Christ." * * * "Cast thy burden upon the Lord, and He shall sustain thee."—Gal. 6:5; 6:2; Psa. 55:22.

Distinct pleasure is in my heart that I am allowed to greet the busy men and women before me for this brief midday service. As has already been announced, these midday services are to be begun exactly at twelve o'clock, and are to be closed at ten minutes before one o'clock. The one design of these services is to help the busy men and women in the heart of the city at the noonday hour by calling their attention daily to those simple, vital things which make for our highest good.

In coming to speak at this first midday service, it has seemed to me that I could bring no more practical word than to talk to you about Life's Burdens. It is the lot of men and women everywhere to have burdens. There is an old Spanish proverb which points a familiar lesson: "No home is there anywhere that does not sooner or later have its hush." The proverb points its own lesson. You cannot mistake it. Sooner or later all men and women have their burdens.

Many of the burdens of men and women may be seen. The deepest and most poignant burdens are not seen. If we knew what fierce battles some men and women were fighting, and what weighty burdens they were carrying, it would teach us lessons of restraint and charity and content-

15

ment beyond any that we have ever known. That very fact should give us pause and caution, even to a marked degree.

The Bible has three words to say about our burdens. Notice them: "Every man shall bear his own burden." "Bear ye one another's burdens, and thus fulfill the law of Christ." "Cast thy burden upon the Lord, and He shall sustain thee." That is all that the Bible says about our burdens, but those three sentences say all that is to be said.

Now, for a little while, let us glance at what the Bible says in its threefold message about our burdens. First, our burdens are non-transferable: "Every man shall bear his own burden." Every life is isolated and separated and segregated from every other life. To a remarkable degree every life is lived alone. You were born into the world alone, and when you shall leave it, no matter where or how, you shall go into the valley of the shadow alone, and between your birth and your death, the cradle and the grave, life is very largely lived alone. No man can perform your duty for you. "To every man his work," the Master teaches us. Not "to every man *a* work," nor "to every man *some* work," but "to every man *his* work." There is a program for you to carry out. There is a niche for you to fill. There is a task for you to face. There is a life for you to live, separated from every other in all the world. Nobody can repent of sin for you, nor can anybody believe on Christ for you, nor can any one make answer at the judgment bar of God for you. We must every one give an account of himself to God.

And that means that nobody is to get lost in the crowd. There is to be no hiding behind others, or behind organizations. Is there any danger more outstanding, in these modern times, than the danger that the individual shall get lost in the crowd? God sees the individual, and the individual must never get lost in the crowd. His eye is upon the one, and the one is to see to it, whatever others may or may not do, that he or she walks that path before the face of God that shall have the favor of God. Whether anybody else does right or not, you must. Whether any-

body else is true or not, you must be. Did you ever read
the diary of Jonathan Edwards? If so, you must have been
greatly impressed with his words—I do not attempt to
quote them verbally—where he penned these two resolu-
tions: "Resolved, first, that every man should do right,
whatever it costs. Resolved, secondly, whether any other
man does right or not, I will, so help me God." That is
the supreme business of every human being, for "every one
shall bear his own burden."

And then the Bible points a second great word for us
concerning our burdens: "Bear ye one another's burdens,
and so fulfill the law of Christ," which means that our burdens are ofttimes community burdens, social burdens, burdens to be shared with others.   Others are to share their
burdens with us. "Bear ye one another's burdens, and thus
fulfill the law of Christ." It is always interesting and
proper to note words of Scripture in their setting. Many
of the fads and fancies and hurtful heresies in the world
have come because the Scriptures have been wrested from
their proper setting. We need always to look at the Scriptures in their setting, and let the Scriptures say what they
meant to say, and mean what they are designed to mean.
Here in this Scripture, where we are told to bear one another's burdens, immediately preceding it, a great verse
stands out for our best consideration. Note it: "Brethren,
if a man be overtaken in a fault, ye who are spiritual restore
such a one, in the spirit of meekness, considering thyself,
lest thou also be tempted." Bear ye, in this way, one another's burdens, the apostle is saying, and so fulfill the law
of Christ.

The primary reference there to this great matter of
mutual burden bearing is to the fact that we should seek
to help those about us who have gone astray. And just
here is the most neglected task of all. Here are we plainly
summoned to go out and give ourselves, without stint or
reserve, to recover men and women who are going wrong.
"If any man be overtaken in a fault," help him. Criticise
him? Denounce him? Throw stones at him? Talk about
him? Nay, verily. "If any man be overtaken in a fault,

ye who are spiritual, restore such a one in the spirit of meekness, considering thyself, lest thou also be tempted."

Even as I call your attention to this point of mutual burden bearing, especially with regard to those that have got out of the right path and are going the wrong path, your minds are now alertly busy, and you call to your remembrance certain men and women who once began well, but who have been bewitched away by some influence from the right path and are going the wrong path. Go after those, to help them. That is what our Scripture says. Just there, my fellow-men, is the most neglected task of all. When men go astray and keep going astray, we are all too willing, too content, to allow them to go on, whereas we are summoned here, by this Scripture, and by the whole message of the gospel of grace, to go out and seek to reclaim, to recover, to restore, everybody that is going wrong.

I am thinking now of a young fellow gloriously converted in my city some time ago, who beforehand had had the miserable habit of swearing—an inexcusable habit, without any defense at all for any man—and yet that habit had such a hold upon him that it seemed second nature to him to swear. By and by he was graciously converted under the call of Christ, and then he talked with the minister, and said: "I think I had better wait for six months or twelve, until I can prove to myself clearly whether I can keep from swearing, before I shall join the church." But the minister said to him: "Not at all. The church is not an aggregation of perfect people. No one is perfect. We are all sinners, saved by grace. You come right on, if you have put your trust in Christ as your personal Savior, and take your place in the army of God, with the rest of the soldiers, and help them, and let them help you." And so he did, and for months there was a devotion about him to Christ's cause that, to the last degree, cheered all our hearts. But after some months the minister missed him from the midweek prayer-meeting, and even from the Sunday services, and he said to his men: "Where is Charles?" And they said: "Haven't you heard?" The minister said: "Not at all. What has happened?" And they said: "Charles was provoked a little while ago to anger in a controversy with one of our citizens, and the hot words came, and the blasphemous sentences fell from his lips, and he is all filled with shame and humiliation, and he has not come to church any more since." "Now," said the minister to the men, "find him. He must be recovered, nor must you cease until he is recovered." But the weeks went by, and he was not recovered, and one day, as the minister went down a certain street, right there before him he saw Charles coming, and Charles saw the minister, and turned quickly down an alley, but the minister said: "Wait a minute, Charles; wait a minute!" And he waited, quite hesitatingly, and the minister said: "Why are you dodging me, Charles?" And with face averted, and by this time covered with tears, he said: "You know. They have told you. Nor is that all. I told you I had better wait a few months before I joined the church. I told you of my frailty, of my weakness. But now I am in the church, and the other day the old anger came back, and I used hot, blasphemous words. I did not sleep at all that night. My pillow was wet with my tears. All through the night I talked with God, and God spoke forgiveness to me, and I went back the next morning and asked the man to forgive me, and he cried with me, though he is not a church man, and he forgave me." "Now," I said, "Charles, would you come down to the prayer-meeting and say about that much to us?" And he said: "If you think I ought, I will." So he was at the prayer-meeting Wednesday night, and when the place was made for him, he was on his feet, and timidly told about what I have just described. You should have seen the men and women gather around him. You should have seen them as they greeted him, and as they sobbed with him, and as they said: "Charles, we will help you. We will forgive you, and you will help us." And he was on the right road again! That is what this Scripture talks about. Whenever anybody goes astray, "you who are spiritual restore such a one in the spirit of meekness, considering thyself, lest thou also be tempted. In this way bear ye one another's burdens, and so fulfill the law of Christ."

But this Scripture has a broader meaning than that. We are not only to make it a point to do our best to recover people who have gone wrong and are going wrong, but we are to share burdens with people all about us, whatever their burdens are. There are the burdens of the sorrowing. Even as I speak, your mind is busy, and you call up some family wrapped about this very midday with great sorrow, or you call up some man or woman about whom the shadows hang with fearful weight this very hour. Go and share such one's sorrow, without delay. Nor is that all. All about us are people with their weighty burdens, burdens terrific, heavy burdens. Go to them and share with them these weighty burdens. There is the teacher. There is the preacher. There is the ruler in the affairs of civil government. Weighty burdens are on their heads and hearts. Do not make it hard for those in places of public trust and responsibility to serve and to lead. Make it easy, with the right sort of co-operation and the right sort of burden bearing.

How may we all help people? "Bear ye one another's burdens, and so fulfill the law of Christ." The most beautiful portrait we have of Jesus is given here in the gospels, in five little words: "He went about doing good." There is the most beautiful portrait ever drawn of Jesus. How may we all help people all about us? First of all, we may help them by living the right kind of lives ourselves. The highest contribution you will ever offer this community and this world is to offer it the right kind of a life. Gladstone never tired of saying: "One example is worth a thousand arguments." One Savonarola turned the tides of wicked Florence. One Aristides, the just man, perceptibly lifted Athens higher. Ten righteous men would have saved Sodom. The people of Constantinople said about John Chrysostom, the golden-mouthed: "It were better for the sun to cease his shining than for John Chrysostom to cease his preaching." The best contribution that you can ever offer to this weary, needy world is to offer it the right kind of a life.

How may we all help people? We are to make it a point constantly—constantly—to believe in people. Every one of us needs the enthusiasm of Jesus, our great Master, for humanity. He came to a man hated by his own race, Matthew, the tax-gatherer, sitting there at the poll tax booth, and He said to him: "Matthew, follow me, and I will make a good man out of you," and from that hour Matthew followed Him. He came to another hated tax-gatherer, Zaccheus, the little man who climbed up in the tree, and pausing under that tree, the Master said: "Come down out of the tree. I will go home with you to-day." And from that hour Zaccheus followed Jesus, a faithful friend of that great Master. Like Jesus, we are to believe in people. I think nothing of that system of espionage which is forever spying out people, to catch up with their weaknesses and their faults. We are to have, like Jesus, great passion and compassion and brotherliness and sympathy for a needy world, and we are to believe in people. A little girl who waited upon her semi-invalid mother, day by day going across the street to get a pail of milk, was crossing the street one day, and the passing car frightened her, and she tripped and fell, and the milk was gone, and a big man laughed cruelly—oh, how could he have done it!—and then he said to the little child, in her dismay: "What a great beating mother will give you when you get home!" And that brought the little girl to self-control, and she said: "Nothing of the sort, sir! My mamma always believes in giving me another chance." So our Master believes in giving men another chance, and we are to have His temper and walk in His footsteps, always.

Nor is that all. We are to make it a point constantly to encourage people. Oh, my brother men, it is a sin for any man on the earth to be a miserable discourager! Discouragement is a sin. Men and women are fighting a big battle, and they do not need weights put on them by discouragement. They need wings put on them, that they may rise and fly, as they grapple with the big tasks that daily confront them. Bobbie Burns, in the heyday of his great power as a writer, saw a little boy following him around in a certain community, and turning to the little boy, Bobbie Burns said to him: "Walter, what do you wish?" And little Walter timidly said: "Oh, I wish that some day

I might be a great writer like you, and have people talking about me like they talk about you." And Bobbie Burns, that great-hearted man, stopped and put his hand on the head of little Walter, and spoke words of inspiration and cheer, and said: "You can be a great writer some day, Walter, and you will be." That little boy was Sir Walter Scott, and to the day of Sir Walter's death, he could never speak of Bobbie Burns except with a sob of gratitude, for Burns spoke the word in season to the weary heart of a little boy.

Yonder was a fire in the big city, and the firemen flung their ladders together, and went up in their brave fashion to the topmost story to rescue the people in such peril, and one after another was rescued by the brave fire laddies. All had been rescued, it seemed. No! Yonder is a white face at that upper window, and they wrapped something about one of the fire laddies, and breasting the fierce flames, he went again to that window, and put the robe around the little woman and started down, but they saw him tremble as the fire raged around him, and it seemed that he would fall with his precious burden, but the fire chief cried to his men: "Cheer him, boys! Cheer him, boys!" And they cheered him, cheer after cheer, and heart came back, and he came down, with the precious life saved. Oh, you and I are to give our lives to cheering a needy world! Ponder this beautiful sentence from Isaiah: "They helped every one his neighbor; and every one said to his brother, Be of good courage."

Now there is one more word to say, and it is the best of all: "Cast thy burden upon the Lord, and He shall sustain thee." If you will read this 55th Psalm, from which that great promise is taken, you will find that the utterer of such promise wanted to flee away. "Oh, that I had wings like a dove," he cried, "for then would I fly away, and be at rest." The burdens were so weighty, the awful conflict was so fiery: "I will just leave it all. I will just throw this thing down, and I will get away. I will flee. I will run. I will give it up. I will not stay with it." Who has not felt that? Who has not felt — "I have had as much of this as I can bear. I will get out of it. I will run. I will fly. I will get away." But that would not win, for when you got away out there in the wilderness, you would have your burden yet, for you have your memory, you have your personality, you have yourself. You cannot thus get away from life's burdens. There is the burden of perplexity for you, no matter where you go; and there is the burden of the consciousness of neglected duty, no matter where you go; and there is the burden of some sin athwart your conscience, like some ghastly cancer, no matter where you go. What are you to do with these burdens of perplexity and neglected duty and sins? What are you to do? Where are you to go? There is only one place. "Cast thy burden upon the Lord, and He shall sustain thee."

How will He sustain you? He will do it in one of two ways. He may take the burden away. Sometimes He does, blessed be His name! You have come sometimes, as have I, into that deep garden of Gethsemane, when that black Friday broke all our plans, and in our dire desperation we have prayed, with the Master: "If it be possible, let this cup pass from me. If it be possible, forbid that I should drink this bitter cup that is being put to my lips." And the cup was taken away, and we did not have to drink it at all. Time and again you have prayed, as you faced a certain great burden, that God would remove it, and He heard, and the burden was taken away. But suppose it is not? And sometimes it is not. Ofttimes it is not. We pray, but there is the burden yet. Now, what if God shall not take the burden away? Then He has promised to come in with divine re-enforcement and help us to bear that burden and be victor, no matter how weighty it is, nor how fiery in its biting power in our life. Paul had re-enforcement. He had a thorn in the flesh. I do not know what it was, nor do you, but it was something very trying. If ever there was a genuine man in the world, it was the Apostle Paul. He was the highest product that Christianity has ever produced. This same man said: "There was given to me a thorn in the flesh." He called it the "messenger of Satan," sent to buffet him, and he said: "I went like the Master in the garden, and thrice did I beseech the

Lord that He would take that thorn away, but He did not take it away at all. He left it, to goad me and harass me and burn me and pain me. But He said to me: 'Paul, Paul, my grace is sufficient for you'"—not "shall be," but "is." "My grace is sufficient for you," here and now, ever-present and never-failing. No matter where you go, nor what shall come, "my grace is sufficient for you." And from that time on you have no more record of Paul's praying that that thorn might be taken away. From that time Paul said: "Most gladly, therefore, will I rather glory in my thorn, glory in my infirmities, that the power of Christ may rest upon me." Said Paul: "I had rather have my thorn in the flesh, which is ever present with me, and have God's added grace, than to be without that thorn and miss that added grace and light and love from God." Now, doesn't that explain much? He will give you increased grace, grace upon grace, if He does not take the burden away when you call to Him to take such burden away.

Oh, my men and women, with your burdens, whatever they are, here is the way out: "Cast thy burden upon the Lord, and He shall sustain thee." Seek not to bear it alone. Seek not to fight out your battle alone. Seek not to solve that perplexity alone. Seek not to stem that flood alone. Seek not to go through that long and bitter night alone. Take the Master into your counsels and into your plans, and turn yourself over to Him, with your burden, whatever it is, and He shall sustain you. One of the great words in the Bible is that fine word "sustain." He shall sustain you. No matter what your burden is—I dare to say it—no matter what your burden is, you shall get sustaining strength from God, and your heart shall surely know it, if you will only cast yourself honestly upon Him.

Have you learned the secret of peace? In a world of burden and battle and perplexity and clouds and shadows and night and death, have you learned the secret of peace? You will never know it until you learn how to cast your burden upon the Lord. I am thinking now of a strong man yonder in the city, whose beautiful wife was taken from him after an illness of just a few hours, and the man was left with a little flaxen-haired girl, of some four or five summers. The body was carried out to the cemetery, where was a simple service, and every heart was broken, the grief was so appalling. And then when the service was over, neighbors gathered around the big man and said to him: "You must come, with this little baby girl, and stay with us for several days. You must not go back to that home now." And the broken-hearted man said: "Yes, I must go right back to the same place where she was, to the room from which she went away, and I must fight it out with this baby right there," and back they went. He told about it all the next day. The baby was late and long going to sleep. Oh, was there ever anything more pathetic than the cry of a bairn for the little mother that will never come back again? Long and late the little one, in the crib there by the bed, sobbed, because she could not go to sleep, and the big man reached his hand over to the crib and petted her and mothered her, as best he could, and after awhile the little girl, out of sorrow for her father, stopped her crying—just out of sorrow for him. And in the darkness of that quiet time the big man looked through the darkness to God, and said: "I trust you, but, oh, it is as dark as midnight." And then the little girl started up her sobbing again, and the father said: "Why, papa thought you were asleep, baby." And she said: "Papa, I did try. I was sorry for you. I did try, but I could not go to sleep, papa." And then she said: "Papa, did you ever know it to be so dark? Why, papa, I cannot even see you, it is so dark." And then, sobbing, the little thing said: "But, papa, you love me, if it is dark, don't you? You love me, if I don't see you, don't you, papa?" You know what he did. He reached across with those big hands and took the little girl out of her crib, and brought her over on his big heart, and mothered her, until at last, sobbing, the little thing fell to sleep, and then when she was asleep, he took his baby's cry to him, and passed it up to God, and said: "Father, it is as dark as midnight. I cannot see at all. But you love me, if it is dark, don't you? I will trust you, though you slay me. With my baby, and my grief, and my utter desolation, I will turn my case over to God." And then the darkness was like unto the morning! God always comes to people who trust Him. Have you learned the secret of peace? Henry Van Dyke points the secret in his poem on "Peace." Mark the words:

> With eager heart, and will on fire,
> I sought to win my great desire.
> "Peace shall be mine," I said. But life
> Grew bitter in the endless strife.
>
> My soul was weary, and my pride
> Was wounded deep. To heaven I cried:
> "God give me peace, or I must die."
> The dumb stars glittered no reply.
>
> Broken at last, I bowed my head,
> Forgetting all myself, and said:
> "Whatever comes, His will be done."
> And in that moment, peace was won.

Whatever your burdens—of sin, or grief, or doubt, or disappointment, or regret, or remorse, or conscious fear and failure—dare to cast your burden, yourself, your all, to-day and forever upon the Lord. Do it now while we pray.

THE CLOSING PRAYER.

O thou Divine Savior and Burden Bearer, speak the word in season to these busy, battling, sinning, burdened men and women, gathered for this brief midday service. Let every man and woman of us, personally and faithfully face our daily task just like it ought to be faced. And let us all consecrate ourselves today and in all coming days, to the last noble limit of ministry, as we seek to help other people to bear their burdens. Forbid, O God, that we shall add to people's burdens. And then let us all come with our burdens, and they are many, and let us cast them, with ourselves, utterly upon that great Savior, who is pledged to turn the very distemperatures of life into triumphs for us, if we will only consent that His will may be done in our lives. Give us grace and help that we may all yield ourselves to thy will, now and forever. And as you go now, may the blessing of the Triune God, even of Father, Son and Holy Spirit, be granted you, all and each, to abide with you through today, and through tomorrow, and throughout God's vast beyond, forever. Amen.

III

NIGHT SERVICE, JUNE 12, 1917.

PRELIMINARY REMARKS.

Before reading the Scriptures, I should like to make two remarks—first, a general remark, and then one quite particular with reference to these services. The general remark is, that Christians ought to be the very best of citizens, and in this time of national, and international, and even world testing, Christians should be on the alert constantly to see how they can best serve humanity's interests. I trust that daily the Christians listening to me to-night are giving themselves to prayer about the World War. Oh, what need for constant and fervent intercession respecting this war! My belief is that we have entered into this war under the highest moral compulsion. We have not entered into it, I must believe, with any lust for revenge, or for gain, but purely, and simply, and solely, in the interest of humanity, at home and the world round, for today and for every after day. Therefore, it behooves every Christian, and every right-thinking citizen as well, who may not be a Christian, to give the most worthy consideration to the personal part that each of us should have with respect to this great conflict. Without ceasing, we should make our appeal to God that He may lead us to do His will. And without ceasing, we should seek in every high possible way, to help our sons and brothers, who are going out from every community to the camps to be trained for the great conflict. And in every way we can, every one of us, as our noble President has said, "should do his bit," in this testing hour,

27

when every human being in this country is involved, and vitally involved, because of the war. I will venture to add this other word, a word which I said to my own people in Dallas a short time ago, that every man and woman in our land, who can do so, should come with noble response to the appeal that is daily heard, touching the Liberty Bonds. Every man and woman who can do so should re-enforce the Government at this practical point. It is a matter reasonable, it is a matter righteous, and I believe that it is a matter profoundly and urgently necessary. It is indeed a high privilege to be the right kind of a citizen. Patriotism is a word of tremendous significance.

Now, a very particular word touching the interests of the meeting. I raise the question with every Christian under the sound of my voice this night: Won't you make it a point, from day to day, to do some definite religious visiting? All about us there are people who are needing, more than words can say, to be spoken to in the right way, concerning personal religion. Won't you thus dedicate yourself for an hour to-morrow? And if it could not be an hour, for half an hour? And if it could not be half an hour, for ten minutes? And if it could not be ten minutes, for as much as one minute, to speak to some human soul about personal religion? I do not think much of a meeting where its activities are limited to the public services. I think very much of any meeting, if the people come to it, and humbly and earnestly seek to have their spiritual strength renewed, and light their torches, and then go out to find somebody in need of God's guidance and help, and speak to that somebody, and seek to guide that somebody into the right way. That is a meeting worth while. Oh, I press it upon you! Won't you do some of the right kind of religious visiting every day of these special days set apart for public services? There is a drifting Christian that you ought to see. He began well back yonder, and something came to bewitch him away from the right path. Oh, how he needs the right kind of a talk! There is somebody whose church membership is not in Fort Worth, but his life or her life is here. The church membership is back yonder in the village church or city church or country church, but the life is here, and the church membership ought to be here, and the activity ought to be here, and the service ought to be here, and the alignment, open and public, for Christ, ought to be here. Do you know such people? Say the right word to them at once. And then, above all that, there are men and women and children all about you, who are going their way without God, to whom you ought to speak. My fellow-men, if the religion of Jesus Christ is worth a straw, it is worth dying for, and, certainly, it is worth living for. The one without Christ is not ready to die, and—what is of probably larger consequence—that one is not ready to live—no, not for a day, nor for an hour. Won't you do the right kind of religious visiting between this and the service to-morrow night? God speed you and help you, I pray.

You are ready to listen for a moment, with reverence, I trust, to two passages of Scripture, the first from the ninth chapter of Mark:

And when He came to His disciples, He saw a great multitude about them, and the scribes questioning with them.

Arguing with them.

And straightway all the people, when they beheld Him, were greatly amazed, and running to Him saluted Him. And He asked the scribes, What question ye with them? And one of the multitude answered and said, Master, I have brought unto thee my son, which hath la dumb spirit; And wheresoever he taketh him, he teareth him: and he foameth, and gnasheth with his teeth, and pineth away: and I spake to thy disciples that they should cast him out; and they could not.

That is what the uproar is about. Your men have failed.

Jesus answereth him, and saith, O faithless generation, how long shall I be with you? how long shall I suffer you? bring him unto me. And they brought him unto Him: and when He saw him, straightway the spirit tare him; and he fell on the ground, and wallowed foaming. And Jesus asked his father, How long is it ago since this came unto him? And he said, Of a child. And ofttimes it hath cast him into the fire, and into the waters, to destroy him: but if thou canst do anything, have compassion on us, and help us.

Miserable prayer, wasn't it? About like many of mine, I am afraid. Think of saying that to God, to the Almighty Savior: "If thou *canst* do anything, have compassion on us and help us!" Jesus said, "You have the 'if' in the wrong place." Mark just what He said:

Jesus said unto him, If thou canst believe, all things are possible to him that believeth. And straightway the father of the child cried out, and said with tears, Lord, I believe; help thou mine unbelief.

That is a glorious prayer. You do not wonder that Daniel Webster wanted it carved on his gravestone: "Lord, I believe; help thou mine unbelief."

When Jesus saw that the people came running together, He rebuked the foul spirit, saying unto him, Thou dumb and deaf spirit, I charge thee, come out of him, and enter no more into him. And the spirit cried, and rent him sore, and came out of him: and he was as one dead; insomuch that many said, He is dead. But Jesus took him by the hand, and lifted him up; and he arose. And when Jesus was come into the house His disciples asked Him privately, Why could not we cast him out?

Well, sure enough, why couldn't they? When Jesus sent forth the twelve, one of the powers He gave them was power to cast out unclean spirits, and they succeeded. And later, when He sent forth the seventy, one of the powers He gave them was power against unclean spirits, and they succeeded. When they came back from one of their tours, one of their reports was: "Lord, even the devils are subject unto us, through thy name." But they failed this time, utterly. So they asked Him, when alone: "Why could not we cast him out?" Mark His answer! Oh, what an answer it is!

And He said unto them, This kind can come forth by nothing, but by prayer.

You observe that the word "fasting" is omitted in the Revised Version.

Now you are ready to hear a briefer Scripture, from the eighth chapter of Luke:

Now it came to pass on a certain day, that He went into a ship with His disciples: and He said unto them, Let us go over unto the other side of the lake. And they launched forth. But as they sailed He fell asleep: and there came down a storm of wind on the lake; and they were filled with water, and were in jeopardy. And they came to Him, and awoke Him, saying, Master, Master, we perish! Then He arose, and rebuked the wind and the raging of the water: and they ceased, and there was a calm. And He said unto them, Where is your faith?

WHERE IS YOUR FAITH?

Text: "And He said unto them, Where is your faith?"—Luke 8:25.

Jesus said unto His disciples, some 1900 years ago, on the storm-swept water, when they were all affrighted and filled with dismay, "Where is your faith?" And Jesus says to a great audience of men and women assembled in Fort Worth, Tuesday evening, June 12, 1917, "Where is your faith?" This is a question that needs to be asked very often, and it needs to be faithfully answered when we ask it, for it is about the most vital matter of all, even our faith.

The conquering weapon is faith. "Without faith it is impossible to please God." His Book so tells us. "This is the victory that overcometh the world, even our faith." We shall not have victory without faith. Of old, God's plaintive question to His Israel was: "How long will it be ere ye believe me?" And that is His question to His Israel this very hour. "O my people, how long will it be ere ye believe me?" The The undoing sin of Christians is their unfaith. We are all along saying, and correctly, that the undoing sin of the unbeliever is his unfaith. "He that believeth not is condemned already, because he hath not believed in the name of the only begotten Son of God," and while he remains in that unbelief must continue to be condemned. Rejection of Christ, unbelief toward Christ, that is the undoing sin. Even so, the undoing sin for Christians is their unfaith. Of old Israel could not enter the Promised Land because of unbelief, and even to-day, and every day, God's people are kept out of many a promised land because of unbelief. We doubt God's ability, or we doubt His willingness, or both His ability and willingness, to help us, and we go our way, groping, and floundering, and failing. It is not only a pity, but it is a sin, deep and tragical, if we are not steadily growing in faith. That was a beautiful tribute Paul paid the church at Thessalonica, when he said: "We are bound to thank God always for you, brethren, as it is meet, because that your faith groweth exceedingly." It will not only be a misfortune, but it will be a sin, if with you and me our faith is not steadily strengthening and growing.

But now the fact confronts us, as pointed by the text, that our faith may be misplaced. The faith of the disciples on that storm-swept water was evidently misplaced. They were disciples of Christ. They were His friends and followers. But their hearts failed, and their faith went down, and they fainted in spirit. Their faith was misplaced. When is faith misplaced? I shall answer that it is misplaced when it is put in human appearances; and we are all along tempted to put our faith in mere human appearances. How we are influenced, how we are swayed, how we are lifted up or cast down, by mere appearances! If the weather be fair, if no lowering clouds come to menace, if all goes merry as a wedding bell, our hearts seem hopeful and our faith buoyant. But that is not the test. How is it when the heavens are darkened with clouds? How is it when the loved one gasps, and the sands of life seem running to the end? How is it when crepe is on the door? How is it when the granary seems scant and the crops have no promise? How is it when appearances are all against us? Our faith is misplaced, if our faith is put in mere human appearances. That was a great saying given by a valiant leader, when he said: "Never take counsel of your fears, or of appearances."

Our faith is misplaced, I go on to say, when we put it in human agency. And certainly, we are greatly tempted, and constantly, to put our faith in human agency. But all along, the Scriptures, by telling illustrations and by pungent precepts, would turn us away from putting our faith in mere human agency. The Bible tells us why God makes choice, as He does, of such remarkable instrumentalities. He has chosen the weak things of the world to confound the mighty, and the reason is given us there in His Book: "That your faith should not stand in the wisdom of men, but in the power of God." A generation or two removed from us, God startled the world by finding a lad yonder in the country place, in England, not yet out of his teens, and God brought him up to the world's greatest city, to great London, and set him right there in its heart to preach His wonderful gospel. Before this young man was thirty, royalty was at his feet, and the British Parliament marvelled at his power, and the lines of his testimony and power had gone out to the ends of the earth— Charles Haddon Spurgeon, the most victorious gospel preacher of all his century, and perhaps of any century since the apostolic times. He was a man uncolleged, and yet God said through him to the world about us: "I want you to look at this man and listen to him that your faith may not stand in the wisdom of men, but in the power of God." Our God is surprising us all along by His strange choice of human instrumentalities. There is the humble country boy. He has never been to the city at all. He is following his plow. He goes to the little country church house, in the quiet midsummer meeting. His heart is moved, his conscience probed, his judgment convinced, his will aroused, and he bows down in humble penitence before Christ, and he is saved. And then he follows his plow still again and strange impulses stir in his heart, and great thoughts burn in his brain. He is thinking about preaching the gospel. He is thinking about going out and telling the world what a dear Savior he has found, and how he would have every man know the same blessed Savior. The years pass on, several of them, half a dozen, a dozen, and yonder is that country lad in a surging city, rallying the tempted thousands of sinning, beaten and wandering humanity, rallying them around the flag of Christ Jesus, the Lord. Who is he? A plain plowboy, clothed upon with the grace and might of the Spirit of God, and in him and through him God is saying to the world: "See him now, and listen to him, and remember, your faith is not to stand in the wisdom of men, but in the power of God." Oh, how it gladdens my heart this Tuesday night, to have the faith to believe that somewhere in this broad country, out on the prairies, or out yonder nestling amid the trees, in some little cottage, a mother folds to her heart a tiny baby boy, and when you and I shall be sleeping beneath the roses, and shall be perhaps forgotten, that boy will be going up and down this country, rallying the wavering, sinning thousands around the flag of Christ, a child out from some home of poverty and need, and God will be saying through him to the world: "See him, now, and listen, that your faith should not stand in the wisdom of men, but in the power of God."

But I think that most of all our faith is misplaced because we limit God. That is a striking expression used in one of the Psalms, where the Psalmist said, concerning Israel of old: "They limited the Holy One of Israel." They "limited God." Mankind can limit God, and does limit Him. At first thought, that seems impossible. The infinite God, filling all immensity, without beginning of days or ending of years, omnipotent, omniscient, omnipresent, eternal—at first thought it seems impossible that He could be limited, and yet He can be, and is, limited. Man limits God, else man is a mere machine, without any more volition than a tree or a stone. Man can say "No" to God, or man can say "Yes" to God. Man can seek God's face, and by Divine Grace become God's friend, and go God's road, and glorify God's great name; or man can be rebellious, and offer his protest against God, and turn his back upon God, and miss the right way, and come to defeat and failure. Man limits God. How does he limit Him? The ways are many. We can limit God even in our very prayers. You have probably heard prayers which had in them a limitation upon God. Full many a time when we pray that prayer "not my will, but thine, be done," our hearts really mean: "Not thy will, O God, but mine, be done." Ofttimes we are found trying to persuade God to come to our notion of things, and accept our view of things, without regard to His wisdom and will. All the while He tells us: "You leave your case to me, and trust

your case to me, and submit your case to me, and I will do
the wisest and best thing possible for you," and yet full many
a time our prayers really mean: "Nevertheless, O Lord, not
thy will be done at all, but mine be done," and in that way we
limit Him.

And then we limit God by our poor lives. Every life is
either a channel or a clog, a channel through which God sends
His blessing, or a clog to hinder and obstruct such blessing. A
human life can be a non-conductor, failing to transmit to others
what God would send through that life unto others. That is
indeed a pathetic picture, where Paul writes one of the New
Testament churches, saying: "For many walk, of whom I have
told you often, and now tell you, even weeping, that they are
the enemies of the cross of Christ." Paul was writing to a
church, and he was saying to that church: "Some of you
church members so walk as to become the enemies of the cross
of Christ." Your attention has been called to that solemn
picture in the last book of the Bible, where Jesus stands outside
a church, begging to be admitted. Listen to 'Him: "Behold,
I stand at the door, and knock: if any man hear my voice, and
open the door, I will come in to him, and will sup with him,
and he with me." Jesus is there, outside a church—outside!
His own people have the door closed, and have Him outside,
and there He stands on the outside, knocking, and saying:
"Won't you let me enter? for I come to do you good, and not
evil at all." "O Jesus, thou art standing, outside the fast-
closed door!" Can you think of anything more heartbreaking
this night than to imagine yourselves keeping Jesus out, keeping Jesus away from some other life, yourself a clog, obstruct-
ing, yourself a non-conductor? He wishes to send through
you a message of life and grace and hope to others, and you
are a non-conductor. Can you imagine anything more serious
than that? We limit God by our lives. Every Christian whose
life is wrong with God positively hinders God and limits God
by that much.

But most of all, we limit God, I dare say, by our unbelief,
our unfaith. Israel could not enter the Promised Land because
of unbelief; and you and I are kept out of many a promised
land because of unbelief, because of unfaith. Jesus wishes us
to believe in Him. The right sort of a man delights to be

believed in. You cannot grieve the right sort of a man in any
other way quite so deeply as to indicate to him that you do not
take him at full face value, as he represents himself to you.
The right sort of a man wishes to be believed in, to be taken at
his word. God delights to be believed in, and the deepest grief
to Him is given Him by our unfaith, our unbelief. We are
told here in the gospels that in one certain community Jesus
could do no mighty works because of the unbelief of the people. Unbelief hindered Him. Unbelief fettered Him, even
Christ Jesus, the Lord. And so He comes to us to-night, saying: "According to your faith, so be it unto you. Where is
your faith?" He comes to us to-night saying: "If thou canst
believe, all things are possible to him that believeth. Where
is your faith?"

We are all along talking about "hard cases." Now, how
foolish and unwise and wrong is such talk, when we think of
God. He asks us: "Is anything too hard for the Lord?" That
was a mighty question Paul asked when he asked: "Why
should it be thought a thing incredible with you, that *God*
should raise the dead?" Granted a God who has all power in
heaven and earth, and who formed the worlds by the word of
His power, granted a Being like that, and where is there any
difficulty or mystery in such a God raising people from death
and the grave? So that our talk about "hard cases" in God's
sight, is all out of place and grievous in His holy presence.

I wonder, my fellow Christians, if in these latter days, our
faith gets much higher for mankind than for the salvation of
the children in the Sunday-school, and the plastic, responsive
young people that are all about us. Where is the faith now
that claims the hardened sinner for Christ? Where is the
faith that claims the old man with the gray about his temples,
far down in the afternoon of life—where is the faith that
claims that man for God? Where is the faith that claims
the man abandoned to sinful and consuming habits? Where
is the faith that claims him for God? Where is the faith
that claims the big business man, great and strengthful,
masterful and powerful, but preoccupied, living as though this
world were all, forgetting that out there a few steps ahead is
the judgment and eternity? Where is the faith that claims
him, from all that preoccupation, for Christ Jesus and His

great salvation? Where is the faith that claims the very difficult case for the Lord Christ? Oh, how we limit God, that we do not go out and claim men, no matter what their hindrances and their limitations and their sins! How we grieve God, if we do not go out and claim them in the name of Christ, even the most difficult cases, for the wonders of His grace and His great forgiveness!

May I tell you the most wonderful conversion that I ever witnessed in all my life? Out in the Middle West, where it has been my delight to go many a time, in the out door camp-meetings, some years ago I went and found in that particular community some very difficult religious conditions. There were more aged people in that community, unsaved, than I have ever witnessed anywhere in all my life, before or since. The religious conditions of the community were hard and difficult. There had been all sorts of pesky religious debates—how miserable they all are, and how inexcusable!—and the people were set and gritty and hard in their relations toward one another. What a tragedy when that is so! I was there some two or three days, and more and more it dawned upon me how difficult all the conditions were. They told me daily about those white-haired men and women, who went groping life's way, without God and without hope. After some days, they told me about Big Jim, the most difficult sinner, they said, west of Fort Worth, even as far west as El Paso. They so described him physically that I could not miss him if he came to the meeting, and they said: "He will come one time to hear you, and then he will swear at you, and rail at you, and curse out the whole meeting, and the preachers and the churches and everybody, and then he will wait a year and come back a year from now to go over the same performance again." That was their report of him. I stood up to preach one evening and in came Big Jim. I could not miss him, from their description. Yonder he sat, far down the aisle before me, at the rear of the great arbor, nor did he take his eye, it seemed, one time from the minister, while his message was being given. At the close of the message, I made the call for men and women who would then and there humbly and honestly make surrender of their poor, undone and sinful lives to the forgiving mercy and help of the Divine Savior, and down every aisle white-haired

men and women came. It was one of those memorable nights,
never to be forgotten. Big Jim kept his seat, nor did he seem
to move. After awhile, the meeting ended, and the people gathered about me, or gathered in little groups to discuss the wonders that their eyes had witnessed that night. One after
another was named who had "come over the line" and made
the great surrender that night to Jesus. And then, ever and
anon, these talkers would make a passing remark about the
presence of Big Jim, and they speculated about his presence,
and about the possibility of his coming any more. One said:
"No; he will not be back. He will swear at our preacher, and
at all the Christian people, nor will he return until next year."
But another said: "Yes; he had a different look on him to-night
from what I have ever seen before. I look for him to come
again. Never did I see him look as he looked to-night." And
so they talked pro and con. Presently the preacher slipped
away from the crowd, for it was late, and wended his way
around the hillside to the little cottage, far removed from
the camping throngs, where he might have quiet and rest,
and as he went around that little mountain side he heard
somebody talking. Oh, it was so earnest! The preacher did
not mean to be an eavesdropper, and yet he seemed chained
in his very tracks. And when he stopped and listened to that
strange talk, he discovered in a moment what it was, and that
there were two of them, and that they were praying, for one,
who spoke for the two, said: "We two, O Christ, agree we
want Big Jim saved, that the mouths of gainsayers may be
stopped in this country. They are saying, O Christ, that Big
Jim is too much for God, that even God cannot stop him. They
are saying that, and we want the mouths of gainsayers stopped,
and the whole land to know that Christ is able to save even the
chief of sinners; and we two, here on the mountain side, late in
the night, give thee Big Jim, believing thy great promise:
'If two of you shall agree on earth as touching anything that
they shall ask, it shall be done for them of my Father which is
in heaven.' For the glory of Christ, simply and only, we pray
you, save Big Jim."

I went quietly on my way. I do not know who they were,
who thus were praying. I never knew. I found my cottage,

and the night passed, and the next day came and wore to night-fall, and I was again under the arbor, facing the mass of people. I stood up to preach and looked everywhere, but Big Jim was not present. But just as I began to speak, in he came, at the same place as on the previous night, and then my message seemed to fly away, and I said: "We will pause and ask God to give the preacher what he ought to say. He does not know. He would speak God's message, whatever it is, to-night, and this man will lead us in prayer that the preacher may speak what, and as, Christ would have His preacher to-night to speak." 'And the prayer was finished, and then the preacher began again, and told simply and only that story of the prodigal son, the easily influenced, impulsive youth, restless, dissatisfied, who went away from home against the protests of wisdom and love, and took his part of the inheritance, and went down the toboggan slide at a rapid pace, and wasted all his substance in riotous living. 'And when his substance was gone, his friends were gone. The hail-fellows-well-met of the other days had fled, and he was down yonder in the swine fields, this lad, feeding the swine, himself eating of the husks wherewith he fed the swine. One day, as the Scriptures tell the story, the young fellow "came to himself." He saw himself as he was. Memory was alert, and the months and the years of his separation from home, came trooping back to his recollection, and the young man said: "I have sinned. I have missed it. This is the way of defeat and death. I will go back to father, and I will confess in his sight and in God's sight how I have missed it, and how I have sinned." 'And then he put that kindling desire into effect, that sublime resolution into action, and he betook himself back the homeward way, and as he came toward the old home, the father saw him, even from afar; the father was waiting, longing to see him; and down the road the father came, and put his arms about the boy, as the boy began his confession, and the father called to a servant: "Bring the best robe for this boy," and to another: "Kill the fatted calf," and to another: "Bring the ring to put on this boy's finger," emblem of the love that never dies. 'And there was music, and there was rejoicing, and there was victory. That was all I said, except that I added: "This story of the prodigal son is simply a picture of the love of God, going out after any soul on earth that has wandered away from God,

which soul God wishes to forgive and recover and save, and
will so save, if such soul will come to Him." And then I said:
"Will the audience remain seated? Without any singing at all,
is there some man here tonight, a prodigal, far from heaven and
God, who says: 'I want God's mercy, and I will honestly yield
myself to God to get it,' let him come and take my hand."

Would you believe it? Big Jim started. Oh, the sight, the
sight, the sight! And presently the men saw him coming, and
hundreds of sobbing men stood to their feet, and sobbed aloud,
and as he came down the aisle slowly, for it was with difficulty
he walked, hundreds of men joined him, and came down with
him. And when at last he got to me and took my hand, he said:
"Sir, I put you on your sacred honor, will the Great Master
save me, if I will give up to Him?" And I said: "Sir, on my
sacred honor, I declare that He will, if you will just honestly
surrender your case to Him." And the men put in with voices,
scores and scores: "It is so, Jim. We made the surrender and
He saved us. You make it, and you will find out for yourself."
And then again, waiting a moment, he looked at me, still holding my hand, and said: "I want you to remember, sir, that you
are speaking to the worst man out of perdition. Would the
Master save a man like that, if he would give up to Him?" I
said: "Sir, on my Master's own statement, I declare to you
that He will save you, even if you are the chief sinner out of
perdition, if you will honestly surrender to Him." And they
punctuated my remark with a chorus: "It is so, Jim. Try it
and you will find out." Once again he looked at me and then
he said, finally: "Sir, when would the Great Master save me,
if I should give up to Him right now?" And I said: "Sir, on
His own word, which many of us have proved, our Great
Master will save you, and your heart shall know that your
sins are forgiven, right now, if right now you will honestly
surrender to Him." And then he turned that big bronzed face
upward, as if looking for the Master himself, and he gasped
out his prayer, just this: "Lord Jesus, the worst man in the
world gives up to you right now."

Oh, I cannot tell the rest! I do not think the angels could
tell the rest. I think if the archangel himself should come down
from those starry heights, that the words of that angel would
be inadequate to tell you the rest. God unloosed Big Jim's

tongue, and he began to talk, and then the old men kissed him, and the old women kissed him, and the young men kissed him, and the young women kissed him, for the chief of sinners had been saved.

What is there wonderful about such a story? Not a thing on the face of the earth, if you will grant that Jesus Christ is divine, and that He came in the flesh to save sinners, and that His divine grace is mightier than any human sin, however long-continued and however heinous. O men and women, you and I limit God because of our unfaith with respect to aged and hardened and difficult and preoccupied cases that are all around us.

But there is another word for me to bring you. How may we strengthen our faith? That is what you and I wish to know. How may you and I strengthen our faith? I have two or three simple suggestions. First, if we would strengthen our faith, we need to make it a matter of prayer. I read you the passage of Scripture telling of a group of men who failed in their faith, and when they got Jesus alone they said: "Why was it we failed?" Mark His answer: "This kind can come forth by nothing, but by prayer." If you are not a man of prayer, you are not a man of faith. If you are not a woman of prayer, you are not a woman of faith. The men and women who do not tread the secret path of prayer are men and women spiritless and broken and without faith. If you and I would have conquering faith, then you and I must make it a matter of constant prayer. Once when Jesus gave His disciples a great task to accomplish, they cried back unto Him: "Lord, if you expect that of us, increase our faith." And so you and I are to come to Him, saying: "If you expect this, or that, or the other great achievement, even the achievement of winning some poor soul, bedarkened and blinded by sin, away from such dreadful path, to God, then increase our faith."

How may our faith be increased? If it is to be increased, then let us plead the promises of God. Oh, how great a privilege to plead the promises of God! Of old, one had a way of talking to God like this: "Do as thou hast said." And when you and I come to pray, we need to fill our mouths with arguments to God, and those arguments are His own promises. "Lord Jesus, here is what thou hast said, and we plead that. We fill our mouth with thine own argument, and we plead that before thy face. Do as thou hast said. Do as thou hast said." What if hundreds and hundreds of these men and women before me, should go apart in groups of two, and should say: "Lord Jesus, here is a case, O, so difficult, speaking after the fashion of men, so difficult, so hopeless, but not at all difficult and hopeless if God will take charge of the case, and, therefore, we two take up thy promise, where thou sayest: 'If two of you shall agree on earth, as touching anything that they shall ask, it shall be done for them of my Father in heaven.' Do as thou hast said. We plead this promise, and rest on it. Do as thou hast said."

How are we to strengthen our faith? I have still another word. If we are to strengthen our faith, then we are to seek the guidance and power of God's Divine Spirit. In this divinest work of all, the work of winning souls to Christ, all along we are to seek the guidance and power of the Holy Spirit. Oh, how wonderful is His guidance, and how marvelous is His power! He does guide His people. There is such a thing as being led of the Spirit of God, and in this divinest work of all, the work of winning souls, we shall miss it utterly and be marplots, if we are not guided and empowered by the Spirit of God. The Spirit of God does teach, guide and empower the servants of Jesus, in this holiest task of all, this work of winning souls to Christ. "When He is come," Jesus has promised it, "He will guide you into all truth." "Ye shall receive power, after that the Holy Ghost is come upon you: and ye shall be witnesses unto me, both in Jerusalem, and in all Judea, and in Samaria, and unto the uttermost part of the earth." O brothers mine, you and I, with all humility and earnestness, want to ask God to guide us in this work we are in, and to give us His own wisdom and power at every step that we take.

> Come, Holy Spirit, heavenly dove,
> With all thy quickening powers;
> Come, shed abroad a Savior's love,
> And that shall kindle ours.

You and I want the guidance and the power of the Divine Spirit in this heavenly task to which we are these days, please God, to put our hands.

Wonderful, how wonderful, is God's leadership by His Spirit and His power, when we yield ourselves to Him! How wonderful it is! A few years ago, I was in Minneapolis, that beautiful city of the Northwest, at one of the Bible conferences for the Northwestern states, speaking there daily for some two weeks, and it was my privilege, while there, to have daily fellowship with that nobly gifted preacher, Wayland Hoyt, one of the first preachers of his generation. I had heard of an incident in his life, and I asked him about it, and he confirmed it. This was the incident: Dr. Hoyt had prepared with unusual care in the other years a special sermon, hoping to reach one of the first citizens in his city on a certain Sunday night, with that same sermon. This citizen was an outstanding citizen, but not a Christian, and rarely came to church. The wife was a devoted Christian and church member. So at the Sunday morning service Mr. Hoyt signalled quietly to the wife, and sent by her a message to the distinguished husband: "Tell him that I ask specially that he will come to-night. I have prepared a sermon, hoping earnestly to help him. Tell him I ask him to come, I wish him to come." The wife gave the message when she reached home, and the husband went to the telephone—he was a gentleman in every instinct and habit of his life—and took down the receiver and called the minister and gave the minister his grateful thanks for his cordial invitation, saying: "Certainly, I will be there to-night. How kindly, how considerate of you to be so interested in me. Certainly, I will be there to hear you." But before the nightfall came a blinding storm filled the heavens, and the floods poured out of the clouds, and the people could not gather. Only a little handful hard by the church could gather at all. The minister made his way to the church and spoke to the little handful, but the one citizen he had thought about and specially prepared for was not there. The minister went home with his heart heavy, and he sat there late and long in his library that Sunday night, and he fell to musing like this: "What a poor out I am making reaching that man!" And then something said to him: "Why don't you imitate your Master and go to the man and preach your sermon to just one man, as Jesus after nightfall preached His sermon on the new birth to Nicodemus, that fine citizen of old? Why don't you walk in the steps of your Master and preach your best sermon to one man?" And that suggestion

fairly boomed like a cannon in his ears and heart. He looked
at his watch. It was midnight. He said: "Why, I could not
go this late at night." And he sat, still thinking further, and
something seemed to say to him, did say to him: "If you knew
that that man's house was in danger, or that his family were in
danger, you would brave any sort of weather, to help them.
Though the storm beat down the avenue, you would breast it,
to go and apprise him of the danger. Why won't you be consistent about the biggest, most important thing of all?" And
then Dr. Hoyt said he found himself putting on his raincoat.
He opened the door and breasted the great storm that still
swept down the avenue. Block after block he trudged his way
through the blinding storm. He said he found himself talking
to himself, saying to himself: "Maybe, the man will say I am
crazy. Maybe I am, but God knows I am trying to do the
consistent thing." Presently he came to the right house, and
as he came toward it there was a light in one of the lower
rooms, and he came up softly to the door, and knocked gently,
not caring to disturb the household at one o'clock in the morning, and in a moment the door opened, and there standing
was the citizen, who had not been in bed at all, and out into the
storm and the night the big citizen thrust his arms and drew
Wayland Hoyt out of the night and out of the storm, and drew
him to his heart, and sobbed over him as a mother would sob
over her children, saying to him: "Thank God, Mr. Hoyt, He
sent you here to teach me how to be saved. I have been there
in my library, reading the Bible and trying to pray. That word
you sent me waked me up and stirred my heart. The storm
kept me from going to church, but I could not sleep. I have
been there reading the Bible and trying to pray, but it is all
dark to me. Jesus sent you to teach me." And Wayland
Hoyt told me that in five minutes his interested citizen was
rejoicing in Christ Jesus the Lord. What if Wayland Hoyt
had not gone? God pity me and you maybe, as time and again
your heart ached with a longing inexpressible for some lost
soul, but you said: "I am unworthy. I am incompetent. I am
unfit." And you deadened your impression, and you went your
way, and such soul went his way, and maybe has gone into
eternity ere this Tuesday night. Oh, seek the guidance of
God's Spirit for this task, and then follow Him!

We are going in a moment, for my message is done. I have a question to ask you, and you will answer it candidly. This is the question: Is there somebody in Fort Worth that you wish to be saved? Is there somebody in Fort Worth that you wish to be saved during these meetings, in which our appeal shall be made to men's judgments and men's consciences? I have no respect for any other kind of appeal in the name of Christ's holy religion. Bethink you now—is there somebody that you wish to see saved during these midsummer days, set aside for some special meetings to help the people in the highest matters of all? Every Christian present who says: "Yes; there is one, or there are some, that I wish to see saved, and by my standing I voice my wish, and ask you and ask others present who pray, to join me in prayer for these nameless ones that my heart thinks about, in these closing moments of this service," stand to your feet. Is there some person or persons whom you would see saved during these meetings, for whom you would have us to unite our prayers this night, and from day to day, that light and leading from God may be vouchsafed unto them that they may be saved? Does my call apply to others? Every man and woman who says: "That represents my heart's earnest desire," stand to your feet. Many have risen. Many persons are evidently now in your thoughts. The Lord teach us to pray for them as we ought!

THE CLOSING PRAYER.

We go now, our Father, at the close of this service, appealing to thee that thy truth, by the power of thy Spirit, may be written in our deepest consciences. O, forgive us for our little faith, for our miserable unfaith. This night we would draw nigh to God. We would pay the price for power with God and for Him, wherever that would lead us, and whatever that would cost us. Whether by death or by life, we would do God's will. Behold the men and women who have risen to their feet to say that they are thinking of one, or thinking of more than one, whom they long to see saved during these midsummer days, in the special daily meetings. O God, fit us to speak as we ought to the people all about us concerning Jesus. Would it please thee for those now praying to pour forth their personal appeal to some soul thought about and prayed for right now? Then let the right person go to such soul and speak God's Word, however timidly. And even though with confession, first of all, for waywardness personal, and inconsistency of life, and incongruity of temper, yet may the soul who loves Christ and loves the soul of the one thought about and prayed for right now, go to such soul and speak as Christ would have the word spoken, to guide such soul out of the darkness and into the light. Holy Spirit Divine, thou Great Revealer of Jesus, come thou and teach us and lead us, and enable us hour by hour, in our talk, in our visits, by the use of the 'phone, by the letter, and in the secret places, when we bare our very souls before God in prayer, to behave ourselves in such a fashion that Christ with smiling face shall look on us, and with blessed lips shall say to us: "I am well pleased."

And now, as the people go, may the blessing of God, even of Father, Son and Holy Spirit, whom we worship as one God, be granted you all and each, to abide with you forevermore. Amen.

IV

NOON SERVICE, JUNE 13, 1917.

THE THREEFOLD SECRET OF A GREAT LIFE.

Text: "Brethren, I count not myself to have apprehended: but this one thing I do, forgetting those things which are behind, and reaching forth unto those things which are before, I press toward the mark for the prize of the high calling of God in Christ Jesus."—Phil. 3:13, 14.

Somebody has well said that "the proper study of mankind is man." The study of biography, therefore, is always a most fascinating and helpful study. Everybody who is normal is interested keenly in the lives of people who have succeeded. We would know all that we may about them, about their beginnings, their struggles, their habits, about their viewpoint in life. This morning I would direct your attention for a little while to the most remarkable Christian of the centuries, namely, the Apostle Paul. He was, and is, the greatest single credential that Christ's gospel has ever produced. One day, in writing to his favorite church, the Philippian church, in a burst of confidence, it would seem, he lets us into the secret of his marvelous life, and we are to study that threefold secret for a little while this morning. Mark his words:

This one thing I do, forgetting those things which are behind, and reaching forth unto those things which are before, I press toward the mark for the prize of the high calling of God in Christ Jesus.

In those words, this greatest of all Christians states the three-fold secret of his incomparable life, and we will do well to look at that threefold secret today. The first element in it is the element of whole-hearted concentration. "This one thing I do"—not a dozen things, not even two things, but "this one thing I do." No life can be very great, or very happy, or very useful, without this element of concentration. Every one

45

should have a work to do, and know what it is, and do it with all his might. Decision is energy, and energy is power, and power is confidence, and confidence to a remarkable degree contributes to success. Many a man in life has failed, not from lack of ability, but from lack of this element of concentration. The whole world is witness to its power. Turn to any realm that you will, and the vital meaning of concentration stands out in all human life, after the most striking fashion.

Take the business world, and the element of concentration there is of prime importance, if success is to be achieved. The very watchwords in the business world magnify this element of concentration. They talk to us about specialization and consolidation, and incorporation, and on and on, giving emphasis in all such words to the meaningful quality of concentration. A short time ago one of the world's most successful business men was waited upon by a group of young men, who sought his counsel about how to succeed, and he gave them this laconic advice: "Young gentlemen, get all your eggs into one basket, and then watch that basket." It was his way of giving emphasis to the tremendous value of concentration. The day for the jack-of-all-trades has passed. A man must do one thing and do it with all his might. The professional man understands that. The lawyer who is minded to reach the topmost rung of his high calling sets himself with all diligence and devotedness to that calling, and does not dissipate his energies on a half dozen other callings, as in the other days men sometimes did. The physician understands that. The day of the specialist has come. The teacher understands that. In all the world about us men understand that this winning element, stated by Paul as the first element, humanly speaking, of his marvelous career, is indispensable to success, namely, the power of concentration —"this one thing I do."

And when we turn to the world of science, and look at the notable scientists, that truth of concentration seems to be written in their lives as with letters of living fire. Edison with all devotedness concentrates his energies in the realm of electricity, and is constantly surprising the world by his marvelous discoveries. And the Wright brothers, with all their devotedness, gave themselves to the mastery of the secrets of the air, and constantly surprised us by their revelations.

When we come to the highest realm of all—the realm religious—this element of concentration there holds sway just as in these other realms. No man can serve two masters. One must be our Master, and Jesus stands above all mankind and says: "If you would be my disciple, then I tell you I must come first. I must come before father or mother, or the dearest loved one of your life. I must come before your own business, or your own property. I must come before your own life. I must be Lord of all, or I will not be Lord at all."

Now, you would not trust your soul's eternal welfare to a proffered Savior who would ask or allow anything less than that He should be first. "Ye shall seek me and find me, when ye search for me with your whole heart." I care not what may be a man's difficulties or doubts in the world religious, if only such man, with definiteness of purpose, with whole-heartedness of aim, shall set himself to seek God's light and leading, I know that he will find Him. "In the day that thou seekest me with thy whole heart, I will be found of thee." Many a Christian man follows Christ afar off, and limps and grovels in the Christian life, because he is seeking to adjust himself in life to giving Christ some secondary place, and Christ will not have it. Concentration is a prime requisite in the victorious life anywhere.

In the second place the great Christian leads us to the consideration of a second secret explanatory of his marvelous career, and that is that he cultivated a wise forgetfulness of the past. It rings like a trumpet blast in this Bible that we are to remember certain things that we ought to remember. That word "remember" rings out like a bugle blast, again and again in the Bible. But along with the factor of wisely remembering there is to go that other important factor of wisely forgetting. Many a man goes hobbled and crippled through life and never does come to the highest and best, because he cannot forget certain things that ought to be forgotten by him.

And what are some of the things that we ought every one to forget? Let me run over a brief list. We ought every one to learn how practically to forget our blunders. What blunderers we all are, and how many blunders we all make! Every man must learn how to forget his own blunders, or he will go manacled and crippled to his grave. The old saying comes in point right clearly, that "the best of men are but men at the best." We are to learn, therefore, how to forget our blunders. Ebenezer was a field of defeat before it rang with the songs of victory. We are to learn how to take our very blunders and make them bridges over which we shall span the chasms and go to better days.

And what else are we to learn how to forget? We are to learn how to forget our losses. In human life losses of all kinds come more or less in our experiences. We are to learn how to get past them, and practically to forget them. I have observed no more painfully tragical sight than a strong, alert man, down in spirit, singing his dirges and chanting his jeremiads because he had lost some property. I am thinking now of a man whose property burned up a day or two after the insurance had expired, and all was a total loss, and there he was without property at all, in the gray of that early morning, and with his face in his hands he kept chanting the pitiful cry: "I have lost all!" Presently his tiny little girl, of four or five summers, came to him, all puzzled, and said: "Why, no, papa, you have not lost all. You have me and mamma left!" And it took that to summon him and to hearten him and to bring him back to sobriety and to right-thinking. No man is to whine and mope and go down because losses come here and there and yonder. But, he is to learn how to get past them and to forget them.

What else are we to forget? We are to learn how to forget life's injuries. It would seem that in this world of ours with its rivalries and competitions and frictions and alienations, it is difficult to get past the injuries that come in human life. And yet I tell you, my brother men, if for any cause you are cherishing hate in your heart, then you have lost the highest perspective of life, and cannot have the highest perspective of life as long as the poison of hate is allowed in your heart and in your life. A man is terribly hindered and has around him a ball and a chain, if in his heart he cherishes something that says: "I will lie awake at nights, and I will turn many a corner, and I will await my day, to get even with some man for some cruel dart that he throws at me." Big men do not hate. Big men do not cherish resentments. Big men put them down and out, and go their way, and refuse to harbor them. They refuse to let them rankle like poisons in the heart, thus to vitiate every high thing that the spirit should hold most dear.

What else are we to forget? We are to learn how to forget our successes. More men have been spoiled by success than you and I can begin to measure. There is danger in success, anywhere, for any man. If a man can bear success, he can bear anything. Easier far can the human spirit bear adversity than it can bear prosperity. It is better any day to go to the house of mourning than to the house of feasting, for in the house of feasting the human spirit is lifted up, and pride always goes before destruction, and a haughty spirit always goes before a fall. When Uzziah of old came to his day of remarkable prosperity, then it was that the Bible tells us his heart was lifted up to destruction. The history of the rich American family stands out like a mountain range, that every third generation of such family goes to defeat and failure and poverty. The first generation wins success, the second generation spends it, and the third generation goes the downward way to poverty and failure. We are to learn how to forget our successes. If a man does not learn what success is for—any kind of success, financial success, political success, social success, intellectual success, any kind of success—if he does not learn what it is for, the day comes for his undoing and his downfall and his defeat.

What else are we to forget? We are to learn how to forget our sorrows—and sooner or later these sorrows come to us, each and all. We are to learn how to forget them. When the sorrows come, we are to learn how to take these sorrows to the great, refining, overruling Master, and ask Him so to dispose, so to rule and overrule in them and with them that we may come out of them all refined and disciplined, the better educated and more useful, because of such sorrows. They tell us that when you break the oyster's shell at a certain place it will go somewhere into the deep and find a pearl and mend that broken place in its shell with a beautiful pearl. Even so, when your sorrow in life comes, you are to learn how to take that sorrow, and so have it woven into the warp and woof of your life that you shall not be weaker and worse for the sorrow, but shall be richer and stronger and better, because of such sorrow. Read every now and then the polished essay of Emerson on

"Compensation." Running all through this world is that clear principle of compensation. The Bible recognizes it: "For our light affliction, which is but for a moment, worketh for us a far more exceeding and eternal weight of glory." We are to lay to heart that sublimest truth that "all things work together for good to them that love God." Yonder in the asylum for the deaf and dumb a visitor went one day, and the superintendent of the asylum said: "Let me show you how bright these little children are, even though they are deaf and dumb. Ask any question you will," said the superintendent to the visitor. "Write your question there on the board, and see the answers that these little mutes will give to your question." He asked question after question, did this visitor. After awhile he asked a cruel question. I wonder how he could have done it. He wrote this cruel question there on the board: "If God loved you, why did He make you deaf and dumb?" Then the little things bowed their shoulders and sobbed for a moment with almost uncontrollable emotion, and presently a little tiny girl came from out her seat there, and went to the blackboard, and wrote under that question these wonderful words of Jesus: "Even so, Father; for so it seemed good in thy sight." Wasn't it glorious? You and I are to take our sorrows, our black Fridays, our lone and long nights, and we are to come to Him and say: "Manage thou these, thou wondrous Friend, who canst turn the very night into morning; manage these for me." And we are to sing with Whittier, when he sang:

> "I know not where His islands lift
> Their fronded palms in air;
> But this I know, I cannot drift
> Beyond His love and care."

What else are we to forget? We are to learn how to forget our sins. If Paul had not learned how to forget his sins he would have been crippled utterly clear to his death. Paul consented to the death of Stephen. Paul persecuted the church. Paul was a ring-leader in sin. Paul seemed to run the whole gamut of sin. He called himself "the chief of sinners," and perhaps he was. If Paul had not learned how to forget those awful sins that mastered him back yonder, if he had not learned how to get past them, then he would have gone with accusing conscience and broken spirit clear to his grave. We shall have about us a ball and a chain, and shall go groveling and despair-

ing and defeated, if we do not learn how to forget our sins.
When we look at the debit side of our life, do our hearts faint
within us? Mine faints within me. But then the Master of
life summons me and says: "Come over here and look at the
credit side, and the credit side will outfigure all that debit
side." And when I come over there I say to Him: "What
dost thou mean, oh, thou gracious Friend?" Listen to Him,
and He tells us: "Where sin abounded, grace did much more
abound." Listen to Him again: "As far as the east is from
the west, so far hath He removed our transgressions from us."
And listen to Him yet again: "I have put your sins behind
my back. I have drowned them in the depths of the sea. I
will remember them against you no more forever." Oh, isn't
that wonderful? Listen to Him again and He tells us: "The
blood of Jesus Christ His Son cleanseth us from all sin."
When Satan comes with his accusing cry, reminding me of
my weakness and my frailty and my transgressions and my
proneness to sin and all that, he can make out his case, I grant
it, but I come back and say to him: "But, sir, where sin
abounded, grace has much more abounded, and in Christ,
whose name is Jesus, I have victory, even over my sins."
"Thou shalt call His name Jesus, for He shall save His people
from their sins." We have a real Savior from sin in Christ
Jesus, and when we trust Him, no more are we to go hobbled,
with ball and chain, because of sin, because Christ becomes our
personal Savior from both the penalty and power of sin.

Years ago, in South Texas, there was a little home in the
country burned down, and before the neighbors could rescue
the family all were burned to death save one little girl, some
nine or ten years of age, and she was badly burned on one
side of her face and little body. The rest were all burned to
death. The neighbors, after a few days, when they had con-
sulted, sent little Mary to the far-famed Buckner Orphans
Home. They advised the noble head of that home when little
Mary would come, on what train, and there good Dr. Buckner
was waiting for her, of course. When she got off the train,
her little eyes were red from weeping, and she seemed intuitively to know that he was her protector henceforth, and she
started toward him saying: "Is this Mr. Buckner?" He said:
"Yes, and is this little Mary?" And then she came and laid

her little head up against his knee, and sobbed with indiscriba-
ble emotion, and looked up at last with that little burned face
and said: "You will have to be my papa and mamma both."
He said: "I will, the best I can, Mary." And then she went into
the Home, and was looked after along with those hundreds of
children. I have been there time and again and preached to
them, and I have seen them come out to greet him when he
would return to them, after an absence. The little tots come
down the avenue, and vie with one another as they swing
around him, each wishing to kiss him first. Along in thàt group
one day came the little burned-faced Mary, and the little children kissed him as was their wont, but little Mary stood off,
several feet away, and looked across her shoulder, watching
the whole affair, sobbing like her heart would break. And
when these little ones had kissed the good man, he looked
across to her and said: "Mary, why don't you come and kiss
me?" That was entirely too much for her and she sobbed
aloud, and then he went over and touched her little chin and
lifted it up and said: I do not quite understand you, Mary.
Why didn't you come to kiss me?" And the little thing had
difficulty in speaking, and when she did speak she said: "O
Papa Buckner, I could not ask you to kiss me, I am so ugly.
After I got burned I am so ugly I could not ask you to kiss
me, but if you will just love me like you love the other children and tell me you love me, then you need not kiss me at all."
You know what he did. He pushed all those beautiful children
away, and took up little Mary in his arms, and kissed the little
burned cheek again and again and said: "Mary, you are just
as beautiful to Papa Buckner as are any of the rest."

Ah, me! I was that burned child once, and sin did it all! I
came to Jesus and said: "I am sorry. My heart is sick about it.
Oh, I have repented of it all." And He said: "I will receive
you, and I will give you the kiss of reconciliation, the kiss of
pardon, the kiss of forgiveness," and I was saved when I came
like that. Now no more will I go fettered and bound because
of sin, because Christ has made me free by His mighty grace,

> Jesus paid it all,
> All to Him I owe,
> Sin had left its crimson stain,
> He washed it white as snow.

Let me detain you for the third word. Paul had a right
anticipation. "Forgetting those things which are behind and

reaching forth unto those things which are before, I press toward the mark for the prize of the high calling of God in Christ Jesus." Paul had a right forward look. My men and women, at this busy noonday hour, I come to ask you, one by one, have you the right aim in your life? What are you living for? What is that hand for? What is the eye for? What is human life for? What is your life for? How are you using your life? How are you investing your life? What is the aim of your life? Does somebody say: "Why, I am taking it one world at a time?" That is not bright. That is not clever. If a man does not include two worlds at a time, then he commits suicide for both. A man is to be a citizen of two worlds, and a man who lives simply for this world, no matter how successfully, how victoriously, how notoriously, if a man lives simply for this present world, he commits suicide in it and suicide for the world endless that awaits us just out there. Oh, include two worlds in your plan!

Let me tell you about three men. One said: "One world at a time for me," and from early morning until dewy eve, he invested all his powers to win success, and he won it, but he died without hope, and without God, taking a leap into the dark with a wail, the memory of which must forever give agony to the hearts that heard it. The second one made profession of religion, but he followed Christ afar off. He put his religion into a little tiny corner of his life. He gave Jesus the small places, and when he came to the last end, with his family and minister around him, the minister was saddened by his awful story: "Sir, I trust I shall get to heaven, but my works are burned up, because I have done little or nothing for Christ. Oh, if I could retrace my life and be the right kind of a man!" And then there was the third man. From life's young morning he dedicated his life to Jesus. He went his way a great business man, but with it all he was the faithful friend of Jesus. He chose Christ as his chief partner, his guide in all things. And when he came down to die, there was a halo of light about his face, and there was victory in his heart, and in his words, and all the men that knew him said: "If ever a Christian has lived, this man is he." Which one of these three men would you rather be? Listen to the words of a modern poet:

A QUEST FOR SOULS

I had walked life's way with an easy tread,
Had followed where comforts and pleasures led,
Until one day in a quiet place
I met the Master face to face.

With station and rank and wealth for my goal,
Much thought for my body, but none for my soul,
I had entered to win in life's mad race,
When I met the Master face to face.

I had built my castles and reared them high,
With their towers had pierced the blue of the sky,
I had sworn to rule with an iron mace,
When I met the Master face to face.

I met Him and knew Him and blushed to see
That His eyes, full of sorrow, were fixed on me;
And I faltered and fell at His feet that day,
While my castles melted and vanished away.

Melted and vanished and in their place
Naught else did I see but the Master's face.
And I cried aloud, "Oh, make me meet
To follow the steps of Thy wounded feet."

My thought is now for the souls of men,
I have lost my life to find it again,
E'er since one day in a quiet place
I met the Master face to face.

O my men and women, you are not ready to die, you are not ready to live, you are not ready for any duty, even for five seconds, if you are putting the wisdom and love and power of Christ out of your life. Be wise, I summon you, and give heed to the supreme things, even in the day when you ought, That day is to-day.

THE BENEDICTION.

And now, as we go, may God vouchsafe unto us every one, His own searching truth, applied by its Divine Author, even by the Holy Spirit Himself, so that we shall from this day forward, put first things first, in the remaining life allowed us in the flesh. Oh, we beseech thee, our Father, that these busy men and women at this noontide hour, may go away with the heart inflexibly fixed to give Christ, the one Savior, the rightful Master of mankind, absolute supremacy in our every heart, and in every life, and in every life plan that we are to have from this day forward.

And as you go now, may the blessing of God, bright like the light when the morning dawneth, and gracious as the dew when the eventide cometh, be granted you all and each, to abide with you today and tomorrow, and throughout God's vast beyond, forever. Amen.

V

NIGHT SERVICE, JUNE 13, 1917.

PRELIMINARY REMARKS.

At the beginning of the service last evening I raised the question with the Christians who were present if they would not set themselves apart definitely to do some earnest personal religious visiting every day during these meetings. Now, I am wondering how many of those Christians who heard that request have to-day heeded it, and to-day have sought to help somebody touching personal religion. All about us there are people who are neglecting the highest things, and yet these people have their heart-hungers and their longings, because eternity hath been set in every heart, and therefore nothing other than the eternal can satisfy the human heart. Oh, I am so anxious, my fellow Christians, that we shall give ourselves during these midsummer days, in this brief meeting, like we ought, to the right kind of religious visiting. I believe—I wonder if you people believe it with me—that every night we come here every Christian listening to me now, can by the right sort of effort bring at least one with you to every night service, who is not a Christian. What if you were to do that? Remember: "Faith cometh by hearing, and hearing by the word of God." What if every Christian listening to me now highly resolved in his or her heart: "As for me, I will do my best to bring at least one with me, every night, who is not a Christian!" Oh, I pray you, pass nobody by. Go after the tallest man in this fair city. Jesus needs him, and surely that man's supreme need is Jesus. Go after the most gifted woman socially in all the city. How the Master needs her, and how she needs Him! Go after the poorest and wretchedest. Jesus would have you pass nobody by. Now, I raise the question with you again, my fellow Christian. Will you not give yourself for an hour to-morrow, to the right kind of religious visiting? There is some duty-neglecting Christian you ought to see. There is some back-slidden Christian that you ought to confer with. And, above all, there is somebody that you ought to talk with who is not a Christian at all. Oh, what an incongruity for a Christian to go his way dumb in the presence of those not Christians! Couldn't you give an hour to-morrow, to this greatest quest of all? And if it could not be an hour, couldn't it be half an hour? And if it could not be half an hour, couldn't it be five minutes? And if it could not be five minutes, couldn't you take one minute to ask some person face to face: "Is it well with your soul?" Be not afraid. Do your best, and God will be with you.

You are ready now, I trust, quietly and reverently, to listen for some moments to the reading of the Holy Scriptures. I am reading from John's Gospel, in the first chapter:

Again the next day after John stood, and two of his disciples; And looking upon Jesus as He walked, he saith, Behold the Lamb of God! And the two disciples heard him speak, and they followed Jesus.

Just one sentence, and that led them to follow Jesus, and you can speak that sentence.

Then Jesus turned, and saw them following, and saith unto them, What seek ye?

What are you men up to? Oh, how candid is the good Master, Jesus! He never misleads. He never deceives. How candid is Jesus! What seek ye? What are you men up to? Why do you follow me?

They said unto Him, Rabbi (which is to say, being interpreted, Master), where dwellest thou? He saith unto them, Come and see.

That is what He always says. That is Christ's standing challenge to mankind—come and see!

They came and saw where He dwelt, and abode with Him that day: for it was about the tenth hour. One of the two which heard John speak, and followed Him, was Andrew, Simon Peter's brother. He first findeth his own brother, Simon, and saith unto him, We have found the Messias, which is, being interpreted, the Christ. And he brought him to Jesus.

A QUEST FOR SOULS.

Text: "And he brought him to Jesus."—John 1:42.

The bringing of a soul to Jesus is the highest achievement possible to a human life. Some one asked Lyman Beecher, probably the greatest of all the Beechers, this question: "Mr. Beecher, you know a great many things. What do you count the greatest thing that a human being can be or do?" And without any hesitation the famous pulpiteer replied: "The greatest thing is, not that one shall be a scientist, important as that is; nor that one shall be a statesman, vastly important as that is; nor even that one shall be a theologian, immeasurably important as that is; but the greatest thing of all," he said, "is for one human being to bring another to Christ Jesus the Savior."

Surely, he spoke wisely and well. The supreme ambition for every church and for every individual Christian should be to bring somebody to Christ. The supreme method for bringing people to Christ is indicated here in the story of Andrew, who brought his brother Simon to Jesus. The supreme method for winning the world to Christ is the personal method, the bringing of people to Christ one by one. That is Christ's plan. When you turn to the Holy Scriptures, they are as clear as light, that God expects every friend He has to go out and see if he cannot win other friends to the same great side and service of Jesus.

"Ye shall be witnesses unto me," said Jesus, "both in Jerusalem, and in all Judea, and in Samaria, and unto the uttermost parts of the earth." The early church went out and in one short generation shook the Roman empire to its very foundation. It was a pagan, selfish, sodden, rotten empire, and yet in one short generation, that early church had shaken that Roman empire from center to circumference, and kindled a gospel light in every part of the vast domain. And they did it by the personal method. The men and the women and the children who loved Christ, went out everywhere, and talked for Christ, in the hearing of those who knew Him not, and the hearers became interested, and followed on, and found out for themselves the saving truth that there is in Christ's gospel. Every Christian, no matter how humble, can win somebody else to Christ. You would not challenge that, would you? Let me say it again. Every Christian, however humble, can win somebody to Christ.

That is a most interesting and instructive story told of the nobly gifted Boston preacher, Dr. O. P. Gifford, who preached one morning to his congregation, making the insistence that it is the business, primary and fundamental, of Christ's people to go out constantly and win others to the knowledge of the Savior. And as he brought to bear his message upon his waiting auditors, with words that breathed and thoughts that burned, the minister came on to say: "Every Christian can win somebody to Christ." When the sermon was done and the people were sent away, there tarried behind one of his humblest auditors—probably the humblest, with reference to this world's goods, for she was a poor seamstress. She tarried behind to make her plea to the preacher that his sermon was over-stressed. Greatly moved she was, the preacher stated, as looking him in the face she said: "Pastor, this is the first time that I ever heard you when you seemed to be unfair." "Pray, wherein was I unfair?" he asked. Then she said: "You kept crowding the truth down upon us that every Christian could win somebody to Christ. Now, you did not make any exceptions, and surely I am an exception. Pray, tell me what could I do? I am but a poor seamstress, and I sew early and late to get enough to keep the wolf from the door for my fatherless children, and I have no education and no opportunity, and yet your statement was so sweeping that even I was included, and in that," she said, "I think you were unfair—the first time I ever knew you to be so." And then, when she had finished her vehement protest, he looked down at her in all her agitation, and said to her: "Does anybody ever come to your house?" She said: "Why, certainly, a few people come there." And then, waiting a moment, he said: "Does the milkman ever come?" "To be sure," she said; "every morning he comes." "Does the bread-man come?" "Every day he comes." "Does the meat-man come?" "Every day he comes to my cottage." Then, waiting a moment for his questions to have their due effect, looking down earnestly at her, he said: "A word to the wise is sufficient," and he turned upon his heel, abruptly leaving her. She went her way, and the nightfall came and she went to her bed to ponder late and long the searching message she had heard that morning. Why, she had not even tried to win anybody to Christ. She had never made the effort. She claimed to be Christ's friend, and yet had never opened her lips for Him at all. She will try, and she will begin with her first opportunity to-morrow, even with the coming of the milk-man. Accordingly she was up before the daylight came, there waiting, if haply she might speak to him some word concerning personal religion. When he greeted her, he made the remark that he had never seen her up quite so early before, and she stammered out some embarrassing reply, not saying what she came to say, and now he had left her, and the gate clicked behind him as he left. Then she summoned her strength and called him back. "Wait a minute," she pleaded, "I did have something to say to you." And when he tarried to hear it, she poured out her heart to him in the query: "Do you know Christ? Are you a Christian? Are you the friend and follower of that glorious Savior who came down from heaven and died, that you might not forever die?" And fairly dropping his milk pails, he looked into her face with anguish in his own, as he said to her: "Little woman, what on earth provoked you to talk to me like this? Here for two nights, madam, I have been unable to sleep, and the burden of it all is that I am not a Christian, and I am in the darkness. If you know how to find the light, you are the one that I need, and you should tell me." And there, in a few brief minutes of conversation, she told him how she had found the light, and he walked in that simple path that she indicated for him. And Dr. Gifford goes on to tell us that before that year was out, that same little seamstress had won seven adults to Christ, not only to the open confession of Christ as their Savior, but to take their places promptly in His church. You can win somebody to Christ.

Have you tried? Will you try? Won't you try, looking to God to guide and help you?

The text tells of a man who won somebody to Christ. The case of an ordinary man is this, and therefore he is chosen, for we are just ordinary people. This man Andrew is not Paul, the outstanding Christian of the centuries. He is not Apollos, that eloquent, winsome man, who could compel people to listen to him, his words were so entrancing. He is just an ordinary, every-day, commonplace man. The Bible makes only three or four passing references to him. This man is the illustration we are to have tonight of the one person going out to win some other person to Christ. Let us fix our eyes upon him to-night, and learn from the story something to help us.

Andrew here stands forth as one who has just found the Savior. How will he act? Two things stand out in response to that question—how will he act? First of all, Andrew is immediately interested that somebody else may be saved. Don't you like that? Isn't that a wonderful example for us? Immediately, this man Andrew is concerned that somebody else may be saved. Oh, there are different evidences, my friends, indicated in these Holy Scriptures, whereby we may pass upon this eternally consequential question, whether or not we have been born again. It may be that at one of these services we will group these Scriptural evidences, and focus them upon this question: "Have I been born again, and what are the Scriptural evidences that I have been born again?" Certainly we might not be able to have a more interesting or profitable study. But whether we shall give ourselves or not to such service, here stands out for us one shining fact, like a mountain peak: If one is born again, that one is concerned that somebody else may be saved. "If any man have not the spirit of Christ, he is none of His." And the spirit of Christ is the spirit of compassionate anxiety that lost people may be saved. Now, Andrew evinces his concern, straightway after he finds the Messiah, that somebody else may find that same blessed, forgiving Savior. Years agone, I was preaching in a series of daily meetings like these, and one Sunday morning, when I made the call for those who would confess Christ to come forward and remain, there came a group down the aisles, and a number waited to be received into the church. When I came to question them about their coming into the church, I came presently to an humble German girl, a servant in one of the families. She was not long from the old country, and her English was barely intelligible, as we listened to it, and I said to her: "My child, why do you wish to join the church?" In her broken English, she made her reply to my question, and her English was so bad that it was well-nigh impossible for us to understand just what she was saying. Then I said to her: "My child, if you won't mind, I will ask you to wait a week, and let us talk with you quietly and carefully, as is the custom with all the young people that come into the church. We would be careful about this great step. The church is for those who have found Christ as their Savior, who know the way, and too much care can hardly be exercised at that point, and I will just ask, if you don't mind, that you will wait and let us talk it over, that no mistake may be made." She readily assented to my proposal, and I passed to the next case, and when I was questioning him presently the child broke out in a sob audible to those in the rear of the large auditorium. All of us were immediately embarrassed. Evidently I had grieved her, and I turned back to her frankly, and said: "Why, my child, I did not mean to grieve you by asking that you wait. That is not anything unusual. The church is doing that sort of thing here constantly. We are asking that the young people talk with the pastor, and talk with the parents carefully, before they come into the church. Coming into the church is one of the greatest steps for a human soul, and it ought to be taken with much deliberation and wisdom. It was for your good, my child and it is not anything unusual that you are asked to wait.' She said, with better English now: "Oh, sir, it is not that that makes me cry! I forgot. I cried because my brother here in this city is such a wild boy, and he is lost, and my heart is breaking. I am so concerned that he shall be saved. Won't you ask everybody here to-day to join me in one prayer that my poor, lost, sinful brother may be

saved? That is what made me cry." And the dear old
senior deacon spoke up, and said: "Pastor, we had better
take her into the church now. She knows the way, and we
need not wait another week." She did know the way, and
there was the outflashing in that conversation, in that last
moment, of her deep knowledge of a forgiving Savior, and
all that audience was swept with her tremulous appeal.
They knew, every Christian there, that this woman knew
the Lord, because of her heart's longing for others to be
saved.

There was another point about this man Andrew, strik-
ingly suggested, when he found the Savior, and that point
is that he went straight home to get his first work in for
his Savior. Now, don't you like that? He went straightway to get in his first work for the great Savior whom he
had just found, in his own home. He went after a difficult
case, let me tell you. He went after his own brother
Simon. Rash and headstrong and impulsive was that man
Simon, and yet plain Andrew, a weakling compared with
Simon, went after that big, strong brother, nor did he
cease until he had brought him to Christ.

Oh, if the limits of this hour allowed, I should like,
my brothers, to pour out my heart in a plea for home
religion. There is an old saying that comes to mind
just here: "The shoemaker's wife is the worst shod
person in the village." Oh, if I might pour out my
heart for a moment in a plea that our homes be ordered like they ought to be in the realm of religion! If
there be one place, let me say it to the parents, where you
should put your best foot forward for Christ, it should be
in your families. I tell you, that is an indictment against
a father if his own boy does not believe in his religion. I
tell you that is an indictment against a mother if her own
girl does not believe: "My mother is the best Christian
in all the world." Oh, that our religion in our homes shall
be outshining and congruous and consistent, even after the
highest and most heavenly fashion! The accent, in my
humble judgment, that most of all needs to be pronounced
this night, throughout this whole country, from border to
border, is an accent on the religion of our homes. As goes

the home, so shall go everything in the social order. The citadel, both for church and for state, is the home. If we shall have the right kind of homes, then shall everything in the social order be conserved and saved, but if our homes shall be beaten down and unraveled and frazzled out by every superficial and foolish thing—God save the mark!— the nation is doomed and the land shall be lost. I wonder what your answer would be, as I look into the faces of Christian parents now, and ask you this simple question: Do you have family prayer at your house? Why don't you have it? You might have measured off to you one round thousand years in which to get up your reasons why a Christian parent should not have family prayer in his house, and when the thousand years had passed, you would come back without the semblance of even one reason. Oh, men and women who love Christ, with your children growing about you, or already fairly grown, is it possible that human life, invested as it is with such sacred meanings and opportunities and responsibilities, shall go passing away, and the chiefest place of all to get in ycur witness for Christ, even under your own roof, shall be overlooked and lost! One of the most menacing signs that you can find in any community, if you are able to find it there, is the decay of family prayer in such community.

I am thinking now of two homes. To the first was I summoned one morning to the burial of their only child. She was a beautiful girl of some fifteen summers. They were not members of my congregation, but of another; but their minister was absent, and, therefore, was I summoned to conduct the funeral. I came to the splendid-looking home, and a vast concourse of people were in and about the house. I asked that I might see the family, and I was taken down the long hall and into the quiet room where the broken-hearted parents sat, and as tactfully as I could, I began to find my way to an apprehension of the situation, that I might the better speak in the funeral service to be had a few moments later. I found in response to questioning, presently, that both of these parents were professed Christians, and then I ventured to tell them that earth had no sorrow that heaven cannot heal, and that they must refuse to turn aside into the abyss of despair and broken-heartedness, because they had a Savior, and they were His friends. By this time the mother was on her feet, and said: "Sir, I have something to tell you that has utterly broken our hearts." I waited to hear what it was, and then she said: "That beautiful girl yonder in her casket, our only child, has been here in our home these fifteen years, and yet in all these years, though her mother is a Christian, and her father is a Christian—in all these years that child never heard either one of us pray one time, sir." And then she waited a moment more, and said: "Sir, our horrible fear is that it was not well with the child, and that her blood will be on our garments." Will you say that it was not? Oh, cruelty of cruelties, inconsistency of inconsistencies, that a child should be in a Christian home fifteen years, and never hear the voice of a parent one time lifted in prayer!

There was another home of which I would speak. I pleaded with the people one morning in the other years, begging them that they put first things first, and that the men who were Christians would pause at the breakfast table for a little season of prayer with the loved ones around them, or in the evening time, when the day was done, that they would gather the circle about them, and speak with the great King and Savior in grateful acknowledgment and in continual plea for His mercies to be granted them. Numbers that morning said that they would change their ways. One outstanding business man, whose voice was often heard in the city, searched me out and said: "Oh, I have lived miserably far from what is consistent and right. I will turn over a new leaf tonight. Family prayer shall be at my house to-night, and every night henceforth." I follow it just a moment more. The next morning, as I crossed the city, I saw his only son about fifteen or sixteen years of age, and as I was traveling rapidly along, the son summoned me, and when he reached me, I saw in his face that there was a deep battle of some sort going on, and I said: "What is it, my boy, that I can do for you?" And then he looked down with face averted, and then looked up with his face covered with tears, and said: "You ought to have been at our house last night." "What happened at your house, my boy? I should like to know." He said: "Oh, you should have been there. Papa prayed last night! Papa had sister and me called into the room, and papa sobbed as he told us he had not lived like a Christian father ought, and papa asked sister and me to forgive him. Neither of us could talk. We did not know what to say. Both of us cried. Papa asked mother to open the Bible for him, and he tried to read it, but he could not, and then papa knelt down and prayed, mostly about himself, and then he said when he got up: 'Children, papa is going to live a different life from this time on.'" And the boy said: "I went to my room and I could not sleep." I said: "Why couldn't you sleep, my boy?" And then, as he leaned over on my shoulder, he said: "I found out last night that I am a sinner, and that I am lost. You do not know how I wanted to see you, that you might tell me what to do." We turned into a little store house, vacant, and there, in a few words, I told the lad how it is that Jesus saves a sinner, and the lad made his simple, honest surrender, and was saved that very Monday morning. You should have heard him the next Sunday morning, when the pastor said: "Tell us, my boy, what started you in this upward way?" He looked across at his father, on the other side of the house, and said: "Papa's prayer last Sunday night started me in the upward way."

Oh, I know it is difficult to have family prayers, my men and women! I know it is difficult, but listen to this: Everything on this earth worth while costs, and you and I must not, dare not, thrust back into some little inconsequential corner in our lives the thing chiefest and commanding that God has appointed for the winning of the world to God.

There is another point for our consideration in the case of this man Andrew. Andrew's act magnifies the place and the power of personal work in the winning of lost people to Christ—the place and power of personal work—and just there are several suggestions for our consideration. There can be no substitutes for personal work. Jesus is depending on His friends to get His gospel made known to a gain-

saying and unbelieving world. He is dependent on His
friends. That is His own divinely appointed method.
There can be no substitutes for personal work! Life must
make its impact upon life. Now, everybody seems to understand that, I have sometimes thought, better than the
church of God understands it. The business men understand the power of personal work. They send out their
drummers up and down the land, to look into the faces of
their customers, real or prospective, and explain their
wares. And certainly the politicians understand the power
of personal work. You let a great issue be on, city or state
or national, with two virile parties each contending for
supremacy, and you will observe that the champions of
these parties send their spokesmen, their representatives,
to look their fellow-men in the face and argue and plead
and explain, if haply they may win their votes. Oh, will
the church of God fail to lay to heart that the chief instrumentality human for the winning of the world to Christ is
the power of personal work? There can be no substitute
for personal work, none at all. Elisha may send his servant Gehazi, with the prophet's own staff back yonder to the
chamber where the dead boy lies, saying to his servant:
"Put my staff on that boy and see if it won't bring him to
life," and the instructions may be carried out, but the boy
will remain in the cold grip of death. Elisha, the prophet,
himself must go, and stretch his own body, warm and puls-
ing, on the cold body of that dead boy. Elisha himself
must make the impact of life upon that dead body. The
Divine Master of life himself gave an emphasis to personal
work beyond anything that I can describe in my simple
discourse this evening. Jesus preached His chiefest sermon
on the new birth to just one man. My fellow-men, if Jesus
thought it worth while to have just one for His congregation, and there do His best work, surely the servant shall
not be greater than his Master. And when Jesus came
to preach His sermon on eternal life, He preached it yonder
to a woman at the well of Samaria — a poor drab of a
woman, about whose character the less said the better, and
yet she had a soul that was to live forever, and when she
came to that well to draw water therefrom, Jesus had His

opportunity, and with words tactful and honest and faithful, He found His way to that woman's conscience, and at the right time revealed himself the forgiving Savior to her. Jesus gave His best service for one soul.

Listen to Him yonder as He tells the story of the shepherd leaving his ninety and nine sheep safely housed in the sheep-cote. Ninety and nine of them were safe, but one was missing, and he left the ninety and nine safely housed in the sheep-cote, and went out after that missing sheep, over the hills and mountains, with his feet pierced by stones and thorns, searching, looking for that one missing sheep. Nor did he give up his quest, until that sheep was found, and the shepherd brought it back and put it in the sheep-cote with the others. What is Jesus saying in this pungent parable? "Oh, my church," the compassionate Savior says, "go out and seek earnestly until that lost sheep is found!" He is saying just that.

Now, all experience and all observation confirm the point that I am seeking to make, that there can be no substitutes for personal work. How shall we save our churches? My fellow Christians, there is one sure way, and that is that our churches be great life-saving stations to point lost sinners to Christ. The supreme indictment that you can bring against a church, if you are able in truth to bring it, is that such church lacks in passion and compassion for human souls. A church is nothing better than an ethical club if its sympathies for lost souls do not overflow, and if it does not go out to seek to point lost souls to the knowledge of Jesus.

But now I come to a practical question. How may you and I win sinners to Christ, as did Andrew of old? That is entirely practical, and this Wednesday evening let us focus our thoughts for a moment on the practical question, how may you and I, like Andrew, win people to Christ? There are several suggestions to be given in response to that question. First of all, let us magnify the Word of God and its Author, the Divine Spirit himself. We are to magnify both the Word of God and the Author of such Word, namely the Holy Spirit himself. The one is our sword, and the other is our power. We are to take this

Word of God and we are to deliver to the lost world about us the message of this Word of God concerning Jesus and the relation of humanity to Him. Our message is made out for us, fortunately: "Preach the preaching that I bid thee." "Preach the Word." The Word of God is to be proclaimed. The Word of God is to be avowed. The Word of God is to be declared. The Word of God is not bound. The Word of God will take care of itself, if only it be faithfully proclaimed. You and I are to come with this Word of God, and without mincing or reservation, are to tell men everywhere that outside of Jesus Christ they are lost, and shall never meet God in peace, if they are not forgiven by this Divine Savior. We are to declare that, and the Lord, in the power of His Spirit, shall apply and shall bring to pass such results as in His wisdom and mercy He deemeth best.

Nor is that all. As we give ourselves to the task of winning souls to Christ, we are with all diligence and devotedness to seek the guidance and power of the Divine Spirit himself at every step. He would guide and help us. You do not have to see the man to-morrow by yourself— that difficult man. The talk you are to have with him is not to be in your own strength alone. Beside you shall stand the omnific Savior, and going with you shall be the counsel and power of His Spirit. You do not have to see that woman in your own poor, unaided wisdom. You are to do the best you can, leaning on the Arm Everlasting, and God's wisdom and God's power clothed upon from His Spirit shall accompany your simple, honest effort.

Again, if you and I are to win people to Christ, then we are to use, like Andrew did, the power of personal testimony. When Andrew found his Savior, he said: "Brother, listen! I have found the Messiah. Let me tell you about Him." And then, with words that thrilled and burned, Andrew told his brother what he had tasted and seen and felt of—Jesus, the long looked for Messiah. My fellow Christians, there is nothing else human quite so powerful as the power of an earnest personal testimony concerning Jesus' experience in your own life, as you tell somebody else what Jesus has been and consciously is to you yourself. You let some man in this audience come down this aisle and stand up and tell us: "This very day I have had definite dealings with God, and know it," and every ear is alert to catch what he says. There is no power like the power of personal testimony. You can tell that neighbor or friend how you heard Christ's voice, and how you responded, and what He said to you, and what He did, and what you have seen and experienced of His grace and love in your own little life. Tell that experience to somebody without delay.

But that is not all. There is no power human like the power of personal love, as we go out to win people to Christ. Oh, do we care for the people round us who are lost? Do we really care? Of old there issued from the lips of one sorely pressed, this plaintive cry: "No man cared for my soul." Are there men and women in Fort Worth who, if we could get at what they think, would say this to us: "They have their churches and their preachers and their Christians numbering many, but nobody ever cared for my soul?" Is there somebody in this community, lost and groping like a blind man for the wall, not ready to die, not ready to live, who in truth could say to us: "I have lived these long years, but nobody ever said that he cared for my soul?" Make that impossible as these days pass. Go with your word of witnessing and pleading and love, and go without delay. There is nothing so powerful in all this world as the power of love. Everybody ought to know the thirteenth chapter of I Corinthians by heart, and in its gracious spirit every one of us ought to live every day: "Though I speak with the tongues of men and angels, and have not love, I am become as sounding brass, or a tinkling cymbal." Do we love lost sinners? Do we care for the young men about us who are coasting the downward road? Do we care for the people whose toil is rigorous and whose lot in life is hard? Do we care for business men and professional men, who are side-stepping with reference to the supreme things, namely, the things of God and the soul and eternity? Do we love these people well enough to go to them and earnestly and alone say to them: "Is it well with your soul?" There is no power in human life like the power of love. The prayer that the psalmist of old prayed is the prayer that you and I ought to pray: "Enlarge my heart." He did not pray that his head might be enlarged. "Enlarge my heart," for out of the heart are the issues of life.

One of the most heart-moving conversions that I have ever known, I witnessed years ago in my city, during the holiday period in mid-winter. There reached me the message that a little Sunday school boy in one of our mission Sunday schools had been accidentally shot by his little neighbor friend, and I hurried to the humble home as fast as I could go, and I found the unconscious little fellow in the hands of two skillful doctors, as they sought to diagnose the case. After awhile, when they had finished their diagnosis and treatment, I asked them what of the case, and they said: "He will not live. The shot is unto death." I asked them if he would recover consciousness, and they answered that he might—that he might live two or three days, or he might not live until morning. I went back the next day, for this first day the boy's father was in the stupor of a terrible drunk. A great-hearted and kindly father he was, too, when he was sober. Oh, the tragedy that many of these big-hearted, capable men allow their lives thus to be cajoled and cheated and destroyed by some evil habit! I went back the next day, and the father was sobering up. He was a fine workman in a harness and saddlery establishment. He was sobering up, and the agony of his case was something pitiful to behold. He would walk the floor, and then he would pause, as the tears fell from his face, while he looked on that little suffering boy, nine or ten years of age. I sat down beside the boy and waited for awhile, and presently the child opened his eyes, and the little fellow was conscious. His eyes were intelligent. His lips moved as he spoke my name, for he had frequently heard me speak in the mission where he went to the Sunday school. I bent over him, and the father came and sobbed and laughed as he observed the consciousness that had come to his little boy. And the father stroked the little fellow's face, and kissed him with all the affection of a mother, and said, as he laughed and cried: "My little

man is better, and he will soon be well." The little face
was clouded as he feebly whispered, saying: "No, papa;
I will not get well." And then the father protested, as
he said: "You will get well, and I will be a good man,
and I will change my ways." The little fellow's face was
clouded, and he kept trying to say something, and I reached
for the man to bend over to catch it, and this is what we
did catch, after awhile: "When I am gone, papa, I want
you to remember that I loved you, even if you did get
drunk." That sentence broke the father's heart. He left
the room, unable to tarry any longer. A few minutes later,
I found him lying prone upon his face, there upon the
ground, behind the little cottage, sobbing with brokenness
of heart. I got down by him and sought to comfort and
help him. And he said: "Sir, after my child loves me like
that, oughtn't I to straighten up and be the right kind of
a man?" I said: "I have a story ten thousand times sweeter than that to tell you. God's only begotten Son loved
you well enough to come down from heaven and die for
you, himself the just, for you the unjust, that He might
bring you to God. Won't you yield your wasting, sinful
life to Him, utterly and honestly, and let Him save you
His own divine way?" And then and there he made the
great surrender. You should slip into one of our prayer-
meetings some night, when the men and women talk about
what Christ has done for them, and one of the most appealing and powerful testimonies you would ever hear is
the testimony of this harness workman, as he stands up,
always with tears on his face, to tell you that love brought
him home when everything else had failed. They criticised him because he drank. They scolded him because
he drank. They railed at him because he drank. They
pelted him with harsh words because he drank. But a little
boy said: "Papa, I love you even if you do get drunk,"
and love won the day when everything else had failed. Oh,
my fellow-men, when everything else shall fail, "love never
faileth." Do you love these lost men and women of Fort
Worth? Then, I pray you, in the great Master's name, go
and tell them that you care for them, and tell it before another sun shall sink to rest in the far west to-morrow
evening.

Long enough have I talked, but I gather up as best I can all I should say for a final moment of appeal. Here it is: Oh, my fellow Christians, let us see to it that you and I, like Andrew, do our best to win people to Christ! What argument shall I marshal to get us to do that thing right now, and to get us to do that thing as we never did it before, and to get us to do that thing these passing days, linking our lives with God with a devotion, and giving ourselves with a humility and a personal appeal, such as we never knew before? What arguments shall I marshal to get us to do that right now? Shall I talk about duty? Then this is our first duty. And what a great word that word duty is! Robert E. Lee was right, that matchless man of the South, when he wrote to his son, saying: "Son, the great word is duty." Shall I talk about duty? My fellow Christians, your duty and mine, primal, fundamental, preeminent, supreme, tremendously urgent, is that we shall tell these around us that we want them saved.

Shall I talk about happiness? Oh, was there ever another happiness on this earth comparable to this—the hearing from the lips of some soul the glad confession that you had said the word to win such soul to Christ? There is no happiness on this earth comparable to that.

Shall I talk about responsibility? What shall I say about responsibility? Your responsibility and mine for these souls about us lost, is a responsibility big enough to stagger God's archangel. You are your brother's keeper. What if you neglect him, and he shall die in his sins? If you shall neglect him, and he shall die in his sins, when you might have won him, then it shall turn out that you are your brother's spiritual murderer. Men can be killed by neglect. Women can be killed by neglect. A while ago there was condemned to death in England a notorious criminal, one of the hardest in all the records of crime. Minister after minister sought to get into his cell before the man's execution, to talk to such man about God and the hereafter, but he steadfastly refused to see any minister. Presently one somehow got into the cell, and began to talk with him, and the poor man, condemned to be executed to-morrow, realized that he was talking at last with a minister of the gospel, and the minister brought to bear his mightiest appeal to that man to turn to God, even in those last waiting hours. The man was stolid and was utterly indifferent, and presently the minister said to the man: "Don't you realize that in a few hours more your life shall be taken and you shall be in another world?" He said: "Quite well, sir, do I realize that my life will be taken, but whether there is another world or not, I do not know, and I have not any concern about that." And then the minister urged and remonstrated and pleaded, and at last the condemned man rose up and said to him: "Sir, if I believed like you say, that a man dying without Christ is lost, and shall be lost forever—if I believed that and had your chance, I would crawl on my knees to tell the men of England, before it is too late, to repent of their sins and turn to God."

Oh, do we believe it, that these men and women about us, and the dear young people under our own roofs, and the devoted husbands, beside whom walk gentle, Christian wives—do we believe that these men are lost, and that these young people are lost? Do we believe it? Then, I pray you, even as I summon myself, let us go to them in the right spirit, pleading with God to teach us, to empower us, to enable us to plead that now, before the day is gone, they may repent of sin and be saved forever.

My message is done when I shall have asked one question. Mark it: Do these Christian men and women listening to me to-night, down in their hearts really wish that sinners shall be saved during these days of special meetings? Probably hundreds here present answer me back: "Sir, that is our deep wish, that sinners may be saved?" But I am going to make it stronger than that. Do these Christian men and women listening to me this Wednesday night say: "Sir, I promise you, yea, sir, I promise God, and in the presence of God and of angels and men, I declare my promise, not only do I desire to see sinners saved in these special meetings, but I will try myself, frail as I am and weak as I am—I will try myself, like Andrew, to win somebody to Christ?" Do you say: "That is my wish, sir, and that is my purpose, God helping me?" Everyone who says that, stand to your feet.

(A great number stood.)

THE CLOSING PRAYER.

Give us thy counsel and comfort, our Father, this hour, when our hearts have been searched by thy Word of truth, and in these last moments, ere we separate, we make our appeal to thee, that we may translate into life, into power, into action, this message from thy Book this night. How we rejoice that many in this presence stand, quietly and humbly, but courageously, to say that they not only desire to see sinners saved, but, what is of far more meaning, they purpose, looking to thee, O God, to help them, to strive personally to win others to Christ, in the hours and days just before us. O Divine Spirit, rest thou upon every head and heart, and be on every tongue, and send us to the right persons, and give us to speak what and as we ought to speak to them concerning their personal salvation. Go thou before us, and prepare the heart, that we shall speak to, and open the understanding, and make the soul to be concerned by thine own life-giving touch, thine own spiritual illumination. Our gracious Father, let these days be days when preachers and laymen, when parents and children, when Christians of every age and name, shall personally dedicate their very best to win the people to Christ. Let this be the time when the people all about us, of all conditions and classes and needs shall have brought home to them the all important truth that to live without God is to live vainly, is to miss the true end of being. Let the truth, terrible and sure, be written like fire in every conscience, that to live contrary to the will of God is to come to defeat and death. And let this be a time when, on the right hand and on the left, men and women and children shall come with honest, earnest and complete surrender of their lives to Christ.

The grace of the Lord Jesus Christ be with you all. Amen.

VI

NOON SERVICE, JUNE 14, 1917.

WHY DO SOULS GO AWAY FROM JESUS?

Text: "Then said Jesus unto the twelve: Will ye also go away? Then Simon Peter answered Him, Lord to whom shall we go? Thou hast the words of eternal life."—John 6:67, 68.

In a very frank way, and with a deep desire to help you, I should like to ask you, one by one, the personal question, What are your relations to Jesus, the Savior and Master? Every one must have personal relations with Him. We must be His friends or His foes. We must be for Him or against Him. What are your personal relations to the Lord Jesus Christ? Are you for Him or against Him?

Once when He was here among men in the flesh, and the multitudes were following Him, and He was teaching them pungently what following Him meant, the crowds were depleted, and grew less and less before His searching teaching, and finally He turned to the twelve apostles, who were following Him, and put to them this plaintive question: "Will ye also go away?" Then Simon Peter answered Him, "Lord, to whom shall we go? Thou hast the words of eternal life."

Our text this morning is that searching question Jesus asked the twelve: "Will ye also go away?" The text suggests two burning questions for us this morning. Why do people go away from Jesus? Where do they go? God give us to face faithfully for a little while at this midday service these two weighty questions.

Why do people go away from Jesus? The fundamental reason is want of grace in the heart, the lack of true faith, the absence of vital Godliness. The Apostle John tells us:

"They went out from us, but they were not of us; for if they had been of us, they would no doubt have continued with us: but they went out from us that they might be made manifest that they were not all of us." But we are back to that searching question, Why do people go away from Jesus? Many do go away from Him. Why? Now, the outward reasons for their going reveal what is in their hearts, and we may glance this morning at some of these outward reasons why people go away from Jesus.

Here, on the occasion of our text, they went away from Him because they objected to His teaching. Through the long centuries, again and again, many have manifestly gone away from Jesus because they objected to His teaching. Read the context here in the sixth chapter of John's Gospel, and you will hear the multitudes as they cry out under His teaching: "This is a hard saying; who can hear it?" And so they turned away from Him because they objected to His teaching. The gospel of Jesus Christ, my friends, is very humbling to poor human nature. Pride revolts at the gospel of Christ. And yet such gospel is not designed to please man, but rather to save him. Jesus comes in His appeal to men, and puts before them the clear demand: "If you would have me for your Savior, I must come first, before father or mother or children or dearest loved ones, or your own property or your own life. I must come first." That is not easy. That is death to self. That is self-crucifixion. And yet you would not have it any other way. Let us make religion easy and we will play it out. Let us make religion hard, even with the hardness of the terms of discipleship laid down by Jesus, and it will be triumphant anywhere in the world.

Why do people go away from Jesus? Full many a time they go away from Him because of the fear of man. That is indeed a biting saying in the Bible, where it is declared: "The fear of man bringeth a snare." Pilate was not the only man who betrayed Jesus, and in that same act betrayed himself through the fear of man. All about us the fear of man plays the most desperate havoc in human life. All through the social order, in the world intellectual, and the world of business, and the world political, and the world social, the highest interests are betrayed, and the supreme call of Christ set aside, through the fear of men. There comes in the tragic power and peril of influence. What can some men mean, and women, by the tragical misuse, the desperate waste, of their highest influence? One waits for another, and one acts because of another, or one does not act because another does not, and all through the social order the fear of man is one of the ravaging wastes of the highest influence that comes to human life. They tell us that in the capital city of one of the older States, in the long ago, a marvelous meeting was led by that eminent American evangelist, Charles G. Finney, probably the ablest evangelist that America ever saw. He preached there some three months, and thousands came to Christ. When he was preaching there one night, the story goes that there slipped into the great audience to hear him the Chief Justice of the highest court of New York State. The learned Justice came out of sheer curiosity to hear a plain, pungent, powerful speaker. It was not his custom to go to church. Not for years had he been at any public service religious, and yet this evening the preacher brought his message to bear on the conscience of this man, taking for his text: "No man liveth to himself," and when the minister had finished his message, he said: "Now, I ask, appealing to your judgment and your conscience"—that is Christ's appeal always—to men's judgments and to men's consciences — His religion does not need any other kind of appeal—when the minister had finished his appeal, he said: "Now, is some man's judgment convinced, and is his conscience searched by the truth spoken to-night, and will he, for his own sake, and for the sake of everybody else whom he may influence, make his public surrender to Christ?" And down the long aisle came the Chief Justice, to make his confession of Christ. When he took the minister's hand, the Justice said: "If you will allow me, I should like even now to turn and speak some words to this waiting audience." And facing them, the dignified Justice said: "If I have any influence over anybody, I beg him to do as I have done, to yield life and all, utterly and now, to Christ." And he called for God's forgiving mercy, that he himself had so long delayed to make that great surrender. It is said that many lawyers at the bar, there assembled in that vast audience, came down every aisle, and stood around the great minister and Chief Justice, and said to the Judge: "O sir, because you have come, and because of your appeal, we, too, will make our surrender to Christ." What if the great Judge had not come? O my soul, I know the man, and you know him, who has not come, and yet, because he has not, there shelter behind him others, who perhaps will continue thus to hide behind him as long as he shall stay away from Christ.

Why do people go away from Jesus? Full many a time they go away from Him, through captious doubts and questions concerning religion. Many people ask, What if this and that be not so? What if the Bible be not trustworthy? What if Christ be not divine? What if there be no immortality for the soul? What if there be no heaven for Christ's friend, and no hell for those who will not have Christ? What if those things be not so? 'And with question marks like that, they turn away from the vital verities of faith, and miss the way of life. Do I speak this midday hour to some man or woman who is in the grip of some serious religious doubt? Then I call to you, do not trifle with that doubt. Probe that doubt, I pray you, to its very depth. Superficial dealing with doubts in the realm of religion is utterly inexcusable. Well has some one said that "doubt is the agony of some earnest soul, or the trifling of some superficial fool." Do not trifle with your doubts. You have too much at stake, if you have doubts, in this lofty realm of religion, to go along carelessly with such doubts. Doubt is caused in various ways and comes from various sources. There is the doubt of the head. Nathanael had such doubt. "Can there any good thing come out of Nazareth?" he asked, and the answer was given him: "Come and see," and he came and saw.

There is the doubt of the heart. Some disappointment comes, beating us into the dust. Some poignant sorrow comes to blind us and to smite us and to check us. John the Baptist had such doubt. Those fine plans and hopes that swept through his mind and heart seemed all crushed as he lay there in the jail, and he sent some of his men to ask the pitiful question of Jesus: "Art thou He that should come, or do we look for another?" Be patient with somebody in doubt, when the dark and cloudy day is on, when the black Friday presses down upon the spirit with its fearful pressure. But I have come to believe, my fellow-men, that doubt is caused by a wrong life more than by anything else in all the world. Time and again when I have come into close quarters with the man who spoke out his doubts and paraded them and defended them, I have found on careful inquiry, full many a time, that underneath and behind that doubt, and evidently occasioning that doubt, was some wrong life. If a man will come with right attitude in the sight of God, he shall be delivered from every doubt, which leads me to call your attention to that great challenge Jesus has given. Notice it: "If any man willeth to do His will, he shall know of the teaching, whether it is of God." That is as broad as the race. That is as comprehensive as humanity. "If any man willeth to do the will of God, he shall know of the teaching, whether it is of God." Let any human being, no matter what the question, what the fear, what the doubt, what the difficulty, assume a perfectly honest attitude toward God, saying: "I want light, and if thou wilt give it, no matter how, I will follow it," such person surely shall be brought into the light. Time and again you have seen, as I have seen, that challenge of Jesus frankly accepted and frankly proved, and men have been brought out of the darkness into the glorious liberty and light of the children of God.

I was in an Eastern city, some years ago, for some two weeks in a daily mission, and every evening when I would finish my message, I said, as was their custom: "If there are interested men and women, who would tarry behind for personal dealings touching personal religion, they will pass through this door into the smaller auditorium, and the rest may go while we are singing the last hymn." I stood there at the door, to greet the people as they passed into the smaller auditorium for more careful and for closer personal dealings, and along with the men who came this particular evening, there came an attractive looking man some thirty-six or thirty-eight years of age, and he tarried at the door to speak with me, fairly trembling as he did so, and yet putting on a brave face. He said to me as he tarried there at the door: "Well, sir, I do not believe a word you said to-night." I replied: "Then, pray, why do you tarry? My invitation was for serious people. My invitation was for men and women in earnest, for those with a desire deep and true to find light and to get help. Why do you tarry?" "Oh," he said, "I thought I would like to see you at close range, and to hear what you said to these men in this room, and therefore I have come along." I felt that I could see underneath all that brave exterior an interest deeper than he was willing at all for me to know, and I said: "You tarry, and when the others are gone, then I should like to have some words with you alone." And so he did, and when the other service was finished, I had him alone, and as I sat beside him I asked him: "What brought you into this place? What gave you these doubts? Whence came all this uncertainty in your spirit concerning religion?" He told me a story that I have neither the time nor the inclination here to repeat. He was the son of a minister in old Virginia. He was reared like a boy ought to be reared, and yet he had got far away from all that rearing, having been absent from home some fifteen years. Then I said to him: "If these things I preach to you tonight are true, wouldn't you like to know the truth of it all?" He made quick response: "Certainly, I should like to know the truth of it all." Then I said: "You can know it. Here is the challenge of Jesus: 'If any man willeth to do His will, he shall know of the teaching, whether it is of God.' " I said: "Now as I bow my head, I will speak to your father's God and to my God, and I will ask Him just to lead you on, and to fill you with desire and purpose to follow His leading." And when I had finished the prayer I said, as we were bowed there at our chairs: "Let us remain bowed, and you try for a moment to pray." He started back and said: "Why, man, I would not know how to begin. I have not tried even in a dozen years." Think of a man's going a dozen years without calling on God! It seems impossible. "I would not know how to begin," he said. I answered: "Then I will frame a sentence for you, like I would frame it for my little child, and you say it after me." And so I did, and he repeated it, and I framed a second sentence, and he repeated that, and a third sentence, and he repeated that, and then I paused and said: "Prayer, sir, is the sanest thing in the world. Prayer is the outcry of a little, needy, finite, mortal being, to a great infinite, omniscient, omnipotent, all powerful, all merciful Being. Tell Him what you would like. Tell Him like you would tell a man something you should hasten to tell him, without any reserve." And then, timidly and tremblingly and haltingly he began his prayer. In a moment or two his words came faster. In a moment or two his sentences rushed like a torrent. He was confessing his sins. He was bewailing his dreadful decline, and memory was burning like fire, and it blazed and burned, as he recalled the old home, with the family prayer, and the father as a preacher, and the mother singing the simple songs of faith. And then he went on and said: "I remember, Lord, the last sermon I heard good father preach. He preached from that text, the cry of the publican: 'God, be merciful to me, a sinner.'" He said: "That is my prayer. Be merciful to me, a sinner. I give up to thee. Help thou a helpless sinner!" And then he was still, and then in a moment more he was on his feet, and I looked up at him and waited for him to make his pronouncement, and then he looked down earnestly at me, with his outstretched hand, and said: "I have found the light!" Of course he had found the light. Any man on the earth who will assume the right attitude toward Jesus shall be brought into the light.

My indictment against the skeptic who prates against the things of God is that he will not be candid about it and go deep enough. Any man in the world, doubter, skeptic, atheist, materialist, whoever he is, who will assume a perfectly candid and obedient attitude toward God, shall surely be brought into the light.

Why do people go away from Jesus? Full many a time they go away from Him through the power of sensual enjoyments. There are two Scriptures that set forth that truth. Here they are: "The pleasures of sin for a season," and this other: "Lovers of pleasures more than lovers of God." Through the power of sensual enjoyment, full many a time men and women miss the upward way and go the downward way to doom and death. And yet this world has in it nothing that can really satisfy the ache of the human heart. That brilliant Frenchman, Sabatier, was right, when he said: "Man is incurably religious." And then the Bible comes on, with its revealing statement, telling us that God hath set eternity in the human heart, and therefore nothing less than the eternal can satisfy the human heart. Temporal things, no matter how many, cannot satisfy the human heart.

This world can never give
    The bliss for which men sigh.
'Tis not the whole of life to live,
    Nor all of death to die.

Beyond this vale of tears
    There is a life above,
Unmeasured by the flight of years,
    And all that life is love.

Nothing short of the infinite and the eternal can satisfy any human heart.

Why do people go away from Christ? Full many a time they go away from Him through the simple, fearful, fateful power of procrastination. They tell us that procrastination is the thief of time, and so it is, but, oh, it is so much more than that. Procrastination is the thief of souls! All about us are men and women who intend somewhere, sometime, to focus their thoughts on the things of God, and to say "yes" to the call of Christ, and yet through the power of procrastination they are hurried on and daily lulled the more deeply to sleep, and the conscience is deadened, and the days go by and the highest things are lost. All about us there are men and women who, when we approach them concerning personal religion, will tell us that they intend to say yes to Christ, that they desire to be saved, that they fully expect this important matter of personal salvation to be settled a little later. But it is a little later that they say. It is to-morrow. It is by and by. Down yonder on the Mexican border, where I have often and joyfully preached to the cattlemen through the passing years, I have heard one cry escape the Mexicans' lips which is revelatory to a remarkable degree of the Mexican character. It would explain why Mexico is so belated in the development of her civilization. That little word that the Mexican uses so frequently is this: "*Manana!*" "To-morrow!" You may crowd upon him this duty, or that, or the other, and he will consent to what you are saying, but in an undertone he will say: "*Manana! Manana! Manana!*" To-morrow To-morrow! To-morrow! And so it is Satan's supreme cry to the human soul concerning religion—"*Manana! Manana!*" To-morrow! To-morrow! And as he cries it, men and women are beguiled and cajoled and deceived, and thus the battle is forever lost for the human soul. May God now arouse this audience from the awful peril of procrastination, that you may turn to God and be saved!

I am coming to our second question briefly. I have asked you, Why do people go away from Jesus? Now to the second question more briefly, Where do they go? Echo answers, Where? Where do they go? Well, if they are Christians and go away from Jesus, as many of them, alas, do, they go into backslidings. Oh, what stories could be told in this fair city about us, and in any other, of drifting Christians, if only hearts were revealed, and we could read all that in them is. Backslidden Christians! David went away from his Lord, and, oh, the hurt of it! Samson went away from his Lord. Oh, the hurt of it! Simon Peter denied the Lord. Oh, the shame of it and the hurt of it! And through the long years the friends of Jesus have listened to siren voices and have gone away from the right path into backsliding. How they have harmed religion! How they have harmed souls for whom the Savior died! How they have harmed themselves! How they have grieved Jesus! Do I speak to somebody here today who is a backslidden Christian? Oh, I exhort you, I summon you, I beseech you, for your own sake and for the sake of everybody else, hasten back to Christ!

I ask you this other question: Where do people go when they go away from Jesus, those that are not saved at all, those that are not born again, where do they go when they go away from Jesus? Jesus tells us in language unmistakable. "Ye shall die in your sins," He said to some who cavilled at His teachings, "and whither I go ye cannot come." You ask me if I believe in the fact of hell. I believe in the fact of hell as much as I believe in the fact of heaven, and I believe in the fact of the one for the same reason that I believe in the fact of the other. The one clear teacher concerning destiny, concerning the hereafter, was Christ Jesus the Lord, and He teaches that every man dying "shall go to his own place." Moral gravity is as real in the world of morals as physical gravity is real in the world natural and physical about us. Every man shall go to his own place when he leaves this world. If a man says to Jesus: "I will go on without you," where Jesus is, such man shall not come. If a man says to Jesus: "I disdain all else, frail as I am and sinful, and I believe on Christ, I can do nothing else, God help me," when such man goes hence, he will go to be with Christ.

Now, if you go away from Christ, pray look at what you give up. If you go away from Jesus you must give up this Book. Christ and the Bible are indissolubly linked together. If you can get rid of the Bible, you can get rid of Christ. If you can get rid of Christ, you can get rid of the Bible. The one is the complement and counterpart of the other. Christ and the Bible are the binomial word of God. If you get rid of Christ you get rid of the Bible, and if you propose to get rid of the Bible, sing no more by the open grave that shepherd's psalm, the twenty-third. Sing no more by the open grave, when you hide your loved ones from your sight, the glorious fourteenth chapter of John: "Let not your heart be troubled." You are done with Christ, if you are done with the Bible, and if done with Christ, you are done with the Bible.

What else do you get rid of when you get rid of Christ? You discredit the testimony of every friend that Jesus has ever had in all the world, and He has had friends many, both great and small. Many of the world's most capable minds have been the devoutest friends and followers of Jesus. Gladstone said he knew sixty of the greatest minds of his century, and that fifty-four of them—scientists, statesmen, mighty men in all callings—were the devoutest friends of Jesus that he ever saw. Oh, this gospel that we preach, my men and women, is not a collection of cunningly devised fables for people silly and thoughtless. The sanest thing on the face of the earth this Thursday morning is for a man or woman to be pronouncedly the friend of Christ—that is the sanest thing of all. Jesus is the needed Savior for the great as well as the weak. Will you look over the world's great names? In the list you will find many friends and followers of Jesus. Look yonder at the list of scientists, and in that list you will see Miller and Agassiz and Proctor, bowing obediently at the feet of Jesus. Look at the world's astronomers, and you will see Copernicus and Kepler and Newton showing their devotion to Jesus. Look at the world's first statesmen, and you will see Washington and Gladstone and others like them, showing their devotion to Jesus. And so through the centuries you will see the earth's first minds devotedly following Christ.

But I would bring the truth nearer you than that. There in the little circles where you and I live, are some whose names never get into the newspapers at all, but you and I believe in them as we believe in nobody else in the world, and they tell us that they have tried Jesus and found Him true. Yonder in the United States Senate some time ago, when a group of senators were at a dinner, as the story was told me by one who knew, one senator looked across to the chiefest senator at that time in the Senate, and said to him: "Senator, do you believe in that old doctrine that a man must be born again to get to heaven?" The senator after a moment's pause made serious reply: "I certainly do. I am grieved to have to tell you that I am not a Christian myself, but I believe in the doctrine of the new birth as preached by Christ." Then the first senator, wincing under the remarkable answer, said to the second, after a moment more: "Pray tell me why you believe in that old exploded doctrine of the new birth?" The senator waited a moment, and his face was serious and a tear was in his eye, as he said: "My mother and my wife have both told me that they surrendered to Christ, and have been born again, and they both live like it is so." You cannot answer that!

I detain you for a final word. If you go away from Jesus you are left baffled and broken in the presence of the three greatest mysteries of all, and I name them, and then we will go. If you go away from Jesus you are left broken and baffled in the presence of sin. You have no Savior if you reject Jesus. He is the only Savior. And the most terrible and obtruding fact on the earth this Thursday morning is the fact of sin in human life. If you get rid of Jesus you have no Savior from sin.

And if you get rid of Jesus you are left beaten and broken, with all the sorrow that is regnant in human life. Pause anywhere and you will hear the undertone of sorrow—anywhere. If you get rid of Jesus you have no delivering friend from the thralldom of sorrow.

And still more, and most of all, if you get rid of Jesus you are left in the presence of death, without light and without hope and without life, broken in the presence of death. When you come to the grave you will need a Savior. Plato and Socrates merely speculated as they looked into the open grave. So did Caesar when he stood up in the Roman Senate. Job asked the question: "If a man die, shall he live again?" Only one person has answered that question. Only one can answer it, and His name is Jesus. He came and bowed His head to death, and went into the dark chambers of the grave, and on the third day after they laid Him in Joseph's tomb, He pushed the grave door open and came out, saying: "Because I live all who trust me shall live forever." Oh, you must not dare to live or die without Jesus!

'Tis religion that can give
Sweetest pleasures while we live.
'Tis religion must supply
Solid comfort when we die.

After death its joys will be
Lasting as eternity.
Be the living God my friend
Then my joys will never end.

Tell me, are you for Jesus? I would be for Him, were I in your place today, if I had to go through flame and flood to follow Him. Be for Him before it is too late! Does He call you today? Follow Him, trust Him, yield yourself to Him whatever your condition or case may be, and His word for you is sure: "Him that cometh to me, I will in no wise cast out."

THE CLOSING PRAYER.

How deep is our joy, O, our Father, that we have such a Savior, even the Lord Jesus Christ, to forgive us and guide us and keep us forever. As we stand here to-day may we promise one another, and above all may we promise Christ to cleave to Him and to cleave to Him forever. And if one is here to-day in the grip of doubt or sin or difficulty of any kind, lead such to be candid and whole-hearted, as such one seeks the way of life, and may such one soon tell us that he or she has found that blessed way and is going with us as we follow Christ.

And as you go now, may the grace of our Lord Jesus Christ, the love of God the Father, and the communion and blessing of the Holy Spirit, be granted you all and each, to abide with you to-day and forever. Amen.

VII

NIGHT SERVICE, JUNE 14, 1917.
PRELIMINARY STATEMENT.

It would be very interesting if we might know the experiences that God's people have had to-day in this community, as here and there they have had conversations with others about personal religion. I am constrained to ask how many Christians gathered in this large assemblage to-night have made it a point to speak an earnest word with somebody to-day about personal religion? Did you do your best? Were you faithful? Then you may gladly leave the result with God.

And now I come to ask if every Christian listening to me will not make it a point—a point of conscience—will not put it upon high principle, to speak to somebody, even to as many as you may and ought, about personal religion, before we come here to this tent again to-morrow night? Can't you give an hour to that weightiest of all matters, the effort to help others in the right care of the soul? And if it could not be an hour, couldn't it be half an hour? And if it could not be half an hour, couldn't it be half a dozen minutes? Tell me, is there any Christian here who, for any cause, should allow to-morrow to pass without speaking to some soul about being right with God? I beseech you, my fellow-Christians, do your best now to help those who need you in the realm of religion. The Lord be your constant inspiration and help in this heavenly work of shepherding souls!

PREPARATION FOR MEETING GOD.

Text: "Prepare to meet thy God."—Amos 4:12.

For quite awhile now there has been a word thrust into prominence, through the press and from the platform, all over this land and in other lands. That word is "preparedness." Its meaning is at once evident. In recent times its meaning has been associated with the realm military, and in such realm its meaning is entirely plain. The word is an equally suggestive one in the realm of education. Oh, what a summons there is to-day to the young people all over the land to get ready for life's work — to be worthily prepared. And this word "preparedness" is an equally worthy word in the important realm of business. And certainly, in the highest realm of all, the realm of religion, this word "preparedness" has an immeasurably important meaning. Our text points the lesson for us in five little words, quite familiar, but to the last degree suggestive: "Prepare to meet thy God."

I shall not now stop to discuss these five words in their setting, but shall begin my message by asking you, one by one, this all-important question: Are you prepared for your meeting with God? Meet Him you must. Your relations to Him are inescapable: "We must all appear before the judgment seat of Christ." It is more serious than that: "So then every one of us shall give account of himself to God." Are you prepared for your inevitable meeting with God?

These five little words suggest for us three infinitely important questions. Let us together ask them and answer them as faithfully as we may this Thursday evening. "Prepare to meet thy God"—why? "Prepare to meet thy God"—how? "Prepare to meet thy God"—when? I have asked these questions as simply as it is possible for me to ask them, so that these boys and girls about me, of young and tender years, may know the points that I am seeking to enforce, for it behooves Christ's preacher ever so to preach, not simply that the people may understand him, but so that they must—so that as they go their ways and speak one to another about what they have heard, or ponder it in their hearts, their hearts shall say: "One thing is certain, and that is, we know what the man was driving at." God help us to-night to speak and to hear like we ought. Above all else, we now would pray for the leading of the Holy Spirit throughout this responsible hour!

Let us consider the first question suggested by the text: "Prepare to meet thy God"—why? It would be enough to say that God commands it. Running like an unbroken thread all through His Book is His command to the children of men to make preparation for their meeting with Him. We could rest our case right there. God commands it. When we know the mind of God about anything, it is the part of the highest wisdom for us to relate ourselves obediently to that command. This is God's command. And shall the poor little creature turn in defiance away from the great and holy Creator? Shall the human, whose life is utterly contingent upon the divine will, turn away from such will and seek to ignore Him? This is God's command: "Oh, ye children of men, prepare ye to meet me!" And when we have His command about anything, then it is the part of the highest wisdom for us to follow that command without reserve and with all devotion.

But the reason for such preparation is revealed to us still further by the revelation God makes in His Book to us. Our condition demands that we shall make such preparation. And what of our conditon? There has come to us in our very natures a moral sickness, the name of which is sin, which has turned us all away from God. Sin is a moral sickness in human life, as real as the hand or the eye is a part of our physical life, and because of that moral sickness, calling for a helper, and because a helper has been vouchsafed, we are to turn to that helper and seek to have healing and recovery from our moral sickness. One little word describes it all, and that word trembled on the lips of Jesus when He was here: "The Son of man is come to seek and to save that which was lost." Oh, what a world of meaning, of horrible meaning, is condensed into that one little word, "lost!" And outside of Christ, that is the condition of mankind. If that could only be realized, how different would be our attitude towards sin and towards

God, who would deliver us from sin's enthralling power. Oh, if that could be realized! One prayer, my fellow Christians, I adjure you to pray, as we gather here from evening to evening, and yonder at noonday in the Chamber of Commerce auditorium—one prayer: "Lord, open the eyes of men and women, that they may see, touch their hearts, that they may feel, their absolute need of God!"

When I was a child—with awful vividness do I remember it—there went throughout the land a shuddering story that a little boy had been kidnaped away from his parents, had been stolen away from his home, had been lost to his loved ones. Not to my dying day can I forget the thrill of horror that day by day went through my childish heart as I heard them discuss it in our home, and heard the neighbors discuss it when they would gather, that a little boy had been lost to his parents. Somebody had stolen him away, and parents were resorting to every possible means to find out about that little fellow, that he might be recovered and restored to his loved ones. When the older people in the country home where I lived would come in from the farms, they would look for the latest paper, if haply they might find some word about that lost little boy—Charlie Ross. And mothers drew their little fellows nearer to them and watched them more closely, as they pondered the direful meaning of the losing from the home of a precious child.

Oh, if that truth could only be passed on and up, like it ought to be, to the realm of religion, and we could lay to heart like we ought what it means for the soul, for the self, for the personality, for the life, to be lost in the sight of God! When we turn to the Scriptures, they are as clear as the light on this momentous point. I quote them now: "God looked down from heaven upon the children of men, to see if there were any that did understand, that did seek God. Every one of them is gone back; they are altogether become filthy; there is none that doeth good, no, not one." I quote again: "There is not a just man upon earth, that doeth good, and sinneth not." I quote again: "All we like sheep have gone astray; we have turned every one to his own way." I am quoting again: "Marvel not that I said unto thee"—moral man though Nicodemus may have been, splendid in his position, cultured in his life—"marvel not that I said unto thee, ye must be born again—except a man be born again, he cannot see the kingdom of God." I am quoting again: "Except ye repent, ye shall all likewise perish." I am quoting again: "There is no difference, for all have sinned and come short of the glory of God." I am quoting again: "He that believeth the Son hath everlasting life; and he that believeth not the Son"—he may have joined the church, he may have been baptized, he may sit with others at the Lord's table, to partake of the emblems of Jesus' broken body and poured out blood—never mind, nevertheless, "he that believeth not the Son shall not see life; but the wrath of God abideth on him."

Salvation is by a person. It is not by a church. It is not by an ordinance, nor by a sacrament, nor by a creed, nor by a ceremony, nor by a form, however beautiful; nor by a man, however clever and pretentious. Salvation is by a person, and that person is none other than the Divine Lord and Savior, Jesus Christ. Whoever receives Him to be His Savior is saved by Him. Whoever turns away from Him does not have spiritual life, but spiritual death.

Note further what is lost. What does it mean to be lost? When Jesus was here in the flesh, He asked the question, one of the most pungent that ever fell from His lips, indeed, if not the most pungent, and this was His question: "What shall it profit a man if he shall gain the whole world and lose his own soul?" Whom was He talking about? He was talking about *you*. "What shall it profit a man if he shall gain the whole world"—not simply this prosperous Tarrant county, not simply this progressive, fast-growing city of Fort Worth, not simply this imperial and powerful commonwealth, so dear to all our hearts; not simply this nation, first of all in the galaxy of nations; not simply this wide-spreading continent, with its measureless resources—"what shall it profit a man"—any man—"if he shall gain the WHOLE WORLD and lose his own soul, or what shall a man give in exchange for his soul?"

What did Jesus mean when He talked about losing the soul? Well, I will tell you, first of all, one thing He did not mean. He did not mean, as is sometimes falsely alleged, that the soul of the wicked at death would go down into darkness and annihilation, to be heard of no more. He did not mean that. Jesus as thoroughly taught the immortality of the soul of the wicked as He taught the immortality of the soul of the believer in Christ. Immortality is never conditioned on character—never. If you shall die in your sins, going down into the grave and to eternity, without Christ, you shall consciously exist in the realm of waste and loss in another world forever, as really as the soul that trusts Christ and stakes all on Him shall go to live at His right hand, and be like Him and with Him forevermore. That man who teaches the doctrine of the annihilation of the wicked is an enemy both to God and to men. Jesus as distinctly teaches the conscious immortality of the soul of the wicked in another world after this, as He teaches the conscious and blissful immortality of the righteous in the heavenly land, which He has gone to prepare for His friends. Oh, if death ends all, it is not such a serious thing to die! If death ends all, then this little life of ours is an awful bundle of contradictions. Would you say that the game is worth the candle, if we must suffer and be pained and have the soul swept with ten thousand vexations and disappointments and horrors, and then drop into the grave at the end of fifty or sixty or seventy years, or more or less, to be heard of no more forever? If that be all, is life's game worth the candle? Oh, my fellow-men, that is not all!

> There is a death whose pang
> Outlasts this fleeting breath.
> Oh, what eternal horrors hang
> Around one's second death!

One of the old Confederate soldiers told me of a young lad who went out from his community to the war of the '60's. The lad was barely grown. He would go to the war, and the mother pressed into his hands a copy of the New Testament, as on his forehead she pressed her lips, and tears and prayers were mingled as she bade him good-bye, urging him as he went to war, to read that little book every day, and follow its precepts, and whether he should come back or fall on the field of battle, if he would follow the light of that little book, all would be well. And the old soldier told how the lad went into the war, and went into battle after battle, never reading the little book at all. They were getting ready to go into one of the most awful battles of that fearful struggle, and the commanding officer was advising his men how to behave, and was saying: "You will play the men now. Many of you will not come back, but you will stand with your faces to duty." And this young fellow was seen with face pale like death, while some of the older men twitted him about his being afraid. They said: "They will about get you, this time, lad, and you are afraid to die, are you? You are chicken-hearted, are you? You are afraid now, are you?" And drawing the little Testament from his pocket where he had carried it, from the inner pocket, he said: "When I went away from home, mother urged me to read this, and I meant to do it, and promised her I would, but I have never opened it. She said if I would follow its light and counsel all would be well, but I do not know what its light and counsel are, for I have not read it. Now I am going into this battle with the awful apprehension that I may not come back again. No, men, I am not specially afraid to die," but then he added, with an awful ejaculation, "My God, I am afraid of what is coming after death, for I have made no preparation for it!" Well might he fear. Well might he start back. There can be no sanity at all, there can be no reasonableness at all, in our coming to the end of the earthly life, and taking a leap into the dark all neglectful and unready and unprepared.

What did Jesus mean when He talked about the soul being lost? He meant the soul's separation from God— just that. "Every man shall go to his own place" when he leaves this world. The law of moral gravity is just as inexorable as the law of physical gravity. Every law of science and philosophy would utterly be disannulled if a man should not reap as he sowed. And if a man turns indifferently and neglectfully away from the claims and calls of God and goes the downward way, his portion must be of the kind of his own sowing. Jesus taught it. You are not willing to defy Him, are you? I am not. Where will you spend eternity? You will spend it just as is your relation to Christ Jesus while you are here in the flesh, on earth, in time. Surely, preparation for meeting God is a matter of transcendent concern. Teach us, oh, teach us, thou Friend Divine, the infinite importance of such preparation to-day!

But I pass to the second question suggested by the text: "Prepare to meet thy God"—how? In answer to that question, I may say that I know the day when you will be saved, if, indeed, you ever are to be saved. I know the day, because God reveals it here in His Holy Word. Listen to Him: "In the day that thou seekest me with thy whole heart, I will be found of thee." Listen to Him again: "Ye shall seek me, and find me, when ye shall search for me with all your heart." Oh, if this Thursday night the man, the woman, the child, is here who is wrong with God, who rises up with high hopes, saying: "This very Thursday night with my whole heart I will seek God," then this Thursday night you shall meet Him and be saved.

There were two plain truths sounded out by Jesus and His apostles, the record of which is kept here for us in His Holy Word, and those two truths are set forth in the two pithy sayings: "Repentance toward God," and "Faith in the Lord Jesus Christ." Here we are, with our moral sickness, with our lapse and defeat and loss and moral failure. Here we are, hostile and disobedient in the sight of God. Here we are, having violated God's law and transgressed His precepts. And He calls to us, saying: "Will you not repent of that evil way? Will you not turn from it? Will you not forsake it? Will you not renounce that evil way and leave it utterly behind? Not only will you be sorrowful for such evil course, but will you not translate that sorrow into action, and forsake the evil way and leave it behind?" That is, by repentance, to turn to God. And then, will you not by faith lean wholly and only upon Christ, the atoning Savior for those who have sinned in the sight of God? Will you not commit yourself to that divinely given Friend, who came, himself the just, to make atonement for us, the unjust, that by His own atoning sacrifice He might make us right with God? Will you not thus definitely by faith take Christ as your Savior? Who-

ever comes, turning definitely away from the wrong course
—and he may make such turning in one moment—and
turning with absolute surrender to Jesus, the Divine Savior
—whoever comes like that to Christ, shall in that selfsame
hour be forgiven and saved. Oh, that it might be to-night,
for every soul here present who is wrong with God! You
set your heart to seek other things, and properly so. You
set your heart to seek success in business, and properly so.
You set your heart to mount the rung of the ladder of
achievement, and properly so. You set your heart to reach
a certain goal out there, noble and worthy, and properly
so. Oh, I summon you, set your heart, by high resolve,
that the greatest matter of all shall not be ignored and
passed by and forfeited by you! Set your heart to seek
God before it is too late.

But we have another question suggested by this simple
text: "Prepare to meet thy God" when? I have asked
you two questions: Why prepare to meet thy God? And
then, next: How prepare to meet Him? And now I am
coming with this third question: "Prepare to meet thy
God"—when? Oh, solemn truth, there are limits that you
must not pass, for if you pass them you do it to your own
deadly and eternal undoing. "Prepare to meet thy God"—
when? There are limits beyond which if you go, the
battle for the soul is lost forever. The Bible is clear at
that point. The Bible is all along reminding us of the
eternal value of this probationary period called time, in
the which period the highest things of the soul are to be
seen to and to be determined upon forevermore. Oh, the
tragedy of being lost just by waiting too long to make
proper preparation for meeting God!

Were you ever yonder above Niagara? If you have
been, some hundreds of yards above that roaring, plung-
ing Niagara, you have seen a strange sign, flung out on
either side of the river, as the river rushes to take that
last awful plunge. You recall it as I speak of it. A plank
with three ominous words is flung out on either side of
the river, and you are arrested as your eye sees those
words — just three: "PAST REDEMPTION POINT."
The meaning of the words is ominous and evident. Oh.

boatman, plying your little boat on the surface of that river, do not get below that sign! Oh, canoeman, floating idly and leisurely on the bosom of that river, do not get below that sign! For a little below the sign the river-bed falls, and the river rushes with the speed almost of the arrow let fly from the bow to take its fearful plunge over the awful precipice. Do not get below that sign. Somewhere in the journeying of a human soul there is that awful sign flung out: "Past Redemption Point." Soul, do not get below that sign! Do not get into that current below that sign!

When ought you to prepare to meet God? What does your best judgment say about it? When ought you to make this preparation for meeting with God? What does He, who was and is the incarnation of infinite wisdom, say to us in response to that question, When ought this preparation for meeting God to be made? He has just one message in answer to that question: "Boast not thyself of to-morrow, for thou knowest not what a day may bring forth." Since I came to this platform this evening, one passed up to me a tragic note saying: "Have a prayer for stricken parents, whose son was torn into shreds by a passing train, on the outskirts of this city, a few minutes ago." We breathe our most earnest prayer up into the ears of our gracious Lord, that He will comfort and heal the parental hearts torn by such a sorrow. The tragedy itself points simply the truth that I am now emphasizing— that in the unexpected hour, the blow falls; in the unexpected hour, the end comes. Therefore, God tells us: "Boast not thyself of to-morrow, for thou knowest not what a day may bring forth."

When ought this preparation to be made? I come to affirm, on the authority of God's teaching, confirmed by all human experience, that to-day and now, every man and woman and boy and girl under the sound of my voice, who is wrong with God ought to see about preparation for meeting God to-day and now. And why so? Let me give you two or three reasons. Judge ye yourselves whether these reasons are worthy the consideration of your best judgment.

You should make your preparations for meeting God to-day and now because you need that your life here and now should be saved. Did you think that I would say, in order that you might be prepared to die? I will say that, but not yet, for that does not come yet. That does not come first. Oh, men and women, there is not a human being before me or anywhere else competent to live life like it ought to be lived for one short second, if such being is in hostile array against God. You are not ready for any duty or any day or any experience, to meet it like you ought, if you are in wrong relations to God, if you are not positionized openly and honestly as the friend of God. So I am coming to say that you should prepare to meet God now, in order that your life, your busy, responsible life, here and now may be saved—your life saved. If I knew that twenty-five years from this Thursday night, I would come back to this growing city, and be right on this same spot, and under a tent like unto this, and this vast concourse of people would be back, and nobody would be missing, and we would all have our wits about us and be in our right minds on that far-off night, twenty-five years from to-night; if I knew that on that night, far-off, when I made the call for you to decide for Jesus and surrender to Him, everyone of you would come then and surrender to Christ and be saved, yet would I pour out my heart to you this Thursday night, and say, come now, that these twenty-five years may not be lost! Come now, that these twenty-five years may not be given to Satan. Come now, that your influence may not be positionized against heaven and Christ and all that is dearest and highest and best. Come now, that your life may be saved to the right side. Come now, that your influence may be positionized where it ought to be. You can no more be separated from your influence over others than you can separate yourself from your shadow as you walk in the glowing sun. Come now, that your influence may be saved! Oh, what do some men and women mean, whose influence is all against heaven and God and the highest life? What do they mean? Years agone, a man was converted under my ministry in my city, after he had reached the age of some sixty-eight

years, and then for the year or two afterward that he was
spared, his devotion to Jesus was something to the last
degree inspiring. Some months after his conversion, I
noticed him at a morning service, profoundly agitated, and
when I dismissed the people he tarried at his pew, and
continued to sob like a heart-broken child, and I went
around quietly to him, when the people had gone, and
asked him to explain his strange and seemingly uncontrollable emotion, and he said: "Why, man, it was your
sermon, your sermon!" And then I remembered my text:
"No man liveth to himself." No man can live to himself. We are taking people up or down with us every
day. We are making it easier or harder for people to
get to heaven every day we live. "It was your sermon,
sir," he said, and then he said: "I am the sad proof of
the tragedy of a wasted influence. I came at sixty-eight
to Christ, and as I came to this church house this morning, I came by the home of my three sons, and I begged
each one of these sons to come to church with me, and
they all shrugged their shoulders and faintly essayed to
smile, and said: 'We guess, father, that we will start to
going to church when we get to be about sixty-eight.'
Then I tried their sons, some of them coming into young
manhood, my dear grandchildren, and they looked at one
another with a wink, and said: 'Grandpa, we guess we
will start to going to church when we are about sixty-
eight or seventy.'" The old man said: "I came on without child or grandchild. I am myself, sir, the awful proof
of the tragedy of a wasted influence." Then he rose up
and looked at me with a pathos I can never forget, and
stretched out his strong arm and said: "I would have
that arm severed from my shoulder if I could turn time
backward and live my life over again—if I could undo my
wasted influence." And then, with a sob never to be forgotten, he said: "Sir, I would be willing to have my head
severed from my body, if I could go back and teach my
little boys by example how a Christian father ought to
live." Oh, the tragedy of wasted influence!

A little boy slept with his father after the mother had
died, and one night the little fellow awakened his father

by his pitiful sobbing—this little six-year-old son—and the
father said: ".Why, my boy, why do you sob?" And the
little fellow did not wish to tell him, but the father urged
him to tell him, and presently the little fellow said: "It
was a bad dream, papa." And then the father said: "Tell
me what it was." And the little boy said: "I would rather
not, papa. It is about you." The father, of course, was
curious now, and said: "Tell me, my boy, what it was."
The little fellow said: "It is about what you have done
to me. I do not think I can tell you." Then the father
coaxed him and mothered him, and said: "Tell papa about
it." And the little fellow said: "Papa, I dreamed that
you, my own papa, had your hand to my throat, and were
choking me to death." God pity us, that is not a dream!
I know parents who are doing that with the souls of their
children. ◆Sometimes it is a strong father, and he would
lay down his life for the welfare of his child, and yet he has
the grip of his parent's influence around the throat of that
child's soul, and the child is missing the upward way.
Sometimes it is a mother. Oh, God, and can it be? The
highest dignity allowed to a human being is the dignity
of motherhood, and can it be that a mother, on whose heart
God lays a precious child for the mother to love and to
guide—can it be that the mother goes her way, forgetful
of the highest, and in those plastic days influences her
children so that they go the downward road rather than
the upward? I am pleading to you to-night for your life.
You will not face life like you ought to face it; you will
spoil it, you will mar it, you will debauch it, you will
prostitute it, you will defile it, if you dare to go your way
without God.

Now I am going to say that second word. You should
make your preparation for meeting God now in order that
you may be ready for life's end, when such end shall come.
And when shall that end come? No angel above us knows
when that end shall come. It may come before midnight
to-night. It may come before the Lord's day shall dawn.
It may come with the gladsome ringing of the Christmas
bells at the next holiday time. When shall I take that
journey down into the valley of the shadow? Only God

knows. Not all of us will be here when the chimes of the Christmastide shall sound so sweetly in expectant ears. I am coming to say, my fellow-men, that there is no wisdom in our going our way to that inevitable end, and then taking a leap into the dark without preparedness, without readiness. There is no wisdom in that. Be ready for the time of your departure from earth. Be ready.

Give heed, I pray you, to this other word: Every day you delay making your return to God, by that much do you add to your difficulty about ever coming. Therefore, should our interest be keyed to the highest for the young people. Oh, how I covet these boys and girls in their teens, and just beginning their teens! How I covet every one of them for God! Wisdom has fled from God's people if they do not put forth their best efforts to save the people while they are young. It is God's time. Listen to Him: "Remember now thy Creator, in the days of thy youth, while the evil days come not, nor the years draw nigh, when thou shalt say, I have no pleasure in them." The voice of God's Book, confirmed by all experience, is that in the morning of life, this biggest question of all—right adjustment to God—should have proper settlement—in the morning of life. Remember it, my fellow-men; remember it, my young people—every day that you delay your coming to God do you add to your difficulties about ever coming at all. Every day that you delay, you increase and strengthen your difficulties. If a man will not do a thing for awhile, then by a law psychological, and physiological as well, after awhile he cannot do it. If through some freakish fancy I should have this arm tied to my body for a dozen years, refusing to use it, and at the end of those years I should say: "Cut the cord and watch me lift the ax and bring down the trees in the forest, as I used to do when a boy," it would be found that I could not lift the ax at all. I would be helpless and impotent to lift that ax at all. I would not lift it—I refused to use it, now I cannot. If through some fancy I should have my eyes bandaged and keep them in the dark for a dozen years, and then say to my friends: "Remove the bandages now, and watch me read as once I read from the book or the paper," you might give me the book or the paper, but I could not read at all. So long was I determinedly and positively in the darkness that light fled away. Every day that a human soul trifles with God's light and turns the back on God, does such soul add to its danger and difficulty and make its probability of salvation less and less and less.

In my city, years ago, as I rode to a funeral with one of our well-known citizens, not a Christian, a man for whose salvation I had yearned, God knows, with a yearning inexpressible, he said to me, as we came back from the funeral, for he was quite reminiscent—we had buried his dear friend—he said: "A strange thing has happened to me, and I do not know how to explain it." Then he added: "When you came to Dallas years ago, I heard you often on Sunday morning, and many a time I went away so stirred that I did not enjoy a mouthful of my midday meal Sunday. But I went my way, saying: 'This matter of religion will get my attention by and by, but I am preoccupied; I am too busy now.' And I have heard you on and on, but less and less, as the years passed. I heard your words awhile ago," he said, "as you stood by the bier of my dear friend, and there was no emotion at all, that I could find in my heart. I have reached a strange place, and that place is that I have no feeling at all, none at all. I do not know what has happened."

I did not tell him what had happened to him, and yet I think I know. The Scriptures are clear as the light that a human soul can trifle with light, and can resist God, and can refuse, and can protest, and can defer, and can wait, until after awhile the human conscience is seared as with a hot iron, and no more is there feeling for such duty-neglecting and light-forgetting soul—no more. There comes in a solemn song that our parents used to sing, when some of us were little tots about their knees. Maybe I can quote that solemn song. Oh, the depth of its meaning!

There is a time, I know not when,
  A place, I know not where,
Which marks the destiny of men,
  To glory or despair.

There is a line by us unseen,
  Which crosses every path,
The hidden boundary between
  God's patience and God's wrath.

To cross that limit is to die,
  To die as if by stealth.
It may not pale the beaming eye,
  Nor quench the glowing health.

The conscience may be still at ease,
  The spirits light and gay.
That which is pleasing still may please,
  And care be thrust away.

But on that forehead God hath set
  Indelibly a mark
By man unseen, for man as yet
  Is blind and in the dark.

And still that doomed man's path below
  May bloom like Eden bloomed.
He did not, does not, will not, know,
  Nor feel that he is doomed.

He feels, he says, that all is well,
  His every fear is calmed.
He lives, he dies, he wakes in hell,
  Not only doomed, but damned.

Oh, where is that mysterious bourn,
  By which each path is crossed,
Beyond which God himself hath sworn,
  That he who goes is lost?

How long may men go on in sin?
  How long will God forbear?
Where does hope end, and where begin,
  The confines of despair?

One answer from those skies is sent:
  "Ye who from God depart,
While it is called, To-day, repent,
  And harden not your heart."

My message is done. I have a question to ask you before I go. How many of you men and women have made preparation for meeting God? And by that I mean simply this, that turning away from yourself you have turned to Christ, and are trusting in Him only and utterly as your Savior. How many of this large throng of people can personally say: "Sir, I have made that preparation. I have heard Christ's call. I have yielded myself to Him. I am trusting alone in Him as my Savior." Every man and woman and child in this press of people that can say: "I have made that preparation, sir, already," lift high your hand just now. [A sea of hands went up.] Oh, isn't it a sight to move our hearts! It looked to me as if almost every hand was lifted. Blessed be God! And yet I must ask another question. Are there men and women in this gathering to-night who could not in conscience lift their hands, thus witnessing that they are on Christ's side? Are there men and women listening to me who say: "Oh, sir, I am wrong with God and know it. I could not lift my hand. I am wrong with God and know it." In the church maybe, or out—a professor of religion once, or maybe never such—but your heart says this: "I am wrong with God and know it. I could not lift my hand a minute ago, but I would lift it on this, that I am wrong with God and know it, and I wish to be right with God, in His own time and way." We will offer our most fervent prayer for you in a moment, ere we go. Do you say: "I lift my hand on that. I am wrong with God and know it, and I wish to be right with Him, and I wish you and all these who pray to offer a prayer for me that I may be right with God, in His own time and way. I would lift my hand on that." As I look this audience over for a minute, do you lift your hand? There where I am pointing, I see you, my brother, and you, dear lady. As I am pointing there to the left, does the hand lift, saying: "That includes me?" Where I am looking yonder, does the hand lift, saying: "That includes me?" I see you, sir. Oh, sirs, breathe a prayer to God to bless these men and women. I see you, lady, and still another, and still another over there. Back to the rear, does the hand lift there, clear to my right? I see you, gentlemen, numbers of your hands.

——Oh, that to-night you would end your delay! Listen to Jesus: "Him that cometh unto me, I will in no wise cast out." Listen again: "Boast not thyself of to-morrow, for thou knowest not what a day may bring forth." And again: "To-day, if ye hear His voice, harden not your heart."

THE CLOSING PRAYER.

Take the service, we pray thee, our Heavenly Father, into thine own gracious keeping, and turn it even as thou wilt. Oh, we cry unto thee, our Father, in the dear Savior's name, in behalf of these interested men and women and children, who this night have said to us: "We are consciously wrong with God, but wish to be right." How we covet them and long for them, that without delay they shall just surrender, simply and honestly, to Christ, that He may be their Savior and Master. Teach them by thy Spirit that waiting has in it nothing but peril. Teach them that by every worthy motive that can move serious people to a great step, now, without delay, they should decide for Christ. May thy Word be bound upon their hearts, where thou sayest: "Him that cometh to me, I will in no wise cast out;" and where thou sayest: "Whosoever will, let him take the water of life freely;" and where thou sayest: "Commit thy way unto the Lord. Trust also in Him, and He shall bring it to pass." Oh, may these men and women and children, wrong with God, but wishing to be right, know, because God shall teach them, that it is Christ's business to save, but it is theirs to surrender to Him, entirely to Him, that He may save in His own way. May they make that surrender even this very night, before they sleep. And if in this throng there were others, who did not witness to their interest about being saved, and yet who are interested, we pray that their interest may be deepened, until speedily they shall find Christ. And if in this place there is one whose heart is not touched with any sense of interest touching personal religion, oh, may the Divine Spirit take of the things of Christ and convict such soul of the supreme and urgent need of Christ's forgiving grace. Take the whole audience now into thine own gracious care, and lead us as thou wilt. How we bless thee that such a vast number of the people present are able to make the great confession that Christ is their Savior even now. May each one go who loves Christ, and speak the word to whom and as Christ would have the word spoken, that others may be helped by us in the hours and days just before us, and helped in the highest and best way. Take this family, stricken with sorrow this very evening, and bind up their hearts with God's own healing comfort and grace.

And now, as you go, may the blessed Holy Spirit brood over you all, and may the love of the Father, and the grace of the Lord Jesus Christ be granted you all and each, to abide with you forever. Amen.

VIII

NOON SERVICE, JUNE 15, 1917.

THE OPENING PRAYER.

Holy Father, deep is our gratitude to thee for thy goodness to us and ours. How wonderful it all seems! Yea, how wonderful it really is! We bless thee for it. And now as we come apart at this midday hour for a brief service, we pray that we may have the touch of thy hand upon us, all and each. We would wait here in thy presence now just like we ought. We would be humble before thee. We would be repentant on account of every evil way, and we would be cleansed from all unrighteousness. We would put our trust unreservedly in God. We would turn absolutely from every wrong course. We would have thee speak to us what thou wouldst have us to hear. We would know thy will, and then we would do it, by thy guidance and help, whatever it costs, wherever it leads. Let there be in the service something that shall help us every one, and that shall make for the glory of thy name. And to-day, and in the days just before us, may we make it our concern, as never before, to put first things first, to seek the kingdom of God and His righteousness, before all else. We ask this in the Master's name. Amen.

A RELIGION THAT IS DIVINE.

Text: "Christ the power of God."—I Cor. 1:24.

A religion without a Divine Savior is a religion incompetent and insufficient for a needy, sinning, suffering, dying humanity. No man has moral sources within himself sufficient to live the life that he ought to live. Systems of ethics and of morals, however beautiful and worthy, will not, and cannot, transform men and women who have the sense of sin in their lives—the sense of moral loss and lapse and failure. A little while ago it was my privilege to speak some ten days to the students of one of the country's largest universities. One day I was waited upon by a group of Japanese students, who desired an interview concerning the relative claims of their country's religion and of our religion. I shall never forget the interview. These Japanese were upper class men in the university. They ranged themselves, some thirty men, in a semi-circle

105

about me, and then they began their questions. How bright, how sharp, how searching, were their questions! And presently they reached the question that they came to ask. They said: "We follow Buddha, and you follow Christ. Wherein does Christ excel Buddha? Buddha teaches this and that," they said, "and Christ, whom you preach, teaches this and that. Wherein do the teachings of Christ excel the teachings of Buddha?" Now, you can see that the issue was sharply joined. You know what I said, I take it. I said: "My fellow-men, Buddha does teach so and so, and standards that he sets up in many cases are beautiful. Christ teaches so and so. But Christ does more. Christ proposes to put a power divine into the life that will yield itself to Him. For illustration: Here are two trains of cars, and at the head of each is an engine. Christ puts His power into that Christian engine, so that it can pull any train of cars, no matter how weighty. Buddha does not talk about putting power into human life. Buddha does not talk about a strength superhuman and unrivaled and divine, which he will put into his followers. He simply holds up a standard out there. Christ holds up a standard and says: 'Come to me, with all your weakness and ignorance and sin; let me save and guide you, and I will help you in your life to realize that standard.' Christianity is the religion of a person, and that person is Christ, and Christ not only points us the way wherein we ought to walk, but He comes to us in our moral weakness and lapse and failure, and says to us: 'If you will honestly commit yourself to me, that I may guide you and master you, I will help you to live the life you ought to live.' And, therefore, Christianity outdistances all systems of human religion, by as much as God outdistances a man." It was good to see the response made by the students from afar to such appeal.

Five little words this morning make our text: "Christ the power of God." They are found in the first chapter of Paul's first letter to the Corinthians.

Let me come at once to the heart of what I wish to say, by asking the question: How is Christ the power of God? I answer first of all, He is the power of God in His own person. Christianity stands or falls with the person of Christ. What Hougoumont was to Waterloo, Christ's person is to Christianity. There have been only three views about the person of Christ—one that He was bad, another that He was mad, and the other that He was what He everywhere represented himself to be, namely, that He was God come in the flesh. When He was here there were those who affirmed that He was bad. They affirmed that He was in league with Beelzebub, the prince of demons. They said: "He hath an evil spirit, and is not to be trusted." And then there were those who affirmed that He was mad. They said: "He is beside himself." They said: "He is crazy." And then there stands out the third estimate of Him—that He was not bad, and that He was not mad, but that He was and is what He everywhere represented himself to be—God come in the flesh.

When Jesus became a man, He said in effect to men, wherever He went: "I am God manifest in the flesh. I am God uncovered; I am God foreshortened, so that a man with all his limitations by reason of ignorance and weakness and sin can find God." The cry of the race through the ages has been: "We would see Jesus. Show us the Father, and it sufficeth us." Jesus came among men and everywhere represented himself as the possessor of the attributes and the perfections of Deity. That Jesus was and is in His own person the power of God is attested by what He said, and by what He did, and by what He was and is. I am compelled intellectually to believe that Christ was more than any mere man, no matter from what angle I look at Him.

Will you look at His words? They attest His deity, "Never man spake like this man." I do not wonder that when Daniel Webster had finished the reading of the Sermon on the Mount, he rose up with pale face and trembling words, and said: "More than any mere man has spoken these words." Never man spake like this man. Christ's teachings concerning the great matters that pertain to life and conduct and man and sin and character and destiny are utterly revolutionary and transforming.

I am also compelled to believe that Jesus is more than any mere man when I look at His works, and one of His appeals to men is: "Believe me, that I am in the Father, and the Father in me; or else believe me for the works' sake." From the cradle to the grave there was in the life of Jesus the outflashings of His divine nature and power. When a little child yonder on His mother's heart the shepherds came to worship Him, and the magi came with their rich gifts to lay before Him. When He was a child of a dozen years, yonder He was in the temple, and the questions that He both asked and answered broke to pieces the superlative wisdom of those learned doctors and teachers assembled in that temple. And when He began His public ministry, the winds and the waves obeyed Him, and sicknesses obeyed Him, and demons obeyed Him, and death obeyed Him. Jean Paul Richter was right when He said that Jesus with His pierced hand had lifted empires off their hinges, and had turned the stream of centuries backwards in its channel. And Lecky, the astute philosopher, was right when he said that the three short years of Jesus' public ministry had done more to soften and regenerate mankind than all the disquisitions of all the philosophers, and all the exhortations of all the moralists since the world began.

I am also compelled to believe in Christ, that His own nature was divine, and that in Him was the infinite power of God, when I look at His character. The standing challenge of Jesus to mankind is: "Which of you convicteth me of sin?" And the universal response to that challenge is stated in the language of Pilate: "I find no fault in Him." Horace Bushnell was right when he said that the character of Jesus forbids all possible classification of Him with any and all other men.

Behold Jesus, this Friday morning, not a Son of man, but the Son of man, for all humanity was summed up in Him. In all other men, goodness is but fragmentary and pitifully imperfect. In the character of Jesus, goodness is perfect and complete, and wanting nothing. If you would look for the highest example of meekness, you would not look to Moses, but to Jesus, who was unapproachably meek and lowly in heart. If you would look for the highest example of patience, you would not look to Job, but to Jesus, who when He was reviled, reviled not again. If you would look for the highest example of wisdom, you would not look to Solomon, but to Jesus, who spake as never man spake. If you would look for the highest example of zeal, you would not look to Paul, but to Jesus, about whom it has been written: "The zeal of thine house hath eaten me up." If you would look for the highest example of love, you would not look to John, who leaned on Jesus' bosom, but you would look to Jesus, who while we were yet sinners so loved us as to die for us. Goodness in men, however wise and pure their character, is fragmentary and imperfect and incomplete. Goodness and perfection stand out in their entirety in the person of Jesus. Men sometimes say to me that they cannot believe in miracles, and in every such case I ask them: "What will you do with Jesus of Nazareth?" He is the miracle of the ages. Jesus of Nazareth—what will you do with Him? He is the outstanding miracle of all the centuries. What will you do with Jesus?

> Forever God, forever man,
> My Jesus shall endure,
> And fixed on Him my hope remains
> Eternally secure.

It was said of Mozart that he brought angels down, and of Beethoven that he lifted mortals up. Jesus of Nazareth does both, and more. Jesus is God's way to man. Jesus is man's way to God. Jesus is the only true Jacob's ladder, by which a sinning man or woman, if he or she will leave sin behind, may mount up to be with God and to be like Him forever. Yes, Christ is the power of God in His own person. I marvel that intellectually every man in the world is not compelled to bow before the person of Christ.

Nor is that all. Christ is the power of God in history. The standing marvel of the ages is Christ himself, the Rock of Ages. An humble prophet of Nazareth has gone up and down the earth, and has more influence, more sway, than all the teachers that earth ever saw combined.

> Hushed be the noise and the strife of the schools,
> Volume and pamphlet, sermon and speech,
> The lips of the wise and the prattle of fools,
> Let the Son of man teach.

Who has the key to the future but He?
  Who can unravel the knots of the skein?
We have groaned and have travailed and sought to be free.
  We have travailed in vain.

Bewildered, dejected and prone to despair,
  To Him, as at first, do we turn and beseech.
Our ears are all open, give heed to our prayer,
  O Son of man, teach.

He is the incomparable teacher of all the ages, and beside Him earth's greatest teachers are as a tapering candle beside a great sun. Christ is the miracle of the centuries, and the church is His monument. The most glorious institution in all the earth is Christ's monument—His church. It is the fairest among ten thousand, and an institution supremely lovely and worthy. And Christ's gospel is the supreme instrument of human civilization. There is not and cannot be any lasting civilization which excludes the teaching of Christ. You may have your systems of government, no matter how compact and militaristic and colossal; you may have your schemes of education, no matter how subtle and clever and adroit and scientific; but all systems human are doomed ultimately to go into the ditch, if the standards and teachings of Christ are flouted and disregarded. The Pan-European war is the demonstration of what I am saying on the most colossal scale in all human history.

And now I am coming to say the most important word of all to you, my brother men, my gentle sisters. Christ is the power of God in human experience. That is the vital word of all. Christianity employs always the scientific method of demonstration, that is, the method by experiment. Somebody once asked Mr. Coleridge if a man could prove the truth of Christianity, and Mr. Coleridge made the simple but complete reply: "Why, certainly. Let him try it." Christ comes to mankind and confidently says to them: "Come and see. Come and try me. Come and test me. Put me to the extremest test. Come and test me and see for yourself, if I do not give you to know that I am the power of God in human life. Come and test me, and you shall sing thereafter, when your fellows ask you what has happened: 'Whereas I was blind, now I see.' Come and try me."

I am thinking now of a young woman, unusually trained and cultured, bedarkened in her spiritual nature by the direst kind of skepticism. She sought interview after interview with the preacher, and one day she said to him: "Sir, intellectually, I just cannot accept your preaching that Christ rose from the dead on the third day, as your Scriptures allege." Presently, the preacher said to her: "Well, what do you think about Christ—waiving for a moment the fact of His resurrection—what do you think of Him?" She said: "He is the fairest among ten thousand. He is the one altogether lovely. I cannot find any fault with Him. Everything about His words and about His works and about His character to the last degree appeals to me." Then the minister went on to say: "If He be the Son of God himself, the power of God in His own personality, if that be so, do you wish to know it?" After a moment's pause, she said: "Assuredly, I do." Then the minister said: "You go alone and tell Him that you are vexed by doubt and held back by questions, but that you wish light, and that you will yield yourself to Him, who has already won your most admiring appreciation; that you will yield yourself to Him, that He may teach you and help you and lead you in any way that He would have you go—just honestly yield yourself to Him. Try Him in that experimental way." She came back the next day with her face radiant like the morning, and said to the preacher: "I cannot prove by outside proof, that Jesus rose from the dead, but my heart knows He is alive, for He has made me alive."

He is to be experimentally tested, my fellow-men. He is to be tested. Let me tell you, I see enough in one week, as do these honored brother ministers of mine about me, to shut us up to the conviction that Christ is the power of God. We see enough in one week in our dealings with men to be shut up to that unhesitating conviction. To illustrate: One day there came to me the news that one of my fellow-workers had gone down in the awful maelstrom of business failure. Fine fellow, rising, battling nobly, but the tides had turned, and down he went, and I went out to his home with my heart in my throat, dreading to see him and his wife. As he met me at the door, he looked years older, but there was no trace of bitterness

on his face or in his eye. He said: "We are glad to see
you. You have heard about it?" I said: "Yes, I have
heard, and I have come out to kneel beside you, and together we will talk to Him who is able to turn the very
shadow of death into morning. No man is to despair or to
worry or to mope because all his property is swept away
in a brief day." He said, speaking quickly: "Oh, no; we
are not bitter about it at all. We did not sleep any last
night. We got up several times in the night, and like two
little children we knelt beside our bed, and we promised
new devotion to the service of Christ. Oh, no, we have not
a bitter thought at all." And from that day to this, and
that was years ago, never have I heard a note of bitterness
or reproach escape their lips, and time and again they have
said to me: "But for Christ consciously in our hearts we
should have been submerged when that black Friday came."

And then, on another day, I was summoned when one
of our citizens lay a-dying, one of the most gifted scientists
I have known, and also one of the noblest Christians. The
sun sank to the west, and the sands of his life were gallop-
ing to the close, and I sat there by him, in response to his
invitation that I come for a final conference, and he said
various and sundry things to me, as I held his hand. I
never shall forget one thing he said. It was this: "Oh,
pastor, go on and preach Christ to men, and nothing else,
for nothing else, sir, will suffice men who are in the grip
of moral loss and failure and defeat. Men do not have
moral resources within themselves to rise and climb. Sir,
preach a divine Savior to a lost world. Preach that only
till the day of your death." That last conversation we
had I can never forget. And then, when he quit talking
like that to me, he said: "I should like to speak to the
children," and the children were brought in, and he had
his word, beautiful and blessed, for every child. And then,
as his wife held that thin hand and bent over him and kissed
the noble forehead, he said to her, with his whispers, as
life's sands hastened to the end: "Mary, dear, you will
know where to look for comfort and strength when I am
gone." She said: "Indeed, I will." Then he said: "Mary,
dear, four different times you and I have marched behind

the hearse to the cemetery, to put away out there, under the flowers, one child, two children, three children, four children, and we came back, and every turn of the carriage wheels whispered to us that the grace of God was sufficient. Now, Mary, dear, when I shall go away, as I shall to-night, you will remember the Shepherd Psalm, and you will remember the fourteenth chapter of John, and you will remember always to call on Christ and be not afraid." And she kissed him, and said: "I will remember. I know whom I have believed, and am persuaded that He is able to keep that which I have committed unto Him against that day." And then he quietly began the recitation of that Twenty-third Psalm, and when he reached that heavenly sentence: "Yea, though I walk through the valley of the shadow of death, I will fear no evil, for thou art with me," he whispered, and we caught it: "See, Mary, He is with me now," and then he was gone to the yonderland. You should have seen her and the children bear their grief without any murmur. God's grace was sufficient for them, and all the people knew it.

And then, on still another morning, my phone rang and one of our young business men said to me: "Be ready. I will be at the door for you with a cab in a dozen minutes. I need you much just now." I was there at the door waiting when the cab drove up, and he jumped out of the cab, his face covered with tears and his agitation something pitiful, and I took his hand and said: "What on earth is it?" He said to me, with a plaintive sob, even with gasps of sobbing: "If you know how to pray, you must pray now, for our flaxen-haired little girl is at death's door, and the doctors give us no hope at all. Sir, if you know how to pray, you will ask God to spare her now." I said: "My friend, I will pray for her, but not the way you suggest. I would not pray the way you suggest even about my own little children. I will ask God, if it can comport with His will, to spare your little girl, but if that be not His will, that He will fortify you and the little mother, and give you grace and strength to face it all." And then he turned upon me wildly and said: "I suppose I could bear it if the little girl shall be taken, but the little girl's mother is an

invalid, and it will kill her if the little girl is taken." I
said: "No, no, my friend; your wife is a joyful Christian.
She has a secret you do not know anything about. She
has a secret that will bear her up and fortify her in the
cloudiest day that ever comes." By this time we had
reached the home, and we went in. The gentle wife was
beside the crib, stroking the little forehead with its flaxen
curls about it, talking to the child as the sands of its life
hurried to the close, and then talking to God. And as we
stood by her, the young father looked at me with a gasp
and said: "Isn't my baby dying right now?" I said:
"Yes, my friend; she is dying right now." And then he
left the room, unable to face the rest. In a few moments
more the little life was gone, and then after a few moments
more the wife said to me: "Where is my husband?" I
said: "I will find him," and I went out behind the cottage, and found him wild in his grief, and when he heard
my footfall he turned to me and said: "It is all over, isn't
it?" I said: "It is all over." And then, with a wail never
to be forgotten, he said: "You will see it will finish my
poor little invalid wife." I said: "Not at all, my friend.
She has a secret you do not know anything about. She
has a power within her above the flesh, superhuman, God's
own power. You come now and see." And we came on
back, and at the door we paused, because she was kneeling
by that baby again, and it seemed sacrilege to enter, as
we heard her praying. She was thanking God for the
little girl, even though she had had her only three or four
years. She was telling the Master that she would always
be a better woman, because He had given her the child.
She was saying that it was "better to have loved and lost
than never to have loved at all." And then she paused,
and I said: "We will go in now, my friend," And as we
entered, she came, the invalid that she was, toward us, and
her face was radiant. There were tears upon it, but there
were smiles deeper than the tears. She put her frail arms
about the big shoulders of her husband, and said: "Poor,
broken-hearted husband, mother is so sorry for you! Mother knows it is all right. Mother's heart is swept with
peace. Little bits of heaven have come down, my husband,

to me. Mother is so sorry for you." Then the big fellow turned to me with the cry: "If Jesus Christ can do that for my frail wife, let me kneel beside my dead baby, and you tell Christ for me that I will give up to Him right now." Of course, Christ saved him then and there.

Jesus Christ can do that. He does do it. Hundreds here will so testify. He is the power of God in human life. Is He your power? God help you, if He is not! Oh, men, my brothers; oh, gentle women, my sisters, is Jesus Christ the power of your life? Is He your personal Savior? Is He your Master, by your own glad assent and consent? Let Him be! I speak to you the sober truth this Friday morning, when I tell you that you may go and drink from every spring on the face of the earth, and you may try the aroma of every flower that earth can give, and you will come back desolate and dispirited and broken, without Christ. Earth cannot heal your malady. Earth cannot cure your hurt. Byron tried it, that brilliant, gifted Byron, and he penned this as the result:

> My days are in the yellow leaf;
>   The flowers and fruits of love are gone;
> The worm, the canker, and the grief
>   Are mine alone!

I read the confession the other day of one of the most prominent actresses to-day on the world's stage. Admirers found her after a brilliant performance, after her appearances had been often encored, and roars of applause had shaken the building—after it was all over, they found her sobbing like a broken-hearted child, and they said to her: "Why woman, you ought to be happy, unspeakably happy, even the happiest of women, because of such applause as your every appearance calls forth." But she answered: "Oh, my heart is broken. My heart longs for something better and surer than this." And it does, because God hath set eternity in the human heart, and the things temporal, therefore, cannot meet the cry of the eternal.

> Oh, where shall rest be found,
>   Rest for a weary soul?
> 'Twere vain the ocean's depths to sound,
>   Or pierce to either pole.
>
> Beyond this vale of tears
>   There is a life above,
> Unmeasured by the flight of years,
>   And all that life is love.

> There is a death whose pang
> Outlasts this fleeting breath.
> Oh, what eternal horrors hang
> Around one's second death!
>
> Lord God of truth and grace,
> Teach us that death to shun,
> Lest we be banished from God's face
> And evermore undone!

Are you willing for Christ to teach you? Are you willing for Him to be your Savior? Are you willing for Christ to be your Savior His way? He will never be otherwise. Are you willing for Him to be your Savior His way, and that He may master your life according to His will, which is infinite in wisdom and goodness? If you are, and will thus yield your life to Him, you shall know that Christ is the power of God in your own experience. Do you say, "Yes, to-day and now, I answer to Christ's call, yielding myself without reserve to Him, that He may have His way with me from this hour forward forever?" How we rejoice with you in your destiny-determining decision, and we leave you with Him, who will never leave nor forsake the soul that trusts Him.

THE CLOSING PRAYER.

And now, as the people go, O Divine Savior, let us every one go, songful in praises, definitely fixed in heart, inflexibly resolved in purpose, that we will cleave to Christ and cleave to Him only and forever. Let us see that we shall feed our souls on ashes if we feed on any other food in this universe apart from Christ. He is the bread which comes down from heaven, which if a soul shall eat, such soul shall live, and live victoriously forevermore. Lord, at this noonday service we would gather up every life here present in our prayers, and by humble, united and submissive prayer, we would bind one another, and by grace divine be bound, about the feet of Christ forever. The Lord keep you all and each, until the day is done, and beyond, forever. Amen.

IX

NIGHT SERVICE, JUNE 15, 1917.

PRELIMINARY STATEMENT.

Before coming to the message of the evening, I would take a moment to urge again, with all my heart, upon the Christians who hear me, all and each, to give yourselves as faithfully as possible, during these passing days, to the right kind of religious visiting. Remember, I pray you, my fellow Christians, that there can be no substitutes for the right kind of personal conversation concerning the Christian religion. All about us people are dying from the lack of personal attention. In sight of our church houses there are such people, and they cross our paths from day to day, and numbers of them, it may be, live under the very same roof with us. Oh, I beseech you, give yourselves these passing days to the right kind of religious visiting. If need be, I beseech you, do the unusual thing to help somebody who needs you religiously.

Some years ago I was preaching in an outdoor meeting in the black lands belt, to multitudes of farmers, and one evening one of those honest, earnest, Christian farmers paused after the service was done to say to me: "If I am not here in the morning and to-morrow afternoon, then you may know that I have gone to my next-door neighbor, who is not a Christian, and have proffered to plow for him, that he may come. He is behind with his work. He has had sickness in his family, and if I go to ask him to come to the services, I know the excuses he will give; so I am going in the morning to offer to plow for him, to do that neighborly act for him. I am going to urge it upon him, and if I am not present, you may know that he is present." And the next day I looked for my Christian farmer, and he was not present, and I preached that day to the man he had sent, for whom he plowed, that such man might come to the Savior, and when the service was done down the aisle came the second farmer, with his face covered with tears, to make his public confession of personal surrender to Christ. A simple thing it was for the first man to do, but wasn't the outcome glorious?

A mother said to me: "If you miss me to-morrow, then you may know that I am sending another little mother, who is not a Christian, for I shall proffer to stay at home and mind her baby, and insist that she come, and if you miss me, know that you have one woman there who needs to hear about Christ." And sure enough, at the close of that service down the aisle came the second little mother, and she said: "When that Christian mother proffered to stay to mind my baby, that I might go to God's house to hear about Christ, my heart went out, and I can no longer hold out against Christ." These are simple things, but see to what tremendous results they lead.

If necessary, I pray you, do the unusual thing, the sacrificial thing, to win somebody to Christ. Make it impossible, I pray you, my fellow Christians—make it impossible for anybody around you to say: "They have their churches, and they have their preachers, and now and then they have their special meetings, but nobody really cares for my soul." Make that impossible. Some time ago a stranger came down the aisle in the church where I am glad to minister, to make his public confession of Christ as his Savior, and to take his place that Sunday morning in the church. He is the most widely traveled man that I have personally known with any intimacy. For some twenty years he has gone around the world writing articles and gathering important information for one of the foremost journals of the East. Twelve different times he has been around the globe. He is a man who knows how to talk as well as write, and I said to him: "Mr. So-and-so, won't you stand up and give your testimony about Christ to the people, without my asking you any questions?" And he gave a testimony that morning that we will never forget. But there was one thing in it that probed our very hearts, and made us stand aghast, almost with horror, and it was this: He said to us that morning: "Though I have been around the world these twelve times in these twenty years, and have touched tens of thousands of lives at close range, in all realms and in all lands, only two people in all these twenty years have asked me if it was well with my soul!" Why the very thought is staggering! And when he had followed Christ that night in beautiful baptism, he said to me, as we came out of the baptismal waters: "I am going to my hotel now to write the most grateful word that I can write to those two men who thought enough of my soul to ask me if I was right with God."

Oh, my fellow Christians, with an earnestness which God would have you feel, and with a faithfulness and with a humility and with a sanity, and with that blessed reasonableness that goes along with the religion of Christ, I pray you now, day by day, on the right hand and on the left, give yourselves like you ought, to the right kind of religious visiting. We will pause now for a moment and pray God to help us.

THE OPENING PRAYER.

We make our appeal to thee, O thou Friend Divine, thou Gracious Father! Forgive us, that, though we have been Christians, many of us, for many years, we have been timid, and worse than that, we have been recreant to duty with respect to this most vital matter of all, the matter of speaking the right word to people, concerning Jesus and His great salvation. We beseech thee that every Christian in this large throng this Friday evening may be personally dedicated from this moment for the days just before us, even as never before, to that highest, holiest business of all, the effort personal to point people in the heavenward way. Go thou with us, to teach and help us in every effort, O thou Spirit Divine. Clothe us with wisdom and patience and let our work be such as Christ will honor, and whatever the result may be, give us to do our best and gladly leave the result with Christ.

We pray for this goodly city, which by leaps and bounds is making its material expansion and progress. Let its spiritual progress be the city's crowning prosperity. Lord, hear our prayer for every house in all this city. Hear our prayer for the great army of laboring men and business men and professional men, who from early morn till dewy eve give themselves earnestly and diligently to the demands of the big battle of life. Hear our fervent prayer for those who rule and minister in the city's affairs. Clothe them with heavenly wisdom and grace that they may rule for the highest good of the people and for the glory of God. Hear our prayer for parents, charged with the solemn trust of rearing their children for present and eternal blessedness. Hear our prayer for every friend Christ has in this city, of every name. May the mercy of God and His grace be abundantly meted out to every such friend of God, and, oh, may we be better friends for Him and better workers for Him with every passing hour.

Hear our prayer for this Friday evening's service. May our hearts be divinely opened by the good Spirit Divine to attend unto that which Christ would have us heed and hear. May the right word be said. Thou knowest, Lord, what such word should be. None of us know, but thou knowest. Guide us, that the right word shall be said, and said in the right temper, and wing it home, we pray thee, to every waiting heart. And may we do to-night with Christ's truth just what we ought to do, and what we will wish we had done when we stand in that day of days to give our personal account to Christ. And we pray it all in His all prevailing name. Amen!

THE TRAGEDY OF NEGLECT.

Text: "How shall we escape if we neglect so great salvation?"—Heb. 2:3.

The Bible calls our attention always to the big questions of life, to the immense questions, to the eternally important questions. For example: "If a man die, shall he live again?" Millions are asking that question afresh in this time of world war and world crisis. Or take this question: "Is thine heart right?" Or take this question: "What shall it profit a man if he shall gain the whole world and lose his own soul?" Or take this question: "What is your life?" The Bible asks the big questions, the transcendently momentous questions. Let us take one of these big questions out of the Bible to-night for our text, a question intensely personal for us all and each: "How shall we escape, if we neglect so great salvation?" There is one word in the text that points the reason why men and women are finally lost, and you have guessed that word, as I quoted the text, or you will guess it now, when I quote it again: "How shall we escape, if we neglect so great salvation?" Now you know the word that points the reason why men and women are finally lost. In this Christian land of ours men and women are finally lost, not because they intend it. Do you suppose anybody really intends, deliberately intends, to be lost, deliberately intends to miss heaven, with all that it has and shall ever be? Do you suppose that any human being deliberately plans, definitely plans, to miss the upward way? Why, then, do they miss it? One little word in our text points the answer: "Neglect." "How shall we escape, if we *neglect* so great salvation?"

The whole world is a battle-field covered over with the wrecks occasioned by neglect. You may behold such wrecks constantly in the world temporal all about you.

How many a time is the sight vouchsafed unto us of young people, with prospect and promise, who in life's morning neglect proper habits, proper training, proper discipline, and go out unprepared for the big battle of life. Oh, if in life's morning, the time for preparation, the time for discipline and the forming of right habits, they would only study and give themselves to those habits that belong so properly and so vitally to youth, how different their life story and battle would be! Often when it is too late, the remorseful memory of neglect burns like some coal of fire!

Or look into the realm of health. The kindly doctor is summoned some day to the loved one under our roof, and he makes his careful diagnosis, and his face is serious, and he makes the suggestion, tactfully but earnestly: "This case calls for a complete change, a change in climate. Conditions here are alarming. Make the change without delay." The skillful scientist advises, but we presume, and the suffering patient presumes. We hope against hope. We wonder if the doctor is not mistaken. And the weeks drag on, and the case suddenly plunges downward for the worse, and the doctor is summoned again, and again makes his careful diagnosis, and his face is now terribly beclouded. Full-fledged tuberculosis holds the patient in its grasp! Oh, neglect, neglect, what mischiefs thou dost work in the realm of health!

And now, when we pass the subject up to the higher realm, the supreme realm, the realm of religion, how tragically and how terribly true it is that neglect there, in that highest realm, gets in its most undoing work. Even we Christians must all along bewail ourselves that our neglect has been so serious. I daresay there is not a Christian listening to me, certainly not one of any extended experience, but whose heart is touched with a twinge of deepest sorrow as you give yourself for a little while to memory, to recollection, and have come trooping back to you the memories of duties neglected, of opportunities forfeited, of privileges that have been allowed to slip away unimproved, which privileges are gone now and shall be returnless forever. Even we Christians must all along be-

wail ourselves that in this manner and that and the other
we have so sadly neglected in the great matters of religion.
We have neglected people. We have forgotten people. We
have overlooked people. We have passed by people. We
have given attention to the smaller things, the slighter
things, the less consequential things; and the vast things,
the supremely worthful things, have often gotten by us,
and through neglect they have gone, and gone to come
back no more.

Have you ever had a religious census taken of this city?
I daresay you have had such from time to time, even as I
have seen such from time to time in my own city. During the last one had in my city there came back into my
hands some six thousand cards. Oh, what revelations
were on those cards! Hundreds of names were on those
cards of men and women who elsewhere had been members
of the church, but who had turned away from their home
back yonder in some other community, the city or the
village or the country place; who had come up to the city
and had got caught in the currents and had drifted with
the tide, and through neglect they had not positionized
themselves with the church at all. Just through neglect
they had gone with the tide and were far away from the
church and religious habits. Here was one who was once
a Sunday school worker, devoted back yonder, but now
that a change of residence is made, he has drifted with
the tide, and no deep religious habits hold him at all. Here
was one who was an officer yonder in the church in another place, but he came to the city, and he was not known,
and others did not specially take hold of him, and he sadly
wandered, and his religious habits were broken. Oh, the
tragedy that has come to many a man just in that way!

Now, I wonder if this Friday evening I am speaking
to Christian men and women who in the other days walked
closely beside the great Master, who came up gladly and
with regularity to the house of God at the time appointed
for public worship, who followed the Christian habits devotedly and conscientiously; and yet you have come to
this city, and the changes have been marked from what
they were where before you lived, and your habits religious

have been broken, and your duties religious have been neglected. Oh, I would lift up my voice, and I would send out to you the most brotherly pleading I can—change that course, and change it without delay! Take your place, I pray you, with God's people. Come back again, I pray you, to the church, which since you have resided here you may have neglected. Take up again, I pray you, the habits that go along with the vital Christian life, and let those habits be again regnant in your life. See to it that in your own house and in your own life such ideals and precedents and standards are lifted up as shall give increasing gladness to your own heart, and as shall be a blessing to all about you. And if you Christian men and women who listen to me, who are positionized in the church with Christ's people, know of such people who are drifting with the tide, duty-neglecting Christians, with their church membership elsewhere, with their church letters in their trunks, with their memberships lapsed, oh, I pray you, give yourselves at that point, in the hours before you, to helping such men and women, who need your counsel and good cheer, and who need your re-enforcement. Every Christian in this community, not positively identified with the people of God, every secret disciple of Jesus in this community, or going his way with his light hidden under a bushel, makes it harder for Christ's people to do Christ's work in this city, and makes it more difficult for sinners about you to be saved. Oh, friend of Jesus, whoever and wherever you are, friend of Jesus, come now and cease your neglect, I pray you, and take your place positively; be positionized conscientiously and consistently, I pray you, with the people of God.

But now I turn away from the appeal to duty-neglecting Christians to address my word to the one here who is not a Christian at all. The tragedy of neglect in your case is a tragedy indeed appalling. How shall you escape, if you just neglect, if you simply neglect, if you merely neglect, so great salvation? Men do not have to blaspheme God to be finally lost. Men do not have to lift up their little fists clinched in the face of the holy and omnipotent Almighty, to be lost. Men have only to go on down the tide, floating, drifting, neglecting, to be finally lost. Neglect is the tragedy of all tragedies in the deadly undoing of human souls.

And now note, I pray you, what is involved in this matter of your neglect. Your salvation is involved. "How shall we escape," our text asks us, "if we neglect so great salvation?" Your salvation is involved. Your salvation! Oh, what can compare with that? Christ Jesus came down from heaven, and He comes yet, in the power of His gospel, to give us His great salvation. Christ comes to save us in our totality. He would save not only our souls, our spirits—Christ would save our lives. Christ would save our bodies. He would save our brains. He would save our influence. He would save our personality. He would save us completely, entirely, leaving nothing out. Christ came to save us from sin unto righteousness, from selfishness unto magnanimity and largeness and nobleness. Christ came to save us from littleness unto greatness. Christ came to save us from the small to the large. Christ came to save us from defeat to triumph. Christ came to save us from night unto day. Christ came to save us from hell unto heaven. Christ came to save us in our whole life, in our service, in our business, in our daily task, completely. Christ came thus to save us. Surely, His is a great salvation.

Oh, my friend, getting to heaven is a very, very important matter, but Christ means a great deal more than that by His great salvation. Christ comes to fit you to live here and now, to fit you for your task, whatever your task is. Are you a toiler at this or that, a man of business, in the professional world—a man of leadership? Christ comes and proffers you His own grace and forgiveness and mercy and divine re-enforcement, that, whatever your sphere, your lot, your post, your task, life may be conserved and saved. Tell me, what is a human life for? What is that hand for? What is the eye for? What is human life for? Christ would save your life to all that is highest and truest and noblest and best. Christ comes to give a completed life. Christ does not come to crib and coffin and confine you in some little, ignoble, superficial,

unworthy life. Christ comes proffering to take out of your
life not a solitary thing except that which poisons and
maims and kills. The sanest thing on the face of this
earth is to be a friend of Jesus Christ. He came to give
His great salvation; and no matter how much a man may
rise, how high he may climb, how great may be his achieve-
ments, man's life is vitiated and the true end of life is
defeated and lost, if a man lives counter to the will of
Christ Jesus, the one rightful Master of mankind.

Napoleon came with his soldiers to cross the desert on
one of his long marches, and in that early morning when
they started across the desert, the historian tells us that
the hot sun came down on the white sands, and the light
and heat reflected made the men pant for water, as they
marched across that terrible desert. In their fierce thirst,
they looked everywhere for water, but the wells were dry,
and no water could be found. Then they looked out there
a little distance ahead and saw a beautiful lake of water,
right out in the desert before them, and they lifted up a
shout of joy, and started in a run toward the water, but
as they ran toward that lake, the lake ran. As they got
nearer, the lake receded and got farther away. It was not
a lake of water at all. It was a mirage of the desert, such
as you and I have seen many a time in this great West.
It was a cheat. It was a delusion. It was a snare. Oh,
my fellow-man, traveling with me through time to an eternity endless, that picture of the mirage in the desert is
the picture of human life at its best, without God. Without God, life is defeated, and its true aim vitiated and
missed and lost—without God. Awful expression is that
in the Bible: "Having no hope, and without God in the
world."

Jesus comes with His great salvation to save us from
our past. Oh, that would be wonderful, wonderful, wonderful! If some power could come into my life and take my
life, with its chapters that I regret to think about, with its
remorseful memories, with its evil hours, with its mistaken
words and deeds, wonderful would be that power, to come
into my life and say: "I will forgive it all, and I will blot
out every evil thing in your past, every one, so that the

record shall be white like the snow." What a wonderful power that would be! Christ is that power. This is His promise: "I will blot out your sins, and put them as far from you as the East is from the West, oh, sinner, if you will come and honestly surrender to me."

But that is not all. Christ saves us in our stressful, eventful, important present. Christ saves us and would save us in the big battle that we are fighting here and now, at the daily task, with the responsibilities thick and many that come to confront us. Christ is man's supreme need now. More than he needs human support, more than he needs bread and meat, more than he needs good health, more than he needs fame, more than he needs money, a human being needs Christ to be the guide and re-enforcement of his daily earthly life. Christ offers to be that for those that will be His friends.

Nor is that all. Christ comes to the one who will honestly be His friend and says to Him: "You need not be afraid of what is coming next. You need not be afraid of the evil tidings that you shall hear. You need not be afraid of some black Friday in the future. You need not be afraid of that grim sarcasm of human life, which you shall face at the close, the name of which is Death. You need not be afraid of what is coming after death. You need not be afraid to face Christ at His judgment bar. You need not be afraid of what is coming during God's great beyond forever. You need not be afraid of anything at all, now or hereafter, if you will only be the friend of Christ. Oh, my brother men, isn't that a salvation worth having? Can you afford for any consideration to leave it out, and pass it by, and do without it?

Now I am coming, in view of all that is involved, to ask you who are neglecting your own highest welfare, your soul's welfare, if you won't cease your neglect, and cease it from this hour? What arguments shall I marshal to help you, to persuade you, to encourage you, if I may, to cease your neglect of your own highest welfare? What arguments shall I summon?

Let me name three. There are many to be named, but at this time let me briefly name three, with a passing word of amplification in each case. First of all, I am coming to say that you should give up your neglect of your own salvation because such neglect is unreasonable. Now, when the preacher comes and make his appeal to reason, what a great appeal it is! That is Christ's first appeal to the children of men. He makes the appeal to reason. "Come now, and let us reason together, saith the Lord." Come now, oh, men and women, and let us reason together. Sharpen your wits now and enter into a controversy with God. Come now and let us reason together. So, then, the first appeal to you to cease your neglect is that your neglect of your spiritual welfare is utterly unreasonable. When the preacher makes the appeal to reason, every sentient, reasonable man ought to open wide the avenue to his mind and say: "I will listen to that appeal." Your neglect of your soul is unreasonable. Can it be reasonable for a human being to neglect God, who made him? Can that be reasonable? Can it be reasonable for me, the creature of a day, with my life utterly contingent on the will of God—can it be reasonable for me to turn my back and turn my heart away from God? Can that be reasonable? Do I not owe to my Maker certain inescapable obligations, and can it be reasonable for me to ignore them and forget them?

And more, can it be reasonable for me, a creature who must face the future, to ignore that future, and fail to make provision for that inescapable future—can that be reasonable? Why, that little squirrel there in the autumn time would teach us. You can see it gathering the nuts and gathering the corn, and storing them away in the hollow tree, so that it shall have provision when the winter day comes and the day of need shall call. The little squirrel teaches us. And the little ant, which we trample all unknowingly beneath our feet, if we would pause and look carefully, we should see it carrying its provisions out there to a common storehouse, that it may have supplies when the day of need and rigorous demand shall call for supplies. And shall a creature made in the image of God—shall a human being, upon whom God hath set the eternal stamp, shall a creature made to live when those stars by night, and the sun by day shall be blotted out forever, and when we live on in a world to come, eternal in its duration—can there be any reason for such a being failing to provide for that great and endless future?

Then I ask your consideration to another argument why you should cease your neglect of yourself, and cease it now, and that is that your neglect of your soul's welfare is not right. Now, when the preacher makes the appeal to right, what a challenging appeal he makes! Oh, what a great word is that word "right!" "Right" is the word that makes history. "Right" is the word that thrills through the ages. This is ever the big question of all: Is this thing right? When the preacher comes and makes the appeal to right, what a commanding appeal he makes to the children of men! I am coming, then, to say that your neglect of your soul's salvation is not right to any creature in God's vast universe. It is not right toward anybody. First of all, I have already hinted at it, it is not right toward God. Surely, you will not contend that it can be right for the creature to ignore and to neglect his Creator. You will not say that that can be right. Some obligations to God are inexorable and inescapable. You will not say that they may be mocked, and that to mock them would be right. Surely, gratitude — what a praiseworthy quality that is in human life!—gratitude should spur every right-thinking man in the world to turn to God, from whom comes every blessing, and say to God: "What wouldst thou have at my hands? After thy mercy and grace and benediction and goodness, gratitude inspires me to respond to whatever thou askest."

There is another argument. Your neglect is not right to yourself. Men owe some duties to themselves. Men owe it to themselves to make the most and the best of themselves. No human being should fling life away, and debauch it, and prostitute it, and trifle with it. Every human being owes an inescapable obligation to himself to make the most and the best of himself. Then would you tell me that a man has the right to-night, while we are worshiping here quietly, such man yonder in the city somewhere, wearied out by sin, or disappointed, no matter what the occasion, to put the deadly gun to his temple and end his mortal life? No, no! It cannot be right. Suicide cannot be justified, and by as much as the human soul outranks the human body in worth, is suicide of soul utterly indefensible and unjustifiable. Every soul rational that shall miss the upward way and go the downward way shall be a spiritual suicide. God is never at fault and never will be, that a rational soul misses the upward way.

But that is not all the argument about being and doing right. I have said that your neglect of your soul is not right toward God, and that it is not right toward yourself. Now I am coming to add this other word: Your neglect of your soul is not right toward anybody else on the face of this earth. We have inescapable relations to one another, and these relations should not be broken and ignored. Our lives are bound up with one another, and we will help or hurt one another every day we live. I tell you, gentlemen, that is an argument to take deep hold upon every normal man and upon every sensitive conscience. You and I are daily helping people upward by our personal influence, or daily we are dragging them downward by our same personal influence. And I speak to you the sober truth when I declare that no human being has the moral right to occupy a position anywhere, in the occupancy of which position he may hurt somebody else. No human being has that right.

In a city where I preached in other years, two young lawyers often were seen in the congregation. They had come from some smaller community to the larger city, there to build their business and to live their lives. Interesting young men they were, partners in the high realm of law. One of earth's most honorable callings is that of the worthy lawyer! I became interested in the young men profoundly. They came time and again to the series of meetings such as these. Night after night I spoke to the people, and those two young lawyers, inseparable young fellows, came night after night to the services. One morning I called upon them at their office to confer with them about personal religion. Happily, I found them alone, and as carefully as I could I felt my way into their lives, and

they were talking after a moment or two rather freely, and
when at last I asked them: "Why are you not openly and
positively on the side of Christ?" they said: "We will give
you a reason. Perhaps you won't think it a good one." I
said: "I should certainly like to know it, whatever it is,
because I am deeply interested in you." Then they pointed
me to Judge So-and-so, one of the most successful lawyers
of the community, and they said: "He is not a Christian.
He is not a church man, and we have taken him for our
model." I said: "You have indeed chosen a splendid man,
but no man in the world should be any man's model. He
is one of the most interesting men I know. I delight to
call him my personal friend. They said: "Well, he rarely
goes to church, he is a first-class lawyer and a very useful
citizen, and we have concluded that if he can afford to
pass personal religion by, with his intellectuality and success and standing, so can we pass it by. That," they
said, "is about all the plea we can give for not being publicly for Christ." I told them other things which were in my
mind, which I need not relate here, but my own mind was
made up as to what I should do, as I left them, and I went
straight to the Judge's office, and fortunately found him
alone. He greeted me cordially, for he was everything
that goes to make the superb gentleman. I said: "I need
not sit down, Judge. You are busy, and so am I. I have
come to ask you a question in ethics." His eyes twinkled
with merriment, as he said: "This is a question for you
preachers and teachers — this question in ethics." I said:
"Yes, and a question it is for the lawyer and the doctor
and the farmer and the merchant and the banker and the
editor, and everybody else." "All right," he said, "what
is your question in ethics?" I said: "Would you say
that a man had the moral right to occupy some position,
in the occupancy of which position he will hurt somebody
else? Does he have that moral right?" And he turned
upon me, with his strong, clear eyes and manly face, and
with conviction surpassing in his voice, said: "No, no!
No man has the moral right to occupy any position in the
occupancy of which he will hurt somebody else. What
is the application of your question in ethics?" And then

I told my story to him of my visit to the two young men, and what they said to me, and how they were even then sheltering behind him. I can never forget his agitation. He went over to the window in the large building, and lifted it on that wintry day, and looked out on the crowds that surged in the streets below. Then he came back, and said: "I cannot answer that question, can I?" I said: "Only in one way, sir. You might be given a thousand years to find the way to answer that question, but there is just one right way to answer it." After a moment or two more of conversation, he said: "I will be at the services to-night," and I bade him good-morning without another word. Day wore to nightfall, and I stood up to preach. I looked everywhere, and yonder were the two young men. I looked carefully again, and there was the Judge coming in, and the young usher gave him a chair to my left. That evening I preached to one man, for if I may win him there is no telling what may be the result upon others. When the sermon was ended, I asked: "Who, for his own sake, first of all, and then for the sake of somebody else who may be sheltering behind him, perhaps all unknown to himself, will make his surrender to Christ? Who will come down the aisle and say: 'That is my case, and that is my decision?'" Down the long aisle came the noble Judge and took my hand, with a seriousness one would never forget, and as he held my hand and talked for a moment, he said: "That question in ethics got me this morning. You had not reached the street, this morning, until I shut the door and locked it, and fell on my knees, and said: 'Great God, has it come to this, that I am staying out of the kingdom of God myself, and by the power of my personal influence, taking others in the downward way? Help me, that my influence may be saved, as well as my soul.'" He had just finished saying all this when I said: "Look, Judge, behind you," and turning, he saw behind him the two young lawyers, waiting until he had finished, to take my hand and to take his, and with a sob in each one of their throats they said: "When we saw you start, Judge, the thing was decided with us."

Oh, my men, my brother men! My brother men! You for your own sake should take the step supreme for your soul. But the issue is infinitely bigger than that. You should take the step for the sake of everybody else. A man's unconscious influence has the largest power of all—a man's unconscious influence—the influence he does not know anything about. It goes out from every man like the fragrance from the flower, and it goes wider and deeper and farther than any human being can even comprehend. It is that unconscious influence that often gets in its deadliest and most undoing work over others. You are positionized. The measure of every one of us is taken in our community. People discuss us, and they think about us. And in that deepest, highest realm of all, in the realm of religion, they take our measure, all of us, in the communities where we live. Our unconscious influence is the most serious of all.

The papers told us awhile ago of a brave little wife who waited through the weeks on her sick husband. She would be awakened by the clock in the night, to get up and give him his medicine. At last she was worn almost to desperation, and scarcely knew what she did, as she got up, hour after hour to give him the medicine. At last, the hour came when, half-awake, she reached up for the vial and poured out the medicine, and put it to his mouth, and no sooner had he swallowed it than he made an outcry to her: "Oh, Mary, dear, you have killed your John! You have given the wrong medicine." And then, as he saw her agony, he said: "Oh, I know, dear, that you did not mean to do it, but this is all. I am finished." And he was finished, before another hour had passed.

My men and women, I am pleading to-night not simply for your soul. I am pleading that that life, that influence, that personality, that manhood, that womanhood, that example, that self, your whole earthly lifetime— forty or sixty or seventy years, or more or less—that your all shall be put on the side where you will not hurt your fellow-men, but where you will help them every day.

But I have still another argument to which I would summon your attention, to constrain you thereby to give up your neglect. I have already said two things. I have said your neglect is not reasonable, from any viewpoint, and I have said your neglect is not right—not right toward God, nor toward yourself, nor toward anybody else. I would now say, from my deepest heart, this other word: Your neglect is not safe. Oh, my heart is heavy here—your neglect is not safe! And why is your neglect not safe? I have already said that you cannot live like life ought to be lived, if you live it neglecting God. It is impossible. Life is maimed and crippled, no matter whose the life, if you presume to live it without God. Your neglect, therefore, is not safe. Moreover, your neglect is not safe because this life is not all. Your neglect is not safe because this little earthly life must have an end. Your neglect is not safe because you must die. Oh, if I could say that so that you would believe it! YOU must die! You MUST die! You must DIE! Will you believe it? And will you address yourself to proper preparation for that solemn event? There are a thousand gates to death, and the easiest thing on this earth is for death to snap the cord of life and send us into the great beyond.

May I tell you the saddest memory out of my young manhood? It comes to me now, on the wings of recollection. It has come to me a thousand times. I had just found Christ, as I was turning into young manhood. I knew very little about Him. About all that I knew was that I had decided for Him. I did not know how to talk to anybody else. The earnest, faithful preacher, genuine to the depths of his heart, sincere as the sunlight, true as truth itself, as every preacher ought to be, spoke to the boys in the school, and groups of them made their decision for Christ. Next to the last night of the meeting had come. I sat beside my desk-mate. He had not yet decided for Christ. I could not any longer be silent, and so I bent over beside Jim and said: "Jim, you go. All is at stake, Jim. You make your surrender. I don't know how to talk to you, Jim, only I would have you go." He looked earnestly into my face and said: "Let me off to-night, George, and if you will let me off to-night, I promise you that, if I feel like this to-morrow night, I will certainly go. Let me off for to-night." I said: "Jim, your issue is not with me, nor is your issue with that preacher who is preaching. Your issue is with Christ, who died for you. He has spoken to you. He has made you serious. He calls you. Make your surrender to Him, and make it now, while you can." He put his face down in his hands, and was moved with deepest emotion, and I bent over him again, and made a second effort. I said: "Jim, if you will make your surrender to Christ, and go down the aisle to that minister, I will walk with you. I will take your arm, if you like, or you can take mine. Won't you do it to-night?" And then resolutely he summoned himself and looked into my face, with purpose in his eye and in his words, and said: "Not to-night. If I feel like this to-morrow night, I will go, but I will not go to-night."

Oh, I wish I could leave the rest untold, but the story would not be done. When the next night came he was not there. The next day in school he was not there. We asked about him, but nobody seemed to know where he was. And then the meeting ended, and the second day came, and the school, but he was not there. Nobody knew why. And the third day, and nobody knew why, and the fourth day; and I said: "I will go by his home to find out why." The mother met me at the door and said: "Why, didn't you know? He came home from the meeting the other night, and before the night was gone, he was stricken with dreadful pneumonia. Oh, he is sick, sir; too sick to see you. He cannot see anybody but the doctor and the nurse and his mother and father." I went around the fifth day, and he was worse. I went around the sixth day, and the mother's eyes were red from weeping, and she said: "We have little hope, sir." I went around the seventh day, and I said: "Let me stay. Maybe I have not done my duty. I have just been a Christian myself a few weeks. Maybe I have not done my duty. Let me stay with him. Maybe he will know me. Let me be near him. Maybe he will be conscious and know me." She let me stay, and the doctors stayed, and the nurse stayed, and the parents stayed, and I stayed. Oh, that long drawn out and never to be forgotten night! Midnight came, and he stirred uneasily there in his bed, and pulled nervously at the coverings that wrapped his bed. Then he began to talk, and we all bent our ears to catch what he said. With his hoarse whispers, and staring wildly, this is what he said: "Not to-night, George! Let me off to-night. I promise if you will let me off to-night I will settle this to-morrow night. I will settle it to-morrow night, if you will let me off to-night, but not to-night. I am not going to-night. I am not going to-night, and you needn't talk further. I will settle it to-morrow night, if I feel like this, but I am not going to-night." In another hour or two the spirit took its flight. Oh, the tragedy, the tragedy, of a man's dying like that! My brother men, I tell you, men ought not to die like that!

What is the issue to which I am summoning your immediate and best consideration? It is a choice between two masters. One is your friend, and the other is your foe. Which should it be? It is a choice between one of two lives. One is a life of ever-increasing usefulness, and the other is a life of ever-increasing waste and hurt. It is a choice between two deaths, the one unafraid and in peace, and the other without preparation and without God. It is a choice between one of two worlds in the great beyond—the world of peace and bliss and hope and life forever, or the world of waste and loss and defeat forever. Which should your choice be? Oh, I beg you to remember, it is your soul that is at stake, and it is your soul that I am pleading for. If, as I came to-night to the tent, I had passed on the outskirts of this fair city some little woman driving a vegetable wagon, and she had driven it off into some deep ravine, and could not extricate her team there in the deep ditch below, if I had come and stood on this platform and said: "Out yonder at a certain place a little helpless woman, selling her vegetables to support her fatherless children, has had trouble with her team, and the team is at the bottom of the ditch, and she cannot get the team up;" and if I had said: "Aren't there men here who will hurry to that little woman, and give her relief?"—men, chivalrous and many, would have been on their feet as soon as I had stated the case. And yet to-night I am talking about your soul, your soul, that will soon be in an eternal world—your soul. Give it a chance! Give it a chance, before it is forever too late!

We are going to pray in a moment, but before we pray I would ask: Are there men and women here who say: "Sir, we are wrong with God and know it and confess it to-night, and wish you to pray for us?" In the church or out, once in the church, or never, once professing religion and drifting, or never having made any profession of religion at all, are there those who say: "We are wrong with God to-night and know it? We would have you and these men and women who pray, to pray that we may be right with God before it is too late?" Do you say: "Yes, I would lift my hand on such call?" Quietly and without any singing now, you will let us see, by your uplifted hands, if you are interested, if God has spoken to you to-night, if you wish to be saved. I am looking now and seeing, and so are these hundreds of Christians around you. Gladly now will we pray for you.

THE CLOSING PRAYER.

We make our appeal, O God, to thee. Great is our joy that so many in this place are for Christ. We would serve Him better henceforth, far better, than we have served Him heretofore. But now we join in one prayer. It is for the men and women about us, who say to us: "We wish you to pray for us, that we may be saved." Lord, as best we can we bring them right now to thee. Oh, teach thou each seeking one that Christ does the forgiving, that He does the saving, but that the soul is to give up to Him, that He may save in His own divine and gracious way. Let that blessed invitation, when thou sayest: "Him that cometh to me, I will in no wise cast out," now take deep hold of every one, and let each one say: "I will not wait, I will not presume, I will not delay, I will not further neglect to yield myself to Christ." Whatever the doubts, whatever the difficulties, whatever the sins, whatever the fears, whatever the questions, whatever the temptations in the life, teach thou each interested soul, O Christ, that thou wilt surely forgive and save, if only such soul will surrender to Thee. We pray that that surrender may be made now, because now is God's time, the wise time, the safe time, and because now might be the only time. Grant, O gracious Lord, that those whom thou hast called to-night, saying "Come unto me," may now by thy grace be given to say: "We will come to-day, even as God bids us come to-day and accept Christ as our Savior forever." We pray it in the great Master's name. Amen.

THE EXHORTATION CONTINUED.

Now we are going to sing that simple invitation hymn, two or three stanzas of it, No. 175:

Why do you wait, dear brother,
Oh, why do you tarry so long?

Before we sing I have a question to ask. Here it is:

Does some man or woman or child here to-night say: "I am a duty-neglecting, backslidden Christian, but God help me, I am definitely resolved right now to end such neglect and to renew my vows with Christ?" Come forward, then, before all the people, as we sing. Do you say: "That is not my case, but it is this—my case is that I am not and have never been a Christian at all. But to-night, seeing my need, realizing my duty, and wishing that this greatest question of all shall be settled, I take my stand for Christ. I yield myself to Him, that He may save me as He wills. I give my surrender to Christ. I have given it. I gave it last night, or before, but I have not made it known, or I will now give it and make it known. Come then and take my hand, as we wait these two or three moments and sing this simple song. Who comes as we sing it?

(Three stanzas were sung, during which several men and women made public confession of Christ, and others came as backsliders to declare the renewal of their vows with Christ.)

THE BENEDICTION.

And now, as we go, our Father, deepen thou the work of grace in our every heart. Deepen it by the searching might of thy truth, applied by thy Divine Spirit. Deepen it hour by hour, so that we, all and each, may now and always give heed as we ought to the highest and the best, even to thy counsels and calls. Strengthen thou all these who came forward to confess their acceptance of Christ as their Savior and Lord. Add unto the company many. And grant that all through this city, during the days just before us, such appeals may be made by the friends of Christ to those who are not now His friends, that before many days shall have passed, many not now His friends may be gladly singing with us the praises of His saving grace. Oh, how we bless thee for thy saving grace! Guide thou and keep all these who put their trust in thee.

And now as the people go, may the blessing of the triune God be granted you all and each, to abide with you forever. Amen.

X

NOON SERVICE, June 16, 1917.

THE OPENING PRAYER.

Because we need thee, O thou gracious Friend Divine, we would again call upon thee for thy guidance and favor. Without any hesitation we make confession of our weaknesses, of our faults, of our sins and sinfulness, of our ignorance, of the many limitations that are upon us, and we plead for thy strength, and for thy forgiveness, and for thy righteousness. O thou Divine Savior, speak to us, we pray thee, at this midday service, life by life, and heart by heart. May we have the word in season, each one of us, this hour, from thyself. Give us, O Father, the consolation and counsel of thy Spirit. Whatever the hurts in our poor little lives, whatever the blunders, whatever the sad chapters, whatever our frailties, whatever our sins, whatever our needs, whatever our burdens, whatever the experiences that are to be for us in the future, certain it is that in them all we need a help above ourselves, and, therefore, do we make our appeal to God. Speak to us this morning, O Holy Father, and may we hear what thou wouldst speak, and may we lay faithfully to heart thine own truth, and may we follow gladly, even from this hour forward, the Lord Jesus Christ, whithersoever He would lead us, knowing that all shall be well, now and forever, for those who trust and follow Him. And we make these requests in the blessed Redeemer's name. Amen.

THE CURE FOR A TROUBLED HEART.

Text: "Let not your heart be troubled: ye believe in God, believe also in me."—John 14:1.

If you were asked this morning to name the most comforting passage in the Bible, what would you say? It would be interesting to know what your answer would be. Many in this presence, perhaps, would name the Twenty-third Psalm, the great Shepherd Psalm, as the most comforting passage in the Bible. Others would mention that oft-quoted verse in the eighth chapter of Romans: "We know that all things work together for good to them that love God, to them who are the called according to His purpose." But probably more of you would select the fourteenth chapter of John as the most comforting passage to be

138

found in all the Bible. Every one of us ought to know that chapter by heart, even as we ought to know many other Scriptures by heart, because some day we may be blind and be unable to read at all, and then if we had hidden away in our hearts many Scriptures, we could read them even though our sight should be gone.

Listen to the opening sentences of this heavenly chapter:

Let not your heart be troubled: ye believe in God, believe also in me. In my Father's house are many mansions: if it were not so, I would have told you. I go to prepare a place for you. And if I go and prepare a place for you, I will come again, and receive you unto myself; that where I am, there ye may be also. And whither I go ye know, and the way ye know. Thomas saith unto him, Lord, we know not whither thou goest; and how can we know the way? Jesus saith unto him, I am the way, the truth, and the life: no man cometh unto the Father, but by me.

Memorize that fourteenth chapter of John's gospel, all of it. You will need it.

Probably our deepest troubles in this world are occasioned by separation from our loved ones. Jesus had just said to that little group of men about Him: "I am going away. Presently we are to be separated. I am going to die." And the announcement stupefied them, dazed them, horrified them. "Isn't there some mistake? He has just said He is going away, and, more, He has just said that He must die. Isn't there some mistake?" They are stupefied. They are horrified. The separations from our loved ones wring our hearts to the deepest depths.

Just a few days ago, I was called to say some words at the grave of a dear, faithful mother, and the grief of her children was so terrible that it seems to me I can never forget it. The oldest daughter did her best to quiet and comfort the several younger children, with no success, and presently she tried a new turn on them. She went up and down the line of children, all bewildered and heart-broken, and said: "Stop your crying, children. Maybe it is all a dream. Maybe we are all at home. Maybe we are in our beds asleep, and will wake up in the morning and find it is just a bad dream, and mother will be with us." And for a moment she thus quieted them.

Oh, the deep wrenchings of heart when our loved ones go away! Jesus had just spoken some words that pierced like arrows the hearts of the twelve men, when He told them: "I am going away." Then He proceeded to comfort them, to point them to the way of light and life, and then it was He spoke this fourteenth chapter of John. Its opening sentence is the text for this morning: "Let not your heart be troubled."

Jesus proceeded in these words to point the cure for a troubled heart. How may a troubled heart be cured? That is an old question. It is as old as the human heart. How may a troubled heart be cured? It is the question of all humanity, of all the ages, of all conditions and classes: How may a troubled heart be cured?

All along there have been given various answers to that question. There is the answer of despair. When trouble came upon Job, wave upon wave, and all was swept from him—first his property, and later his children, and later his health, and later his friends—finally his wife said to the husband: "Curse God and die." That is the answer of despair, and the answer of despair is not a cure for a broken, troubled heart. The poor suicide takes that course—the course of despair.

Different causes make for the despair of the human spirit. Sometimes it is business reverses, and the man's spirit is broken, and down he goes, and he cannot recover himself any more, and despair grips at the throat of his soul. Sometimes despair is occasioned by a shattered confidence. Oh, how terrible a thing it is to have our confidence in somebody fundamentally shattered! Sometimes one's despair comes because of ill health. What weakness men's poor spirits feel when their bodies are in the grip of disease! What allowances we ought to make for those who are sick! What pity and patience and forbearance we ought to exercise towards people racked with pain! Just here is an exhortation every one of us should earnestly heed.

But full many a time the answer of despair follows the course of sin. I was in a Southern city a little while ago, speaking for a half-dozen days, and my host drove me by two beautiful residences—two of the fairest in the city— and told me that in one home had been a mother and in the other had been a father, and these two, because of sin which had made itself known, and was making itself known throughout the city, to the shame of both homes, had entered into a death pact, that they would each at a certain hour take the suicide's course. And they carried out such death pact. Oh, how terrible is the course of despair for a human heart when such heart has grievously sinned!

There is another answer proposed as the cure for a troubled heart, and that is the answer of stoicism. And what is the doctrine of the stoic? The doctrine of the stoic is, to steel your heart against all feeling. The doctrine of the stoic is to put your tears all away and refuse to cry. The doctrine of the stoic is to deaden your feelings, and make your heart like a rock. The doctrine of the stoic is to be sublimely indifferent, no matter what comes. With rigid face, like a stone, go on, steeled against it, indifferent to it, with your heart shutting it all out. That is the doctrine of the stoic, but that doctrine won't cure a broken heart.

If you have read carefully the stories of Darwin and Huxley, those world-famed scientists, you will find the confession, in the latter end of the life of both those notable men, of sorrow that they had so steadfastly steeled their hearts against that which was tender, against that which was gentle, against that which warms the heart, against that which provokes tears, against that which kindles the flames on the altars of emotion and sentiment and the finer feelings. Both of them bewailed the fact that they had pursued that course. The doctrine of the stoic is not the doctrine to cure a troubled heart. Sooner or later the heart will find it out, sometimes in the gathering shadows of old age.

Then, again, Epicureanism is proposed as the cure for a troubled heart, and the doctrine of Epicureanism is: "Forget all your trouble. Plunge into the realm of pleasure. Sound all the depths of pleasure. Go the whole gamut of pleasure. Forget, forget all your troubles. Leap out into the deepest depths of pleasure, and there revel and swim in those depths, and put out of your sight and out of your mind all thought of sorrow. Drown it all in the realm of pleasure." But that won't cure a broken heart.

When I was preaching awhile ago in another community one day there came to the service a young widow, robed in black, and the minister whispered to me: "That is an unusually sorrowful case. Her husband was assassinated here a few months ago, all unexpectedly and wickedly, and she carries a broken heart. She is a woman of culture and of a noble family, and much appreciation is cherished for her here in this city, but she gropes in the darkness with her broken heart." And then he went on to tell me that her friends took her, when the awful tragedy fell and smote her heart into the dust, and carried her away to Florida, in that midwinter time, and they said to her: "We will take you down there to one of the beautiful hotels, in the midst of the orange groves. We will take you there where music shall be heard, and where all that is gay and beautiful shall echo and re-echo in your ears, and you will forget all this sorrow in a little while. Come with us and you will forget it all." And the poor, bruised, broken-hearted woman went with them, but she came back months later with that same broken heart. You cannot cure the heart in any such fashion.

There has been proposed still another answer as a cure for a troubled heart, and that is the answer of denial. There is a fundamentally false philosophy abroad in the land, which proposes to cure a broken heart by denying that there is any brokenness of heart — that there is any trouble at all. Now, that busy, noisy and fundamentally false philosophy simply denies the facts, and proposes to get past the difficulty by denying the facts. It denies the fact of sorrow, the fact of suffering, the fact of sin, the fact of death. It denies them all. But you cannot cure a troubled heart by simply denying that there is any trouble. The facts are here. All about us is the solemn fact of sin, and the fact of suffering, and the fact of tears, and the fact that a black Friday comes ever and anon, and the fact of the long and lonely and sleepless nights, and the fact of bewilderment and confusion, and the fact that all unexpectedly we are again and again beaten down into the dust by the flail of disappointment. We cannot cure the trouble by denying the facts.

Where can we get our trouble cured? Just one way, at just one place, from just one source, and it is stated for us here in the glorious fourteenth chapter of John: "Let not your heart be troubled: ye believe in God, believe also in me." Jesus here states the cure for a troubled heart. Jesus is himself the physician for a troubled heart. Nor is there any other anchorage and re-enforcement and healing and recovery and peace sufficient for any troubled heart, if you reject Jesus and put His counsel and comfort far aside. "I am the way, the truth and the life. No man cometh unto the Father but by me." "Put your case in my hands," says Jesus. "Come, with your sorrows and your vexation and your disappointment and your surprise, and your reverses, and your consuming grief, and the pain of your spirit which never ceases; come to me, and I will cure your troubled heart, and I will unfailingly re-enforce you, if you will come to me." Christ is humanity's cure for a troubled heart.

Have you a troubled heart? Is there in your life one experience and another and another, every thought of which brings a stab to your heart, or the deathly pallor to your cheeks? Have you a troubled heart? No matter what the occasion, there is one source to get it healed, and that source is Jesus. He is the one mediator between God and us. He is the daysman unto whom we may come, and unto whom we may confide our all, without any hesitation or reserve. Christ is the cure for a troubled heart.

Now, my fellow-men, why should you and I thus stake our all on Christ? If you ask me if I have, I answer you modestly: "I have staked my all on Christ." Living and dying, and in God's vast beyond forever, God help me, I can do no other. I have staked my all on Christ. Now, why? Why should we stake our all on Christ? He tells us: "I am the way, the truth and the life. No man cometh unto the Father but by me." Why should we come to the Father by Christ? Why should we accept Christ as our daysman, our umpire, our arbitrator, our mediator?

Why should we take Christ as our physician, our leader, to be our friend supreme, and stake our all upon Him?

First, because Christ in His own personality is entirely worthy. Christ has vindicated His claims to our absolute confidence. Christ in Himself attests His own worthiness to our absolute confidence. Can you find any fault in anything which Jesus ever said? Pray, tell me what it is. Did there ever fall from His lips any word that you can gainsay and condemn? You can condemn the sayings of any other from whose lips words have ever fallen. Can you gainsay any word that ever fell from those gracious lips? Can you gainsay any work that Jesus ever did? Did He do anything when He was here in the flesh, and in these nineteen centuries since He went back to His Father has He done anything for the world that you can gainsay and complain of and condemn? Is there anything in the person of Jesus, in the character of Jesus, in the life of Jesus, that you can gainsay and condemn and set aside? Jesus in His own personality is the attestation, the authorization, the corroboration, the demonstration of His claim to human trust and human confidence, without any hesitation or reserve. Christ in His own personality authenticates His absolute right to human trust, without any reserve, from every human life.

And, more. If Jesus shall go away, and we shall set aside His counsel and leading, we are left bewildered utterly and broken in the world in which we live. What that sun is to the vast physical world this midday hour, lighting up the world's darkness everywhere, Jesus is that, and more, in our world of morals, in the needy world of humanity. When He says for himself: "I am the light of the world," He makes no pretentious and vainglorious claim. Jesus is the light of the world. Will you take the world's big questions and answer them? You are utterly bewildered and in the darkness if you take Jesus away, and if you fail to take His answer. Take the three questions that this hour most baffle and perplex poor humanity, and Jesus gives the only satisfying answer for each of them and all three of them. There is the question of sin, and the question of sorrow, and the question of death. If you take

Jesus Christ away and disregard Him, you are left utterly
bewildered and baffled and broken in the presence of those
blinding and burdensome mysteries — sin, sorrow and
death.

What will you do about sin, if Jesus be disregarded
and taken away? What will you do about sin? Oh, my
fellow-men, the one tragedy in all the world this hour is
the tragedy of sin. The one unbearable yoke that is on
humanity everywhere is the yoke of sin. The most terrible
and obtruding fact this Saturday morning in all the world
is the fact of sin. Now, what will you and I do with the
fact of sin, if Jesus be disregarded and taken away? No
man within himself has moral resources sufficient to meet
life like it ought to be met, to live life like it ought to be
lived, and to die at last like one ought to die, and to make
personal answer to God as each must make such answer
in the after world. No man has moral resources within
himself sufficient to overcome and be the master of sin.
Jesus comes in, the great physician, saying: "I did not
come to call the righteous, but sinners, to repentance. If
you will commit yourself to me, I will make you a new
man." Jesus alone can save us from sin.

Speaking awhile ago in one of our larger American
cities, one day friends brought to the service where I was
speaking at midday to the busy citizens, an ex-registrar
of one of America's largest universities. He had gone into
the depths of poverty and failure and shame because of
drink. Oh, how I pitied him, and how my heart yearned
after him! You do not throw stones at such men, do you?
That is not the way to win them. That is not the way
to win anybody. Oh, go down to them, and with a brother's hand, and a brother's heart, and a brother's pity, and
a brother's patience, and a brother's re-enforcement, seek
to win them, not by driving, but by the winning con-
straints of love. So they brought this man to the service,
and when the service was done they tarried behind in a
little room, and I was introduced to him, and I could see
in a moment how wretchedly he had fallen, and though
he was terribly shattered by the down-dragging power of
drink, I could see yet the traces of the strong man that

he had been, and glimpses of the wonderful man that he
could be. There we sat conversing, and he said to me:
"Sir, I seem done for. I seem to have lost the battle. I
seem unable to extricate myself from the dominant passion
of drink in my life." Does it surprise you to hear that he
was the son of the chief justice of one of our highest courts
in one of our American states? Superb had been his opportunities. Quite honorable was his record in the university from which he had been graduated. But now he
had fallen to the depths. I will tell you what I told him
at last. I told him the story that Henry Drummond tells,
who won the same sort of a man once, from the depths
to the heights, to Christ Jesus. Drummond was resting in
a quiet home in the hills of Scotland, after an extended
meeting that he had been holding in one of the Scotch universities. When he had been some three or four days in
the quiet of that home in the hills, he said to his host
and hostess: "I must go now and get the next train for
my next engagement." They said: "We are not going
with you to the station"— a journey of three or four miles
from the house—"we are going to let you go alone with
our driver. Drink has brought our driver to the depths.
He is an unusual scholar," they told Mr. Drummond. "He
is a rare gentleman," they told Mr. Drummond, "and we
are going to leave him with you. He is in the clutches of
helplessness because of drink, so he tells us. He is in the
grip of despair about himself, so he will avow to you.
Maybe you can help him, and so we will leave you with
him." Drummond climbed out of the carriage, up on the
seat with the driver, just like he should have done, and
then, in his own winsome, gentle, gracious way, Drummond made his way to that defeated fellow's conscience
and heart. Presently that driver was confessing his weakness, and failure, and lapse, and sin, and downfall, and defeat, and when Drummond had heard it, all Drummond
said to him was this: "What if I, who drive beside you,
were the finest horseman that ever drove a team of horses;
what if I could control the wildest span of horses that ever
pulled a carriage, no matter how strong, no matter how
restive; what if these horses driven by you were such a

span, and they rushed around this mountain road, and you could not restrain them, you could not control them, you were helpless, and I said to you: 'Man, give me the reins and I will control them,' what would you do?" The man saw the point in one moment, and turning to his new-found friend, he said: "Oh, Mr. Drummond, is that what Jesus Christ proposes to do for a man defeated and down? Does He just wish me to give Him the reins to my life?" "That is it," said Drummond. "Let Christ have the reins; though your sins be as scarlet, He will make them as white as snow. Though your heart and its weakness be poured out like water, He will fortify you with a power which is above men, and you will go your way, clad with a strength which is superhuman." From that hour that defeated fellow walked in the conscious strength of his Savior, and a little later was at the head of one of the chief places of trust and usefulness in all fair Scotland's borders. Christ was his deliverer from sin. "Thou shalt call His name Jesus, for He shall save His people from their sins."

If you are without Jesus, you are left baffled and helpless in the presence of sorrow. You can hear the undertone of sorrow everywhere. You can feel and see the awful reign of sorrow on every side. The other day, one of our young carpenters in my city had me go with him to Oakland, where we put away our dead. He had lived just a little while with his beautiful wife, and they had recently brought to completion a lovely little home, and prospects like some rosy morning gleamed before them, because they were well and industrious, and their hearts were filled with love and hope. In one brief night she sickened and died. He said to me, as we turned away from the freshly-made mound: "Oh, man, I had just got ready to live, and all this has come!" What was I to say to him? What would you have said to him? What should I say to you, if that were your position this morning, and I stood beside you as your friend? "There is one who can turn the very shadow of death into morning. There is one who can take life's tears and attune them to the sweetest music, and His name is Jesus."

At another time, there in the big hospital, a dear mother died, and I was with the husband and several children. Oh, the grief was heart-breaking! It seems always to be so when a mother dies. And then that little oldest one, twelve years old, mothered all the rest, and went to her utterly broken-hearted father, and put her arms around him and said: "Papa, I will help you. Papa, we must do better than this. Papa, you and I love Jesus. Papa, I will help you take care of these children." The family was taken home, and the next morning we got ready for the funeral, and that little twelve-year-old girl, the most motherly child for her years I ever saw, mothered all those five little ones through it all. Then we went to Oakland, and the funeral service was had, and the kindly men came to let down the body gently into the grave, and I felt somebody pulling at my coat. I looked, and there was the little motherless twelve-year-old girl, and she said to me, with an agony that would break your heart: "Oh, Mr. Truett, if Jesus loves us, how could He have allowed this?" What could I say? I said: "Little woman, I cannot explain it, but let me tell you, my child, some day when you get to the Father's House above, and you shall sit down by Jesus, He will explain it all to you, and when He explains it, you will know it is all for the best, for He tells you, 'What I do thou knowest not now, but thou shalt know hereafter.'" You take Jesus away and we are helpless to comfort or be comforted in the day of broken hearts.

There is one more mystery to baffle you, and it is the chiefest mystery of all. What shall you and I do when we walk down into the valley of the shadow of death, if Christ be taken away? Caesar stood up in the Roman Senate and said: "If there be anything beyond death, I do not know. If there be anything beyond the grave, I cannot tell." Jesus went down into the grave and explored its every chamber, and then on the third day He came back from the grave with the keys of death and the world invisible swinging at His girdle, and He says to you and to me: "You cleave to me, and you need not be afraid of death and what death can do to you." The other day I saw a man, not a believer in Christ, bid his little curly-haired girl of six years good-bye, and as he kissed her little face and fingered the curls about her ears for a moment, he turned away with seemingly utter desperation, saying: "Good-bye, little tot, forever!" And then, in a moment more, came the frail little mother, and she stroked the forehead and kissed the little girl's face again and again, and blessed God for the little girl, even though for only a few years. Life was richer and sweeter and better every way because of that child, she kept gratefully declaring. Then she kissed her, and said: "Good-bye, for just a little while, little tot. Mother will see you right soon, and be with you beyond the sunset and the night." She could say it because of Jesus.

Men and women, Christ is the Light of the world. Let us follow Him! Oh, let us follow Him! Let us follow to-day and forever! Let us sing with the poet:

So, I go on not knowing,
    I would not know if I might.
I would rather walk with Christ in the dark
    Than to walk alone in the light.
I would rather walk with Him by faith
    Than to walk by myself with sight.

Settle it now as we pray that Christ shall be your light, your Savior and Master, from this hour until death, and beyond forever.

THE CLOSING PRAYER.

And now, Holy Father, as the busy men and women go, may every one be definitely fixed in purpose: "As for me, Christ shall be my Savior and Master." All about us are weighty questions. It is not easy to live, and the journey of the earthly life is soon ended, and then we pass into a land that shall never end. O Jesus, we would follow thee faithfully all the days, and then when we come to the valley of the shadow, we would have thee with us, and thy rod and thy staff to comfort us, and when the mists from off the sea of death come up into our faces, and we hear the echo of the breakers of that sea, O thou loving Savior, be thou the Pilot for us all, and bring us safely to the Father's house above, to the home of many mansions, where we shall be with Jesus, and be like Him forever. How we bless thee for answering prayer, and for saving souls, and for keeping us in the love of God!

And as you go now, may the blessing of the triune God go with you to be your defense and inspiration, now and forever. Amen.

XI

NIGHT SERVICE, SUNDAY, JUNE 17, 1917.

PRELIMINARY STATEMENT.

Just one design is in my mind concerning these services, and that is to help the people, if and as I may, and to glorify the matchless name of Christ. We would do the people good, and not evil at all, in these services, and to such end, we ask that God's people shall not only seek to make the public services what they ought to be by their attendance, and by bringing others here, and by prayer for the preacher and for the people, but also that they will seek, personally, all through this fair city, every day during the week, and in every way that they can, to help the people religiously. There are people whom you know, to whom you ought to talk concerning personal religion. There are drifting Christians, going down with the currents, and they need your earnest, brotherly entreaty, that they may stop before their further loss and waste of happiness and usefulness. And there are people who know nothing at all, experimentally, of the forgiving grace of God in the human heart. Jesus came to save them, and you and I need now to speak to them the best we can, as lovingly as we can, as faithfully as we can, that we may help them now. Very grateful, indeed, is the preacher that the large audiences, these several evenings, have co-operated so heartily. We have had well-nigh perfect order, in this large outdoor meeting. When a mother needs to withdraw with the child that frets and disturbs, or if some one is ill and needs to withdraw, by just a little thoughtfulness upon the part of those going, and especially upon the part of the rest of us who tarry, all of us making it a point not to be diverted, not to look about— by just a little thoughtfulness even in a large outdoor throng like this, we can have well-nigh perfect order.

And now as I come to speak to you for the evening, I should like to direct your undivided attention to the text:

THE PERIL OF RESISTING GOD.

Text: "Who hath hardened himself against Him, and hath prospered?"—Job 9:4.

That is a question from the book of Job, in the ninth chapter. If you shall forget all else that I say this Sabbath evening, I pray God that you may not forget this text. Mark it again: "Who hath hardened himself against Him, and hath prospered?" The very suggestion in the text is surprising, startling, even amazing. The suggestion is that human beings may harden themselves against God, and do so to their present and eternal hurt. The very suggestion, I say, is exceedingly startling. "Who hath hardened himself against God?" Against God! He is our Maker. Can there be any wisdom in one's hardening himself against his Maker? Does one need any other proof of the deadening and undoing power of sin than that sin could come into a human life and harden such life against its Maker? He is our best friend, and yet men and women, through the power of sin, through its deceitfulness, are hardened against God, their best friend.

The wonder grows when we remember that we whose lives are utterly contingent on God's holy will, are hardening ourselves against a Being of infinite power. If God should withdraw His moral support for just one minute from the strongest man that listens now to my voice, such man, sitting or standing, would gasp and in one moment be in the embrace of death. And yet men and women harden themselves against that Being of infinite power.

He is a Being of infinite wisdom. He knows us altogether. There is not a secret in a single heart in all this vast throng this Sunday night, but that such secret is thoroughly known to the omniscient God. Oh, if such fact could only be real to us for just a moment, surely it would give us pause, and give us as best we may to cease from our every evil way.

In the war of the 60's, one of the officers of the Southern armies was taken a prisoner, and kept for quite awhile in a federal prison. In his memoirs he recounts his prison experiences. He tells us that he was guarded day and night, and that he could not look up, neither to the right, nor to the left, night or day, but that eyes were watching his every movement. He tells us that if he started in his dreams and was rudely awakened from his sleep, standing over him and watching him were eyes that never ceased to observe his every movement. He tells us that of all the experiences, torturing and terrible, through which he passed in that fearful, fratricidal war, that one experience of eyes watching him all the time was the most torturing experience of all.

Oh, my brother men, if the truth could only come home to us properly, this very hour, that God sees us and knows us altogether, and that for everything in our life, whether public or secret, He will bring us into judgment at last, what a difference such fact would make in our conduct before Him!

And how the wonder grows yet more, when we remember that men and women harden their hearts against a Being of infinite goodness! I could understand how men would make a straight fight with Satan, seeking to resist him and put his devices all away, when they remember that Satan is man's persistent and never-ceasing enemy, and that Satan means mischief, and mischief only, and not good at all to any and every human being. When men and women find out the awful power of Satan to hurt a human life, for to-day and for to-morrow and for the eternal beyond, I could understand how men and women would rise up with a fixed resolve, and say: "Satan shall not have our service. He shall not have our allegiance. He shall not have us. We will break with him and put him away." And yet, wonder of wonders, men do not break like that with Satan, but men break with God. that Being

of infinite goodness. He holds our lives in the hollow of
His hand. Every mercy that comes to us in life, from
the largest down to the very smallest, He is its giver and
sender. He means good, and good only, and not evil at
all, to us every one. Oh, how can men and women harden
themselves against a Being like that, infinite in kindness
and patience and goodness and forbearance toward us?

That is, indeed, a pathetic picture in the earthly life of
Jesus. One day He had preached to the people His wondrous words of light and hope and wisdom and love, and
as the day wore towards evening, they gnashed upon Him
in their rage, and they took up stones wherewith to stone
Him, and Jesus turned to the crowd that sought to stone
Him, and spoke to them these plaintive words: "Many
good works have I shewed you from my Father; for which
of these works do ye stone me?" That is to say: "Do
you stone me because I am telling you the right way to
live? Do you stone me because I am counselling you to
break with every wrong thing, because wrong brings
nothing but hurt, and cannot do good at all? Do you
stone me because I point the way of hope and love and
life to people groping in the dark? Do you stone me because I speak the words of cheer to people downhearted
and fearful? Do you stone me because I open the gates
of promise and of hope to people who need a constant and
all-helpful friend? For which of the works that I have
done do you stone me?" That is the question that the
Master asks to-night of this vast concourse of people, assembled in Fort Worth. "Oh, man or woman, not on
my side, but on Satan's side, what have I done that provokes you to be against me, your best friend?" What does
your heart answer to such question?

How do people harden themselves against God? The
ways are many. I may indicate just a few of those ways
that are commonest, and you will think of others that I
may not, because of the limits of this hour, mention at
all. How do men harden themselves against God? Full
many a time do they do so, because of the power of sin
that strengthens in the life the longer that such sin is indulged. Human life is not stationary. Men go up or down.

Men are constantly climbing or descending in human life. Therefore, God's admonition is given that people shall be saved while they are yet young: "Remember now thy Creator, in the days of thy youth, while the evil days come not, nor the years draw nigh, when thou shalt say, I have no pleasure in them." The longer that sin is indulged, the mightier, the more strengthful, the more binding does it become in a human life. You may take any sin, no matter what, and the longer that sin is given rein and allowed to run riot like it wishes, the more that sin grows and strengthens. Take the sin of drink, and I do not mention that because I think it is the worst. Heaven knows that it is bad enough, and yet there may be other sins far worse. But take the sin of drink, for illustration. Do I speak to some man here who drinks, perhaps to excess? Let him not be afraid that I shall speak one cruel word concerning him. I shall not. The rather would I come to him, and stretch out to him a brother's hand, and say to him: "May I not help you?" I would help him if I could. But do I speak to some man here who drinks to excess? Let him retrace his past days, even back to the first day when he began that ill-fated habit. He was probably well-reared. He was warned against the subtle power of the habit of drink. A dear mother, when he went away, pressed her kisses through her tears upon his face, and besought him to steer clear of that undoing habit— drink. And other voices, father's and teacher's, and still other voices, warned him against the deadly peril that there is in the habit of drink. Doesn't he recall it all? And then there came a time when he was away from home, and when he was urged to take his first drink. He re- members even now, as I speak of it, how his hand trembled as he put that cup to his lips, and he thrust his eye to the right and to the left, if haply some face out of the past would come forth to forbid his taking that ill-fated step. And then he had taken his first drink. Oh, that was the beginning of the down-dragging of his life! The first drink is the drink that makes the drunkard—not the last. And the years came on and the habit strengthened. Do I speak to such one here to-night?

There came to my home, a little while ago, one of our citizens for whom I have long felt the deepest religious interest. It was two o'clock in the morning when my doorbell rang, and when I answered, I said to the man: "What on earth brings you here at this hour of the night?" He came into the hall at my invitation, and said: "You can see, can't you?" And I could see. I did see. He was then in the clutches of drink. His fearful habit had its terrible hold upon him at that same hour. Then he said to me: "I have come because I want to hold your hands, and get down at your knees, and have you swear me in the sight of God that I will break such habit, for I must break it ere it shall utterly break me." Then he said: "I have just come from home. I went home a little while ago, late in the night, and my little wife had one talk with me that broke my heart, and breaks it when I call it to mind. She said to me: 'Husband, you have broken my heart. If you do not desist soon, I shall be gone, for I am completely crushed, even in health, by your course.' And while she was talking," he said, "my old mother heard us, and came from her room across the hall, frail and aged, and put her arms about my shoulders, and sobbed her broken heart out on my neck, and said: 'Son, if you do not quit soon, mother will go to her grave believing that her son is doomed for a drunkard's death.' And no sooner had she talked like that than my little daughter came, in the grip of typhoid fever, where she had been for weeks unable to sit up, and yet she had heard the conversation, and was so moved that the child, just beginning her teens, somehow got to me, ere I knew it, and was clutching at my coat, a little skeleton from her sickness, and she said: 'Papa, you are breaking the hearts of us all, and killing us all. If you do not quit soon, we will all be dead." And the big fellow sobbed aloud and said: "I cannot quit. I am helpless. I am so driven and beaten and weak, I cannot quit." Now, sin does that. You let it loose, you give it the reins, and it will vitiate, it will pull down, and it will deaden and destroy. I repeat again, I do not name that sin because I think it is the worst. There are others, perhaps more deadly, more undoing than that. I take that to illustrate the point that the longer sin is indulged, the more terrible does it become in its power to deaden and harden the heart.

How do men and women harden themselves against God? Full many a time they do it through the power of public opinion. The longer I live and study men and women, and see their conduct, the more am I convinced of the truth of that solemn saying in the Bible: "The fear of man bringeth a snare." Oh, what power there is in public opinion! One waits for another. One acts because of another. One is silent because another is silent. Just there comes in the awful peril and power of influence. The man who does not care about his influence over somebody else surely must be a fool or a monster, or both. We must be forever careful about our influence over others, for by our silent influence, day in and out, we are taking people up with us or we are taking them down. We are making it easier or making it harder every day we live for other people to live, as is our influence over them. You do not wonder that when George Whitfield was converted, he prayed as his first prayer: "Oh, God, forgive me for my wasted influence over other people!" George Whitfield had been a ring-leader in sin. He had led many people astray, but when he had found Christ for himself, he fell down before Him and cried out: "Oh, God, forgive me for my misused influence over other men!" Surely, he could not have prayed a saner prayer than that. And you do not wonder that still another man, a little while ago, when they told him that he was dying, that his last hour had come, gathered the covering about him and sought to hide his face, and said to the people, out of the pitiableness of his condition: "Yes, and when I am gone, as the doctor says I soon shall be, be certain to gather up my influence and bury it in the grave with me." But that is the very thing that cannot be done. Your influence is going on now, and will go on and on, when you shall sleep beneath the flowers. Oh, the power of influence! That ought to give pause to every serious man and woman in the world.

I would rather be nailed up in my coffin, strong and

well as I am this Sunday night, and buried alive, than to
live a life that would damn somebody else. Human influence is that serious and that terrible.

I was preaching in a series of meetings in one of our
cities some time ago, and I noticed a young fellow, for
three of four consecutive evenings, far down the hall before me, a lad, I should say, of some sixteen years. When
I asked: "Are there people to-night interested in being
saved? Will they lift the hand or stand?" This lad for
three or four evenings made response without any delay.
Then another evening came, and there he was, but he made
no response, and indeed seemed indifferent. Then the
next meeting came, and I looked for him, and I found him
at last, but far to the rear of the hall—evidently indifferent,
deliberately indifferent. I could read it in his face. And
when the service was concluded that night I hurried
around, if haply I might find the young fellow, to have a
word with him, and fortunately I found him, and took him
aside, so that I could have a word alone. I said to him:
"I have seen you in the audience, and my heart has been
strangely drawn to you. For two or three evenings, you
indicated that you wished to be a Christian, and now for
these past two evenings you have said by your face and
conduct that you are indifferent to such matter. Pray
tell me what has happened." Then he looked up into
my face, and plaintively said: "I think I had rather not
tell you. I was interested," he went on to say. "I was
deeply concerned by what you said. I did tell you that I
desired to be a Christian, and I meant it, but I have reached
a different conclusion. I think I had rather not tell you
why." I said: "My lad, I should not like to take any advantage of you at all. I would not for my right arm wittingly
take an advantage of any man or woman who comes to
hear me preach. I would not like to be impertinent, but
I should like to know what has come to turn you away
from facing that open gate to the heavenly world and to
the better life. Something has come. I should like to
know what it is, that I may help you." Then he said:
"Very well, I will tell you. My father is Dr. So-and-so.
My father never goes to church. I never knew of his being

at church in all my life. I have decided to follow my father,
and not follow you at all. My father is to me the most
splendid man in the world"—just what a boy ought to
think about his father, if possible. "My father," said the
boy, "is my model man. He is the cleverest man I know,
and the strongest man I know, and I have made my choice,
and I am going to follow my father, and I am not going
to follow you. Father says by his example that the Christian religion is not worth while. I am going to say it, too,
as long as my father says it. That has changed my course,"
said the handsome lad.

Oh, wasn't it pitiable, even heart-breaking? I said some
other things to him, and among them I said: "Come on
to the services, and I will do my best to help you yet,
and I will do my best to help your honored father, and I
want to think about it through the night." My sleep was
troubled, the whole night through, about that unusual case,
but when the morning came my mind was made up: "I
shall go to see the father and introduce myself to him, and
cast myself upon God for wisdom to have some words
with that father, about what is involved." And when the
morning came I made my way to his office, and fortunately
found him alone. I was the first to arrive. When I introduced myself to him and found that he was the man I
was seeking, he turned upon me with beaming, searching
face, and said: "Certainly, you have not come for yourself. You are evidently not a sick man." I said: "I have
not come for myself at all. I have come to have a word
with you about your own boy." And then he was all
alert in his attention, and he said: "Do you know my
boy?" I said: "Slightly." Then he said: "Isn't he a fine
boy?" I said: "I should say that I never saw a finer one.
My heart is drawn out to him profoundly, and I have come
just to have a frank word with you about your boy." He
said: "In what way? To what end?" Then I said: "I
am preaching for a few days in your city." "Oh," he said,
"I see. I have noticed something of it in the daily papers."
I said: "Your boy has been hearing me, Doctor, for several nights, and your boy seemed deeply serious for three
or four nights, and indicated his seriousness, and then he

deliberately put such matter away. His deliberate purpose was written in his very face and voiced in his conduct, and I sought him out last night and had a word with him. He was exceedingly reticent, and he was grandly loyal to you, but when I asked him why he had deliberately determined to turn away from the call of Christ and the Christian religion, he made answer that you, his father, were his model, his beau ideal, his pattern, and he had decided to follow you, and not follow me, nor follow anybody else. I have come just to tell you that, and to ask if you do not have too much involved to let the matter stand like it is?" His face was colorless almost in a moment, and then he walked the room under terrific pressure for another moment, and then he turned to me and said: "That is the heaviest blow, sir, I ever received." And then I said to him: "Doctor, what do you think you ought to say about it?" He waited a moment, and said: "When is your next service?" I said: "At ten o'clock, this morning." He said: "I cannot go at ten, because of an engagement for a needed operation at the hospital. When is your next service?" "This evening, at eight o'clock." Then he looked at me with strength of purpose, and said: "I will be in your service to-night, and I will give this matter immediate attention. I think I know what to do, sir. I will see you to-night." I bade him good-morning without another word. I had said all I ought to have said, it seemed, on that first visit. The day wore to nightfall, and I stood up to preach, and my eyes searched the press of people everywhere. Is that father present? Yonder he is. He is just coming in now, and the usher is giving him a chair, far to the rear. That evening I preached to one man. Oh, if we can get him, we are likely to get his fine boy, and we may get many because of the two! When I had finished my sermon, I simply raised this question: "Is the man here who, on high principle, for his own sake first, and then for the sake of somebody sheltering behind him, will now and here take his step Christward, and give his heart's surrender to the call of Christ? Is he here? Let him come down the aisle and take my hand in token of such surrender to Christ." And the father was on his feet, and down the aisle he came, and there went through the audience something like an electric thrill, for everybody there seemed to know him and profoundly respect him. Now he had reached me here at the front, and he took my hand ,and the first word he said was: "My boy got me. What you told me about my boy this morning got me." And then he went on and said: "When you left me, I shut the door and locked it, and I knelt down in my room and I tried to pray, as I have not done in years, and I said: "Oh, God, forgive me, for not only am I staying out of the kingdom of God myself, but I am keeping my own boy out. Has it come to that? Forgive me, and not another hour will I wait to make my surrender, to turn my case over to Christ, the Great Physician, that He may forgive me and save me His own way." I said to him: "Look, Doctor, behind you!" And there, standing behind him, following him down the long aisle, was that handsome boy, and the boy put his arm around his father's neck, as a little child fondles its mother, and, sobbing, said: "Oh, papa, I am glad you came, and I have come, too. I wanted to come, and I waited for you."

What if that father had not come? God save the mark! I know fathers who have not come, and the boys have not come, either, and now and then I know a mother — oh, can it be? A mother! Sweetest name of all, next to the name of Jesus! A mother! A mother!—now and then I know a mother who does not come, and her best friend, Jesus, is set aside. By the power of her influence, however silent, she says to the children of her own being: "This great matter of personal religion is not great at all!"

Oh, influence, how many thou art destroying! How many thou art turning away from God! If I am speaking to-night to parents, father or mother, who are not Christians; if I speak to-night to citizens, whoever they may be, not Christians; if I speak to-night to young men or middle-aged, or to one with the gray about his temples, not Christians, oh, my friends, my friends, my friends, I send my voice out after you, do not misuse your influence, and cause it to hurt with eternal hurt the lives of people around you!

How do people harden themselves against God? Full many a time they do it by raising captious doubts and speculative questions about religion. They do it by asking questions about religion, and asking them superficially, and then not staying to answer them. They say, for example, What if this be not so? And then they do not delve into the matter, to probe it to see if it is so. They say, What if there be no God? They say, What if Jesus Christ be not trustworthy? They say, What if the Bible be not God's guide-book for men, to lead them homeward and heavenward? They say, What if there be no heaven for the people who will not have Jesus? They say, What if these much talked of matters be not so at all? And then, like an ostrich, they hide their heads down in the sand, and they do not see, and will not face the facts. I wonder if I speak to-night to some skeptic, no matter how dark and deep his skepticism; to some doubter, to some disbeliever, concerning the things of Christ's holy religion? If I do, I call to him as his brother man, oh, my friend, you can know the facts about Christianity—you can know the facts. If a man be a doubter, a skeptic, an atheist, a materialist, an agnostic, who flings all religious belief to the winds— if his case be that darksome and that terrible, I come to him to-night to say that he can get light and will get it, if he will just be candid with God. Professor Bushnell got it—that famous teacher in Yale. In the days when he was a most popular teacher there, and also an outstanding disbeliever concerning religion, a young preacher went to Yale, to preach two weeks. For days and days there seemed to be no response to his preaching. The young fellows heard him, but there was no response heavenward, so far as the minister could tell. A little later he had diagnosed the situation. The young men were hiding behind Professor Bushnell, the most popular teacher in Yale, and the minister sought out Professor Bushnell and said: "Professor Bushnell, if these things that I am preaching are so, wouldn't you like to know it? If Christ be praiseworthy, wouldn't you like to know it? If Christ does change men who trust Him, and forgive them, and put a power super-human in their lives, wouldn't you like to know it?" And Bushnell, after a thoughtful pause, said: "Certainly, I would like to know it, if the thing be reliable and praiseworthy." Then said the minister: "You can know it, if you will just be candid." "How?" said Professor Bushnell. "Take Christ's own challenge," said the minister, "and here is that challenge: 'If any man willeth to do the will of God, he shall know of the teaching, whether it is of God.'" "But," said Bushnell, "I do not know how to start. I do not know that there is any God at all. How could I start?" Said the minister: "Start like this: 'Oh, God, if there be such a Being, give me light on this matter of religion. If thou hast any interest in my getting light, and if thou wilt give me light, no matter how it comes, I will follow such light wherever it leads!' Take that clue, and you will find God." Professor Bushnell said: "I will take it." Three days afterwards, Bushnell came back and stood on the rostrum of the old chapel and said to his students: "My men, I have a wonderful thing to tell you. I laughed to scorn all that this man preached, and all the rest of them, and the churches. I have found out that I was in the darkness and they were in the light. Oh," said Bushnell to his students, "I have put God to the test, and I know that He is the Savior, and I am henceforth His disciple and friend forever."

Men can know, my fellow-men, whether Christ and His gospel are true. I see this challenge of Jesus put to the test and gloriously found out, week after week. It was my privilege a few weeks ago to speak for five days to the students of our State University at Austin—a really great university, which should have the loyal support of every citizen in our State. While there, I was not only speaking publicly—I was dealing privately with those scores and hundreds of young men and women. There sought me out one day one of the seniors in the law class, and he said to me: "All that you are preaching and all that religion proclaims is as dark to me as the darkest midnight." I said to him: "If there be reality and truth in the religion of Christ, wouldn't you like to know it?" He said: "Indeed, I would. I would like to know the truth, whatever it is." Then I said: "I will give you a clue. Tell God,

if there be one, that you want light, if He has any concern
for you to have it, and tell Him that if He will give it,
no matter what it costs, nor where it leads, you will follow
that light, and you will find it." It was not long until he
came back from his quest, his face shining like the morning, with this public confession: "I have found out in my
heart that God is, and what is better, I have found out
that God has forgiven me and saved me." Yes, yes, men
can find the way of light if they will only be candid. If
you are in trouble about questions religious, come with
absolute candor, and say: "Lord God, here I am, an eternity-bound being, and I want light from God, in God's way,
and if He will give it, I will walk in it," and you will get
light.

How do people harden themselves against God? They
do it through the theory that they will save themselves.
The thought of their own self-salvation leads many, it is
to be feared, to harden their hearts. And what shall I say
at that point? Can any man save himself? Can any woman
save herself? Can a soul wrong with God save himself?
Such soul can cross the storm-swept ocean from one shore
to the other on a straw for a boat as easily as you can
save yourself without the grace and mercy of God. Oh,
soul, if a sinner could have saved himself, then Jesus, the
Son of God, would not have come down from heaven and
died on a cross, the most horrible death that earth hath
ever known. If a sinner could have saved himself, that
cross is a work of supererogation, that cross is a mistake
and a crime. Because sinners cannot save themselves,
therefore did Jesus come. And when He comes He tells
us: "I am the way, the truth and the life. No man cometh
unto the Father but by me." He tells us: "Marvel not
that I tell you, unless you are born again, you cannot even
see the kingdom of God." He tells us: "Except you repent, you shall all likewise perish." He tells us: "Neither
is there salvation in any other: for there is none other
name under heaven given among men, whereby we must
be saved." Oh, soul, never, never, can you save yourself!
Do not be hardened in heart at that vital point.

How do men and women harden themselves against

God? Full many a time they do it on this wise: They do
it by looking around them, and pointing their finger at
alleged poor Christians and hypocrites, that they can find
all about them, on the right hand and on the left, and
in that way they harden themselves against God. And
what shall I say at that point? Are these who are unbelievers able to put their finger down on poor Christians
all about them? Are these who are unbelievers able to
put their finger down now and then on some hypocrite in
the church? Are they able to do it? God pity us, yes, they
are! And are there poor Christians in the churches, and
is there now and then some pretender in the churches?
God save the mark, yes, yes! But what of that? Oh,
come now, I pray you, be consistent. Will you throw all
the money away, because there are counterfeiters in the
land molding false money? Will you throw the good
money away, because counterfeit money is sometimes in
circulation? Come now, will you throw all the fruit away
because you discover some decaying fruit there in the
basket or the barrel of fruit that you purchase? Pass it
on up higher. Come now, will you fling your soul out
into the night which will never have any morning, because
somebody around you is not living the Christian life like
that Christian life ought to be lived? I call your attention
yet a moment more to this serious point. God calls your
attention to it in this solemn language. Listen to Him.
I quote it now: "Therefore thou art inexcusable, oh, man,
whosoever thou art that judgest: for wherein thou judgest
another, thou condemnest thyself." Are you able to put
your finger down on some faulty, defective Christian, or
some arrant pretender? What of that? Jesus looks down
upon you and says: "After I died for you, and offer to
save you with mine everlasting salvation, will you discard
me and destroy yourself, because somebody around you
does not live up to the proper standard of the Christian
life?" Oh, soul, be done with such trifling!

How do people harden themselves against God? Most
of all, I think, just at this point, namely, at the point of
procrastination. They tell us truly that procrastination is
the thief of time. Ah, me! it is so much worse than that.

Procrastination is the thief of human souls. Procrastination steals human souls away from hope and life and eternal peace. All about us there are men and women wrong with God, and when they are approached, they will confess it; they will grant their duty and their need; they will express their desire; they will confess frankly that they desire to be saved; they will tell you promptly: "I mean some day, and not far off, to give my soul its proper attention." But they drift with the tide, and through the power of procrastination not only is time stolen, but their souls are stolen, and thus are they finally lost. Oh, the tragedy of it—the tragedy unspeakable of such procrastination!

When that ill-fated ship went down long years ago, the Royal Charter—a ship in its time corresponding to the Titanic, that was wrecked a little while ago in mid-ocean—when the Royal Charter was burned, that strong ship had toured the waters of the world, and had on board a distinguished company of passengers, and they were to land finally on their return voyage at Liverpool, and great preparations were being made in Liverpool to welcome them home. Many of the passengers were Liverpool citizens, and homes were being put in order, and, indeed, the whole city was being put in order to welcome the returning and cherished passengers. And yet on that last night, just a few hours before they reached Liverpool, the ship caught fire, and despite all the efforts to save it, the ship sank to the depths of the sea, nearly all of the passengers drowning with the sinking ship. Only a few escaped to tell the terrible story. The morning came, and all Liverpool was agog with interest to welcome the people, not knowing of the sinking of the ship, and then the few survivors came ashore, and told the awful story to the people. Then the story had to be carried to the homes in Liverpool. Dr. W. M. Taylor, one of the first ministers of his generation, tells us that he was commissioned to carry the story of the sinking ship to one of his families, and to tell the little wife that her devoted husband and the father of her children would come back to his earthly home never again. The minister said he went on such journey with his heart in his throat, and when he reached the home and rang the

bell, a little flaxen-haired girl came and welcomed him
laughingly, and merrily said: "Dr. Taylor, papa is to be
here, and mamma is getting him a fine breakfast, and you
will stay, and I will run and tell mamma." And she
scampered away to tell her mother, and then the mother
came in and gladly bade him welcome, and said: "Oh,
you have come at the right time! Husband is to be here
in a few minutes." And then she started back. She said:
"What on earth is it, Dr. Taylor? What has happened?
Do not keep me in suspense. Why do you look like you
look?" And he took her hand in his and said: "Little
woman, I am the bearer of evil tidings. The ship has gone
down, just a little distance from the shore, down to the
depths of the sea, and your husband is drowned there
with the rest." She looked at him a moment, he said, and
her face turned pale with the whiteness almost of the
snow, and rigid like a stone, and then she uttered one
piercing cry and fell unconscious at his feet. This was
her cry: "Oh, God, he got so near home, and yet will
never come!"

That is the parable, and that is the picture of men and
women in this gospel land of ours, who hear, and who feel,
and who know, and yet who, through procrastination, will
miss the upward way. Oh, soul, do not longer procrastinate! Do not longer delay, with this eternally important
matter of your personal salvation.

I have a moment more to ask your attention before we
shall go, and you will give it the best attention you can,
despite the passing, ringing fire bells—a moment more,
and you will give your earnest attention, for the text is
not quite done. What shall I say? Listen to the text
again: "Who hath hardened himself against God, and
hath ever prospered?" Do you know one who hath hardened himself against God and hath ever prospered? Do
you know one? Oh, that word "prosperity" is a charmed
word! That word "prosperity" is a hypnotic word. For
prosperity men rise early and toil late. For prosperity men
sail the rolling seas, men tunnel the mountains, men seek
to make every sort of discovery, in order that they may win
prosperity. What is prosperity? What a charmed word

it is! There can be no real and abiding prosperity if we set ourselves to neglect God and His proffered salvation of our needy souls. "Who hath hardened himself against God, and hath ever prospered?" Do you know one? Do you know one who hath set himself against God and stayed so set, and yet has really prospered? Do you know one? Did Cain prosper, who took his brother's life? See him as he went a pariah into the forests! Did King Saul of old prosper? Did Balaam prosper? Did Ananias and Sapphira prosper? Did Judas, who sold Jesus for thirty pieces of silver? Do you know one of your acquaintances who has hardened himself utterly against God, and has really prospered?

Let me tell you how one of the chiefest business men of the West died a little while ago. He had his son to sit beside him, and said to the rest: "I have some words with my son," and holding that son's hand in his own frail, dying hand, he said to his son: "Son, you are holding the hand of the greatest failure of any man of the West." And the son said: "No, no, father; your name on the wires would make the business world quiver throughout the great West." He said: "Very true, my son, but I have lived as though time and the world were all, and I am dying now with unpreparedness, and all is dark. I am the greatest failure of all, for I have lived simply for earth and for time."

One of the best known citizens of Texas, who gave his heart to Christ when he was nearly eighty years old, said to me the last time I saw him, just before his departure— and his name is a household word in Texas: "Oh, sir, my life was almost totally lost. I did not come to Christ till right in the fag end of life. I did not come until the sun was going down in the west. Yes," he said "Christ has saved me, but, oh, to think, sir, that I have given nearly all my life to the wrong side!" Doesn't the picture make your heart shudder?

What is the conclusion of this whole matter? I sum it up in some final sentences. There can be no real and abiding prosperity for a human soul that is set against God, no matter how much he claims, no matter how wide his swath of power may seem to be, no matter who he is. There can be no real and abiding prosperity, if the human heart be set with disobedience against God. At last it comes down to ashes, and it cries with one of old: "My soul feedeth on ashes." And mark you this, my men and women; mark you this: When the battle of the soul is finally lost, all is lost. There are some battles that can be regained, but not the battle of the soul finally lost. Therefore Jesus' arresting question: "What shall it profit a man if he shall gain the whole world and lose his own soul?" Some losses have compensations, but the loss final of the soul has no compensation. When Francis the First lost the battle of Pavia, he got his broken, scattered men together, and sobbed like a child with them, and said: "Men, we have lost all but honor;" but having honor left, they could go to the battle again. Some losses have compensations, but not the final loss of the soul. Some losses can be repaired, but not this loss. If you shall take your way down into death and into eternity, without making a surrender true and honest to Christ, the battle is lost. Christ himself so tells us: "Ye shall die in your sins: whither I go, ye cannot come."

What arguments shall I marshal this night to summon this audience to give the right attention to the call of Christ for the salvation of the human soul? What arguments shall I marshal? Shall I talk about duty? Here is your first duty—to see after the safety and welfare of your soul. Shall I talk about need? He is your chiefest need. More than you need money and position and friends and health, and even physical life, do you need to be a Christian. Shall I talk about influence? Your position for Christ shall help others upward, and your position against Him shall take others downward. Shall I talk about happiness? Here is your supreme happiness. Shall I talk about usefulness? Oh, what can compare with living a life so as to be useful in the broadest and deepest and most constructive way?

Oh, my friends, my friends, harden not your hearts against Christ! Before I let you go away very soon I am coming now to ask: Has this vast audience made peace with Christ? Have the men and women before me, who have heard with such patience and attention to-night, for which I thank you so gratefully, made their peace with God? Are the men and women under the sound of my voice at peace with God, through Christ?

Now this night, before you sleep, even here and now, as you stand to manifest your desire to be saved, as the Lord liveth, if you will honestly surrender your case to Christ, you shall here and now be born again. No matter what your fears, your sins, your weaknesses, your doubts, your temptations—no matter what was your yesterday, no matter what your to-day, no matter what shall be your to-morrow, you shall be saved, forgiven, born again, as the Lord liveth, if you will honestly surrender your case to Christ. End once and forever the great matter by your personal acceptance of Christ as your Savior, just now, while we pray.

THE CLOSING PRAYER.

And now, O Lord, ere the crowd disperses, we would gather up every life, and as best we can present it to God, and pray Him in Christ's name to put His hand of mercy and forgiveness and salvation on every needy life in this vast throng. Here, all about us, are men and women who say to us: "We are wrong with God and know it, and we wish to be right with Him." O God, teach them now that it is Christ who makes the case right. Teach them that no man can work the great change which a sinner in God's sight must have, in order to meet God in safety and peace. Teach them now that salvation is of the Lord. Grant that now all these interested men and women may turn to Christ, and before they put their heads upon their pillows to sleep to-night, say simply: "Here, Lord, we give ourselves to thee, 'tis all that we can do." Thank God, it is all Christ asks, but He asks that. He asks for honest, absolute surrender. May every seeking soul answer Him back: "Then I give it. With my doubts and fears and sins and difficulties all, I will surrender to Him. Living or dying, no matter what may come, I will surrender my case forever to Christ, the appointed righteousness and Savior for needy, helpless sinners." Lord, let these men and women, a multitude about us, thus surrender to thee to-night. And if in this presence there were those too hesitant and timid to express their desire to be saved, but whose hearts do wish to be right with God, O, draw them, too, and save them, too. And if in this presence there is one man or woman or child indifferent to Christ's call, indifferent to Christ's death, indifferent to the inevitable day of personal death, indifferent to human influence, indifferent to the testing that is coming at God's judgment bar, indifferent to the life to be lived here and to the death that shall follow such life, indifferent to eternity—O, our Father, if there be one to-night in the great press about us who is indifferent to these high calls of heaven and of God, by the power of thy Spirit teach and lead such one to-night to be profoundly concerned to find the true way to live and to serve God. And may this mighty throng be bound as one life about the heart of God, so that it shall be well with every one, living, dying, and beyond forever. Deepen this work in all our hearts. Time flies. Sin is busy, and death works all about us. Remind us profoundly, O Lord God, that to-day is the day of salvation, that to-day is the day of grace, that to-day is the day of spiritual opportunity. God give us to seize to-day, and to use it like we ought, to use it even while we can.

And now, as the people go, may the blessing of God, even of Father, Son, and Holy Spirit, be granted you all and each, to abide with you forever. Amen.

XII

NOON SERVICE, JUNE 18, 1917.

PRELIMINARY STATEMENT.

My heart has been warmed and cheered from day to day, by the large number of busy men and women who have felt inclined to come to this midday service. It is deeply significant that such throngs have it in their hearts to come to this noonday meeting. I would daily propose to the Christian men and women before me that we give ourselves unstintedly to helping the people religiously, throughout all the week before us. I pray you to forget it not that there can be no substitutes for personal work in behalf of people who need God. I pray you to remember it, that all about us are men and women who are drifting away from the right, because of the lack of the right kind of personal appeal from the friends of God. The highest title that Jesus gives His people is the title of "Friend." I am speaking to many friends of God at this Monday meeting. O ye friends of God, do your best to win other friends for Him these passing days! Bring them to the midday meetings. Bring them to the night meetings. Have the right kind of conversations with them. And above all, beseech God for the light and leading of His Holy Spirit in this work that we are all trying to do, both publicly and privately.

THE DEADLY DANGER OF DRIFTING.

Text: "Therefore we ought to give the more earnest heed to the things that were heard, lest haply we drift away from them."—Heb. 2:1. (R. V.)

And now to the morning message. If you were asked the chief danger to us all, what would your answer be? It would be interesting to know your answer. What is the chief danger

170

to us all? The Bible tells us. It is the danger of drifting away from the path of duty and of right and of safety. That is the chief danger for us all, and there is a Scripture which points that for us, which I quote you:

"Therefore we ought to give the more earnest heed to the things which we have heard, lest haply we drift away from them."

There is your revealing word, that word "drift." "Therefore we ought to give the more earnest heed to the things which we have heard, lest haply we drift away from them." The chief danger for us every one is indicated there in that little word "drift." It is the danger of drifting away from the path of duty and of right and of safety—simply the danger of drifting. That is the chief danger of us all. There are many expressive figures in the Bible touching human life. In one place we are asked the question: "What is your life?" and the answer is given us in the very next sentence: "It is even a vapor, that appeareth for a little time, and then vanisheth away." It is like a morning cloud dissolved in the sun. In another place the Bible compares life to the swift ships of the sea. In another place human life is represented as the grass that groweth up in the morning, but on the evening of that same day the grass is cut down and withereth. Again, it compares life to the eagle that hasteth to its prey. There is no more impressive and expressive figure for us, for human life, than this figure here of drifting. You can see it. The life boat goes down the stream. The current bears it on, and that is the faithful picture of human life. And because of the ease and the danger of drifting, therefore we are warned here by the Word of God to take heed to the things we have heard, lest haply we drift away from them.

This warning is for us all. Not one of us may be absolved from it. Not one of us but that urgently needs this warning concerning the peril of drifting. It is a warning for Christian people, I should say, first of all. Every Christian needs to heed this warning here given against the awful peril of drifting. The Bible is filled with admonitions to us right at that point. "Watch and pray, that ye enter not into temptation." How often the Bible rings with that bugle call! "Wherefore, let him that thinketh he standeth, take heed lest he fall." How that truth is emphasized in the Bible! How we are warned against the snare of pride, and how the fearful consequences of pride are set out before us in the Bible! What foes we are reminded of in the Bible that lie in wait to entrap us, and to deceive us, and to sidetrack us from the right path! There is our own flesh, and we are never to lose sight of the fact that though the spirit is born again, when we believe on Christ as our Savior, yet the flesh is unregenerated and will be unregenerated until it shall be raised from the dead. These redeemed spirits live in houses that are not yet regenerated, and we are never to lose sight of the fact that we must reckon with our flesh as we go along in the Christian life. And then there is the world about us, with its amusements and its spirit against God. And then in addition to that there is a great evil personality in the world, whose name is Satan, bedarkening and deceiving and misleading, and seeking in every way he can to seduce us from the right path. Here is this great triple alliance, the flesh and the world and Satan, and we are to watch all the time, or we shall, by these influences which this triple alliance shall suggest, drift away from the right path. We are exhorted to war a good warfare. We are exhorted in the Bible to fight the good fight of faith. We are exhorted in the Bible to put on the whole armor of God that we may be able to stand, and, having done all, to stand.

Now, we are not to lose sight of the fact, my fellow Christians, that the Christian life can be lived shabbily or it can be lived gloriously. We are not to lose sight of that fact. We can follow Christ afar off, or we can walk beside Him, and be His conscious friends and comrades and fellow-workers. We are not to lose sight of that solemn truth—the Christian life can be lived shabbily or it can be lived gloriously. Oh, the supremest tragedy, I think, in all the world is that so often saved people, people born again, people who shall at last reach heaven—the tragedy is untellable and incomparable, I think, that even saved people live the Christian life shabbily. All about us, what revelations there would be if men's hearts were uncovered, and we were to trace the stories of their declensions, their departures from Christ, even after He saves them! All about us there are pictures of men and women who began the Christian life well—oh, how hopeful was their promise!

-and yet they were bewitched away from that blessed course, and they have gone drifting and floating. They have floated with the tide, and have neglected to stem it. And the great apostle here summons us, challenges us, to watch, that we do not go down the currents with that easy flowing tide.

Why do Christians go away from Christ? The reasons are all about us. If a Christian neglects the vital duties and habits that go along with the Christian life, then he will go drifting down that stream. Let a Christian neglect church attendance, and he will soon be into trouble. "Not forsaking the assembling of ourselves together," is an injunction ringing in the Bible like some mighty trumpet. Let any Christian be careless on that point of constant, habitual, high-principled church attendance, and he will soon be in trouble. Let any Christian neglect the vital matter of secret prayer, and he will soon be in trouble. There can be no substitutes for secret prayer. Let a Christian neglect the vital habit of daily turning to the Word of God to get therefrom God's counsel and comfort, and such Christian will soon be in trouble. The Christian life has its reasonable and vital habits, just as the physical life. Let the physical life be ignored and maltreated, and the physical life shall be preyed upon, and shall be victimized with declining health. And the Christian life in just the same fashion shall be beaten upon and undermined, if the habits that go with it are ignored and forgotten.

How do Christians get away from the right path and go drifting down the stream? Sometimes it is because of business reverses. I have lived long enough in a modern city—twenty years in one pastorate—to see how men are often crippled and thrown into the deep currents because of business reverses. Full many a time men's hands hang down and their hearts faint when business reverses come, and they seem shattered and broken and oftentimes fearfully crippled in their faith, when business reverses come. Business men need God's wisdom and help, every day and hour, in their daily business.

And then sometimes it is a sorrow that comes into life, a blinding, bedarkening sorrow, a crushing sorrow, that causes people to drift away from Christ. Sorrow has one of two effects in a life. Sorrow embitters, sorrow sours, sorrow takes life's sweetness out; or sorrow makes the beaten one draw nearer to the Lord and cling the more closely to Him. Full many a time when a sorrow comes—this or that or the other sorrow—the soul turns away from the source of healing and comfort, and goes drifting down the stream, missing God's proffered help for any soul that will wait upon Him.

And then full many a time drifting away from God comes on because the soul is wrong in its relations toward some other human being. I have lived long enough to find out that the wounds and the hurts and the frictions that come to the human heart, out of wrong relations between man and man, make up one of the saddest chapters in human life. Let a man be wrong in his heart toward another human being, and such man is crippled dreadfully in the sight of God. There is no place in the human heart for hate, if a man is going to get on well with God. A man loses the sense of perspective, a man's vision is blurred, a man's life is all poisoned, if he gives place in his heart for hate toward any human being. I have lived long enough to see that life's frictions and rivalries and competitions and contacts and collisions often turn human beings away from God. I know two brothers who have not spoken to each other in years and years. Both of them are nominally church members. I asked each of them, at separate times, just a little while ago: "How are you getting along in the Christian life?" and each one answered in effect: "Oh, sir, bad enough. It has been years since I have had any peace or power as I have tried to pray and tried to serve God." It could not be otherwise. The brothers quarreled over their father's will, and they parted asunder, with anger each toward the other, and they have gone on in such fearful course through the passing years. Oh, my brother men, human life is too big for that, too worthful for that, too important for that. God's favor is too valuable for that. Our holy religion is too precious for that. We are to come like old Abraham came and spoke to his nephew, Lot, when the herdmen of Lot and the herdmen of Abraham were quarreling and were divided, and Abraham said to his nephew: "Lot, my boy, there must be none of this. Let there be no strife between your herdmen and mine, between you and me. We be brethren. You go your way and I will go mine. You take your

pastures and I will take mine. We will not have any strife."
The human heart that would serve God must come to the place
where it will not be sidetracked from the path of happiness
and duty in the Christian life by collision with or animosities
toward some other human life. Full many a time drifting
comes just at that point. There come some experiences into
the human life which shatter confidence, and which make the
soul stand back aghast, and which raise a score of questions
about religion, and down the stream the life goes, and church
attendance is given up, and church habits are broken, and on
and on and on with the tide such poor life goes floating down.
Oh, it is pitiable and it is terrible!

And sometimes the Christian life gets all wrong with God
and goes drifting down the stream because of admission into
it of some wrong thing—of some secret sin. I am thinking
now of a well known man whose case puzzled numbers of us,
and when we looked into it at last we found he had accus-
tomed himself in the secret place, without even the knowledge
of his wife, to an ill-fated drug, that bedarkened and deadened and turned him away from the right path. Let a man
admit into his life any evil thing, and coddle it, and pamper
it, and keep it there, and he is all sidetracked from the right
course, and down that stream he will go drifting. Some
secret sin will shrivel and wither his peace in the sight of God.
"If I regard iniquity in my heart, the Lord will not hear me."
Oh, how pitiable and how terrible it all is! At last such
Christian, all broken and drifting, and to the largest degree
useless, shall come up empty-handed in the sight of God. It
is an awful thing to be saved just by the skin of one's teeth.
It is an awful thing to think of meeting Christ empty-handed,
with the works of our life all burned up, but they shall be,
if they are not in harmony with the will of God.

Do I speak today to drifting Christians? I pass my eye
and hand down every pew before me, and would pause at the
door of every heart. Do I speak to drifting Christians? Turn
your boat up-stream, whatever it costs, whatever the price.
Oh, my drifting fellow Christians, turn your boat up-stream!
You have too much at stake to go on like that. Whatever the
price, whatever the cost, turn that boat up-stream. Set yourself with a resolution deathless: "I am going to recover my

feet. I am going to retrace my wrong steps. I am coming
home. I am coming back to my Father's house. I will burn
the bridges." Turn your boat up-stream, oh, drifting Christian!

But I have a word more for the one who is not a Christian. There, is to be sure, a great peril to the Christian that
he shall drift, but I have a serious word to the one not a
Christian. There are currents to make you drift, and they are
terrible. There are currents in this stream on which your
boat floats to beat you down and to keep you away from
heaven and away from God. What are those currents?

There is the daily atmosphere that is about you, the atmosphere impregnated with worldliness and with materialism,
with all their down-dragging pressure and tendency. There
is the subtle atmosphere about you to keep you away from
God. How difficult in some atmospheres it is to pray! How
difficult in some atmosheres to think seriously! All about
us is the down-dragging atmosphere, to make us forget sin
and death and the judgment and the world to come, and our
personal accountability to God. The atmosphere about you
may easily cause you to drift. Such atmosphere tells us:
"When in Rome do as the Roman does." The very atmosphere about you constantly inclines your boat to go down
the stream.

What other current is there to cause your boat to go down
the stream? There is the daily task. We are preoccupied.
We have our hands full, our heads full, our hearts full, our
lives full. There is the daily task. Over there in Luke's gospel Jesus gives a faithful picture of human life. He spoke a
parable to them, saying: "The ground of a certain rich man
brought forth plentifully, and he thought within himself, saying, What shall I do, because I have no room where to bestow my fruits and my goods? 'And he said, This will I do;
I will pull down my barns and build greater, and there will I
bestow all my fruits and my goods, and I will say to my soul,
Soul, thou hast much goods laid up for many years. Take
thine ease. Eat, drink and be merry." Wasn't it fine? Oh,
no, it was not fine. This man forgot that his soul could not be
fed on corn. This man forgot that he was doomed to die.
This man forgot that he must answer God. This man said:

"I will say to my soul, Thou hast much goods laid up for many years. Take thine ease. Eat, drink and be merry. No matter if the drouth comes, no matter if no crops are made, I have enough for years. I will not worry. Take thine ease. Eat, drink and be merry." But God, who is the unseen but real factor in every human life, said to him: "Thou fool, thou fool, this night shall thy life be required of thee. Then whose shall those things be which thou hast provided? So is he that layeth up treasure for himself, and is not rich toward God." A man's daily business, profitable and proper business, a man's daily tasks, profitable and proper, if he does not watch, shall make him lock God and light and heaven out of his life and miss all that is highest and best, and bring him to doom and death.

What other current is there to make you drift? There is the deadening that comes from familiarity with religious things, to make men drift. I said to a sexton in one of our cemeteries: "Doesn't this daily digging of graves depress you?" And he said: "Not now, sir, not now. When I first began to dig these graves out here, I was blue from night until morning and from morning till night. I went to my bed at the end of the day's work, to dream through the night about digging graves, and I dreamed about seeing the big caskets, and the tiny caskets, and all, but now, sir, I have got past all that. I could lie down in the midst of these graves now and sleep without any disturbance. I have been in it so long, I have touched it so much, I have become so familiar with it, it makes no impression upon me at all."

Oh, that deadening power, if we resist light from God! That is a fearful Scripture which says that the gospel is the savor of life unto life, or of death unto death. A man hears the gospel and resists it. He is weaker and worse off than ever before. The gospel is the savor of life unto life, or of death unto death. There is the undoing power, the deadening power, the corroding power, the wasting power of familiarity with religious things.

And along with that is the deadening power that comes with time. A business man, who has made good in the world's big affairs, a splendid man in many ways, said to me a little while back, when I talked to him about religion and the higher call, after we had talked perhaps two hours: "Sir, you think I have won in life." I said: "Yes, in a way, you have." "Well," he said, "the world would say I have won in life, with all this business success," and then he turned upon me with his care-worn face and said: "I would give every dollar I have if I could cry about personal religion like I used to when I was a sixteen year old boy. But," he said, "I have given myself, I have given my life, I have given my hands, I have given my brain, I have given my blood, I have given my manhood, I have neglected my family, I have given my all, to win, and I do not seem to have any feeling any more at all." And he is not yet quite fifty years of age. Yes, yes, the currents are all about you to beat you down.

There is another serious word to be said, and that is that we can go drifting down the stream and not know it. Many a Christian is terribly backslidden in his heart and does not realize it. You remember the story about Samson. Samson wist not that his strength had departed from him, and when he went out to grapple with his task he was utterly paralyzed. His strength was gone, and he wist it not. You remember that description of Israel of old—gray hairs were upon his head, but he did not know that he had gray hairs. A man can drift and be far down the stream, almost to the rapids, almost to the frightful plunge over the precipice, and not know it at all.

Oh, soul, wrong with God, I am coming in this last moment to beg you to turn your boat up-stream. Is there anything in your life wrong in the sight of God? Do you wince when you think of bringing your life to the gaze of Heaven—to the inspection of God? Do you wince? Then I pray you, be candid, and I pray you, be serious, and I pray you, be purposeful, and I pray you, be determined, and I pray you, be highly resolved. I pray you, turn that boat up-stream. You have too much at stake to go longer and further down the stream. Act up to the light you have. A noted woman, in the darkness, terrible darkness religious, said to one: "What on earth shall I do? Everything about religion is dark as night to me? What shall I do?" And that one whom she questioned gave her back this wise answer: "Oh, lady, act as if God were, and you shall come to know that He is." And in just a few hours she came back, His surrendered, trusting child. My fellow-men, my gentle women, act up to the light you have.

Have you drifted? Are you drifting? Is there something in your life wrong in the sight of God. Is your boat going down the stream? I pray you, I challenge you, I beseech you, I summon you, I call to you—turn your boat up-stream and turn it without delay, and turn it before it is too late.

A young fellow heard a preacher in the other days, and was greatly moved, and the preacher said: "When you have a religious impression, the time to act upon it is right then. The time when you hear God's call, in the which you ought to respond is right then." And the young fellow walked down the aisle and publicly made his surrender to Christ, saying: "It shall be right now that I take Christ as my Savior," and he went back to the saw-mill in the mountains where he worked, and the boys said that next morning he sang all the morning. Religion in the heart makes men sing. The boys said that he sang all the morning, as they moved the great logs to the saw-mill, and as he went singing all that morning—the first morning that he had ever known what it was to be Christ's trusting disciple and follower—about noon his body was caught somehow in the machinery and crushed and mangled, so that a little while thereafter he went away into dusty death. When they got him out he faintly said: "Send for the preacher, that preacher in the church house at the foot of the mountains last night." The preacher fortunately was soon found and hurried up the mountain to the mill, and he bent down by the side of the dying fellow, and took his hand and said: "Charley, I have come. What would you like to say?" And with a smile on his face that was never on land or sea, he faintly pressed the minister's hand and said: "Wasn't it a glorious thing that I settled it in time?" Oh, my men and women, my men and women, I beseech you, in the great Savior's name, turn your boat up-stream before it is too late! "Now is the accepted time. Now is the day of salvation." Let it be your time—your day. Lord, save thou the people and they shall be saved!

THE CLOSING PRAYER.

And now, Holy Father, as the people go out from this midday service, may they go to practice the truth they have heard. May they go to put into life the summons, the challenge, the exhortation, the entreaty of God's Book, which has been brought us this hour. May the drifting Christian say: "As for me, whatever others may or may not do, God help me, I am going to turn my steps in the right way to-day." May such one say with Joshua: "As for me and my house, we will serve the Lord." O, we pray that the drifting Christian, no matter what caused the drifting, nor how and where it began, may such Christian this day come back and walk humbly with Christ, and be saved from those burning memories, and those accusations of conscience, which ever follow waste and drifting in the Christian life. And still more do we pray, Lord Jesus, that the soul in this place that is going down life's stream, without hope and without God, not saved, not ready to live, not ready to die, not ready for any world, all wrong with God, wrong with the moral universe, wrong with time, wrong with eternity, wrong with earth, wrong with heaven, wrong in every right respect, because wrong in the chiefest way—may such man or woman now be helped of God's grace to say: "As for me, this day, God help me, my life is going to be linked with the will of Christ." May every soul in this presence wrong with God, now say: "As for me, this day I will seek the Lord, and I will follow Him wherever His light and leading shall point the way." Deepen this work of grace profoundly in the hearts of this multitude this midday hour, O thou life-giving Lord, and all through this fair city, may God, by His Divine Spirit, make many a visit to-day, summoning the people in the upward way.

The grace of the Lord Jesus Christ be with you all and each as now you go, to abide with you forever. Amen.

XIII

PRELIMINARY REMARKS.

Again and again does the duty and the privilege need to be urged upon all of the great Master's friends that we shall give ourselves, one by one and from day to day, the best we can, to the right kind of religious visiting. 'Tis a glorious thing. 'Tis nobly constructive. 'Tis the right kind of thing in a meeting, when God's people not only make it a point to come to the public services, but make it a point to go away from the public services and as best they can speak to the people about Christ and His great salvation. You recall that cordial and beautiful invitation that Moses gave to Hobab, his kinsman: "Come thou with us, and we will do thee good." That invitation ought to be given by Christians day by day: "Come thou with us, and we will do thee good." They are all about us, those who need such personal appeal. They are our neighbors. Some of them are our own loved ones, living under our own roofs. They are our fellow-citizens. They are our friends. They are strangers within our gates. They are the poor and the rich, the high and the low. Day in and out, the right kind of religious visiting, by which is meant the right kind of conversation concerning personal religion, ought to be had by Christ's friends. Do it, I pray you, my fellow Christians, to the last limit of your power. Speak the word in season to others, from day to day, who need to hear from your lips the right appeal concerning personal religion.

It is a deeply interesting study to glance at the faces of people assembled in an audience like this, from evening to evening. I have found myself searching the audience, as I do every audience, and my heart is moved by the diversity of faces, for what is quite so interesting as a human face? It has been specially interesting to note that all ages are coming to the services; the older people, with their white hairs and their stooped shoulders, and the strong, middle-aged men and women, now grappling with the big battle of life, and the young men and women, beginning to know something of the seriousness of life, and then the happy boys and girls. How blessed it has been to see the boys and girls in these several evening services, and still more blessed to mark how they listen! I look about me and note in the audience this evening many boys and girls, and find my heart lifting up a prayer for every boy and every girl, and find my heart lifting up a prayer for every young man and woman. Oh, how I covet the young people for Christ! It is God's time for them to come, while they are young, for Jesus not only wishes to receive us into heaven when we shall die and leave this world, but He wishes us also to live like we ought while we are in this world. He desires not only to save our souls, but He would save our lives here and now. And, therefore, how reasonable, how wise, that we should be inexpressibly concerned for the boys and girls, for the young men and women.

WHAT SHOULD WE DO WITH JESUS?

Text: "What shall I do then with Jesus which is called Christ?"—Matt. 27:22.

I would take a text this evening that I would have every boy carefully to hear, and every girl, and every young man, and every young woman, and the older men and women, because the text is a personal question, from which there is no getting away, an old question, a question asked by Pilate. This is that old question: "What shall I do then with Jesus?"

Pilate had to face that question, and he trifled with it, and he made shipwreck of himself because he trifled with that question. And everybody that trifles with that question shall make shipwreck of himself or herself for time and for eternity. "What shall I do then with Jesus?" That question is yours and mine, just the same as it was Pilate's, and we must answer that question, just as surely as he was called upon to answer it long ago. Now I am coming to ask these young people and these older people, to-night, and all of us, and each one of us, how shall we answer this question: "What shall I do then with Jesus?" How shall we answer it?

Sometimes the best way to answer a question is to ask other questions, and that is the way I am going to do to-night with this question. I am going to ask you some other questions, so that by asking these other questions we will be led up to see what we ought to do with this question we have to-night for our text: "What shall I do then with Jesus?"

And this is the first question I would ask: What can I do with Jesus? Do something with Him I must. I cannot evade that question. I cannot avoid it. I cannot escape it. Do something with Jesus I must. Neutrality respecting that question is impossible. Now, what can I do with Jesus? I can accept Him as my Savior, or I can reject Him and turn away from Him, just as this man Pilate did. I can crown Him as my Savior, or I can crucify Him morally in my heart. I can put Him away and have nothing to do with Him. I must do one of those two things. There are not three things to be done about Jesus, but one of two things. I shall either be His friend or His foe. I shall either accept Him as my Savior or reject Him. I shall either follow after Him or turn away from Him. I shall either say "Yes" to Him, or "No" to Him. I shall either be for Him or against Him. Now, I must do one of those two things.

That brings us to the second question I would ask: Who is to decide the question for me—"What shall I do then with Jesus?" Who is to decide that question for me? There is but one somebody in all the world to decide that question for me. Who is that somebody? Certainly not my foes, if I have any, are to decide that question for me— and I trust that I have none. Certainly not my friends—

and I trust I have friends—but however many, or however few, or however true they may be, no friend that I have in this world can decide that question for me, but I myself must decide it. Nor will I be forced to decide it. I will not be coerced to decide it. I will not be compelled by force to decide this question. Jesus comes and stands before us and asks: "What will you do with me? Do something with me you must. What is it going to be?" Nobody will compel me. Nobody will coerce me. Nobody will drive me. Nobody will force me. I myself must face that question, and I must answer it. Now there comes in the highest dignity of human life, and there comes in the greatest danger to human life. The highest dignity of human life is that a human being can say "Yes" or say "No" to God. A little human being, fashioned by the great Maker, can say "Yes" or say "No" to God, and will say one of those two things when God makes His call. That is the highest dignity allowed a human being and at the same time that is the greatest danger that ever comes to a human life. No danger can compare with that. I can take this awful power of choice that God has given me— and the highest prerogative of human life is the prerogative of choice—I can take that and I can ruin myself with it. I can ruin my life; I can ruin my soul; I can ruin all pertaining to me, by flinging choice down into the ditch and making the wrong use of choice. Certainly, God is never at fault that a soul makes the wrong choice. God is never at fault that a soul misses the upward way.

Listen to God as He talks about it. He takes a great oath by himself, saying: "As I live, saith the Lord God, I have no pleasure in the death of the wicked; but that the wicked turn from his way and live;" "Turn ye, turn ye, from your evil ways; for why will ye die, oh, house of Israel?" Certainly Jesus is never at fault that a soul misses the upward way. Look at Jesus yonder, weeping over the city of Jerusalem, and as He weeps, He utters that plaintive cry: "Oh, Jerusalem, Jerusalem, how often would I have gathered thy children together, as a hen gathereth her brood under her wings, and ye would not! Behold, your house is left unto you desolate." Jesus is

never at fault that a soul misses the upward way. If I
shall miss the heavenly way, if this boy shall, or that girl,
or that young man or woman, or the middle-aged man or
woman, or the oldest man or woman here to-night; if any
of us shall miss that upward way, which I pray God to
forbid—yet if any of us shall miss the upward way, the
fault will not be God's fault, but it will be our fault.

And now that brings me to another question: What
does it matter what I do with Jesus? Does it matter at
all? I have already said: Do something with Him I must.
Do something with Him I will. I will be for Him or
against Him. As certainly as I live and breathe, do something with Jesus I must, I must. Now, what does it matter
what I do with Him? Does it matter at all? And if it
matters, how does it matter? Wherein does it matter
what I do with Jesus? I am coming to say that it matters
vitally in three great respects. Let us see what they are.

First of all, it matters vitally to you personally, in
your own life, what you do with Jesus. Jesus comes offering to forgive your sins, if you will surely trust Him.
Jesus comes offering to give you a new heart, if you will
trust Him as your Savior. Jesus comes offering to change
you with a change that must be within you, if you would
meet God in peace. Jesus does all that. If you come and
give yourself up to Jesus as your Savior, then in His own
way, He will change you and forgive your sins, and put
His power within you, and give you His great salvation.
Surely, that is a matter of unspeakable concern to you.
What you do with Jesus determines whether you shall be
saved. If you do the right thing with Jesus, you will be
saved. If you do the wrong thing with Jesus, you will
miss the upward way and be forever lost. Surely, that
is a matter of supreme moment for you, what you shall
do with Jesus for your own self.

But that is not all. What you do with Jesus vitally
matters about your relations to everybody else. What
you do with Jesus vitally affects the life you are to live
and the influence you are to wield down here in this world.
Jesus came, as I said a moment ago, not only to save our
souls and to bring us home to heaven when this life down

here is done, but Jesus wants to save our lives, wants to save our influence, wants to save us, and have us on the right side here in this world—here and now. And what you do with Jesus not only matters for yourself, but it matters in your influence over everybody else. If I should ask these young people to-night this question: "Do you desire to be useful? Do you wish to live the life most useful?" your answer would be given without a moment's hesitation, and with uplifted hand you would say: "Sir, I desire to live the useful life, to live the most useful life that it is possible for me to live while I live in this world." Well, the most useful life is utterly impossible if you do not do the right thing with Jesus. If you do not take Jesus to be your Savior and Master, the most useful life is utterly impossible. Jesus comes wanting to save our life, our influence, have us on the right side, so that our powers may not be misplaced, and be misused, and be wasted. Jesus wants to save us in the life that we live here and now, in its relations towards other people.

An old man was saved when he was just eighty years old. Not many people live to be that old. Perhaps very few of us in this company will live to be eighty. Three score and ten is man's allotted life. But this old man that I am thinking of lived to be eighty, and at eighty he was gloriously converted to Christ. Like a little child, he said "Yes" to Jesus when Jesus called him, and then he lived four years more. He lived to be eighty-four years old, and you might ask him when he was eighty-four years old how old he was, and he would tell you that he was "four years old." His great-grandchildren would sometimes get around him, and they would say: "Grandpa, how old are you?" And the dear old man, with his voice trembling, would say: "My children, grandpa is four years old." And they would laugh and nudge one another, and would say: "Why, grandpa, you are eighty-four." "No," he would say, "I am four years old." And they would laugh again and say: "Why, grandpa, you are eighty-four." And then he would stop and explain to them, every time: "No. my children, grandpa lived eighty years without God. Grandpa lived eighty years without being the friend of Jesus. Grandpa

lived eighty years going the wrong road, putting his life
on the wrong side, on the side of sin and Satan, and he has
lived just four years on the right side, just four years on
Jesus' side, and, therefore, grandpa insists that he is just
four years old." Now, there was deep truth in what he
said. He was making the point that I am making to-
night—that Jesus wants to save our lives, and our lives
are not saved to the highest if they are against Jesus, if
they refuse Jesus, if they reject Jesus, if they turn away
and fail to follow Jesus.

But more is yet to be said. What does it matter what
we do with Jesus? It matters something else, very important. I have said it matters for our own salvation what
we do with Jesus. And then I have said it matters for
the life that we live in this world what we do with Jesus.
Now I make bold to say this other word: Where we are
going to spend eternity is dependent upon what we do
with Jesus. Now, isn't that a momentous matter? Where
shall I spend eternity? Eternity, oh, thou great eternity!
Where shall I spend eternity? I will spend eternity according to what I do with Christ, and according to what I
do with Christ here in this world, before I go into eternity
at all. Now, isn't that a stupendous matter? And isn't
that a matter to take hold of the hearts of these young
people, and these middle-aged, older people? Where shall
I spend eternity? I will spend eternity according to what
I do with Christ here in the world, here in time, here in
the flesh, here on this earth.

If you have ever been to the Jerry McCauley Mission,
yonder in New York City, you will recall that as you entered it, your attention was arrested by a striking motto,
there in plain view before you, and this is the question of
that motto: "If I should die to-night, where would I go?"
Every man and woman that comes in sees the placard
there on the wall: "If I should die to-night, where would
I go?" I ask this audience, this Monday night, to ask
themselves, one by one: "If I should die to-night, where
would I go?"

You would go into eternity according to your relations
here to Christ. Christ said to some people who caviled

at His teaching when He was here: "Ye shall die in your
sins; whither I go, ye cannot come." Christ distinctly
teaches us that our relation in eternity will be determined
by our relation here in time to Christ. How serious, how
momentous, how tremendous, is that thought! If I am
to spend eternity in blessedness and peace, then that matter will be determined here in time by what I do with
Christ. And if here in time, I reject Christ, forget Christ,
leave Him alone, do not come to Him, do not say "Yes"
to Him, do not surrender to Him, and die in that state of
mind and heart, where He goes I cannot come. It is the
clear and unspeakably solemn pronouncement of the Scriptures, whenever the question of destiny is touched upon
in the Scriptures. "As the tree falls, so shall it lie." "He
that is unjust," says the Bible, "let him be unjust still."
"He that is filthy, let him be filthy still." "He that is righteous, let him be righteous still." "He that is holy, let him
be holy still." What I do with Christ here in time, on
earth, this side of the grave, will determine where shall
be my eternity.

I have asked you three questions, and I have just one
more to ask. I have asked you three questions, trying to
help you answer this question of our text: "What shall
I do then with Jesus?" First, what can you do with Jesus? You can accept Him or reject Him. You can say
"Yes" to Him or "No" to Him. Second, what does it
matter what you do with Jesus? It matters vitally for
yourself. It matters vitally for the life you are to live in
this world. And it determines where you will spend your
eternity in the world after this. Who is to answer this
question for us? We have looked at that question also. Nobody in the world can answer that question for us, but
each one for himself, for herself, must answer it. Now,
I am coming to ask one more question in the discussion
of this pungent question. Here it is: When should I decide this question, "What shall I do with Jesus?" Your
question and my question, the inescapable question, the
inexorable question — when should this question, "What
shall I do with Jesus?" be decided? Shall it be decided yes-
day? It cannot be now. Yesterday is gone, and shall

never come back again. Shall it be decided to-morrow? We do not know anything about to-morrow. We have no promise of to-morrow. The Bible distinctly prohibits our building on to-morrow. "Boast not thyself of to-morrow; for thou knowest not what a day may bring forth." When, then, should this question be decided? There is only one time. The Bible tells us that time. "To-day is the day of salvation." "Now is the accepted time." "To-day, if ye hear His voice, harden not your heart." The time wherein this question of what I am to do with Jesus is to be settled, the time for its right settlement is to-day, is here and now, because that is God's time. When we know what is God's time, we should address ourselves to it without any delay.

Why should we settle this question of what we are to do with Jesus to-day—to-day and now? I have already said because it is God's time. Whenever we know God's time, we should adjust ourselves to it, obediently and promptly. This is God's time. He knows the best. He tells us: "It is good for a man that he bear the yoke in his youth." He tells us: "Remember now thy Creator in the days of thy youth, while the evil days come not, nor the years draw nigh, when thou shalt say, I have no pleasure in them." This is God's time, and, therefore, my concern grows deeper every hour that the young people all over the land may come to Jesus while yet they are young. Oh, as surely as we live, wisdom has fled from our churches, if we do not sound out, as we sound out no other note in the world, that the time in which people are to be saved is in life's morning, and not in life's evening, and not in life's middle time. The time is in life's morning. "Remember now thy Creator, in the days of thy youth." Why? He tells us: "While the evil days come not, nor the years draw nigh, when thou shalt say, I have no pleasure in them." The time for us to come to Christ, oh, my young people, happy boys and girls, happy, hopeful young men and women, the time for us to come is in life's morning, because that it is the habit-forming time in life. Our habits shall be crystallized soon. I have seen many people when they were converted to Christ and confessed Him publicly before the people, and yet just a few have I ever seen who came to Christ when the white hair was about their temples—just a few. I spoke a little while ago to some 1200 Christian men, a few over 1200 by actual count— just Christian men—a special message I was asked to give for Christian men—and I asked that group of a little over 1200 Christian men: "How many of you came to Christ after you were forty-five years of age?" How many do you suppose stood up? Only three after they were forty-five. "How many of you came after you were forty?" Thirteen. "How many of you came after you were thirty years of age?" Less than fifty. "How many of you came to Christ before you were twenty-one?" And over 1100 stood to their feet, saying: "We came to Christ before we were twenty-one."

Oh, it is God's counsel for us to gather into His fold the happy young people in the morning of life! It is God's time. It is the habit-forming time. They are forming their habits quickly now. Life is plastic now. Life is renascent now, responsive now, malleable now. After awhile it will be set in its ways. The adage comes in just there which says: "As the twig is bent the tree is inclined." You can go and bend down the little bushes and swing them this way and that, but in after years you may go back, and there are the strong, stalwart trees, which will bend neither this way nor that. They are set at last, fixed at last, by the fearful power of habit and growth. That is the parable and picture of human life. Oh, ye parents! Oh, ye teachers! God's time is for us to win the young people to Him while yet they are young.

The story goes that a certain king once ordered one of his subjects to make him a chain, and the blacksmith went and made the chain a certain length, according to the order of the king. And when the blacksmith brought the chain to him, the king ordered him to go back and make the chain twice as long, and the blacksmith obeyed him and brought back the chain twice as long. Once again the king bade the workman to take the chain and make it still twice as long. And the blacksmith obeyed him, and brought the chain to the king, and the king said to another subject, or other subjects: "Take this man and wrap him in this chain, and bind him and destroy him." Now, that is the parable and picture of habit. Satan does his best to keep these boys and girls, and young men and women, from coming to Christ in life's early morning. He is forging that chain of habit longer and heavier, tighter and stronger, every day, and the years pass on, and habit tightens, and its coils grow closer about the people, until at last they seem set and fixed in their ways, and little is the probability, far out in life, that they will ever come to Christ at all. God's time is while they are young. I have already said it is the useful time—and we want to be useful. One little life we have down here—forty years or fifty years, or more or less. Why live it at all, if we are not going to live it in the right way? We will be cumberers of the ground; we will not only hurt ourselves, but we will hurt everybody else, if we live this life in the wrong way. One little life to live! Oh, the glory of living it in the most useful fashion, which cannot be unless we are honestly for Jesus Christ.

There is yet another word to be urged upon you: You should come to Jesus now, and rightly settle this question of what you will do with Jesus now, because now is the safe time. Now might be the only time. I think I had better stress that for a moment, and stress it even for the young people who sit in this audience, looking up into my face, and listening so attentively, along with the older people. The matter of coming to Christ should be settled now because now is the safe time, and now might be the only time.

May I tell you about preaching to my own young people a special sermon some time ago, one morning, to the Sunday school? The doors were shut, so that the Sunday school would not be disturbed, and I preached a sermon of some twenty-five minutes to the younger people there, and when I had finished I asked who was ready then and there to decide for Christ? When I asked that, I said: "I want all such to come and take my hand, those of you who are ready now to say 'Yes' to Jesus, who will trust Him, that from this morning He may be your Savior."

And numbers and numbers of the young people came, and
along with that group came one of our girls, some twelve
or thirteen years of age, a serious and beautiful child.
Soon the service was concluded, and the day went by, and
the week went by, and I stood in my pulpit the following
Sunday morning, and when I had concluded the sermon
at the regular eleven o'clock service, a man came from
the outer door through my study, and touched me, and
said: "Before you go to your luncheon, you are wanted to
go to Nellie's home. They are going to take her to the
hospital. She is desperately ill, and she wants to see you
before she goes to the hospital." "Certainly," I said, "I
will go with you right now." I went with him speedily
to the home where Nellie lived, and there she was waiting
to see me before they carried her in the ambulance to the
hospital for the serious surgical operation. When I sat
down beside her I said: "What do you want to say to me,
Nellie?" She drew her handkerchief over her face, as if
to conceal the soft tears that bedewed her cheeks, and I
waited so that she could take her time and say what she
wanted to say to me in her own way. "What have you
got to say to me, my child?" I said again. And then she
said: "I don't know that I will come back from the hospital. I am very sick." I said: "Well, Nellie, what if
you should not come back?" And she said: "That is just
what I want to talk with you about. If I do not come
back—and something tells me that perhaps I won't—if I
do not come back, I want you to know that it is all right,
and I want you to tell my Sunday school class of girls, if
I do not come back, that I was not afraid. I want you to
tell them that on last Sunday, when you preached to the
girls and boys, I decided for Christ, and I am following
Him; I am trusting Him. I said 'Yes' to Him last Sunday, and meant it, and if I do not come back, I want you
to tell the girls in my class that I went away and was not
afraid, because I had decided for Christ." I said: "I hope
you will come back all right, Nellie, but I am glad to hear
you say all that, my child, and we will be praying for
you. I will pray for you now, and then I will be thinking
of you this afternoon and to-night." The day wore away

and the night came on, and I preached in the evening and went back to my home, and at midnight word came from the hospital, saying: "Nellie desires to see you very much." I said: "Certainly; I will be there very soon," and very soon I was there. Things had all gone to the bad with her, and her pulse galloped like some runaway horse. I sat beside her, and said: "What have you to say now, Nellie?" And she said: "I cannot go back home, and I caanot get back to the Sunday school and to church any more, and I want to ask you again to tell the girls in my class that I was not afraid, that I was ready, because when you preached a week ago, saying: 'Now is the accepted time to decide for Christ,' I said: 'It shall be my time.' " Wasn't it a glorious thing that I could tell the people that a little girl of a dozen years, when she heard Jesus saying: "Now is my time for you to come to me, now is the best time, now is the safe time, now might be the only time," a little timid girl said: "It shall be my time. I will surrender to Jesus, and trust Him now and forever to be my Savior?"

I am coming in a moment to the close of the sermon, but I have a question to ask you, before you leave the tent to-night. What have you done with Jesus? What will you do with Him? Do you say: "I am ready to-night to trust Christ; I am ready to-night to do the right thing with Christ; I am ready to-night to answer that question properly, 'What shall I do then with Jesus?' I will take Him for my Savior; I will be for Him from this hour, and no longer will I be against Him?" Then come and tell us of that great decision, as now we sing.

THE CLOSING PRAYER.

And now as we go, we pray thee, our Father, to put thy gracious favor upon these who publicly confess their acceptance of Christ as their personal Savior, and let them go to live for Christ like the Christian life ought always and everywhere to be lived. And, O, put thy Spirit profoundly upon those who desired thus to come but have held back. Show them how great a matter this is, how eternally and urgently important a matter this is, of doing the right thing with Christ, and for Him. And may these young people—how we covet them every one for Christ, from the morning of their lives—may they all and each from this night forward faithfully trust Christ, and follow Him in all His appointed ways for His friends. And all through this city, deepen thou, we beseech thee, the interest in all our hearts to be and to do in thy sight according to the counsel of thy holy will. How we bless thee for thy goodness and mercy to us! Let such goodness cause us daily to be more zealous for our Lord.

And now as the people go, may the blessing of the triune God be granted you, all and each, to abide with you forever. Amen.

XIV

NOON SERVICE, JUNE 19, 1917.

PRELIMINARY STATEMENT.

A series of daily, special meetings, such as these now in progress, are vitally important for God's people — for those who are already Christians. Such meetings are pre-eminently worth while, indeed, are altogether necessary now and then, for God's own people, for it is easy for Christians to drift, and to have their habits in the Christian life broken, and to go down life's stream, failing to give worthy testimony for Christ, and at the same time missing the peace and the power which ought to be in the Christian life. Meetings like these are often necessary for Christians, to summon us, to challenge us, to bring us back where we shall have our spiritual strength renewed and made deeper and larger. But we should not be content, as Christians, that the meetings shall be limited to that. We should look about ourselves daily, and give ourselves to serious thought and service for others. We should put forth our efforts in the most thoughtful and diligent way to help those about us who are not Christians. What opportunities we have in a modern city like this—what opportunities to help daily those who are not Christians! Most of the men and women before me this Tuesday noon, I take it, are Christian men and women. My heart would be profoundly warmed, if I could believe and be assured that every Christian here to-day would do his or her best to-day and to-morrow, and from day to day to help those about

194

you who are not Christians. You should not neglect any-body. The humblest, the poorest, the lowest, the tallest man in town should each be spoken to, in the proper fash-ion, concerning his personal relations to God. The woman most needy, the most neglected, the most capable, the most devoted to the social world, should each be appealed to, and every such life sought for the side and service of Jesus. Do I raise an unreasonable question when I raise the ques-tion if every Christian before me cannot and will not make it a point to bring with you to-night to the big tent, a group of people who are not Christians? And if it could not be a group, couldn't you find one person, and when you find that person, and bring that person with you, prob-ably sitting beside him or her—that can be determined in each case, as may be deemed best—pray as you bring such person, that the preacher may speak what and as he ought to speak to help that person? We are not to get away from that scriptural truth that "faith cometh by hearing, and hearing by the Word of God." I ask it most earnestly, my fellow Christians, if you will not, all and each, make it a point to bring with you to-night a group of people, or, if not a group, then one person not a Christian, to the daily services? How delighted we are to see these great throngs of Christians at the public services, the largest proportion of Christians, I think, that I ever saw in public services! But how deeply desirous we are that the Chris-tians shall bring with them from service to service those that are not Christians! How we long to help them! We would do them good, and not evil at all. "And they that be wise shall shine as the brightness of the firmament; and they that turn many to righteousness, as the stars for-ever and forever." Pay the price, I pray you, to be per-sonal soul winners.

THE SUPREME OFFERING TO CHRIST.

Text: "Amasiah who willingly offered himself unto the Lord."—II Chron. 17: 16.

And now, as I come to speak this morning, I wonder, as I look over this throng, just how much every life here means to the world. Would you have your life to count for the highest and the best? Then such life cannot count for the highest and best if it be not yielded to the guidance and mastership of the Lord Jesus Christ. There is a sentence in the Bible that points this truth for us, to which our attention is to be directed to-day: "Amasiah, who willingly offered himself unto the Lord."

You ask, Who was Amasiah? If you will read the context, you will see that he was the chief officer in the reign of good King Jehoshaphat. Next to the king himself, this man Amasiah was the first man of the kingdom. So important was he that 200,000 picked men were put under his command, and Amasiah stood next to the king in position. Now, this important man, situated in this eminent place, "willingly offered himself unto the Lord."

It is a glorious thing when men and women of leadership are pronounced and positive friends of the Lord. It is a glorious thing when the outstanding lawyer is the modest, faithful friend of Christ; and the skillful doctor, who has such an opportunity to bless the world; and the patient teacher, who occupies such an eminent place of responsibility and opportunity; and the alert editor, likewise strategically situated for wielding the most tremendous and commanding influence; and the aggressive business man, with people under him, whom he directs; and on and on and on, in all realms. What a glorious thing when people in position of leadership, as was this man Amasiah, make it a point to be pronounced friends of God! For the most serious thing in all the world, my men and women, is this matter of personal influence. The most significant thing about life is for life to be positionized properly, and the most tragical thing about life is for life to be positionized wrongly. Day in and day out, by the quiet emanation of our influence, we are taking people up, or we are dragging people down. Glorious then is it, beyond words, when a man or a woman is the known, positive, faithful friend of Christ!

Let the example of this man Amasiah teach us to-day. There are two or three simple, but greatly important lessons in his story, that we may well study this morning. First, Amasiah put God's cause as the first thing in his life. Surely, that was right. Where should he have put

it? Where should the men and women before me this
Tuesday noon put God's cause? We must put it somewhere. We must give it some place. We do give it some
place. Where should we put God's cause, in our personal,
every-day life? Now, we take often the most superficial
view, as we face that question.

I saw a symposium a little while ago in one of the
clever magazines, where answers were given to the question: "What is the great need for the church to-day?"
The answers given to that question were ludicrous, for
the most part, if the matters talked about had not been
so serious. One gave as his answer: "The great need for
the church, to-day, is that it shall have larger numbers."
Surely, he missed it widely. Never one time does God
put the emphasis on numbers. Indeed, we are distinctly
warned in the Bible, both by direct statement and by implication, concerning the snare that there is in numbers.
David of old took the census of the kingdoms of Israel
and Judea, and plunged the nations into the direst disaster, because while taking his census, he and his people
took their eyes away from God, and down the people went
into the ditch of disaster. It is not how many we count
that tells, but how much do we weigh? It is not quantity
that tells, but quality. It is not duration that tells, but in-
tensity. Once when Henry Drummond was holding an
institute for a group of Christian men, following his address he gave a quiz for the men, and presently one of them
asked: "Mr. Drummond, isn't the first need of Christianity to-day that it shall have more men behind it?" And
quick as a flash the keen man made answer: "No, not
more men, but a better brand." Jesus cannot command
big situations with little people. I dare to affirm to-day
that Jesus is most of all hindered by little people, and,
therefore, there comes the ringing challenge of the Bible:
"Quit you like men"—not like fops, not like dandies, not
like prigs—"quit you like men." Jesus waits for the
strength, the robustness, the masculinity, the power, the
personality of men laid on His altar, to win victories that
shall shake the world.

Then, in that same symposium to which I have re-

ferred, one made answer that the great need for Christ's
cause is that it should have more money. That answer is
as wide of the mark as is the first. Nowhere in the Bible
does the emphasis fall upon money as the chief requisite
for the triumph of God's cause. Money is a powerful factor everywhere, in religion as well as in the daily affairs
of men. I have no sympathy at all with that outcry that
is sometimes heard against money, against men who make
money, against men who have money. It is the cry of the
thoughtless, and sometimes of the anarchist, and for it I
have no sympathy. A man who can make money ought to
make it, legitimately, to be sure, honestly, rising early in
the morning and toiling late at night. But as men make
money, they are to remember that challenging word spoken
by Moses, when he said: "But thou shalt remember the
Lord thy God; for it is He that giveth thee power to get
wealth." We are to remember that money is to be a servant, and not to be our master at all. I can quite well understand how a certain rich woman in the country felt
awhile ago, when she lay a-dying, and at last piteously
appealed to the physician to know if that were death that
she was then facing, and had his answer that it was. Then,
seeking to draw the covering about her face, some who
were present said that over and over again the rich, self-
centered woman wailed out her cry: "Oh, how I dread
to meet God when I remember how I have trifled with
my money!" And well she might, for she must answer at
God's judgment bar for every dime that she has had. Do
not be deceived—money is not the first thing in the kingdom of God! It is often an unmitigated curse, the lust
for which turns many from the better way, and pierces
them through with many sorrows.

What is the first thing for the triumph of the kingdom
of God? It is pointed here in the case of this man Amasiah. He put God's cause as the first thing in his life. He
crowned his life by putting God's cause therein as supreme. It was the same kingly word said by Jesus long
afterward, when He preached His great sermon, saying:
"But seek ye first the kingdom of God, and His righteousness: and all these things"—bread and meat and sufficient

to wear—"shall be added unto you." "Seek ye first the
kingdom of God, and His righteousness." "Seek ye first"—
not secondly, not thirdly, not incidentally, not partially,
not optionally, not in subordinate fashion. Put "first" the
kingdom of God, and His righteousness, and then you can
go afield anywhere, absolutely assured that the best thing
is going to come to you.

Later along, that incomparable Paul illustrated the
same truth, when he said: "To me to live is Christ." Or,
freely translated, he said: "For me to live is for Christ
to live over again." "That is to say," said Paul, "in my
own little life, the best I can, I am to reincarnate the spirit
and teachings and purposes of Christ, and to live literally
for Him." "I am not my own at all," said Paul. "I am
Christ's. I belong to Him by a threefold claim. He cre-
ated me, and then He died for me, and then He preserves
me, and I belong to Him by that threefold claim." "My
brain is not mine," said Paul; "it is Christ's. Let me
mind what I do with Christ's brain. My hands are not
mine; they are Christ's. My feet are not mine; Christ
bought them with His blood. Let me mind where I take
Christ's feet. My heart is not mine, but Christ's. Let
me mind what I love with Christ's heart. My life is not
mine, but Christ's. Let me see to it that I take Christ's
life and put it where, and live it as Christ's life ought to
be lived."

Now this man Amasiah points that grandly telling lesson for us, and he did it in what we call a secular calling.
He did it yonder in the army, and if there is a difficult
place, I should judge, for men to stand up and be four-
square for God, it would be in the army. And yet there,
this strong man put God's cause first—there in the army—
which leads me to say that the distinction that we sometimes seek to make between what we call the "sacred and
the secular" is an improper distinction. There can be no
secularities in the right kind of a Christian life. You are
just as much called to be the right kind of a Christian here
on Tuesday, as you are yonder, Sunday morning, in the
house of God, with the hymn book in your hand, lustily
singing praises to His name. And I will dare to affirm

that if Christian men and women are going to be more careful and conscientious at one place than another, then out in the market place, in the shops and factories and stores, in the court house, in the busy marts of trade, in the circles where men constantly touch elbows with the world, let them there see to it that they are the right kind of Christians. If they are going to make a difference anywhere, let the better way have pre-eminence out there, as they touch elbows with the world.

I see glimpses, I think, of that glorious day coming when God's men and women will, out in the big world, shine there for Christ and witness there for Christ, so that daily their lives shall have increasingly winning power over the world about them. Some years ago it was my privilege to speak for ten days in another state, in one of the largest and noblest of our American churches. In such congregation was the leading shoe man of the world, who was also a devout Christian. Morning by morning, and night by night, he was faithfully in his place in the meetings. One day as we were going away I asked him: "If you should put your life passion in one sentence, what would that sentence be?" He smiled and said: "If you had come to my office, like I have asked you, you would know, for I have it there in my office on a cardboard. You had better come over and find out." I went on with him, and presently we were there in his office. There was his life passion, on the cardboard, in six little words. Some of these business men have, perhaps, been in his office and have seen them. Six little words voiced his life passion. If you have been there, you will recall them. Here they are: "God first. Family second. Shoes third." That is exactly right. You put it any other way, and you will make trouble. That arrangement is exactly right: "God first. Family second. Business third." God first, before father and mother and dearest loved ones. God first, before man's business, certainly. Making a living is a mere incident. Making a life is what we are in the world for. God first, our family second, and then our daily task third.

An interesting story is told of one of the great pork packers of the Northwest. One was introduced to him

one day and did not quite understand who he was, and
asked him at once: "What is your business?" The big
packer made answer, with modest face: "I am a Christian, sir. That is my business." The man questioning
him reddened a little in the face and said: "You did not
understand. What is your daily work? What is your
main concern?" And the packer made answer, with his
own face reddening, because he was modest, and said:
"My business, sir, is to be a Christian, but I pack pork,
sir, to pay the expenses." Oh, men and women before me,
our business in this world and life of ours is to be the
right kind of friends for Christ. That is our one, supreme
business. Amasiah points that lesson for us.

Amasiah points a second lesson, to which your attention is briefly directed. Our text says: "Amasiah willingly offered himself unto the Lord." Note that carefully.
See what this man Amasiah offered his Lord: "Amasiah
willingly offered himself" — himself — to the Lord. And
that is the supreme gift. The highest contribution that
any man or woman can make to this needy world is to
live in it the right kind of a life. One Savonarola turned
the tides of wicked Florence. The people said of John
Chrysostom, that glorious preacher in Constantinople: "It
were better for the sun to cease his shining than for John
Chrysostom to cease his preaching." This man Amasiah
gave his life to the Lord. Now, there is the crux of the
whole matter of living the Christian life.

I go every year to the cattlemen of the West, to their
annual camp meeting, and have been thus going to them,
for a week every year, for fifteen years. The most interesting week I ever live, in some respects, is that week;
and among the most interesting men — the biggest, the
finest, in many respects, that I have ever touched, are
those stalwart men. Sometime ago, when I was out there,
I preached to those men, some 1200, hidden away in a cliff
of the mountains, one morning, on the text: "Ye are not
your own. Ye are bought with a price: therefore, glorify
God in your body, and in your spirit, which are God's."
One of those big fellows who heard that day had not been
a Christian long. When the service was over he locked

his arm in mine and said: "Let's go for a walk. I have
something serious to say to you." We went up the canyon,
about a mile and a quarter away from the camp. After
we started, he did not say another word for quite awhile.
His great chest rose and fell, as if some seething furnace
were beneath it, as, indeed there was. I waited for him
to speak; I did not venture to question him at all. When
we were a mile and a quarter away from the camp, behind
a large ledge of rock, he turned and faced me, and said:
"I want you to pray a dedicatory prayer for me." "What
do you wish to dedicate?" I asked. Slowly he began to
talk, and the tears began to stream from his eyes, and he
said: "I did not know until this morning that all these
thousands of cattle that I have called mine are not mine
at all, but every one belongs to Christ. I did not know
until this morning that all these miles and miles of lands
over which my cattle have browsed are not mine at all,
but that every acre belongs to Christ. You see, I have
not been a Christian long, and I do not know much about
the Christian life. I have learned to-day, as never before,
what the Christian life means. Now I see that every hoof
of all these thousands of cattle belongs to Christ, and every
acre of all these lands over which they browse belongs to
Christ, and I want to take my true place in God's cause.
I want you to tell God for me that I will be His trustee
from this day on. I will be His administrator on His estate. I will try to live from now on like such an administrator ought to live. And when you finish telling Him
that for me, you wait. I have got something to tell Him
myself." We knelt there behind the rock, like two children, and I said: "Master, this man bids me tell thee
thus and so, thus and so." And he assented and consented,
while I spoke the sentences to God. When I had finished
I waited, and he put his face down to the ground and
sobbed. I waited and waited, and on and on he sobbed,
and presently he gasped out his prayer. It was this: "And
now, Master," he said, "am I not in a position to give you
my bad boy? His mother and I seem to have no influence
at all over him, but I have given you my property to-day,
and I will henceforth be your administrator on your estate,

and now won't you take my boy in the same way, and save
him, and save him soon, for your glory?" We went back to
the camp, and the day wore to evening, and I stood up
again to preach to the men. Nor had I spoken fifteen
minutes until that wild son, on the outskirts of that crowd,
stood up before us all, came toward his father sitting there
at the front, and as he came and as we looked, he said:
"Papa, I cannot wait until that man is done his sermon.
I have decided for Christ!" And this Scripture, that hour,
was plain to our hearts: "Delight thyself also in the Lord;
and He shall give thee the desires of thine heart." Oh,
what power a man has with God, when such man comes
to Christ and says to Him: "You can get me for any
field, for any journey, for any task, for any duty that you
wish. Master, I am yours—to go and to say and to be
and to do, just as thou wilt." What a power he has in
the world!

Notice the text again: "Amasiah offered himself willingly." There was no coercion, no conscription, no draft-
ing. He offered himself willingly to the Lord. Oh, men,
my brothers! Oh, women, my sisters! What a glorious
thing for men and women to rise up and say, without being
coaxed and coerced and compelled and drafted and con-
scripted: "Christ can get my best, and I am going to
give Him my best!" What a power that man or that
woman is! What a power! One of two factors dominates
every life. Either self is the dominating factor in life, or
God. Mark it! The self-centered life is doomed. No matter how brilliant, how clever, how powerful, how achiev-
ing, the self-centered life is doomed. That is true of a
nation. The self-centered nation is going on the rocks.
That is true of an organization. The self-centered organization will finally collapse and be doomed. That is true
of a family. No matter how clever and brilliant and influential, if such family be self-centered, the day of its
doom comes on. Even as doom came to Lot's family, the
self-centered home is doomed, no matter how brilliant.
The imperial Gladstone was probably right when he said:
"Napoleon had the keenest brain that was ever packed into
a human skull." And yet Napoleon died like a dog in the

ditch, after he had made Europe cower and cringe and tremble before him. Why? He was self-centered in life from first to last. What did he care to walk with cruel foot over the heart of his beautiful Josephine? What did he care to sacrifice a hundred thousand soldiers, if only he could carry out his self-centered and fiendish ambition? The self-centered life is doomed. No matter what the calling, the position, the power, the self-centered life is doomed. But the life linked with Christ, the life that says "Yes" to Christ, the life that says: "Thou, oh, Christ, canst have thy way with me. Thy plan I wish. Thy program I accept. The road thou wouldst have me travel, make it plain to me and I will take it"—that is the life victorious. That is the life that wins. That is the life of glorious conquest on any field.

Before you leave this hall to-day, let me ask you, my men and women, if you have fully settled it that you want Christ's will brought to pass in your life? Any other course has in it regret and ever-increasing distress. Is it fully settled with you that you want Christ's will brought to pass in your life? George MacDonald, that sturdy Scotchman, phrased it in his simple poem: "What I Said and What Christ Said." Maybe I can quote his lines:

I said: "Let me walk in the field."
He said: "No, walk in the town."
I said: "There are no flowers there."
He said: "No flowers, but a crown."

I said: "But the skies are black,
There is nothing but noise and din."
And He wept as He sent me back:
"There is more," He said, "there is sin."

I said: "But the air is thick
And fogs are veiling the sun."
He said: "But hearts are sick,
And souls in the dark undone."

I said: "I shall miss the light,
And friends will miss me, they say."
And He answered: "Choose to-night
If I am to miss you, or they."

I pleaded for time to be given.
He said: "Is it hard to decide?
It will not seem hard in heaven
To have followed the steps of your Guide!"

Then I turned one look at the field,
And set my face to the town.
He said: "My child, do you yield?
Will you leave the flowers for the crown?"

> Then into His hand went mine,
> And into my heart came He,
> And I walk in a light divine
> That path I had feared to see.

Oh, my brother men, you will miss it unspeakably, you will miss it irrevocably, you will miss it so that memories will burn and conscience will bite like some devouring serpent, if you are not for Christ. Wouldn't you like publicly to-day to say: "God help me, I would be for Him, I will be for Him, and to-day I yield myself to Him to be for Him till life's day is done?" Every soul that says: "I say that," come tell us now, as we sing the hymn.

THE CLOSING PRAYER.

How we thank thee, O, our Father, for thy marvelous goodness to us! We go now with a prayer deep and fervent to God, that He will give these men and women who confess Christ to-day to live for Him simply, honestly, straightforwardly, conscientiously, consistently, till the earthly day is done. Some here to-day have wandered far from God. Yea, Lord, who in this presence has not wandered? But we want to return, we would now leave ourselves in Christ's hands, like a little child rests on its mother's heart. Forgive our every evil way, O Lord, and from this hour take us by thy hand and guide us by the counsel of thy Spirit, so that we shall go where, and speak what, and live as the great, good Savior would ever have us to do. And may the soul in this house all wrong with God, bedarkened and troubled, who has missed the right way, has wasted life, has wasted influence, be taught of thee that it is not too late yet to be reconciled to God. Speak to such now and say to that one that God will forgive him, and will put his feet in a sure place, and God will help him to be strong and true, and right, and safe, if only he will surrender his life to Jesus, the welcoming Savior and Lord.

And now may this whole multitude go to-day to speak as they ought for Christ, to-day and every day, and to give His cause their best love and loyalty and strength as long as they shall live in the flesh.

Keep us, O thou covenant-keeping God, in the love of Christ, and faithful to His holy will, till the day is done. We pray in His all-prevailing name. Amen.

XV

NIGHT SERVICE, JUNE 19, 1917,

PRELIMINARY REMARKS.

A letter has just been handed me from a mother, who says she has been attending these services, and has received a large blessing from them. She says in the letter that her son is away in the training camp, getting ready to respond to the country's call to war, and she greatly desires the prayers of the Christian people here assembled, for the salvation of that son. I can well believe from what she says about him in the letter that he is, indeed, a noble son, the pride and joy of his mother's heart. It will surely be a proper thing for us now to pray for him, and for all the other sons who have gone out from this community, like him, in response to the country's call. I would pause just here to ask if there are other parents present, whose sons have gone away to the training camps to make ready to serve the nation in this world crisis? We will unite our prayers in just a moment for those sons.

I wonder if there are not parents all through this great throng, who have sons and daughters who are not saved. I should like to ask every parent present, father and mother, for whose unsaved child or children you would like to ask for prayer, along with these that have just been mentioned, the soldier boys that are away from home; every parent in this midst, who has a child not a Christian, whom you would see saved in God's time and way, to stand quietly this moment. Many are standing.

One eye sees and knows all that is represented by this standing multitude. The Lord teach us to pray! May we pray now, with heads bowed.

THE OPENING PRAYER.

Just because we need thee, O thou great and gracious Father, we would call upon thee yet again, before the message of the hour is to be brought to the people. We would be in thy presence here, waiting upon thee, just as thou wouldst have us. We would turn from every evil way. We would follow the Lord just as He points the way and from this very moment.

And now we would unite our prayers for all our soldier boys, who have gone from us in response to the nation's call. Lord, shield them from evil and so teach them concerning the things of God that they shall be God's men, the soldiers and friends of the great Savior, living for Him, loving Him, and following Him where'er they may be called in response to His will. May those who are now Christ's friends be better friends to Him every day, and in thus serving Him may they bless their comrades with eternal blessing. And may all those who are not Christ's friends—those represented by parents here to-night and similar sons throughout our great country—we pray that upon them all may be brought to bear such worthy Christian influences that every one of them shall be speedily won to Christ, and then go to live for Him with all the fulness and usefulness of the Christian life. In these unusually anxious and responsible days, may all these young men be taught of the Lord and find their strength in His control.

We beseech thee to look with favor upon all these parents to-night, who have witnessed to the fact that they have some child dear to their hearts who is out of the ark of safety. O, first of all we pray thee to bless these parents! In their own hearts, give them all and each to be right with God. If any parent has come short of duty in the training of the child, may such parent set about from this very minute to redeem the time, to pursue the wisest possible course in the immediate future, so that the best shall come to the child. Oh, we pray that the immeasurably solemn responsibility of parenthood may be borne in upon us all, so that all parents in this presence shall address themselves, with all sincerity and diligence and devotion, to advise and to lead and to pray for and help their children in the highest way, even in that way which shall have God's approval.

Speak, we pray thee, Lord, to the waiting multitude. Search our hearts. Deepen within us the sense of eternal things. Oh, deepen within us the sense of the value of time, and the mighty meaning of personal influence, of personal responsibility. Write the lesson deeply in our every heart that each man is his brother's keeper, and that if we neglect, and evil comes to such brother, God shall require his blood at our hands. Oh, let us see what a great thing it is to live—to live in that high way, in that sublimely faithful way, that God commands and that the interests of humanity about us so imperiously demand.

God be gracious to us now! Without thee we can do nothing. It is not by might, nor by power, but by thy Spirit, O Lord, that these blessed things are done for the children of men. We would not put our confidence for one moment in arms of flesh. We would put it altogether in the living God. May He take us by the hand, and wield the service to-night as He wishes. May He give the preacher to speak what and as Christ would have him speak. May the people's hearts be opened divinely, so that they shall hear and respond just as Christ would have this multitude to hear and respond. Find us to-night, O Lord, every one of us who has come to these pews. Oh, find us, heart by heart, and life by life, and incline us to the upper and better way. If duty has been sadly neglected, may we be unwilling from to-night to continue in such neglect. If backslidings hold Christians here, may they now rise up with a high resolve and come back to Christ. If men and women have long halted between two opinions, whether to come to Christ or wait longer, may they put away the matter of waiting and come now. May the boys and girls of tender years—how we love them and would commend every one of them to Jesus—may they to-night be unwilling longer to wait to say yes to Christ. And may God's will, whatever that is, wherever that leads, whatever that costs, be done by us all, throughout the entire service to-night. For Christ's sake. Amen.

THE DOOM OF DELAY
Text: "He lingered."—Gen. 19:16.

Deeper than any words I can say may indicate is the

desire of my heart so to speak that I may help the people. No other concern have I, in speaking in Fort Worth, or speaking anywhere else, if I am able to read my heart. I would do the people good, and not evil at all. The longing is ever present with me, and inexpressible, that the people may have the crown and climax of life, which is true religion. ⬤That was a pungent thing a little boy said to his father: "Papa, is your soul insured?" "Why do you ask, my boy?" "Because I heard Uncle George say that you had your life insured, and your house insured, but he was afraid that you would lose your soul, because you seemed to have no thought for your soul. Papa, won't you get it insured right away?" The little fellow fired a center shot when he asked that question. How true it is that men and women do insure their lives, and insure their houses, as they ought, and sometimes insure autos, and yet the eternal claims of the soul are passed recklessly by. ⬤That question asked needs ever to ring in our ears: "What shall it profit a man, if he shall gain the whole world and lose his own soul?" What does it count, if a man shall rise high in the world of business, or in the world of statecraft, or in the word social and intellectual, if such man forgets to give heed to the highest claim of all, and lives and dies without the favor of God, and without conserving the welfare of the soul? What does it all matter? How solemn is the thought that men and women come to public worship like this, and hear and feel and think and desire, and yet through the power of delay miss the upward way, and lose that which is of eternal value. The text points such a case as that. You need not forget the text. It may be easily remembered, because there are just two words in it: "He lingered."

It describes the conduct of a man whose name was Lot, who occupied wrong relations, and God sent angels to warn him to cease from such wrong relations, and pursue the right path — the path of importance and wisdom and safety for himself and others. And yet, though he was warned faithfully by God's messengers, there stands out the ominous signboard in his life, on which are written two little words: "He lingered."

Evidently, this man Lot is the exact counterpart of men and women in every community where the gospel is preached. Faithfully are they told of their danger and their duty. They are warned concerning the peril that there is in lingering. And yet they wait and presume and float down the current, until at last all that is highest and safest and best has been forfeited and lost. I wonder, as I begin to speak on this admonitory theme, if in this large press of people this evening I am speaking to men and women, to parents, to middle-aged men and women, to older ones with the gray about their temples, to young men and women, to happy-hearted boys and girls, who are lingering concerning the highest things, when duty and safety and need and right and happiness and usefulness would urge them to cease such lingering. If I speak to some who are lingering to-night with regard to the highest and all-important matters, oh, for you would I send out my most earnest entreaty, and to God would I lift up my heart, that your lingering may cease, and cease before too much has been lost—yea, before all has been lost.

This case of Lot has in it many lessons, but two or three emerge from the story, to which I would now call your attention. May the Divine Spirit help me, and may He help you, that speaker and people alike may do God's will in this service! You will notice, first of all, what this man Lot did. One little word describes it. He "lingered." After he knew his duty and had been told of his danger, yet he "lingered." That is Satan's supreme masterpiece with which to deceive and to destroy mankind. It lurks in the little word "linger." Satan's supreme scheme to blind men and women and mislead them, and seduce them from the right path, and utterly defeat them and destroy them, is stated in that one little word, "linger."

One who had fearful melancholia dreamed that he died and went away to that world of waste and loss and night, the name of which is hell, and that down there he saw and heard the conclave of evil spirits in that world of waste, as these evil spirits counselled and plotted how they might best destroy the world of surging people, who had not yet died. And in his dream, he said, one proposed: "Let us go back to the world and say everywhere: 'There is no God.' And if we can get that fixed in the minds and hearts of the people, that there is no God, we will have them utterly unanchored and at sea, and we shall destroy them." But the other evil spirits answered in a chorus: "We cannot win with that." The fool hath said in his heart, "No God." And, oh, what a foolish person he is! It would be far more reasonable for you to say that this watch, with its machinery, all regular and orderly, just happened, than for you to say that this great world, with its order and symmetry and harmony, peopled with living, rational, human beings, just happened, and that no God was behind all and the Creator of all. So the evil spirit said: "We cannot win with that theory."

And then another one proposed: "Let us go back to the world, and everywhere sow down the subtle suggestion that the Bible is an untrustworthy book, and if we can dislodge the confidence of the people in the Bible as God's Book, His God-breathed revelation to men, they will be at sea, and we can win them and destroy them." But the evil spirits answered in a chorus, so the dreamer tells us, that they could not win with any such plea as that. Every effort has been made to destroy the Bible, but in vain. Men have bound it. Men have burned it. Men have chained it. Men have done all that they could to get rid of the Bible, but its leaves are scattered to the four winds of the earth. Above all, it is hidden in human hearts. So the evil spirits said: "We cannot win with that. We cannot thus get rid of the Bible."

Then another one said: "This is my suggestion. Let us go back to earth, and say to mankind everywhere that there is no such world as hell, the world of waste, the world of loss, the world of soul defeat, no such place as that. Let us say it everywhere. Let us say that God is too merciful and good to allow anybody to be destroyed and lost, and let us teach that everywhere, and then with that subtle doctrine of deception we will mislead and destroy the world." But the evil spirits answered in a chorus: "We cannot win with that." Down in the human conscience is written the consciousness that as men sow, so shall they reap. Men know that. Men know that vice and virtue cannot have the same harvest. Men know that a praying, God-fearing, God-serving man must have a different harvest from a man who neglects God, and is prayerless, and flagrantly disobeys God, and puts Him out of his life. There is a difference in the harvest, and men know it. So they said: "We cannot win with that. Down in the human consciousness there is a little monitor called conscience, that makes its painful insistence that as men sow, so shall they reap. We cannot win with that doctrine."

And then one of the evil spirits, so the dreamer tells us, rose up after a moment and said: "Eureka! Eureka! I have it! I have it! Let us go back to the world and say everywhere that there is a God, and that men are responsible to Him, and that the Bible is His Book, the revelation of His will, the signboard to point men in the upward way; and let us say that there is a world of waste and defeat, the name of which is hell, which responsible human beings shall have for their home, if they turn away from God's proffered mercy, and refuse to accept Him as He stretches out His hand with forgiveness and salvation; say that men shall die, and shall be their own destroyers. But when you have said all that, say one more word, and say it everywhere. Say to sinners everywhere just this word: 'Time enough yet!'" And then the dreamer said that all hell applauded, for that was the masterpiece concocted by Satan to destroy the world. That is Satan's masterpiece to destroy the world. He comes with his subtle suggestion, saying: "Be not in any haste about religion. Don't be anxious about that really important matter just yet. Linger about it. Take time about it. Delay about it. Procrastinate. Time enough yet!" And with that fearful, specious teaching, Satan is destroying men and women about us as nothing else can and does destroy the needy children of men.

Oh, may I come this evening and pause by the heart of every life in all this great press, and as a personal friend—for I would be that to every human being on this earth, to help him if I might—may I pause there and ask you: "Is not this matter about which you linger entirely too important for you to continue such lingering? Isn't the matter of your soul's duty and safety and need and welfare a matter too important for you to keep on lingering?"

Suppose that you were involved in some important business transaction, and I should come to you and propose that we go to the sea, or to the mountains, for two weeks of recreation and rest, and that you leave all that and come with me, you would look at me and say: "I should like to go, and under ordinary conditions, perhaps I might go, but I am just now passing the papers for an important trade. Both sides are ready to sign them up, and I cannot leave until all this is closed." And suppose I come back and urge you: "You can put that away. That can wait. It can wait a week or ten days, and when you come back you can sign the papers and pass them and have it all concluded." You would stare at me as you wondered if I were not utterly abnormal, in the face of all that you had told me about the readiness to close the transactions that had been having your attention. Suppose that there were illness in your body, serious in its encroachments, and the doctor came and looked you over and said: "You must immediately give your case attention. I find serious, even ominous signs in your body. You must immediately give your case attention." How unreasonable for you to laugh in his face, and put his warning away, and go as of yore! You say: "Certainly, either would be unreasonable, of the illustrations you have named." And yet I come tonight to talk to you about the lingering of your soul with reference to its highest claims and duties and needs. Tell me, can it be reasonable for you to linger over that? Was not Jesus right when He said: "Seek ye first the kingdom of God, and His righteousness, and all these things shall be added unto you?" Was not Jesus pre-eminently right?

Years ago, in some special meetings, I became deeply interested in a young law student, who was going away presently to the law school at Austin. I sought him out for a quiet interview and said to him: "What are you going to do about this first question, the call of Jesus to

be your Savior and the master of your life?" He said:
"I have definitely decided, in these meetings, that it is the
sanest thing in the world to be the friend and follower of
Jesus; and I have gone on further and decided that just
as soon as I get my diploma from the law school at Austin,
straightway I am going to seek the Savior and begin serving Him." You know what I said to him: "What if you
do not come back from the law school at all? What if
you never complete your law preparation at all? What
if those three years are not to be allowed you? Hadn't you
better make sure now of the supreme matter? With your
wits about you, calm and clear, hadn't you better make
the supremest decision ever allowed a human soul to make,
namely, to say: 'Yes, Lord Jesus, who died for sinners,
I yield to thee. Save me, and from this hour guide me in
thine own way.' Hadn't you better take that first step
now, and let these smaller matters be properly related to
such pivotal decision?" And then, after he had waited a
moment or two, he looked up into my face and said: "I
will take that first step right now. Right now I surrender
to Christ. I will confess Him in the public service this
evening." And he did so confess Him that very evening,
and a few days later went away to the State University
law school at Austin. It was less than three months until
his body came back to North Texas in a casket. Only one
short week of pneumonia had hurried him from time into
death and the grave. He had chosen the better part before it was too late. Oh, men and women, oughn't you
to put first things first?

And tell me again, isn't this matter of lingering a matter that vexes you the more it is crowded upon you? What
pleasure is there in indecision? How terrible a thing for
us to be continually agitated with a big question that must
be decided, and yet we are not decided! This man Lot
did not find lingering pleasant, for the Bible tells us that
"he vexed his righteous soul from day to day with their
unlawful deeds," as he went drifting with the tide. Tell
me, can there be any pleasure in lingering with reference
to the most important question that you will ever face?
Here is a question that is inescapable. Do something

with Jesus you must, you will. Now, can it be pleasant to you to say: "I will keep putting Him off, and saying no, and lingering with respect to His call, and putting it indefinitely away?" Can that be a thing to please your mind? How terrible a thing is the spirit of indecision with reference to any question!

Oh, I would pause at every lingering heart here to-night, and look up into your faces, as a friend, and probe you with questions as to why you linger about the most urgently important matter of all! Do you tell me: "Sir, I am lingering because I have no interest in religion at all?" Oh, no! Not one in this place, I think, makes answer like that. Not one in this place looks me now in the face saying: "That matter of Christ's call has in it no appeal for me, and that matter of my soul's welfare does not interest me a jot." Nobody here makes a suicidal answer like that. Time and again you have thought about being saved, about having your sins forgiven, about being right with God, about being ready if the summons should come to go hence, ready for whatever should come. Time and again you have thought of all that. Time and again your heart has had its deep and serious hours of reflection and high purpose. Time and again you have said: "I must give this matter of personal religion the right attention." Time and again you have written down the resolve: "I must by and by look after this first question of all, even the salvation of my soul." Oh, it is not that you do not care that you linger—it is not that.

Is it this—does somebody say: "I am lingering because I cannot see how it is that one is born again; I cannot understand the philosophy of how a soul is saved by a crucified and risen Savior?" Do you say that is why you linger, because you cannot understand how it is that one is saved? Neither do I understand it. Neither does anybody else. The wisest Christian philosopher on the face of the earth cannot explain to you how it is that one is born again. The how of everything is veiled with mystery. The lowest form of life is utterly impossible of analysis and explanation by the greatest thinker and philosopher of all. And here the highest form of life—spiritual life—life which God gives the soul that accepts Christ as a Savior—that highest form of life is utterly impossible, in the way that it is imparted to man, of human comprehension or understanding. That scholarly man who came to Jesus, when Jesus was here in the flesh, one evening when the twilight had gone and nightfall had come—that fine man, Nicodemus, who came to Jesus to talk with Him about these spiritual matters, when Jesus told him, "You must be born again, or you cannot even see the kingdom of God," said just what you and I have said—"how can one be born again?" Mark Jesus' answer: "The wind bloweth where it listeth"—that is, where it pleaseth—"and thou hearest the sound thereof, but canst not tell whence it cometh, and whither it goeth; so is every one that is born of the Spirit." You and I are to come confessing our sins, and turning from them by repentance — forsaking them, renouncing them, and to make honest, absolute surrender of our poor, sinful lives to Christ, saying to Him: "Savior, I give up to thee. Save me thy way." And He will grant His forgiveness, and He will by His own divine power give us that new birth, without which one must ever remain blind concerning Christ's great salvation.

That nobly gifted editor of Atlanta, Georgia, Henry Grady, a great publicist, a thrilling orator, a humanity-serving citizen, one of the South's most honored sons, got far away, right in the zenith of his power and popularity, from Christ. Like many others similarly situated, he neglected the things of Christ and drifted with the tide. Far back yonder when he was a boy, he made a profession of religion, and for awhile observed the religious habits, but when his remarkable fame and career came on, he neglected the Christian life, and went drifting with the tide. They told me, when I was speaking in Atlanta some years ago, this beautiful chapter out of his great life. When he had made one of his loftiest speeches, on one occasion, and plaudits from North, South, East and West were coming to him on every wire, he slipped out of the office of "The Constitution," his daily paper in Atlanta, saying to his associates as he left: "You need not know where I am, but I am going to find mother to-night in the little home,

I have something to say to her. I will be back in the morning. You need not know where I am." And he took an out-of-the-way road to his mother's cottage, and when he reached it, he said to his mother: "Mother, all these plaudits, all this fame, all this notoriety, all this popularity, all this applause—that does not satisfy my heart. Mother, I once thought that I was a Christian, but if I was, I have got far away from God, and I have come back, mother, to ask you if I may not kneel down at your knee, and be a little boy again, like I was when I was at home with you, and say my simple prayer, like I used to say it every day when the day was done. And then, when I have said my prayer like that, I wonder if you won't take me to my bed, and tuck the cover around me, just like you used to do when I was a little boy, and then, when you have tucked the cover around me, if you won't bend down over me and pray for your little boy, for God to teach him and guide him and help him, just like you used to pray for me when I was a little boy." And that is exactly what happened in that little home that night. Great Henry Grady knelt at his mother's knee, like he used to do as a little boy, and said his simple, boyish prayer, like he used to say it long years before, and then his dear old mother escorted him to his room and bed, and she tucked the cover about him, and bent over him, with tears and prayers, commending her boy to the great Savior. And then she kissed him, like she used to do, and left him alone. And in the gray of the early morning, Henry Grady came from his room, and found his mother, and there was a light on his face fair like the morning light, and he said: "Mother, I was a little child last night, and felt out after Jesus, and He met me and has spoken peace to my poor, wandering heart."

Oh, souls not right with God, come as little children to Him, this evening! Be a little child and come to Jesus. Oh, lawyer, over there, or doctor, or carpenter, or merchant! Oh, wandering man or woman, with your mind all puzzled and perplexed and shot through with the questions, be a little child to-night, and say: "Lord Jesus, I know that I have moral lapse and loss and sin in my life, and that I do not have moral resources within myself suf-

ficient to be the man or woman I ought to be. Lord Jesus,
I will surrender to thee. Save me thy way." And, as the
Lord lives, He will save you this very night. Oh, do not
linger, but come to Him! "Except ye be converted, and
become as little children, ye shall not enter into the kingdom of heaven."

The chief reason, I summon you to remember, why
souls are lost is wrapped up in that word "lingering," that
word "delay," that word "to-morrow," that word "procrastination." "He lingered." He just lingered, and the
ill-fated results followed. And while you and I linger,
convictions within us get feebler and fainter, even every
hour we linger. And while we linger, our desires and impressions, kindled within us by the truth and Spirit of
God, yet resisted by us, wane and get less and less. And
while we linger, the difficulties strengthen about us and
multiply. While we linger, habit hardens and character
crystallizes—while we linger. Oh, the tragedy of it!

The naturalists tell us about a little plant called the
"sensitive plant," the most sensitive plant, they tell us,
that grows in all the vegetable world. You may touch that
little plant, and it will vibrate in every limb and leaf, as
with the vibrations of some fine-stringed violin. You may
keep on touching it, and it will vibrate every time you
touch it, but less and less and less, every time you give it
a touch. Keep on touching it, and there it vibrates, perceptibly, but the vibrations are less, they are fewer, they
are slower, with every touch. After awhile that sensitive
plant, under the repeated touches, refuses to vibrate any
more. The plant has at last been touched to death, and
there it hangs, in every limb and leaf and tendril, all flabby
and unresponsive. It has at last been touched to death.
Oh, human soul, that soul of yours is more sensitive than
the finest stringed violin! More sensitive is that soul than
the vegetable plant that I have just described. And that
soul is touched, that soul is called, that soul is played upon,
that soul feels, that soul vibrates, that soul responds, that
soul argues, that soul trembles, but that soul lingers. Now,
Satan does not care how much you tremble, nor how much
you feel, if you will only linger, for lingering is the way

of doom and failure and death. God give you to cease
your lingering, God give you to stop your lingering, this
very hour! Oh, Breath Divine, bestir these lingering souls,
that their lingering now may cease!

There is another thought in the text, to which we now
advance, far more serious than this first thought, to which
your earnest attention has just been called: Lot's lingering doomed other lives, even those of his own heart and
home. Oh, that is to my mind the most awful thought
to be contemplated by the human mind. Lot's lingering
doomed his family. You read there the story in all its
contextual relations, and you will see how Lot's lingering
dragged that family of his down into the deepest ditch of
ruin and defeat. Lot went to his sons-in-law, when at
last he was awakened to get out of the city, called thereto
by the warning of the angels, and he said to those sons-in-
law that they must hasten, for danger was imminent and
overwhelming for the city. And those sons-in-law laughed
him to scorn. They mocked him to his face. They called
him an old dotard. He had lingered too late, he had waited
too long, and his influence was contemptible with those
sons-in-law, when at last he sought to recover and save
them. And even Lot's wife, warned solemnly not to look
back as they made their haste from the city, looked back
and met her ill-fated doom. Oh, Lot, head of the house,
if thou hadst been the man thou oughtest to have been,
that woman would not have looked back, and that fate
would not have come! Thy lingering hast wrought her
doom!

And then Lot went on with only two of his children,
two daughters, and the after-story of those two daughters
is the most shocking story in all this Holy Bible. Lot's
house went down, wrecked and doomed and lost, because
Lot lingered. That is the most terrible picture in all the
Holy Bible. It brings you and me face to face again with
the awful power of human influence. One person helps
another or hurts another, just by human influence. Gladstone never wearied of saying: "One example is worth
a thousand arguments." Your example and mine every
day takes people up or takes them down. Oh, influence,

influence! Is there any other question quite so serious in the world for human minds to contemplate? Jesus gives the picture of one who causes through his influence somebody else to stumble and miss the right way: "It were better for him that a millstone were hanged about his neck, and he cast into the sea, than that he should offend one of these little ones." Oh, parent, is your child going the broad way because of you? Oh, friend, is your friend or acquaintance going the broad way because of your position, your influence, your example? Oh, soul, for your own sake, first, personal religion is the supreme claim, and then for the sake of others, whom you must hurt or help, whom you must take up or drag down, you must not, dare not, be careless about your influence. And the supreme influence is the influence of example.

I was speaking awhile ago in one of our Southern cities, and one of the members of the National Congress was in the audience, one evening, a man of much weight and worth, but not a Christian, and that evening I was preaching on the text: "No man liveth to himself." When I gave the call for public confession of Christ, that congressman's conscience was probed to the depths. He acted up to the light he had, and walked down the aisle and said to me: "God forgive me that I did not do this when I was a young fellow, but I do it at last!" And no sooner had he done that than it looked as if half the congregation would follow him down the aisles—young men, and middle-aged men, and boys — as they saw that conspicuous citizen come like a little child and make his surrender to Christ. Oh, soul, you intend to come. Hasten, I pray you, not simply for your own sake. For the sake of somebody sheltering behind you, waiting on you, not acting because you have not acted, hasten, I pray you, to make your return to God.

Now I call your attention a moment more to the instrumentalities that were used to cause Lot to give up his lingering. God sent His angels to Lot to warn him, to beseech him, to counsel him to give up his lingering, to leave that place of wrong relations, where his feet were fast in the mire. God sent angels to help Lot. Whom

has He sent to help you and me? His messengers are
many. Angels, I doubt not, for the Bible teaches it, play
a significant part in human lives. But there are other
messengers that God sends, and they are near at hand,
and you and I may perceive them and know them. There
is the Holy Bible. Oh, what an influence the Bible has,
with its pungent calls to men! Sometimes just one sentence grips the human conscience and turns it away from
darkness to light, from the wrong road to the right. Call
to mind some of its pungent words: "Prepare to meet thy
God." "Seek ye the Lord, while He may be found. Call
ye upon Him while He is near." "For the great day of
His wrath is come; and who shall be able to stand?" "How
wilt thou do in the swelling of Jordan?" "So then every
one of us shall give account of himself to God." With
Scriptures like these, the human conscience often is probed,
and turned by even one sentence of Scripture, from the
wrong to the right way.

And then how often God sends us His messenger of
preaching. Oh, what strange effects has preaching! Many
a time the preacher is thought by the hearer to be personal, to be acquainted with all that is in the hearer's life,
and to be actually describing the life of the hearer, and
the hearer winces under such personal description. Time
and again men have sought me out as I have left my pulpit, and have said to me alone: "Who told you about my
condition, that you laid it bare here to-day?" And I have
said: "Why, I never heard of your condition. No living
soul has ever breathed a word to me about your condition."
They said: "What then does it all mean?" And I have
answered: "It means that God knows about it, and God
has guided His preacher, who said: 'Lord, the preacher
does not know what to preach, but thou knowest. Give
him the message which thou wilt take and apply to the
human conscience,' and God took the message and with
it found the human conscience." What strange effects
preaching has! One wrote me this from Birmingham,
Alabama, the other night: "I heard you when you laid
bare my case in that sermon. Somebody had told you all.
I went back to the hotel, in your city, but could not sleep,

and I took the train and I have reached Birmingham, and here in the hotel in Birmingham, at midnight, I have found Christ, and I am writing to tell you that your sermon was not in vain. I wonder who told you about me." Nobody told me about him. I had never before heard of him. I did not know he was in the audience. But the omniscient God knew he was in the audience, and sent the message and fitted it home to his heart by the Divine Spirit, who shows the soul the way from darkness to light.

Sometimes, ofttimes, God's messenger is home influence. Did you ever hear Mr. Torrey, the far-famed evangelist, tell what an awful unbeliever he was when he was a young man, how he went to the deepest depths of infidelity and scouted everything—the Bible, Christ, God, heaven, hell, immortality—everything like that? And his dear mother yearned after him, and loved him, and pleaded with him, and prayed for him, and after awhile he said to his mother: "I am tired of it all, and I am going to leave and not bother you any more, and you will not see me any more. I am tired of it all." She followed him to the door, and followed him to the gate, pleading and praying and loving and weeping, and then at last she said, as her final word: "Son, when you come to the darkest hour of all, and everything seems lost and gone, if you will honestly call on your mother's God, you will get help." He went his way in his darksome and terrible infidelity. Deeper down he went, day in and out, and month in and out. And he said the months went by, and he was 427 miles from his mother's home, in a hotel in a certain town, unable to sleep, wearied with his sins and wearied with life, and he at last rose up in the early morning, and said: "I will get out of this bed, and I will take the gun there from my valise, and I will put it to my temple, and I will end this farce called human life." And as he got out of bed to do that dreadful thing, the last word that his mother had said came back to him: "Son, when your darkest hour of all comes, and everything seems lost, call in sincerity on your mother's God, and you will get help." And Torrey said he fell beside his bed and said: "Oh, God of my mother, if there is such a Being, I want light, and

if thou wilt give it, no matter how, I will follow it." He
had light within a few moments, and hastened back home.
And, to follow the story just a moment more, he said that
when he got back home, thinking he would surprise his
mother and come upon her unexpectedly, she came down
the walk to the gate, laughing and crying with uncontrollable joy, and said: "Oh, my boy, I know why you are
coming back, and I know what you have to tell. You have
found the Lord. God has told me so." Oh, the power of
a mother's prayer! Oh, the power of a father's prayer,
the power of a brother's prayer, a sister's prayer! Oh,
the power of a wife's prayer, when she links herself with
God! And full many a time God's good angel to bring
one back from the darksome and downward way is somebody's prayer, who says: "Lord, spare this soul a little
longer. Give this soul a little more respite, a little more
time." Prayer, how mighty it is before God when it is
sincerely offered!

Sometimes it is a providence that calls you. Sometimes
God's blessings come robed in black. Sometimes sickness
terrible is at the gate, at the door, within the house. Sometimes a loved one's life hangs on a thread. Sometimes
your own life has been hanging on a thread. And through
all these providences, God is saying: "Set your house in
order, and do it in time. Do it before it is too late. Do
it while you may. Cease your lingering, and come to God."

And over it all, and through it all, and above it all,
God's good Spirit is the chief agent of all to woo men and
win them to come to Christ. Every desire in your heart
to be right with God was put there by His good Spirit.
Oh, do not resist that light-bringing, life-giving Spirit, I
beseech you!

Now I am coming to ask you, won't you refuse to go
on with your lingering? Won't you cease from your lingering and come the upward way? Won't you this hour
rise up with a grand decision? How grand decision is!
In one great hour Esau lost all by a wrong decision, and
in one great hour beautiful Esther gained all by a right
decision. How grand decision is! Won't you summon
yourself with a fixed decision and say: "My lingering in

the wrong road, exposing and imperiling my soul and my influence over others, stops to-night, and I make my return to God?" Won't you thus cease your lingering? Won't you end your delay! Won't you stop that cry about "to-morrow," about "by and by," and say: "It shall be to-night for me that I make my return to God?" Oh, I pray you, linger not too late!

I was in Galveston preaching, before that first horrible storm came years ago, the awfulness of which made the whole world stand aghast. I was there just a little while before that storm, preaching in a series of meetings, and when I came to the last night service that I could attend, I pleaded longer than usual that night, thus hoping to reach five men who had heard me several nights. Other men came forward, confessing Christ, but none of those five. When the people had stood up at my summons for the benediction, I turned to them to plead again, remembering it was my last service: "Won't those men who have waited come now?" And one of them started, and came down the aisle, announcing his decision for Christ. And then I said: "Won't others come?" And a second one came and stood by me, at my invitation. And then I said again: "Won't others come?" And a third one of those men came and stood beside me. Then I waited and said: "Won't other men, who know they ought to surrender to Christ, ought for every high motive that can move a thinking man to take a great step, won't you take that step and come?" And the other two men stepped out into the aisle and came forward, and we had all five of them. In a moment or two I dismissed the audience, and soon was hurrying on an outbound train for my home. And then, in a few weeks, came that fearful storm that swept thousands of people into the engulfing waters. Later, when I got in touch with a friend over the long distance phone, to ask what I could do for him and his, he said: "Do you remember how you pleaded in your meeting that last night?" I said: "Surely, I can never forget it." "Do you remember how you lifted up your voice and sent it out for the five waiting men?" I said: "Yes; tell me what has happened to them." And then I heard the sob in his throat, as he said: "All five of them, sir, have gone down in the whelming flood and are drowned." And then, as I waited a moment more, he said, with a sob distinctly audible: "Oh, sir, what if you had not pleaded a little longer? What if they had not come?" And I ask again: What if they had not come?

What if you do not come before it is too late? What if you linger one second too long? Lingering one second too long to come to Christ is as ruinous as lingering an eternity too long. Oh, this Tuesday night, won't you cease your lingering and say: "My decision is given?" Do you remember the description given of Cortez's invasion into Mexico, long ago, when there was such destruction wrought by such invasion that ill-fated night? Do you remember the description given of that awful night by the historian who sets out the story? Three little words stand out to tell the fearful story: "The sad night!"

Oh, Savior, is this to be that sad night about which some soul here shall have to say: "I heard. I felt. I knew. I was taught. I ought to have acted. I knew it well. I said, 'I will linger.' I said, 'I will wait.' I said, 'Not yet.'" Shall it be written down concerning you: "The sad night!" God forbid! Be not afraid to surrender to Christ. Be not afraid to decide it. Be not afraid, little girl; be not afraid, my boy, to say "Yes" to Christ. He saves. If you trust Him, He will take you and save you. Be not afraid, oh, man or woman, young or older, or even aged; be not afraid to make your surrender to Christ. Be not afraid, oh, duty-neglecting Christian, to rise up with a fixed resolve and retrace your steps and say: "I will redeem the time. I will renew my vows with Jesus." Be not afraid, oh, backslidden Christian, far out in the cold and in the night; be not afraid to return now to the forgiving Savior. Jesus' invitation to the wanderer is sweeter than the strains of an aeolian harp. Whosoever to-night, in all this place, wrong with God, in the church or out, who wishes to be right with Him may be absolutely assured that Jesus waits to be gracious unto all such persons, and to bless and to save them.

If your heart has given its acceptance of Christ as

your personal Savior, and you have not yet made it known, or if your heart now makes such acceptance of Him, come before all the people, while now we sing, to tell us of your decision that He shall be yours and you shall be His, to-day and forever.

THE CLOSING PRAYER.

And now, Holy Father, as the people go, take thou these who come confessing their return to Christ, their surrender to Him, and make life glorious for them from to-night. Let every saved soul grow stronger and stronger, because it rests utterly on Christ to save, and follow obediently all the light He gives. And may the soul be so fortified with Christ's own conscious grace and help that from to-night each of these shall go to live in the most victorious way for Christ. And the Lord grant, as now we separate, that there may be bound upon every heart in this place, all through this throng, the worth and weight of eternal matters, in such an impressive way, that every one in this place who is wrong with Christ, may to-night, with whole-heartedness, seek to be right with Him. Set before every heart here the assuring promise: "In the day thou seekest me with thy whole heart, I will be found of thee." May this be that day for all this throng! Deepen this work of saving grace in all our hearts, our great Savior —mightily deepen it in all our hearts—so that we shall have hearts burning with passion and compassion for souls about us, even as Christ would have us think and feel and act toward them and for them. And give us to speak the word in season to them, and to pray the prayer acceptable before thee in their behalf, as the hours come and go.

And now, as the people go, may the blessing of the triune God be granted you all and each, to abide with you forever. Amen.

XVI

NOON SERVICE, JUNE 20, 1917.

PRELIMINARY REMARKS.

That is a very suggestive sentence in the Bible, which says: "I was glad when they said unto me, Let us go into the house of the Lord." That same word is the word, I trust, that is being daily passed on by the Christian men and women before me, to others about them, Christians and non-Christians. Very thoughtfully, and as we can find the opportunity, the invitation needs to be passed to those about us: "Come with us." It should be a fixed habit in every Christian life to find out people who do not go to church, and thoughtfully and earnestly ask them to go to church. "Faith cometh by hearing, and hearing by the Word of God." "How shall they hear without a preacher?" "It pleased God by the foolishness of preaching to save them that believe." There can be no substitutes for preaching. Daily, one of the reigning habits in every Christian life should be to ask people about them to come with them to hear the preaching of the gospel of the grace of God. But we should do more than that. That is consistent and blessed and important, but that is not enough. We should, in the right way, ask the people about us, if it is well with their souls, if their sins have been forgiven of God, if they have been saved, if they have been born again, if their hearts know what it is to rejoice consciously in Jesus as their personal Savior. That kind of conversation ought to be had by Christian people, men and women, day

in and out, even with every opportunity. There is a right
way to talk with people about their souls. Such talk
means humility and carefulness and prayerfulness and a
deferential consideration for the one with whom you are
talking. How Jesus respected personality and honored it,
when He stood before it, divine as He was, making His
calls and claims to be allowed to be Savior and Master!
You will bring with you a group to-night to the big tent,
won't you, who ought to be brought to the meeting? And
if it cannot be a group, cannot each of you Christians bring
one person that you ought to bring? And all along won't
you be in prayer that the preacher may speak just what
he ought to speak, and in that temper in which Christ's
gospel ought always to be spoken? And, more, won't you
be in prayer unceasing that the good Spirit Divine will
open the heart of the one you bring to attend to the word
that may be heard? God lead you and help you, as you
give yourselves to the divinest quest of all—the winning
of the lost to Him!

A CONQUERING FAITH.

Text: Luke 5: 16-27.

I should like this morning to direct your attention to
a very suggestive incident about this first matter of all—
the winning of souls to Christ. Will you not give reverent
heed to it as I shall read it? I read you from the fifth
chapter of Luke's gospel:

And He withdrew himself into the wilderness, and prayed. And it came
to pass on a certain day, as He was teaching, that there were Pharisees and
doctors of the law sitting by, which were come out of every town of Galilee, and
Judea, and Jerusalem: and the power of the Lord was present to heal them.
And, behold, men brought in a bed a man which was taken with a palsy: and
they sought means to bring him in, and to lay him before Jesus. And when
they could not find by what way they might bring him in because of the multitude, they went upon the housetop, and let him down through the tiling with
his couch into the midst before Jesus. And when Jesus saw their faith, He said
unto him, Man, thy sins are forgiven thee. And the scribes and the Pharisees
began to reason, saying, Who is this which speaketh blasphemies? Who can
forgive sins, but God alone? But when Jesus perceived their thoughts, He
answering said unto them, What reason ye in your hearts? Whether it is easier,
to say, Thy sins be forgiven thee: or to say, Rise up and walk? But that ye
may know that the Son of man hath power upon earth to forgive sins (He said
unto the sick of the palsy), I say unto thee, Arise, and take up thy couch, and
go into thine house. And immediately he rose up before them, and took up that
whereon he lay, and departed to his own house, glorifying God. And they were
all amazed, and they glorified God, and were filled with fear, saying, We have
seen strange things to-day.

The whole incident is taken for our brief study this
morning.

We have in this incident, first of all, a picture of Jesus in prayer. Before He went to do any great work He gave himself always to a season of prayer; and after He had wrought a work and had withdrawn from the publicity of it, He betook himself again to the quiet place to pray. Oh, the master example for us in prayer is Christ Jesus, our Savior and Lord! The locust that eats up our power as Christians full many a time is the locust of neglected prayer. If the Master had need to pray, how much more the need for His disciples!

And we have in the record of the incident an expression quite striking: "The power of the Lord was present to heal them." Jesus was in a certain building teaching, and it was thronged to its utmost capacity, and there were Pharisees and doctors of the law sitting by, who were come out of every town of Galilee, and Judea and Jerusalem. The striking expression you will note again: "And the power of the Lord was present to heal them." It does not say that the power of the Lord did heal them. It says: "The power of the Lord was present to heal them." They did not wish to be healed. As a matter of fact, those Pharisees and doctors of the law, sitting around, were there to cavil, to criticise, to carp, to complain, to deride; were there to find fault. And yet God was there in His power to grant healing and forgiveness and grace, if only their attitude to Him had been of the right sort.

Oh, it is a solemn thought, my friends, that when we gather for worship anywhere, in the name of Christ, the power of the Lord is right there to heal the people. If only such case shall assume the right attitude to God, then shall healing surely come. How it ought to touch our hearts! How it ought to solemnize them! How it ought to humble us! How it ought to move us to prayer, that every time we meet and offer any prayer, God is there to heal and will heal, if only the right attitude shall be assumed by the hearer toward Him!

Here we have the arresting incident, that four people combined to bring one person to Christ, for Christ's mercy and help, and the whole occasion is rich in lessons. Two or three will suffice for us this midday meeting. The first

is that some cases require extra effort to get them to
Christ. There are some cases in this fair city that will
never be won to Christ unless extra effort if put forth to
win them. The ordinary effort will not reach them. The
passing, commonplace effort of one person will not reach
such cases. There are cases here and there and yonder
that require extra effort, if they shall ever be won to Christ,
and this incident points this pungent lesson and we need
earnestly to study that lesson to-day.

Now, to be sure, many cases—I think, most cases—are
brought to Christ by individual, personal effort. One person goes out after another and brings that other to Christ.
Andrew went after his brother Simon, much stronger than
Andrew, self-willed and impulsive and strengthful; and
yet modest Andrew brought his strong and aggressive
brother to the Messiah. Time and again is the lesson written large for us, in human experience, that one person
may go out and bring another person to Christ. Some of
us in our pastorates see that truth illustrated week by
week.

I am thinking this moment of a timid mother, who
came to my study, with her little eleven-year-old girl, just
a few weeks ago, to say to me, in modest but earnest sentences: "I have brought my little girl to talk with you
about coming into the church next Sunday morning." And
then I turned to the child, and sought as tactfully as I
could, to elicit from her what she knew about Jesus, and
she told me her straightforward story. Her mother, the
Saturday night before, had taken her aside, and with careful, prayerful words had explained to the little daughter
what being saved meant, and how a sinner is saved alone
by Christ, and the little girl said: "Mother, I will take
Him right now for my Savior," and her decision was given,
and with her eyes moist with tears the beautiful child,
looking at her mother, said: "Mother won me to Christ
Saturday night. When they were all away from home
except mother and me, mother brought me to Christ."
Oh, I imagine that a legion of angels watched around that
home, as the mother did the sublimest thing possible for
a mother to do, when she pointed her child in the way of

life. And the company of angels, I doubt not, hurried back to the starry heights above, to tell the hosts up there: "The kingdom is coming, because we saw and heard a mother teaching her child the way of life."

On another morning, just before I went into my pulpit to preach at the eleven o'clock hour, there was a knock on my church study door, and I opened it, and there stood a faithful Sunday school teacher, and she had two of her boys, each about twelve or thirteen years of age, and she said: "Pastor, I should like for you to talk with these two boys. They think they would like to join the church this morning, and I should like for you to question them, to see if they are ready for that great step." And then I questioned them, and they were soon earnestly telling me, in answer to my questions, how this Sunday school teacher had hunted them out, and had talked with them personally and alone during the past week, and how she had so explained the necessity and the happiness and usefulness of being a Christian, that they could not say no, and had said yes to Jesus. They knew that He was the Savior, and not somebody else, and not something else, and they were trusting alone in Him. Their way was clear, their confession beautiful, their knowledge of Jesus evident, and they came into the church that day. How glorious that a Sunday school teacher understands: "I am a shepherd of souls, and I must watch as one who must give account, and I cannot, must not, dare not, ignore the highest claims of these in my class, namely, their spiritual needs."

And then sometimes a friend goes out and wins his friend to Christ. Oh, what proof of friendship is comparable to that, where one person goes to another, and in humble, careful, winsome, prayerful words, seeks to win that other to Christ, and succeeds! What finer proof of friendship than that!

And how glorious when the Christian wife seeks ways, with all humility and diligence and prayerfulness, to win her unbelieving husband to Christ! One of those unbelieving husbands, who held out long and late against Jesus, said to me recently, when he came to talk to me about coming into the church: "Oh, sir, the tears, the very tears

of my Christian wife haunted me, as she would say just
a little to me about how she yearned for me to be a Chris-
tion, about how she prayed for me. She said just a little,
but her very tears haunted me."

Most people, I take it, are brought to Christ by one
person. But there are cases that require more than one.
There are cases that require extra effort. There are cases
that require combination, consolidation, co-operation, even
of the noblest sort. Our Bible study to-day presents such
a case. Here was a paralyzed man. He could not get to
Jesus at all. He was unable to betake himself there. One
man could not get him there. It was a task too difficult
for two men, and so it came about that four men combined
to carry that man, on his bed, sick man, bed and all, into
the house where Jesus was teaching, that the great and
gracious Healer, as well as Teacher and Lord, might cure
this man. When they came to the house where Jesus was
teaching, it was so thronged that they could not get in.
Oh, the pathos of the whole scene! The house was
crowded with people, who did not care to heed the Christ
themselves—who carped and caviled and criticised, if haply
they might find fault with something Jesus should say or
do. They were not willing to go into the kingdom themselves, and worse than that, they crowded the doorway
and blocked the entrance, so that others, who did wish to
reach the Master, should be kept out. So these four came
and could not enter. No place was allowed them to enter.
But, not to be deterred, they took that man, bed and all,
to the housetop and removed the tiling, and let him down
through the roof, bed, sick man and all, right at the feet
of Jesus. And when Jesus saw their faith, He said unto
the sick man: "Thy sins are forgiven thee." He did the
first thing first. He put forth His power for the cure of
his soul first, and then the cure of the body came afterward, and we are never to lose sight of this divine order.
The supreme thing is for men's sins to be forgiven. The
supreme thing is that men's souls may be made right in
the sight of God. Jesus first of all cured this man's sick
soul, and then later cured his body.

Will you think earnestly on this record of how this

man was brought to Jesus? Four men combined to bring him, and, I repeat, there are cases about us that will never be brought to Jesus, except by combined and extraordinary effort. And we need to see them and find them and combine to help them. These four were necessary to get this dreadfully difficult case to Christ. It was a task too much for one, too much for two. It was a task requiring the four, and such cases are about us, and this morning I am seeking to give emphasis to the doctrine that such cases, though difficult and pre-occupied, and far away from God's favor and forgiveness, ought to have our most conscientious, most co-operative, most capable attention. There is not the case of a single man or woman in Fort Worth, no matter how pre-occupied, or absorbed, or old, or wicked, or sinful, no matter what the case, or who the case may be—there is not one that God's people ought to pass by, arguing: "Their cases are too hard, too difficult, too hopeless." There is not one such case.

One morning I preached in another city, and said: "I wish you would do the unusual thing to win souls; I wish you would do the extraordinary thing. I wish you would go to cases maybe that nobody has spoken to about Jesus for a whole generation." And four men tarried behind and said: "The most difficult case in this community is a half-paralyzed man. With extreme effort, he drags along, with his crutches and a man supporting him, and he is the most blasphemous sinner in all this city." I said: "Gentlemen, I would have you go after him. You bring him to the outskirts of this meeting, and put him in a comfortable chair, and God help me, I will do my best to help him." And so they went, four of them, and at first he mocked them. He derided them. He laughed at them. He jeered at them. He swore at them. And then at last he listened a little more seriously, and then he pleaded his inability, he pleaded his pitiful impotency, and then at last, the men said: "We will come and carry you. We love you that much. We will put you on the outskirts of the congregation so you shall not have anybody to run over you or to take advantage of you." And so they brought him, and they whispered to me that he was there, and told me where he sat, and I observed him in a moment, and that day I preached to one man—impotent, paralyzed, broken and helpless—about the wonderful mercy of God, to make a man over, to transform him, to reconstruct him, to re- deem him, to recover him, to forgive him, to fit him to live, to fit him to die, to fit him for earth, to fit him for heaven. Jesus does all that, if only a man will come to Him in the right way. And then I said: "Is there some man here, all broken and beaten and defeated, who would like to be right with God. Maybe he has waited long. Maybe the sun of his life is far in the afternoon. Maybe the sun is now sinking low toward the western hills. Now, if such man is here and he wants to be right with God, God waits to be gracious to him. Does he wish to be right with God? Will he lift up his hand and let me see?" And the first hand to go up was the hand of the half-paralyzed man. Then I dismissed the people a few minutes later, and sought him out, and before the men carried him away, the man had humbly made his surrender to Christ. Oh, it was well, for the days were just a few until the second stroke came and carried him into eternity. The extraordinary thing ought to be done for such people, all about us, and done speedily and unceasingly.

I am thinking now of a noble lawyer in Waco. I shall mention his name. If he were living, he would not object. He is now in God's house above. His family, I doubt not, would not object to such mention of his name. This noble lawyer and outstanding citizen was Judge Waller Baker. These lawyers present all knew him. Some years ago, when a preacher preached in Waco, he said to his audience: "Oh, men, do not go on in the ordinary, commonplace way, in the winning of souls. Go after a case difficult. Go after a case long neglecting, pre-occupied, too busy to come to God; go after him, and if you do not do the extraordinary thing, and put forth the unusual effort, you will not even arrest his attention. Go after him." And when the ser- mon was done, another lawyer in the audience, himself a distinguished jurist and Christian citizen, gathered some men around him and said: "If three of you men will join me, we will go after this great lawyer." They combined,

the four of them, and they went that afternoon. The lawyer was preparing a difficult case, and he had left word
with his stenographer, in the outer room: "Do not admit
anybody to my inner room at all. I must not be disturbed.
A serious case is on me now." But the stenographer had
left the room a minute before they came, and she was
not there to forbid their going in, and into the room they
went, and then they knocked on that inner door, and it
opened, and there was the lawyer, with his coat off, deep
in the preparation of that serious case, and he said: "How
did you men get past my stenographer?" They said: "We
did not see any stenographer." And so they were in the
office, and the door was shut, and he said to them: "Gentlemen, there must be something very serious that can
bring you four men here." The great Christian lawyer
made answer: "There is, Mr. Baker; the most serious
matter in the world, and I will speak first, and I want first
of all to ask you to forgive me, that I have been such a
poor Christian, that I have not talked with you more earnestly about Christ and His supreme claims, and your need
of Him. But we have come, we four men, to ask if you
won't cease all your procrastination, and if you won't, for
your own sake, and for Waco's sake, and for the world's
sake, and for Christ's sake, to-day yield yourself to Christ."
And then the second man made his plea, and the third
man said his say, and the fourth man made his appeal, and
then the first man said: "If you won't mind, let us kneel
down and all of us be little children, and we will ask God
to help you to burn all the bridges, give up indecision and
delay, and do the extraordinary thing—yield yourself right
now to Christ." And down they went on their knees, and
all four of them prayed, each for a moment, and when they
rose up Mr. Baker said: "Gentlemen, I cannot, will not,
hold out against this. I do surrender to Christ. May God
forgive me that I did not do it long ago. I do surrender to
Christ. Oh, it is so unselfish for you four men, my friends,
my neighbors, to come after me like this! I do surrender
to Christ, now and forever." Wasn't it glorious? Now,
just a little while after that, I was in Los Angeles, speaking there in the Temple Auditorium, and one morning,

when I had finished my sermon, I saw before me a sympathetic face in the press of people, and when I had said the benediction at the close, quickly he came to me. It was the same Waller Baker, out there on the Pacific coast, getting some needed rest, and he said: "They have told you about what I did?" I said: "Oh, I know all about it, Mr. Baker. Thank God!" He said: "At last I am on the right road—at last!" He went on to San Francisco, perhaps that night, or a day or two later, and I returned to my Texas home, and before I reached my home, when I reached El Paso, the daily papers had chronicled the news that the evening before, as Mr. Baker was leisurely walking down the streets of San Francisco, he sank down from heart failure, and a few moments later was dead. When I read it, this was my first thought: What if four men had not gone to him as they did, a few weeks before, to win him to Christ? Oh, I am pleading that you, citizens and neighbors and friends, shall, in the right spirit, link yourselves, with God to guide you, and empower you, and go after these long neglected cases. Pass not one of them by. Some of them are rich, but their money won't suffice their souls. Some of them are having a feverish time in the world social, but society will not ease the ache of a sinful, suffering heart. Some of them are in office, are pre-occupied, and every minute is crowded as they clutch after the prizes that lure them on, but these prizes, each and all, cannot ease the hurt of the sinning soul.

I am summoning you this morning to do both the difficult and consistent thing—to go after such cases all about you. And now as you bethink yourselves, case after case will stand before you. I am beseeching you that you will combine with the other man, and you twain shall plead that promise of Jesus: "If two of you shall agree on earth as touching anything that they shall ask, it shall be done for them of my Father which is in heaven." If you need two, let there be two to go, all unadvertised, but in the quietness and patience of Christ. Oh, how the grotesque, and the absurd, and the spectacular in religion cheapens and harms! Our Master's cause does not need any of that. In the beautiful spirit of humility, with quietness, without ostentation, without parade, but patiently, prayerfully and faithfully, we should give ourselves to this Christly task. I summon you to it to-day, even as I summon myself, that our conduct in the days to be may be far more consistent than it has been in the days that are gone.

Now, the lessons in this incident are many, and they are written large for us. Let us do the unusual thing, if that be necessary to get the attention and win the heart of some soul tha* has missed the upward way. Let us combine and co-operate. Let us pray together and go together, if haply by such earnest effort we may win that difficult case. Pass no case by. Leave no case unapproached, unhelped. Take them as you can see them, and bethink you concerning them, and do your best to win them to Christ. Oh, my brother men and my gentle sisters, let us care for human souls these passing summer days like we ought!

How is it that we are often keenly sensible to physical distress, to the cry of the body, and yet of the deeper distress of the soul we are often unmindful and insensible? Why is it that we do not care like we ought for human souls? For one reason, I say we do not care because we do not sufficiently realize their condition. Oh, if we realized that outside of Christ the battle is lost for a human soul, surely that realization would bestir us to make the best effort for them possible. Many a time we are quiet and uncommunicative touching human souls, because we realize so keenly our own unworthiness. Let me be personal for a moment to say that if I had waited until I felt worthy to approach a human soul—worthy in myself—I would have been dumb as death on such subject all these years I have been a Christian. I never saw the day that I felt worthy, for one second, to speak to anybody about his soul. I must say, with the apostle of old: "I know that in me, that is, in my flesh, dwelleth no good thing." If I had waited until I felt personally worthy to join the church, I should never have joined any church. If I had waited until I felt personally worthy to preach the gospel of the grace of God, I should never have preached one time. Oh, we are not to preach ourselves at all, but to preach Christ Jesus the Lord. Many a time we ought to begin our conversation with an humble confession of our own pitiful frailties and weaknesses, and then go on to say to the friend whom we approach: "I do not preach myself—you must understand that. I preach Christ Jesus the Lord." All our worthiness comes from Christ Jesus, "who of God is made unto us wisdom, and righteousness, and sanctification, and redemption, that, according as it is written, He that glorieth, let him glory in the Lord."

Two business men on the outskirts of the city lived side by side. One was a church man, and had been for long years, and the other a non-church man. The church man went to church every Sunday morning, and the non-church man went never at all. But they came into the city from its suburbs every week day morning, on the trolley, to perform their tasks in the city, and through the long years they went back and forth on the train together every week day. It came about, in the strange providence of God, that both were sick unto death at the same time. Each lay upon the dying bed the same day, and the non-church man's wife, herself a Christian, was in such an agony about him that she was constrained to say: "Husband, wouldn't you like for a good Christian man to come and talk with you about religion—you are very sick." And he slowly shook his head and said: "Not at all. My neighbor, Mr. So-and-so, is a church man, and in all these long years we have ridden thousands of miles together, and we have talked about every subject upon which men converse, but he has never said a word to me about religion. Why, there could not be anything in it, if a church man, who has been with me hundreds of days and has traveled with me thousands of miles, has never essayed to speak to me one word about religion. If he could pass such subject by through these long years, and be silent about it, I will go away just like I am." And so he died. Oh, if we would realize as we ought the peril and the worth of souls! The hour will be gone in two minutes more. Oh, if we would realize as we ought the peril and worth of souls! Won't you parents realize before it is too late?

I went to a dying son in Dallas, and did my best to

win him, and finally I said to him: "Oh, my boy, how much your father is interested in you!" And then searchingly he looked at me out of his deep, sad eyes, and he said: "What is that?" I said: "Your father is so interested in you. He sobbed about your religious condition to-day as we talked. I have come to you at his request." And then he looked at me long and hungrily, and said: "Isn't that strange? Father never said a word to me about religion in all his life." Strange? Why, it is horrible! Strange? Why, it is atrocious! Strange? Why, it is monstrous! Strange? Why, it is criminal! Why, that kind of conduct feeds hell on hope, and is enough to put crepe on the door to God's heaven above! Parents, speak the all-important word now to your children. Oh, my fellow-men, citizens, toilers at all life's tasks, professional men, business men, speak the right word now to your friends! Oh, ye who love the Lord, get you to-day at this task, like you ought—this task of winning souls!

THE CLOSING PRAYER.

And now we appeal to thee, O God, who heareth prayer, to lodge thy truth in our every heart. O, make us to be right in thy sight, concerning this greatest of all causes—that of winning lost people to Christ. We would repent of every evil way ourselves. We would bow our hearts to the very dust, because we have been so inconsistent, so frail, our lives so incongruous as Christians, saved and called to win souls. We have been so often neglectful of duty. We have allowed little things to turn us from the plain course of right. We have allowed people to hurt our testimony for Christ. We have allowed checkered experiences thus to hurt us. O Jesus, Master, blessed Savior, make these thy people to be right in thy sight this day, and fit them for their matchless task of pointing people to the heavenly way. And we pray thee for thy saving favor upon all this city. O, grant that during these midsummer days the people may hear in the right way, from lips which God will anoint, the right sort of appeals concerning personal religion. And may the difficult cases—the hardened, the aged, the sinful, the duty-neglecting, the deeply backslidden, the God-forgetting, whoever and wherever such people may be—may they all and each be properly approached by these friends of God, to the end that every such case may be won to Christ. And may there be no vain confidence in arms of flesh for this superhuman task. May our confidence all be stayed on God, and may He guide us and empower us at every step by His own omnific Spirit, so that, night and day, we shall do His will these passing days.

And as you go now, may the blessing of the triune God, even of Father, Son and Holy Spirit, be granted you all and each, to abide with you forever. Amen.

XVII

NIGHT SERVICE, JUNE 20, 1917.

PRELIMINARY REMARKS.

Through these several days of the meeting, many touching requests have reached us, by letter and otherwise, asking specially for prayer for certain specified objects. I wish I had time to read you these many requests. Time and again, parents have requested that groups of Christians in these meetings, would join the parents in prayer for their sons and daughters. Time and again, modest, shrinking, but devoted wives, have asked certain praying ones quietly—and that is the better way for it to be asked—that they would join them in special prayer for their husbands. And friend after friend, a large group of friends, have presented their friends, saying to men and women here and there in the meeting: "Won't you join us in special prayer for these friends?" Now I indicate these requests in this way, that you may be much in prayer for them all. Note after note has reached me, in which the request has been made that the whole multitude be asked to join in special prayer for definite persons. The limits of the hour would not allow for such notes to be read, even if it were proper to read them, but the fact is a most challenging call to us to be much in prayer. I should like for us in a moment to make mention of these requests, every one, to Him who knoweth all about each case, in a special prayer. And yet before we offer that prayer, I should like to give others the privilege of voicing, in just one moment, when I shall indicate, their special requests for prayer. I shall put it by groups, by sections of people, as I ask that question. I should like, if there are parents here, whose children are not yet saved, and you would have all these who pray to join you in prayer for them, to witness to such desire by lifting the hand for a moment, as my eye shall glance over the audience. I see—there are many hands that are lifted. That is, indeed, an appealing sight. I should like again to see every person here whose heart has some person or persons for whose spiritual welfare you yearn, for whose salvation you pray, and you would like for us to join you in such prayer, manifest it by lifting your hand as my eye shall again glance over the audience. Oh, there are many! And in this choir, let me see. I trust every member of this choir loves Christ. How indebted we are to them for their devotion! Very helpful is the part that they render in a meeting like this, and we are profoundly grateful to them. Your every hand was lifted. There were many, many, many wishes voiced by the uplifted hands, just now. God saw and knows about every case that was indicated by such uplifted hands. Let us pause a moment to speak to Him now, in their behalf.

THE OPENING PRAYER.

We would wait upon thee, O God, yet a moment longer, at the throne of grace. We bring thee all these requests for prayer, and pray thee to visit each one with light and love, with mercy and grace, in thine own time and way. Regard, we beseech thee, these parents, whose uplifted hands witnessed to the alarming fact that they have children who are out of the ark of safety. O, may parental interest for the salvation of such children be so quickened and deepened by the Spirit of God, that all these parents will, by precept and example, go to the utmost of devotion to win their children to Christ.

And we unite our prayers with those of these wives, who in one way or another have indicated their deep concern that their lost husbands might be saved. O, strengthen thou the faith of every Christian wife whose husband is an unbeliever, and speak to such unbelieving husband through the wife, or in any way thou wilt, thou sovereign Savior, so that he shall be saved. O, grant that these Christian wives may not always have to go life's way alone in the deepest, highest things, but may they have their husbands with them, that wife and husband, the mother and father, together may journey on in the heavenly way, and there bring with them those whom thou hast given them.

And we pray with every friend here to-night, whose uplifted hand witnessed to the fact that he or she had some person or persons for whose salvation they would pray. We would unite our prayers with them, for every person represented. And if it would please thee, O Lord, for these men and women to go in person and speak to such lost ones concerning Christ and His great salvation, whatever their modesty, whatever their timidity, whatever their sense of unworthiness and of unfitness, yet let them go, clinging to Christ to guide and help them. May there be such worthy personal attention to souls, such right approach to souls, by these all about us who care for souls, that God will come with divine reinforcement, and make their witnessing triumphantly effective in winning many to Christ. Lord, help every one, here and there and everywhere who is engaged in this great work. Quicken our consciences until they shall burn with personal concern for the salvation of the people. May every one of us utterly refuse to allow the painful consciousness of our unworthiness and our unfitness to deter us from the holiest work of all—the converting of sinners from the error of their ways. Give us ever to remember that we watch for souls as they who must give account to God. May we so watch that when we give our account to God we shall give such account with joy, and not with grief. And may the Divine Spirit guide us in all these visits, in all these conversations, in all these approaches to human souls. We would utterly yield ourselves to Him for His light and leading. We would be led, literally and utterly and only, of God. We would have divine wisdom to guide us at every step, so that we may do that only which will please Christ our Lord.

May the service to-night be altogether under the divine direction. May the preacher speak just as Christ would have him speak. May he have the temper that will have Christ's approval. May these hearts all be opened by the great, good Spirit Divine, so that they shall heed the word that shall be spoken. In all this throng of people, may the men and women, and even the boys and girls, now open their hearts and minds, that they may respond just as God would have them respond, to the call of His own truth. May His will, whatever it is, be accomplished through us and with us this night. We pray in Christ's conquering name. Amen.

THE CONFESSION OF SIN.

Text: "If we confess our sins, He is faithful and just to forgive us our sins."—I John 1:9.

This is the text: "If we confess our sins, He is faithful and just to forgive us our sins." It is from the first chapter of John's first epistle. Its primary application is manifestly for Christians, as the context indicates, but its gracious truth may be applied to all who sin, and are therefore in need of God's forgiving mercy.

Somebody has well said that the three hardest words to say like they ought to be said are these: "I have sinned." You will grant the truth of that saying upon a brief moment's reflection. The three most difficult words to say like they ought to be said are these three: "I have sinned." And yet confession of sin lies right at the foundation of our coming to Christ. If one be not a sinner, then for him there is no Savior. For him, Christ's gospel does not have any appeal, if one be not a sinner. Jesus tells us: "They that are whole (or well) do not need a physician, but they that are sick." And again Jesus tells us: "I did not come to call the righteous, but sinners to repentance." And again He tells us: "The Son of man is come to seek and to save that which was lost."

Oh, are you a sinner? Then I preach to you a Savior, for Jesus came to seek and to save sinners. Forgiveness of sins is a real experience. Sin is as real as your hand or eye. Sin obtains with every rational soul. The forgiveness of sins is as real as the sin itself. The Lord Jesus Christ came to grant forgiveness of sins. Forgiveness of sins is a personal experience—a real personal experience. There can be no forgiveness except between persons. That chair could not forgive you. That tree could not forgive you. That beast of the field could not forgive you. Forgiveness is always between persons. Now God, the Great Person, comes to you and me, the little, finite, human, mortal, dependent, sinning persons, and says to us: "If you will turn to me with right attitude, I will forgive your sins." Oh, I ask you, one by one, as my eye sweeps the audience: "Have your sins been forgiven of God?" Could you lay your hand upon your heart and say: "I have the consciousness within me, that God has forgiven my sins?" I would press that upon you, one by one—have your sins been forgiven of God? And I would pray you, do not stop until you can give a complete, satisfactory answer to that great question—have your sins been forgiven of God?

Our text tells us, "If we confess our sins, He is faithful and just to forgive us our sins." Be not deceived, I pray you, my men and women, on this crucial point, the reality of sin, and the inescapable fact that sin must be confessed in the right way, if we are ever to get forgiveness for our sins. Be not deceived at such crucial point, the fact of sin in your life and mine—the awful fact of sin. There are two chief causes that conspire to deceive us at this point, and the one is the ignorance that we have of our own hearts. Who has ever sounded the depths of his own heart? Who knows every secret expression and bias and motive of his own heart? No one but God has ever sounded the depths of a rational, responsible, human heart. So the proneness is constant with us not to know our own hearts. God tells us in His Word, pointblank, that "the heart is deceitful above all things, and desperately wicked: who can know it?" That is the solemn asseveration of God's Word. "The heart is deceitful in all things and desperately wicked." That is God's own indictment of the human heart.

And now, if we will pause to consider how the human heart treats God, we will see how wretchedly sin has played havoc with the human heart. Look at the attitude of the human heart toward God, in two ways. Look at the ingratitude of the human heart toward God. That sin, the sin of ingratitude, is one of our commonest sins, and surely one of our wretchedest, one of our most heinous sins. Oh, the sin of ingratitude, anywhere, how base, how bad it is! How terrible is the sin of ingratitude of a child toward its parent. "How sharper than a serpent's tooth it is to have a thankless child!" said the great dramatist. Ingratitude anywhere is a terrible, most represensible fault. Ingratitude even among men is despicable, and when we relate it to our chiefest, our supremest benefactor, even to God, how base, how terrible, is ingratitude seen to be in His sight. God gives our lives, and crowns us with every mercy and blessing, from the largest to the least, and yet we are forgetful and indifferent and ungrateful toward that infinitely benevolent Being. If there were no other motive to bring every rational person to the feet of Christ, this motive ought to bring us all—the motive of gratitude. With such a Friend and such friendship, such mercy, such patience, such kindness, such forbearance, such a Friend ought to have from us our best devotion and love. The human heart is deceived by sin, and that drowns the expression of gratitude to God.

And then the human heart, in its deception, may be seen in our disobedience toward God. Obedience is a mighty principle, that everywhere must work its mighty sway. You let obedience be trifled with in the home, and the home will go to rack and confusion and ruin. You let obedience be trifled with in the school, or trifled with in the army, and chaos will follow such trifling. Now when we think of obedience in the highest realm of all, even obedience to God, which is the chiefest and first duty of every human life, and when we remember that God, the holy Lawgiver, with His laws and precepts for human guidance and government, is trifled with and disobeyed, how terrible is the fact of sin, that it could make us to be both ungrateful and disobedient in the sight of God!

And then our lack of recognition of the undoing power of sin in human life comes from another cause, and that is, ignorance of God's Word, which Word reveals God's will for the children of men. The one supreme standard by which all conduct and character and creeds shall be tried is by God's Holy Word. God's Holy Word is the guide-book to point men and women in the right way forever. And yet ofttimes we do not know what that Word says, where that guide-book points. But when we open its pages to see what God says about mankind, there it is, luminous as the sun in the heavens at noontime. When we open the Scriptures, there stands out the solemn word of God: "God looked down from heaven, to see if there were any that did good, and there was not one, no, not one." We open the Scriptures and read again: "There is not a just man upon the earth, that doeth good and sinneth not." And we open the Scriptures again and read them: "There is no difference. For all have sinned, and come short of the glory of God." And again we open the Scriptures: "Marvel not that I say unto you, except you are born again, born from above, you cannot even see the kingdom of God." And we open the Scriptures and quote them again: "Except ye repent, ye shall all likewise perish."

Now, we are often ignorant of what the Word of God says about human conditions and human character and human need and human destiny, which ignorance does not excuse us; and because of such ignorance of God's Word and of our own heart, we do not realize as we ought the undoing and destructive power of sin in human life. Oh, my fellow-men and women, I pray you, let us all take our proper place at God's feet, and realize as He would have us, the awful fact that sin has come with its crippling power into our every life, and we must have deliverance from such sin, we must have absolution from it, we must have forgiveness for it, we must turn from it to be saved from its fearful penalty and power.

And now, our text points the way for our forgiveness and recovery: "If we confess our sins, He is faithful and just to forgive us our sins." Here we are face to face with the solemn matter of confessing our sins. How shall we confess our sins? Solemn matter that! If we will confess our sins in the proper way, we shall have forgiveness for them, and we shall be saved out of them and in spite of them, and peace here and forever shall be our portion. How then shall we confess our sins? The Bible points the way for us, and we will look at that way to-night. The Bible indicates the wrong way, that we may be warned concerning such way and refuse to walk in it. The Bible gives us case after case of men who confessed their sins, but in the wrong way, to their own hurt and undoing and destruction. Let us look at such wrong way, pointed in the Bible for us that we may be warned and not take such way. I call your attention to two or three cases that the Bible holds up for our warning and counsel.

Pharaoh confessed his sins, but in the wrong way. Pharaoh was the king, as you recall, down in Egypt, and the time came when, under heavy pressure, Pharaoh made confession of his sins. You remember the circumstances, do you not? God had sent Moses a little while before this occasion, to tell Pharaoh, the king, that he must let the children of Israel go out of Egyptian bondage to their appointed land yonder, which God had promised His chosen Israel. Moses stood before Pharaoh, the king, and gave the king the message from God, and Pharaoh scouted it all. Pharaoh scornfully mocked it all. Pharaoh said: "Who is God, that I should obey Him?" Pharaoh said: "I am a king myself. Leave my presence," said Pharaoh to Moses; "I will do as I please with these slaves. They shall yet grind at my mills, and they shall yet do obeisance to the bidding of my people." And Moses went his way. But God has His own ways of making His authority and righteousness effective. You recall that there came plague after plague, until ten plagues fell upon Egypt in swift succession. You remember that the water was everywhere turned into blood. You remember that the cattle on the hills and in the valleys were stricken with murrain, so that presently they lay dead everywhere. And on and on the terrible plagues fell over Egypt, until the last and culminating plague came, namely, the first-born in every Egyptian family, whether of man or beast, lay dead in one night. And when the morning came there was wailing throughout Egypt, from one border to the other, for the first-born, both of man and beast, lay dead in every Egyptian family.

At last Pharaoh was serious, and he sent for God's man, Moses, and when Moses confronted him, Pharaoh said: "I have sinned. Go tell your God to stay these clouds of wrath and trouble that are falling upon my people. I have sinned. I relent. I change my way. I yield to God's great call. Tell your God that, and I change my way." And Moses prayed, and the clouds lifted and the sunlight came again throughout Egypt. And then Moses started with the children of Israel to the land of Canaan, which God had promised them. Yonder Moses goes, with that nation of spiritless slaves following at that valiant leader's heels. Yonder they go. Would you believe it? Pharaoh took it all back. Pharaoh summoned his men and sent them in swift haste after Moses and the retreating Israelites, and said to his men: "Re-capture, recover them all, and bring them back, that they may yet grind at our mills." And you remember how they pursued the retreating hosts led by Moses, until they came to the Red Sea, and God by a miracle opened that sea, and Moses with the hosts crossed swiftly, and then the reckless, presumptuous champions of Pharaoh plunged into the opened sea, and the standing mountains of water came down to submerge them, and they were destroyed. Now, this case is typical of the hardened sinner, and such are to be found, I fear, in every community in this gospel country—the hardened sinner; one who under pressure feels and hears God's call, and relents and concedes, and makes his promises, and yet puts them all away and goes deeper into sin and darkness than ever before—the type of the hardened sinner.

Oh, I wonder if I speak to such! How difficult such case is! Years ago I was ready to close the midweek prayer-meeting where I was pastor, and I had lifted my hands for the benediction, and the people were standing, and just then there came rapidly to the church door one of our physicians—a noble, Christian physician. Oh, how great a thing for a physician to be a devout Christian, and how important! He came in and waved his hand and said: "Pastor, have the people to be seated. I have a statement to make." And we were seated, and then he told us of one of our well-known citizens, whose wife was a devoted Christian and member of the church. He told us how ill such man was, and how he, the doctor, had just left his bedside, where five doctors had had an extended consultation, and the decision of those five doctors was that, speaking after the fashion of men, the great citizen had already passed beyond the reach of materia medica, and would die before morning. "But," said this doctor who came to the prayer-meeting, "I believe in God, and that He can turn the battle back from the gate when all hands human are helpless." Don't you prize a doctor who talks like that? Then said the doctor: "We told this citizen just what his case was and is, and he was utterly horrified, for he is not prepared to die. For a moment, he grasped after something, and finally he said: 'Isn't this the night, Wednesday night, when the people meet at the church to pray?' The doctor said: 'Yes, it is.' Then the sick man said: 'Doctor, you hasten down there and tell those people where my wife goes to church—tell those people who pray—that I solemnly promise that if God will spare me, and raise me up from this sick bed, when the tide is turned and I am well, I will go to God's house, and I will seek His face, and I will follow the light He gives.'" The doctor told the story, and I said: "Every head will be bowed. We will pray for him." And I led the people in that prayer, and we commended him to God, and we begged that he might live, on the one ground, that when recovered he might make good his pledge, he might redeem his promise, and live thereafter in harmony with God. The next morning early, the doctor phoned me that the tide had turned, and that the man was incomparably better, and would undoubtedly live; and day by day that was the word that came from his sick bed, where no one was allowed to enter, save the doctor and the nurse and the wife. At that time, I visited another community, to aid in some gospel meetings, and was gone some two or three weeks. When I came back, and made inquiry, they said: "He is out on the streets, and practically well," and a few minutes after my inquiry, I met him on the street, face to face, and I hurried to him, and took his hand, and rejoiced with him with most grateful joy. And then I said to him, for it was Saturday: "You will be at God's house with us to-morrow." I yet held his hand, and he winced and said: "Oh, no! I am behind with my mail. I have a large number of letters unanswered. I have lost so much time, I must put in to-morrow looking over that mail." And I still held his hand and searched his heart, as I looked through his eyes, and said: "Oh, no, my man! You will, of course, be at God's house to-morrow, I take it." He winced yet more, and his face colored crimson, and he said: "I know what you are thinking about." I said: "Indeed, you do." He said: "I was in a close place. I had to do something, and do it quickly, and I did as I did. But I cannot be at church to-morrow. I am behind with my work. I will be there later, when I get up with my work. I cannot be there to-morrow." I still held his hand, and I said: "Man, man! You have come back from the very gates of the grave. You have been spared, evidently, in answer to prayer, on your high pledge that when God recovered you, He should have your best. Come to God's house to-morrow, and give heed according to your serious pledge to Him." He fairly rushed away from me, as he said: "Oh, I cannot! By and by I will. I cannot now. Business engrosses me now." And he was gone, and the weeks went by, and he never came, and a group of citizens were making ready to go on a trip to the East, a group of business men, and they stood there in the depot, waiting for the train, all chatting happily, when suddenly this man trembled, and put his hands to his face, and before the others could realize what was happening, he fell with heavy fall there on the depot floor. The ambulance was summoned, and the doctor, and they carried him away to his home. But the hours were just a few, until apoplexy had done its work, and all unconscious, the man went out into the other world to reap the harvest of his own sowing. The physican called me and told me the tragical ending a little later, and for days and days there was only one Scripture that swept through my soul— this Scripture: "He that being often reproved hardeneth his neck, shall suddenly be destroyed, and that without remedy!"

Such man is the type of the hardened sinner, the sinner,

who, under pressure, makes his high pledge to God, and
then puts it all away. Such sinner, one day, finds a black
Friday enshrouding the whole home. A loved one is ill
almost unto death. The black shadows throw themselves
everywhere about the place, and the man's heart is in his
throat, and he goes out alone and utters one cry, over and
over again. He walks alone, saying two little words, and
those words a cry: "Oh, God! Oh, God!" And on and
on he says just that: "Oh, God! Oh, God!" And then,
later along, he gives his high pledge that, if God will turn
the battle back from the gate, he will repent, he will turn
to God. And that vow is heard, and God's mercy is shown,
and the battle is turned back from the gate, and the black
Friday passes, and the man, with his pledge, goes his way
and forgets it all. Oh, do I speak to somebody in this vast
throng to-night who has forgotten his vows, who has murdered his covenant, who has strangled his good resolution?
I pray you, summon yourself again to the right consideration of that serious promise made in the other days.

There was another man who confessed his sins, but to
no good purpose. That man was Balaam, the false prophet,
whose story is told for us in the Old Testament. You recall the circumstances under which Balaam confessed his
sins. He was in the presence, one day, it would seem, of
a good man on his death-bed, and that scene made an
impression upon Balaam that provoked his cry of the confession of sin. He saw a good man there in the death
chamber, passing away, and it moved Balaam to his heart's
depths—a sight that is never to be forgotten, to see a good
man die, or to see a bad man die. It is a sight from which
there is no getting away. When I see how my people can
die, I come back to my pulpit brave as a lion to preach
Christ's gospel to the world — when I see how Christ's
friends can die. So it would seem that Balaam saw a good
man die, and he came out of that death chamber with the
cry: "I have sinned. Let me die the death of the righteous, and let my last end be like his!" That was his promise; that was his prayer; that was his wish. Would you
believe it? The very next day Balaam took it all back.
The very next day Balaam summoned about him a group

of men whose avowed purpose was to exterminate from the face of the earth all of God's prophets and people, and get rid of them every one—the very next day.

What about this man Balaam? He is the type of the undecided man, the type of the vacillating, hesitating, irresolute, wavering man; and that is the most difficult type of all, I have thought, to reach with the gospel—the man one day serious, and the next day putting it all away; one hour saying: "I have sinned. Let me die like a good man ought to die," and the next day mocking it all. He is the type of the wavering soul. How difficult to reach such soul with the gospel of grace! For convictions not followed get fainter and die. Impressions not followed blow away like the blossoms are blown from the trees in the orchards in the springtime. Every time a conviction to do a duty is felt and not followed, the life-blood is let out and the soul is weaker. Every time one's duty on any subject is clear and plain, and the man hesitates, through policy, through fear, for any cause, he is weaker thereafter in his deepest manhood. Oh, soul, wavering, irresolute, undecided soul, how difficult to reach your soul with the gospel! The alarm clock you set to wake you in the morning will wake you, if when you hear it you will obey it and rise from the bed promptly in response to the summons. But you let that alarm be sounded, and you turn over and say: "I will sleep a little more; I will take a dozen minutes, or half an hour," and trifle with the clock like that, and keep that up a little while, and you may put that clock under your pillow at last, and it will give its alarm as usual, but you will sleep the sound slumber, and will not respond at all. Oh, like that there comes in the awful power that undoes the soul, when one hears and feels and knows that duty calls, and yet puts it all away, as did this man Balaam.

There was another man I would name, who confessed his sins to no good purpose, but made his case worse, and that was that man Achan, a soldier in Joshua's army. You recall the circumstances, do you not, under which he made his confession of sin? A soldier he was in Joshua's army, and specific directions had been given for the guidance

and government of such army, and there was a fixed penalty, severe and terrible, if such directions should be trifled
with by the soldiers. Away they went to the conflict, led
by Joshua, and yet, strange to say, Joshua's army, brave
and mighty, was completely routed, and the hearts of his
men were poured out like water, and they fled like the wild
beasts of the hills, and Joshua was on his face, ashamed
and broken-hearted because of the shameful defeat. And
God said to him: "Get thee up, Joshua, and search the
army, and thou wilt find the reason for the fearful failure." And you recall that the whole army was searched,
company by company, regiment by regiment, man by man,
the whole army, and at last the searchers came to the last
company, came to the right man, and put their finger on
the right man, who was the culprit, who had made the
mischief, who had wrought the awful defeat, and this man
was led away to meet his awful penalty in death. And as
he was thus led away, poor, doomed Achan blurted out
his confession, "I have sinned," as they led him away to
the awful penalty of death. Oh, I do not need to follow
Achan further, to ask what became of him! I do not know.
But I do need to say, with all the emphasis with which I
can marshal words to say it, that I personally have little
confidence in death-bed confessions, when the soul is leaving the suffering body and going out into eternity. I will
not be understood as saying that a dying man may not truly
repent of his sins and be saved. He may. The Bible gives
us one case where a dying man did truly repent—the thief
on the cross—and Jesus made answer to him: "To-day
thou shalt be with me in Paradise." He did repent, but
the Bible gives only one example of one in the last hour
who repented of sin. The Bible gives only one example—
one, that people may not utterly despair, and only one, that
people may not recklessly presume.

Oh, men and women, with your wits about you, with
your judgments clear, with your consciences sensitive and
responsive, I pray you, in such a time as this, calmly and
deliberately and thoughtfully, face the question of what
you will do with God. I follow Achan just a moment more,
for Achan could not die to himself. I have been saying,

according to the Scriptures, that no man can live to himself, nor can any one die to himself, and Achan is an awful illustration and demonstration of that momentous truth. Read the story of Achan and you will come across this awful sentence: "That man Achan perished not alone in his iniquity;" and read the story a little further, and a little more closely, and you will find that thirty-six men went down with Achan to his awful fate. Oh, influence! When will we be done with influence? We will be done with it not at all. We will be done with it nowhere. You can no more be separated from your influence than you can be separated from your shadow as you walk in the sun. Achan did not die alone, but took thirty-six men down with him to dusty death. Oh, influence! How serious, how momentous, how terrible, is the fact of influence! I wonder if a parent could have another hell quite so horrible as for a child to look the parent in the face, father or mother, and say to such parent: "You brought me here by your own example!" Could there be another hell quite so terrible as that? I wonder if there could be another remorse quite so consuming for any man or woman, as for some soul in the world hereafter to say to such man or woman: "I imitated you, and you brought me the downward way!" I pray you, oh, I pray you, save your influence to the right side!

I have one more case to present, telling how sin is confessed, but that is the right case. I could present a number, but one will do. There is a right way whereby to confess sin, and if we confess our sins in that right way, we shall have forgiveness. What is the right way? One case will illustrate. I take the story of the prodigal son, the most familiar story, perhaps, in all the Bible. You remember how he went away from home, and wasted his substance rapidly in riotous living, and went down, and down, and down, and was at last yonder in the swine field, feeding the swine and eating of the food wherewith he fed the swine. But one day he came to himself, and he followed such self-awakening with thought, with resolution, and with action, and he brought himself back the homeward way.

Look at his case just a moment. First of all, the Bible tells us that he came to himself. He came to himself at last, far from home, down yonder in the world, in the field of waste and failure. He came to himself. How significant that expression: "When he came to himself." Oh, Spirit of God, give the people to come to themselves, religiously and spiritually! He came to himself, and he bethought himself: "Back yonder at home, they have plenty and to spare, and here I am starving among the swine. What wretched waste is my portion!" said the prodigal. But he did not stop with that. He was filled with sorrow over his course, and said: "I will go back and tell father, and in the sight of God make my confession that I have sinned against father and against heaven, and no more am worthy to be called my father's son. I will take a place unknown as one of the hired servants, and I will go back and make that confession of my wrong, my waste, my sin." Right there are the beginnings of repentance. He sees his wrong course. He acknowledges his wrong course. He sorrows over his wrong course. Right there are the beginnings of repentance. But then he rises up, for that is not enough, and he makes a great resolve, and the resolve was this: "I will arise and go back to my father, and make my confession full and complete." What wonders are wrought by resolution! Mountains are transformed into molehills by resolution. What wonders are wrought by resolution! He rises up and says: "I will! I will! I will decide. I will choose. I will make up my mind. I will!" Oh, how grand a thing is resolution! Alexander was asked how he conquered the world, and he said that he conquered it by making up his mind, and then by not delaying to act when his mind was made up. And Lowell magnifies this truth when he sings:

> Once to every man and nation
> Comes the moment to decide,
> In the strife 'twixt truth and falsehood,
> For the good or evil side.

This prodigal son made up his mind. But that was not enough. The Bible tells us in the next sentence that he acted. In the next sentence, the Bible tells us that he arose and came to his father. Now, that is vital. That is the gist of the whole matter. He arose and came. It is not enough to wish. It is not enough to desire. It is not

enough to feel. It is not enough to long. It is not enough
to purpose. It is not enough to resolve. The very gist
of it is to rise up, as did this prodigal, and act. He arose
and came. You know the rest. You know how he was
welcomed. You know what he received. The old father
was waiting for him and looking for him down the long
road, which road the boy had traveled when he went away.
And one day, the old father saw the son coming; when
the son was yet a great way off, that father's eye of con-
stancy and love discerned him, and down that road the
father went hastily to meet that returning son. Down the
road the father went, and up the road there came the son,
and when the son was yet a great way off, the father saw
him, and ran toward him, and had compassion on him. The
father took that son, now all rags and shame, to his fatherly heart, and the son began his confession: "I have
sinned, father, against you and in the sight of heaven. I
have made shipwreck of my life." And the father said to
his servants: "Bring the best robe for this our son." And
to others: "Kill the fatted calf and provide for this son."
And to another servant: "Bring the ring to put on his
finger"—the ring, emblem of the love that never ends. And
the welcome given to the returning son was unspeakable,
and the sweetness and power of it all is such as to melt
all our hearts.

What is that story? What does it picture? Just this:
It is a picture of how much God wishes to forgive any
person anywhere, who would come to Him and have His
forgiveness. As I come to the last moments of this message, I am coming to ask, are there men and women here
who say: "We are wrong with God, but we wish to be
right with God?" Do they say, whether members of the
church or not: "We are wrong with God, but we wish to
be right with God; we wish our sins forgiven; we wish
to be recovered from the wrong road and the wrong life?"
In the church or out, professing religion or not, do they
say: "We are wrong with God, but in God's own time
and way, we would be right with God?" A little while ago
I asked those who had special objects for whose forgiveness and salvation they would have us unitedly pray, to

witness to such fact, and many were the uplifted hands which gave such witness. Now, I would ask, are there souls here who lift their hands to say: "I am wrong with God and know it, but I wish you to pray for me, for I wish to be right with God, in God's own time and way?" Before we have a moment of prayer my eye sweeps the audience to see if souls are here to-night who say: "Yes, I lift my hand, that you and others may speak to God for me, for I am wrong with Him, but wish to be right." My eye will search the audience for just a moment, to ascertain, if candidly and earnestly, hands are lifted to witness to the fact: "I am wrong with God, but I wish you to pray for me that I may be right with God in God's own time and way."

This is, indeed, a solemn moment. There were many uplifted hands. God be merciful to you, and forgive you! He surely will, if you will only turn to Him now in the right way.

Now, listen! You wish to be right with God. Oh, He wishes it for you a thousand-fold more than you can wish it. God wishes your life to be made right a thousand-fold more than you wish it. God wishes it enough to give His Son to die for you! Be not afraid just now to surrender your all to Him, oh, man, or woman, or child here to-night, saying in heart: "I am wrong with God." Be not afraid just there to surrender your case to Christ. He does the forgiving, but you are to give up to Him. He does the saving, but you are to decide that He may. He does the changing within you that is necessary, but you are to yield to Him that He may. Be not afraid to make that surrender to Him now, to be His from this hour, forever.

Outside of one of our cities, some time ago, a train was wrecked, and a crowded Pullman of people were killed in that frightful wreck, and every man on such Pullman train was a citizen of the city, except one man. He was a stranger, and they did not know him, and they carried those bodies back to the city and had a funeral service for them all, there in a large hall. Women and men came, and took their last look at that row of caskets, their last look on the faces of their beloved. And wives and sisters and daughters came, and bent over the caskets here and there,

and imprinted the last kiss—the kiss of love upon the faces
of the loved ones. But nobody kissed that stranger's face.
Nobody knew him. But presently there came a little
woman, aged and poor. She had looked at the other faces,
and had watched their loved ones kiss them, and seeing
everybody pass by this stranger's face, she bent over that
face a moment, and looked intently, and then she sobbed
as she said: "I will kiss him once for his mother's sake!"
And she gave her kiss. Oh, soul, far more quickly than
that does the Lord wait to give you His forgiving kiss—
the kiss of reconciliation, the kiss of pardon, the kiss of
peace, the kiss of salvation, if you will only yield yourself
to Him! Be not afraid to do it now!

Yonder in London, an aged woman heard that glorious
preacher, William Dawson, say one night, that Christ
wanted to save the worst man in London, and would save
him, if such man would just give up to Christ. And the
little, aged, kindly woman, who was always trying to do
good, went out to see a man whom she knew, dying on his
pallet of straw, dying from consumption, and she told him
what the preacher said — that Christ wanted to save the
worst man in London. The man would not accept it, but
shook his head. The man was very sinful in life and hard in
heart. The man said: "It could not be so. I am that worst
man, but Christ has no love or interest in me." Then the
gentle woman went back after the preacher and said: "You
must come to help him. I cannot. I am unable." And
presently, William Dawson was there bending beside him,
and Dawson said: "How is it, friend?" The poor fellow,
there in his place of squalor and wretchedness, answered:
"I am not your friend, and you are not mine. I do not have
any friends, and I am not entitled to any." But Dawson
went on with gentle words, and said: "Yes, I am your
friend, and therefore have I come;" and he talked on and
on, and said presently: "That is not the best of it. Jesus,
the great Savior, is your friend, and loved you enough to
die for you, and if you are just willing, He will take you
and save you, even in this awful plight to which you have
come." And the man listened, and the man's heart softened
and responded, and he said: "Oh, if it could just be so! I

would like to be forgiven. I would like to be saved, if He would just do it!" Then Dawson quoted some of the great promises: "Come now, and let us reason together, saith the Lord: though your sins be as scarlet, they shall be as white as snow; though they be red like crimson, they shall be as wool." And again: "Whosoever will, let him take the water of life freely." And on and on Dawson talked, and then he said: "My friend, I will pray for you, and while I pray, you just tell the Savior what a poor sinner you are, but that you will just give yourself up to Him, that He may be your Savior." The poor fellow made his surrender, and deep was his joy and peace, while they talked afterward. But presently, he said to Dawson: "I could die in absolute peace, if just one thing were granted me." "What is it?" asked Dawson. The man replied: "I am the black sheep of my father's family. I committed an awful crime when I was a young fellow, and broke my parents' hearts, and disgraced my home, and when at last I went home, father was stern. He met me and said: 'Joseph, if that is the best that you can do, there is the gate, and you need not embarrass us by your presence.'" And said Joseph: "I took him at his word, and I did not go about them any more. I went into the deepest sin. I have come to the depths of sin. But now at last I have turned to Christ, and in His marvelous mercy He has forgiven me. If I could just hear father say: 'Joseph, I will forgive you, too,' I could go away without one cloud." William Dawson said: "Where does your father live, and who is he?" The dying man told him, and William Dawson said: "I will try to find him." And across great London, William Dawson went, street after street, over long distances, and at last he reached the right street, the right home, and he rang the bell, and the door opened, and a white-haired old man, venerable and dignified, stood in the door, and William Dawson asked his name. He was the right man. Then William Dawson began: "I have come to tell you about your son Joseph," and the man's hand was up, like that, repellant and quieting. "I once had such a son," said the old man, with his face white from bitter memories, "but he shamed us all, and I showed him the door and the gate,

If you have anything, sir, to say about him, there is the door and the gate for you!" William Dawson paused. What could he say? He waited a moment more and said: "Well, I will go, sir. I am sorry. Your son Joseph is dying, and will soon be dead, and God has forgiven him, and he longs for you to tell him that you forgive him, too." And then the proud head of that father came down, and he cried out as with a great pain: "Oh, man, is my Joseph dying? My little Joseph? My boy, who used to sit on father's knee? My boy is dying and wanting me to forgive him? Oh, man take me to him as quickly as you can!" William Dawson said they hurried over that city as fast as cab and car could take them, and after awhile they had reached the place, and the old man was beside his dying Joseph, and took up that skeleton in his arms, and embraced him as a mother presses her child to her heart, and sobbed out his own broken heart. And the dying Joseph said: "Father, God has forgiven me. I know it. Poor sinner that I am, I have surrendered to Him, and He has forgiven me. Oh, father, I just wanted you to forgive me, too!" The father said: "My boy, my precious boy, if I had only known that you wanted me to forgive you, never did I see the day that I could have held out against your wish that I should forgive you!"

Tell me, will a man forgive, and God be hard-hearted and unresponsive? The one thing the great pitying Father in heaven wants to do this hour is to forgive every man and woman in this press of people who wants to be right with God. Just give up to Him. He will forgive in His own way. Just pray this simple prayer and follow it: "Here, Lord, I give myself to thee; it is all that I can do." It is all He asks. It is all He wishes. Do that, I pray you. Do that while you may. Do that while you wish to do it. Do that here, in this place of prayer, even this very hour.

Two voices are here to-night, two voices, and I can hear them now. The first voice makes its cry: "Not yet!" You know where that voice comes from. It is Satan's voice: "Not yet! Not yet!" It is the way of death. "Not yet!" Oh, listen not to it! Put it away. There is another

voice that can be heard, if you will only listen: "I will!
I will! I will, God help me! I will, and I will now!" We
are going to sing that gospel song: "Jesus is tenderly calling thee home, calling to-day, calling to-day." As they
sing, I stand here to greet you. Is the man here, or woman
or child, that says: "I am that person who has been wrong
with God?" In the church or out, does one say: "I have
neglected duty. I have broken vows. I have sinned. I
have wandered. I have drifted. I have gone into backsliding. I am that person in the church. I want to renew
my vows. I want Christ to make my case right, and I will
surrender to Him, and renew my vows with Him, publicly
to-night?" Come and take my hand.

But does somebody say: "No, that is not my case?"
Does somebody say: "This is my case: I have already
surrendered to Christ, but I never did make it known. Here
to-night I will make it known?" Does somebody say:
"That is not my case yet. This is my case: I want to
surrender to Him. I want His forgiveness. I want Him
to save me, and to-night He offers to save me, if I will just
come to Him, just decide for Him, just surrender to Him;
I will gladly surrender to Him now." Do you say: "That
is my case?" Then come and take my hand. Is the case
here that says: "One of those three cases includes me?"
Come, take my hand, as they earnestly sing this gospel
song, before our final prayer.

THE CLOSING PRAYER.

We go now, O gracious Father, with hearts profoundly grateful to thee, for
thou art good and ready to forgive, and thou art plenteous in mercy unto all who
call upon thee. We commend these who seek thee and yield to thee, one by one,
and every one, to thy mercy, praying thee that from this night their surrender
to thee may be a complete and an eternal surrender. We pray also for men and
women who have said they want to be right with God, but are hesitating to
come to Him. They are in life's middle time, numbers of them, strong and
mature in mind and body, and there are others, young men and women, who are
seeking the Lord. O, we commend every one to thy mercy—to thy leading.
Give that to-night they shall come utterly and finally and decisively to the end of
their waiting, and that each one shall say: "As for me, to-night and forever,
from this hour, I give myself to Christ, that He may be my Savior and Master
forever." Day by day, and hour by hour, give thy people, Lord, to speak and
to do and to pray according to thy righteous will.

And now as we go, may the blessing of the triune God be granted us all
and each, even as He deemeth best for us. For Christ's sake. Amen.

XVIII

NOON SERVICE, JUNE 21, 1917.

PRELIMINARY STATEMENT.

The word spoken a moment ago by the honored pastor touching the wisdom and necessity that we Christians, one by one, shall to-day give ourselves to thought and to effort and to prayer, to help others about us, who are in wrong relations religiously, is a word that ought to sink deeply into our every heart. How great a thing it is to help people in this highest and best way, even in the upward way! God takes our efforts, frail as they are, and infirm, and if we give them earnestly to Him and for Him, His blessing upon them is sure. "He that goeth forth and weepeth, bearing precious seed, shall doubtless come again with rejoicing, bringing his sheaves with him."

THE MINISTRY OF SUFFERING.

Text: "Who is among you that feareth the Lord, that obeyeth the voice of His servant, that walketh in darkness, and hath no light? Let him trust in the name of the Lord, and stay upon his God."—Isa. 50: 10.

The Bible has a message for every life, no matter what its duty or test or need. The vitality of the Bible is indestructible. No condition nor exigency of human life comes, but that the Bible has a word to meet it exactly. In every congregation such as this, there come always to such services some who have been called to walk the vale of suffering and sorrow and tears. Numbers and numbers have paused at the close of these midday services, to tell me of certain

260

deep burdens they were bearing, or certain sore griefs that
they were suffering, of certain deep perplexities that confronted them. I am to bring you a promise this morning—
one of the most comforting and precious in the Bible. It
is in the fiftieth chapter of Isaiah, the tenth verse, and
you will keep it, because you will need this promise: "Who
is among you that feareth the Lord, that obeyeth the voice
of His servant, that walketh in darkness, and hath no light?
Let him trust in the name of the Lord, and stay upon his
God."

May I tell you how I came to find that promise? We
are all along coming upon promises that we did not know
were in the Bible. What a living book it is! And how
increasingly wonderful it becomes, the more we read it and
study it! I was in one of the Texas cities some years ago,
preaching in some daily meetings, and my attention was
called to the devotion to Christ of a noble mother in that
congregation. I had rarely seen anything to rank with her
devotion, and in many ways my attention was called to it.
Some months went by, and there came from that city to
my city, another mother from that church, and presently
I asked her about the first mother. She said: "I came
especially to see you about the first mother. Her case is
unspeakably pitiful. It is this: She has come to the place,
because of trouble, sorrow and suffering, where her spirit
seems all beaten into the dust, and she is without light. If
you ask her the question if she trusts Christ, she will answer without hesitation, in the words of Job: 'Though He
slay me, yet will I trust Him.' But," said the second
mother, "this first mother is in deep darkness, and is without light. I have come to you to ask if there is some suggestion you can give her out of God's Word." That is
how I came to find this text. Now you are ready to hear
it quoted again. Mark it, for you will need it: "Who is
among you that feareth the Lord, that obeyeth the voice
of His servant, that walketh in darkness, and hath no light?
Let him trust in the name of the Lord, and stay upon his
God." "Who is among you that feareth the Lord,"—the
fear of the Lord is the beginning of wisdom—"that obeyeth
the voice of His servant, that walketh in darkness, and

hath no light?" That was her case, exactly. What is to
be done? The rest of the verse tells us: "Let him trust in
the name of the Lord, and stay upon his God."

You will be glad to know, to trace the story just a
moment further, that this promise was the message God
used to recover this bedarkened, sorrowing mother, and
to thrill her heart again with glorious peace.

Let us look at that promise a little while this morning,
because sooner or later all our feet must go down that vale
of sorrow and suffering and darkness and tears, and this
text describes a condition that will sometime come to us
all. What is the condition? Here is one that fears the
Lord, and obeys the voice of His servant, and yet walketh in darkness, and hath no light. That is the condition
that sometimes comes to us in our earthly experience, and
that condition is sometimes the severest test that ever
comes to us. Darkness is always trying to us. Darkness
is trying to us physically, especially when we are ill, and
agitated, and disturbed. Oh, how sick people dread the
night and long for the morning! Surely, they will be better
when the light comes! And when we come into the realm
of darkness religious, how terrible such darkness becomes,
and how glorious is light when it streams down on our
darkness!

It raises an old question, as old as Job, and it may be
older: Why do tears and sufferings and darkness come
to those who are the friends of God? We can understand
why trouble would come to the man who is not God's
friend and refuses to be, for as a man sows, so shall he
reap. If he sows to unbelief, the reaping must be of a
character with the sowing. We can understand why the
godless man, the man who will not be God's friend at all,
would come to the harvest of distress. We can understand
that. But that is not the difficult question. The question
is: Why do sufferings, and darkness, and tears come to
those who are the friends of God?

Now, sometimes there is an off-hand, superficial answer given at that point. Sometimes when a Christian is
seen to be in darkness and trouble and tears, the superficial

critic pounces upon him and says: "This trouble comes as the result of some sin." The Word of God is not that cruel. The Word of God does not teach that doctrine. That doctrine is as false as it is cruel, and as cruel as it is false. When you turn to the Word of God, it is perfectly clear. Listen:

"Whom the Lord loveth He chasteneth, and scourgeth every son whom He receiveth. * * * If ye be without chastisement, then are ye bastards, and not sons. Furthermore, we have had fathers of our flesh which corrected us, and we gave them reverence: shall we not much rather be in subjection unto the Father of spirits, and live?" And then the beautiful words of Jesus are in point just here, where He says: "As many as I love, I rebuke and chasten." So you see, a part of the program and plan and experience of human life is chastisement, is trial. "In the world." said Jesus, "ye shall have tribulation." It is one of the most expressive words in the Bible. But He goes on to say: "But be of good cheer; I have overcome the world."

But now we are raising the question: Why do the friends of God pass down the vale of suffering and darkness and tears? There are some partial answers, to which our attention may be called briefly this morning. I say partial answers. They must be partial. The full-orbed and complete answer we must wait for until we shall read it yonder in the golden glow of the land and life above. But there are partial answers, why trouble and trials and tears and darkness and suffering come again and again to the friends of God here in this world. Let us glance at some of these partial answers.

For one thing, trouble, if rightly used, enables us to honor God. Trouble, then, is a trust, and we are so to receive it. We understand about other things being trusts. There is the man of education; he must answer for those superior attainments. There is the one who can sing so that hearts are enchanted by the music; that singer must answer for that gift. There is the man of money, and the man of money must answer for it. The men who make money must answer for that capacity. Whatever our gifts or capacities, all of them are to be received as trusts from

God, to be used in His name, to help humanity. Now, along with other trusts comes trouble. Trouble is to be received, however it comes, as a trust, and we are to bear it, we are to meet it, we are to go through it, we are to face it like we ought, as a trust from God, to be used for the glory of His great name.

You recall Job's manifold and fiery trials, that patriarch in the land of Uz, that conquering business man, and that faithful friend of God—Job, the man whom God so approved and applauded. One day Satan impiously said to God: "If you will give me a chance at your man Job, I will shake his religion out of him, and I will make him deny you." Said Satan impiously to God: "Your man Job is serving you because of sheer selfishness. He knows, in the crude saying of the world, 'which side of his bread is buttered,' and therefore is he proposing to serve you. Give me a chance," said Satan, "and I will make him deny you." And God said to Satan: "I will give you carte blanche at Job. You may do anything you please to him except to kill him." And then the awful testing began. There was Job, all unacquainted with the colloquy between Satan and God, happy and prosperous in all his surroundings. And then there came a dark-robed messenger, which took from him all his property; and I tell you, when you strike a man in his property you have dealt him a staggering blow, and some men seem never to recover from such blow. What a pity that 'tis so! Then there came another messenger, saying that this trouble had come to Job—his servants were all taken away, and then there came another messenger, telling him the awful tidings that his children, all and each, had gone down into dusty death. But stricken and beaten to the very dust though that father was, he simply made answer through the darkness: "The Lord gave, and the Lord hath taken away. Blessed be the name of the Lord." And then there came another black-robed messenger, and Job was stricken in his health, so that from the crown of his head to the soles of his feet, his body was one festering mass of affliction and suffering. And when his erstwhile friends in the days of his prosperity came to see him, so grievous were Job's sufferings, that those men sat around him for seven days and did not deign to open their lips, so terrible was Job's plight, and when at last they did speak, they said, in effect: "Job, you are the worst man out of perdition, or this never would have come to you." Miserable comforters were they all! Job said to them: "Gentlemen, your diagnosis is incorrect. I do not know why this awful aggregation of troubles has come down to swallow me up, but let come upon me what will, though He slay me, yet will I trust in Him." And God brought Job out of all those troubles, and made the latter days of his life incomparably more glorious than the former, and you and I are to-day strengthened by the very recitation of how God sustained Job in the black Friday that long ago came to his life.

There was a time in my life, when for days and days, the only book I wanted to read was the book of Job, and I read it through and through and through, that book of Job, that tells how the human heart is swept in its deepest depths of suffering and darkness, and yet how God blesses it and brings it up and out and sets the soul again in the high place of safety and peace. Trouble rightly borne honors God. Mind, when trouble comes, how you behave. No matter what the trouble is, mind how you behave. Many a man has dishonored God when trouble came. No matter what the trouble is, no matter what brought it, no matter who brought it, no matter how it came about, God is dishonored if a Christian does not bear his fiery trial like he ought to bear it. You are being tested for God, and you will dishonor Him egregiously, or you will honor Him gloriously, according to your behavior when trouble is on. Remember that.

I am thinking now of a Christian girl who married a noisy, disputatious unbeliever. Serious matter that! Oh, when will the people as seriously view this destiny-shaping question of marriage as it ought to be viewed? When will parents be as careful in their teaching about it, and young people as careful in their decisions about it, as they ought to be? This dear girl, a glorious Christian, was wooed and won by a handsome young fellow, but he was a scorner of

the things of God, and she went into that atmosphere. His
father and mother and his grandparents were likewise stout
unbelievers, and all of them lived in the same big home.
And then there began a daily trial of that girl's faith. The
most insidious attacks were made on her faith, from this
angle and that, but she held calm and steadfast and true
to Jesus during all of that first year of their wedded life.
She had to make her way to the house of God alone, but she
went, and that went on for about a year, when one day,
as she moved about the duties of the kitchen, her clothing
caught fire, and before they could reach her and put out the
fire, she had received burns from which she died, a few
hours later. But while she lived, she was conscious to the
last, and she bore her sufferings with all the glorious devotion of some mighty martyr for God. Never a word of
reproach or bitterness escaped her lips—never one word.
She went on quoting God's great and precious promises
to the last, and when it was evident to her that she was
going, she stretched out those charred, blackened, once
beautiful hands and arms, and tried to put them around
her husband's neck, and said: "Poor Charlie, the thing
that tries me, and the only thing, about going away, is
that I have not lived long enough to teach you and your
dear parents and the dear old grandparents, that Jesus is
real and sure, that He is a Savior, and that He does help
us, and that He is our refuge in every time of trouble and
need." And then she went away, and the funeral was had,
and the body was left to rest yonder in the cemetery. The
family returned to the home, and the day died down to
nightfall, and there by the open fire sat the bereaved ones,
when presently the young husband stirred and said to his
father and to his grandfather: "Mary had what the rest
of us do not have, and I am going to seek her Savior."
And the father said: "My boy, you are right. I know it.
I feel it. She has taught me that, and I will seek Him,
too." And the old grandfather stirred, and put his staff
out, and came over to the son and grandson, and laid his
hand on the head of each, and said: "My sons, you are
right. Mary did have what the rest of us do not have, and
I am going to seek her Savior, too." And in three days

those men had found Christ, and numbers of their loved
ones around them. A little woman, called to pass through
the vale of deepest darkness and suffering, honored God
through it all, and her testimony was irresistible. Mind
how you behave when trouble is on you! If you carp, and
cavil, and criticise, and murmur, and are evil in your
speech, oh, how you will dishonor God! Trouble rightly
borne will surely honor God.

Why do darkness and sufferings and tears come to
God's people? There is another partial answer. They
furnish an occasion for God to bestow His grace. If I may
so put it, they give God a platform on which to stand and
work His great work. For example, there is a lawyer,
well trained in the schools, and he has received his diploma and is ready for his noble calling. Now, if he is to
evince his skill in legal learning, he must have his case.
Yonder is a doctor who has been graduated after years of
painstaking study. If that doctor is to demonstrate his
skill in materia medica, he must have his case. Even so,
the Lord Jesus Christ, if He is to show men what He can
do for them, in the black Fridays, in the darkest vale, in
the most dreadful hour, then the hour of trouble and darkness must come, that He may come and extricate us therefrom.

How often is that truth illustrated! Paul had his thorn
in the flesh. I do not know what it was, but it was something serious, you may be sure. He called it the messenger
of Satan, sent to buffet him, and thrice Paul besought the
Lord to take away that thorn in the flesh, but it was not
taken away, and after that, Paul said: "I am glad I have
it. I glory in it, because God has given me more of His
grace than I ever would have had, but for the thorn, and
so I will take the thorn and the added grace, and be enlarged in my knowledge and experience of God."

Why does trouble come to the child of God? Many a
time it is the strange way of preparing such friend of God
to be a helper of others, as such person otherwise never
could have been. There is no teacher like experience. I wonder if we really and deeply learn anything at all, except
as we learn it in the realm of experience. And so trouble

often comes and we pass through it, and we are fitted as we pass through it to be helpers as we never could have been but for such trouble. Paul discusses that particular doctrine when he says: "God comforteth, in all our tribulations, that we may be able to comfort them who are in any trouble, by the comfort wherewith we ourselves are comforted of God."

I am thinking now of two young mothers. The baby of the first one died after a brief illness, maybe a day and night, and I was summoned to the funeral. She and the husband were not Christians. They were quite worldly and quite godless, so I had a difficult time, indeed, in reaching them and speaking to them. I went with them, in their brokenness and desolation, to the cemetery, and came back with them. I said to them: "You will come to God's house, and you will get comfort there." And so they came, and in a few Sundays both of them came into the light and were saved, and they took their place in the church and made faithful followers of Jesus. Months went by, and one day I was summoned to another funeral. The second little mother was called to put away her flaxen-haired little girl. She was utterly despairing and desolate in her grief. She, too, was an unbeliever. I read the sweetest Scriptures I could find to help her, but she did not seem to hear a word I said. At last, as the quartette began to sing, the first young mother I have described, came quietly from the place where she was, and took her place beside the second mother, and put her arms about her and gently said: "Oh, Jennie, dear, it is going to be all right!" And Jennie answered back: "Why, Mary, it cannot be all right! Everything about it is bad and dark and wrong! It cannot be all right!" "But," said the first mother, "I passed through this, and I know what you are passing through, and God called me, and through the darkness I came to Him, and He has comforted me, and He will comfort you, Jennie, dear. You cling to Him and He will bring you out." And the first mother did more for the second mother than I could have done, maybe in days and months, for the first little mother had traveled that road of suffering herself. Oh, it is often that way, my friends! The world's

highest blessings often come out of its deepest sorrows and
trials and tears. Heaven itself can be entered only by way
of the cross. There is no way to get there except by the
cross of Christ.

Did you ever read J. M. Barrie's charming little book,
"Margaret Ogilvy?" Everyone should read it. There is
one chapter in it on "How My Mother Got Her Soft Face."
The author is really talking about his own mother. The
story is that the oldest son in the family went away from
home, when he reached his majority—went out to the big
world to fight the battle of life for himself. Letters came
and went, through the months of separation, between the
son and mother, and one day a wire came to her that the
son was desperately ill, and she had better come at once.
She hurriedly packed her valise, and started to the railroad
station, some miles away, committing the tasks of the home
to the younger children, to do the best they could with
them; but before she reached the station, there came a
second messenger boy with the telegram, telling her that
her boy was dead, and they were sending his body home
on the next train. The body came and the funeral was
had, and the mother moved about the house, her face be-
tokening a sorrow too deep for human speech. But after
some weeks, they saw that her face shone with a light
that was never on land or sea. Not a murmur escaped her,
no bitterness, no complaints, no harsh words; hers was
a patience like unto Christ's patience. And when some
neighboring woman lost her boy or her girl, when sorrow
came to a neighboring home, Mr. Barrie said, five miles
away, ten miles away, twenty miles away, forty miles
away, the suffering and sorrowing one said: "Send for
that woman who has the soft face. She will know what
to say to us, for she has passed down the vale of suffering
herself." Oh, my friends, suffering is often the way whereby we are fitted to help a broken, bruised, sinning, suffering world, as we never otherwise could help it!

Why do sufferings and tears come to us? There is another word. Many a time, it is a necessary discipline for
us in the building of our own character. Mark you, God's
great concern is for our character—for what we are, not

what we seem to be. God's great concern is for our inner, deeper selves. Over and again, trouble is God's disciplinary teacher to give us that experience that shall refine us and teach us and cleanse us and fit us, that we may be and do in God's sight what He would have at our hands. The highest conception of life here is that it is a school, and you and I are the pupils at school, and God has many teachers, and one of His teachers that comes robed in black is suffering, is trial, is deepest, darkest testing. David said: "It is good for me that I have been afflicted, that I might learn thy statutes." Oh, we need, my fellow-men, to be disenchanted! Ease is the bane of everything that is good. We need to be disenchanted, so that our trust shall not be in the flesh, nor in the world, but stayed on the living God.

I am thinking now of a little woman who was happily married, and two children were given her, and she lost both of those children, and they were buried in the same grave, and then she went down with complete nervous collapse, and for long months, even for some years, she was helpless as a little child, and had to be fed by loved ones, who ministered to her. One day, as her little auntie, who was a joyful Christian, was feeding this little helpless woman, who was unusually despondent on that particular morning, the little woman said: "Oh, auntie, you say that God loves us. You say it, and you keep saying it. Oh, auntie, I used to think He did, but, auntie, if He loves us, why, why did He make me as I am?" And the little auntie, after kissing her gently, waited a moment and said: "He has not made you yet, my child. He is making you now!"

When through the deep waters I call thee to go,
The rivers of sorrow shall not overflow,
For I will be with thee, thy troubles to bless,
And sanctify to thee thy deepest distress.

When through fiery trials thy pathway shall lie,
My grace, all-sufficient, shall be thy supply,
The flame shall not hurt thee—I only design,
Thy dross to consume, and thy gold to refine.

There is one word more. What are we to do when the trouble is on? The next tells us. "Who is among you that feareth the Lord, that obeyeth the voice of His servant, that walketh in darkness, and hath no light?" What is that one to do? Here it is: "Let him trust in the name of the Lord, and stay upon his God." There is your anchorage. It is not anywhere else. You will grope and flounder and be in the ditch anywhere else, my friends. Some of you have been called to pass through deep troubles—fiery troubles. You will fatally err if you go anywhere else but to God. There is the anchorage. If you have an anchor for a ship, you do not keep the anchor in the ship, when you need to anchor the ship. You take the anchor and put it down out yonder. So our anchor is not within us at all. We are anchored to Christ. Listen to His promises: "Because I live, ye shall live also." And again: "I will never leave thee, nor forsake thee." And again: "And, lo, I am with you alway, even unto the end of the world." That anchor will hold. And if you do not stay upon God in the dark and trying day, you have serious cause to suspect whether you have ever really trusted Him at all. Trust Him in the dark day, because God's grace and promises are designed for dark days, just as those great ships are built yonder to withstand the stoutest storm that ever drives the seas. Why should you trust God on the dark and cloudy day? Because such a faith will glorify God. With your submission to God's will, patient, meek and uncomplaining, with your clinging trust, like Job, saying, "I will trust Him, though He slay me;" saying, "Whatever comes, I will follow Him the best I can, whatever the vale through which I walk"—if you will trust Him like that, you shall be a blessed witness for God.

Why are you to trust Him on the dark and cloudy day? Because it won't always stay dark and cloudy, thank God! Sure are His promises that "the day will break and the shadows flee away." "Weeping may endure for a night, but joy cometh in the morning." "For our light affliction, which is but for a moment, worketh for us a far more exceeding and eternal weight of glory." It won't stay dark. There comes a sweet, fair morning, tinted and glinted with all the favor of God, and you are to look forward to that morning, and cling to Him, and go your way, knowing that all shall be well.

The hour passes in two minutes more. Tell me, was

this message for somebody here to-day? Oh, receive it and follow it! Is some heart here to-day perplexed and bedarkened? Take the text, I pray you, and go with it, making it your own. Take one step at a time, and then take another step, and then take another step, and He will bring you into the fair day, and you will sing with the poet:

> So I go on, not knowing;
> I would not know if I might.
> I would rather walk with Christ in the dark
> Than to walk alone in the light.
> I would rather walk with Him by faith
> Than to walk by myself with sight.

Stay yourself upon Him to-day, and from this day forward cleave ever to Him with unhesitating trust, and then may you sing with the psalmist that the Lord will perfect that which concerneth us, because His mercy endureth forever.

THE CLOSING PRAYER.

Our blessed Heavenly Father, bind the word that each of us needs to hear and heed upon our deepest heart. May we walk like we ought, in our day and generation, for the glory of God. May our tempers and deeds be always such as shall cause the people to take knowledge of us that we are Christ's, and that we delight above all else to do His holy will. May we always have that mind which was in Christ. And, O, by example as well as by word, let us glorify Christ continually, each of us, till life's day is done. Bring the one that is in the darkness here to-day just to stay all on God, and everything shall be well. Teach us that no matter what the darkness that may come—the trial, the tears, the disappointments to beat us into the dust—no matter what the fearful surprise, the sore wrenching of the heart, the awful bitterness of spirit—no matter what—God's grace is and shall ever be sufficient for us. And let all these men and women say: "We will trust Him, though He slay us, and to-day we will cling to Him with new trust and new hope and new passion and purpose in obeying His will."

And now as you go, may His grace fill your every heart and His wisdom guide your every step, forevermore. Amen.

XIX

NIGHT SERVICE, JUNE 21, 1917.

PRELIMINARY REMARKS.

Before I read the Scriptures, in a moment, I would pause to say that a shadow lies across my heart, because my visit here cannot be much longer at this time, with these two cherished pastors and churches, and with the people of this community. If it were possible for me to do so, I should tarry here for several weeks, in daily services, but an exacting engagement, that I cannot in conscience put aside, makes it impossible for me to tarry, save for two or three days more. The Lord willing, I shall be here to-morrow, speaking at noon in the Chamber of Commerce auditorium, and to-morrow night here, and again at noon in the Chamber of Commerce auditorium, and I shall be back again for two Sunday services, the Lord willing. Quite well do I understand that in a city like this, or in my city, or in any other city, it is altogether desirable that special meetings be continued daily for weeks. One of the very significant things about Mr. Sunday's meetings, as I have seen them at close range, is that he tarries for weeks and weeks and weeks, making his daily appeal. I shall be here these two or three days, as I have indicated, the Lord willing. I cannot tell you how deep is my wish, my prayerful wish, to help the people who come to these services at noonday and at night. And I cannot tell you how deep is my prayerful wish, that every Christian may be a fellow helper to those who are not Christians. There are many you can see and bring

273

with you to these remaining services. The parent can prayerfully see what can be done for the child; and the teacher can prayerfully see what can be done for the class, or for the single pupil; and the neighbor can see, and the friend can see how you can help friend and neighbor. Oh, I beseech you to put your best into these two or three days, expectant that God will send still larger blessings upon us.

HOW TO BE SAVED.

Text: "And there was a certain nobleman, whose son was sick at Capernaum. When he heard that Jesus was come out of Judea into Galilee, he went unto Him, and besought Him that He would come down, and heal his son: for he was at the point of death. Then Jesus said unto him, Except ye see signs and wonders, ye will not believe. The nobleman saith unto Him, Sir, come down ere my child die. Jesus saith unto him, Go thy way; thy son liveth. And the man believed the word that Jesus had spoken unto him, and he went his way. And as he was now going down, his servants met him, and told him, saying, Thy son liveth. Then enquired he of them the hour when he began to amend. And they said unto him, Yesterday at the seventh hour the fever left him. So the father knew that it was at the same hour in which Jesus said unto him, Thy son liveth. And the father himself believed, and his whole house."—John 4:46-54.

This evening I should like to speak the simplest word within my power on the all-important theme, "How to Be Saved." I take it that the overwhelming majority of this audience are saved people, for which I give devoutest thanks to God. Maybe there will be something in the message for them to-night. They will prayerfully heed it, I trust. But especially do I desire so to speak that the one here who is not saved, or who is puzzled about it, who does not quite understand, but wonders if he or she is saved, will receive help.

A little while ago, one of the great English preachers was asked this question: "If you were to put in one sentence a message of counsel to your brother preachers in England and around the world, what would that sentence be?" I was wonderfully impressed with his reply. This was his answer: "Oh, brother preachers, make it plain to the people how they are saved." It was a vital message, wasn't it? Suppose, oh, Christian friend, that some unsaved friend should meet you to-night or to-morrow, and should ask you to tell him how to be saved, what it is to be saved, what would you say? Could you "make it plain to the people how to be saved?"

I am to read you a brief statement of how a man came to Jesus, when Jesus was here in the flesh, and stated his case, and received the needed blessing from Jesus. Let us all look at that case right carefully; let that little child listen carefully, as well as the grown person. Faith is illustrated here in this story that I am to read. I do not know a simpler illustration in the Bible, of faith in its several degrees, in its several expressions. The children will notice it— and I have been so grateful that the boys and girls have listened just like the grown people. God bless them, all and each, the boys and girls, as well as the young men and women, and the older people. Now you are ready to listen carefully to this Bible story:

And there was a certain nobleman, whose son was sick at Capernaum. When he heard that Jesus was come out of Judea into Galilee, he went unto Him, and besought Him that He would come down, and heal his son: for he was at the point of death. Then Jesus said unto him, Except ye see signs and wonders, ye will not believe. The nobleman saith unto Him, Sir, come down ere my child die. Jesus saith unto him, Go thy way; thy son liveth. And the man believed the word that Jesus had spoken unto him, and he went his way. And as he was now going down, his servants met him, and told him, saying, Thy son liveth. Then enquired he of them the hour when he began to amend. And they said unto him, Yesterday at the seventh hour the fever left him. So the father knew that it was at the same hour in which Jesus said unto him, Thy son liveth. And the father himself believed, and his whole house.

Surely, that is one of the simplest stories about faith, to be found in all this blessed Book of God, one of the simplest explanations of what it means to come to Christ, and get what we need from Christ. Faith is here illustrated.

Let us look to see how this man came to Jesus. You are to note the steps, and you and I are to come in exactly the same way. There are three steps here in this story. They are so simple that a child of just a few years can understand them. God grant that the child, and the strong man, and all of us may see the truth to-night in this simple story!

This man sought Jesus' help. This man took Jesus at His word. And this man found out that Jesus had done what He said He would do. Now, it could not be any simpler than that, could it? This man sought the help of Jesus, and when Jesus told him what to do, he took Jesus at His word, and then later along he found out that what Jesus said was so. Now, there is faith from the first to the last. There it is, from the tiniest beginning to its victorious culmination. Oh, that the Divine Spirit may make

it so plain to-night that never again after this Thursday
night shall we stumble and pause on the great matter of
what it means, and how it is, to be saved!

First of all, this man sought Jesus' help. He was a
day's journey away, in another community, and he heard
that Jesus was in this given community, and the man
came the day's journey to the place where Jesus was, seeking Jesus' help. Isn't that intelligent and reasonable? This
man needed Jesus' help, and he sought it. He came a day's
journey, and stood before Jesus to seek the help that he
thought Jesus could give him. How reasonable that is!
How intelligent that is! Now, we act upon that principle
every day. Business men seek success. There is some
object you desire. You seek it. You do not fold your
hands and sit there stolidly and say: "Oh, well, if it is to
come it will come," and let it go at that. The farmer does
not pursue any such course. The merchant does not pursue any such course. The carpenter does not pursue that
course. Nobody who has a given object to reach pursues
any such course. This man sought Jesus Christ. How intelligent! How reasonable! If you had sickness in your
family, you would not sit with folded hands and say: "Oh,
well, if this loved one is to get well, he will, anyway," or
"she will." You do not deal with it that way. You seek
help for that loved one. You find a physician. You search
for medicines. You seek help, that the sick one may be
cured, may be recovered. How intelligent that is! So
here is a man who wants Jesus' blessing, and he seeks for
it. That is the very quintessence of reason and intelligence.
That is what the Bible bids us do about this supreme matter of being saved. Seek after it. The Bible has great
sentences bearing upon that point. "Seek ye the Lord,
while He may be found, call ye upon Him while He is
near." And take this sentence: "In the day that thou
seekest me with thy whole heart, I will be found of thee."
Oh, if this Thursday night, the girl or boy, the young man
or woman, the older man or woman, in this place, with
the whole heart seeks the Lord, then this night you shall
be saved. If with the whole heart you seek the Lord for
one second, you will be saved. Couldn't you do that? This

man came to Jesus, seeking Jesus' help. You see this man's mind was made up. His purpose was fixed. This man said: "My boy down yonder is ill, and if there is help to be had for him, I must seek such help. I must get it. All the remedies used for my boy have proved futile and unavailing, but I have heard that one whose name is Jesus can cure the sick, and my boy, my blessed boy, is hard by the gates of death, and if Jesus can cure him, I must seek Jesus and state the case and beg for His help." You see, this man's mind was made up. "I am going to try Jesus out," said this man. "I am going to go to the limit in my effort to get His help." His mind was made up. His purpose was fixed.

And then, when he came to Jesus, this man prayed. Prayer is just talking to God. Anybody can pray. The sanest and most reasonable thing in the world is prayer. Prayer is the cry of the little, finite, mortal, dependent human to the great God, able, and willing, and merciful and mighty. Prayer is the cry of a little one whom God made, to that great God who can help, and wants to help, and offers to help. Prayer is coming to Him, saying: "I would come and have thy help. I would come in the right way, and I would receive thy help, for the right purpose." That is prayer. Anybody can pray. Oh, do you pray, my friend? How long since you prayed? To-night, the man or woman or child here, who is wrong with God, can cry from the heart, even while I am speaking: "Lord, help me! Lord, forgive me! Lord, save me! Do for me what needs to be done, I humbly pray." Anybody can come to God like that, and that is prayer. That poor publican that the Bible tells about, put his prayer into one sentence, but, oh, how pleasing to Jesus was that prayer—that one sentence: "God be merciful to me, a sinner." And Jesus said: "This man went down to his house justified, rather than the Pharisee who stood and prayed with himself," but made a long and meaningless and formal prayer. Anybody here can pray the publican's prayer. Suppose you pray it right now. Suppose you let your heart pray it. Suppose every one of us right now lets our heart pray it, as the preacher would let his heart pray it:

"God be merciful to me, a sinner!" Did everybody join in that? Won't you let your hearts join in that prayer, so suitable, so important for us every one? Now let us join in it as the preacher voices it again, and leads it: "God be merciful to me, a sinner!" Will you come to Jesus like that?

And this man was very earnest, very serious, in his appeal to Jesus. He said to Jesus: "Sir, come down ere my child die. Let us not talk. Let us not parley. Let us not cavil. Let us not delay. Hasten with me. Come down ere my child die." How earnest he was! And that is the way for us to pray. We are to be earnest, with our minds and hearts made up about the thing we need and would have from the gracious and merciful Savior. We should be earnest. But now, mark it, there was a weakness in this man's prayer, in this man's appeal, and I am going to call your careful attention to it right now. What was the weakness? This man dictated to Jesus how He should help him. He said to Jesus: "Sir, come down ere my child die." He said in effect: "Come and go home with me. Come where you may see the boy. Come where you can touch his beating pulse and look into his suffering face. Come down. Come, go home with me." And Jesus said: "Why, man, won't it take signs and wonders before you will believe?" Said Jesus to the father: "Why, you are dictating to me how to help you. You are even putting limits and boundaries about the method of my help." Jesus said to him in effect: "Oh, nobleman, if I will heal your boy, won't you consent that I may heal him my way?" Now, isn't that reasonable? Let us call that nobleman. "Nobleman, if Jesus will show mercy to your boy, won't you let Jesus show mercy in His own way, without any advice or counsel or direction at all from you?"

The nobleman saw the point. The nobleman saw that if Jesus was going to take that case, then the father must relinquish the case to Him, must turn the case over to Him, must commit the case to Him, and there it is. Call to the man: "Oh, nobleman, if Jesus will heal your suffering and terribly sick son, won't you let Jesus do it His own way?" And so I pass the word to every one here, who

wants the help of Jesus, to every one here who wants to
be forgiven and saved: If Jesus will save you, won't you
let Him save you His way? He will never save you any
other way. You must come to the point where you will
say: "Yes, Jesus, I yield. I give up. I trust. I surrender. Save me your way." He will never save you any
other way, and you must come to that point.

May I take a little leaf out of my own poor life? When
I was a young fellow, seeking Jesus, the way was all dark
to me. I could not understand how to be saved. Oh, if
somebody had sat down beside me when I was a lad, and
had told me the simple way to be saved, I think I would
have walked in it! I remember one day I was alone, and
for hours and hours this was my prayer: "Lord, deepen
my feeling. Lord, make my eyes to be fountains of tears.
Lord, fill me with remorse and misery and condemnation."
I prayed like that, supposing that if I reached a certain point
of awful, deplorable remorse and regret and wretchedness
of spirit, surely Jesus would then take pity on me. Why,
that was not the way for me to come to Jesus. The way
for me to come to Jesus was to come to Him and say:
"Lord Jesus, here I am, a sinner, and I cannot save myself. Thou hast taught it, and surely thou knowest. I
have found out in myself and of myself and by myself how
weak and frail I am, how insufficient I am to save myself.
Lord Jesus, thou doest the saving, thou sayest it, and thou
sayest: 'Come to me without delay, and I will come to
you, and I will save you.' Lord, I turn the best I can from
every evil way, and I give up to Jesus, that He may save
me His way, and I give up right now. Dark or bright,
no matter what comes, I will give up to Jesus." Oh, if I
had come like that, when an interested boy, I would have
found Christ, as I did find Him when my feet were turning
into young manhood's morning. I did find Him, when
quietly one night, sitting in an audience like this, an earnest preacher pleaded that Christ might be given His own
way to save the soul, that the soul, needy and helpless
and unable to save itself, would make honest surrender
to Christ—utter surrender. I sat back there as you sit
back there before me now, and I said: "Lord Jesus, it is

all as dark as it can be. I do not see through it. I cannot understand it. I am making no progress. I am getting nowhere. I am drifting with the current. Dark or bright, live or die, come what may, I surrender right now to Christ." Right there is the place to be saved, and nowhere else. Right there! Won't you let Him save you His way? Won't you, oh, husband and father; won't you, oh, mother and wife; won't you, young man or woman; won't you, my boy or girl, let Jesus save you His way, by your own consent? Won't you tell Him: "Yes, Lord Jesus, I say 'Yes' to your call?"

Now, you see the second point. When the man saw the issue, when it was joined, when the man saw that he must turn the case over to Jesus, Jesus said to him in effect: "If you will turn that case over to me, that I may save that boy my way, then that boy shall surely be healed." Now comes the beautiful point of the story. The Scriptures here tell us, as I read them to you: "And the man believed the word that Jesus had spoken unto him, and went his way." Right there a soul is saved, and nowhere else—right there. The man took Jesus at His word. The man closed the matter with Jesus. Jesus said: "If you will commit that boy to me, I will save him. Will you do it?" He said: "I will do it." And Jesus said: "Go your way; your boy lives." And the man took Jesus at His word and went his way. Right there a soul is saved.

Won't you take Jesus at His word? What word? Any word that He speaks to you, calling you to Him. His promises are countless almost as the stars in the skies above us—His glorious promises. If you will take any one and follow that to Jesus, and say: "I will take you at your word. It is 'Yes' to your word. I will give up to you"—whoever does that, Christ will take that person, then and there and forever, and be your Savior. What word? Oh, there are many! Take this one—I dare say that uncounted tens of thousands of people have come to Jesus on this plain promise which now I quote: "Him that cometh to me I will in no wise cast out." There is enough gospel in that one promise to bring every rational human being to Jesus for salvation. "Him that cometh to me I will in no wise cast out." That is for you, and you, and me, and all the rest. "Him that cometh to me!" "If anybody will come to me, and just give up to me, I won't cast that person out," the great Savior declares. Or take this promise: "Whosoever will"—how simple that is—"whosoever will, let him take the water of life freely." "Whosoever is willing," says Jesus, "for me to be your Savior, and you will just give up, if you are just willing, I will take you that very moment, and you will be mine, and I will be yours." Or take this sentence: "The blood of Jesus Christ, His Son, cleanseth us from all sin." One is in this audience who was brought by that verse to Jesus. A man with the gray about his temples has told me about it. That verse brought him. "The blood of Jesus Christ, His Son, cleanseth us from all sin." The man heard it and said: "Well, if it is Christ's blood that cleanses me, then I will give up to Christ, and let Him save me in His own way," and Christ saved him then and there.

Or take this beautiful sentence: "Come unto me, all ye that labor and are heavy laden, and I will give you rest." I wonder if millions have not come in response to that invitation. Or take this promise: "Commit thy way unto the Lord"—oh, but it is a sinful way, you say, a marred way, a bad way, a wrong and improper way—never mind, whatever your way is, "Commit thy way unto the Lord, trust also in Him, and He"—not you, not the church, not the preacher—"He shall bring it to pass." What does He say? He says: "Come and commit your case, whatever your sin, or doubt, or fear, or temptation, or need, or weakness, or difficulty, or evil memory, or accusing conscience—no matter what, commit your case to the Lord, and He will take you and forgive you and save you. He says just that. Could language be plainer?

Oh, soul, don't you see it? Isn't it plain? Do you answer me back: "Oh, sir, but this is my difficulty?" State it. What is your difficulty? Why are you not tonight Christ's friend and follower? Name your difficulty. Whatever your difficulty is, I do not care what it is—it may be exceedingly trying—whatever your sin, your

doubt, your fear, your anxiety, your temptation, your weakness, your past, your present, your future, if you will honestly surrender your case to Christ, He will manage you,
the difficulty, the sin, and everything about it. He does
the saving, but you are to surrender. He never saved one
that did not give up to Him. He never saved one rational
soul that did not say: "Yes, Lord, I will surrender. I
will decide." He never saved one that held back and refused to surrender to Him. And He never failed to save
any soul in this world, no matter how bedarkened, how
troubled, how sinful, how difficult, if such soul just said,
and meant it: "Here, Lord, I will surrender to you that
you may save me." Oh, isn't it simple—the way to be
saved? The little girl there knows when I quote that sentence: "Commit thy way unto the Lord," what it means.
The little girl would know what I meant if I said: "Child,
take this letter and commit it to the postoffice." She would
understand that. That child would understand it. That
boy would understand. "Commit this letter to the postoffice," and the child would take it there and commit it
to the postoffice. The man there would understand about
taking his baggage yonder to the train, and having the
baggage checked, and he would get his little check there
for it, and behind that baggage that he checked would be
the weight, the authority, the responsibility of that whole
railway company. Jesus comes saying: "Here is the
check. I will give it to you, if you will commit your way
to me. I will take your case and save you, and you may
keep this check and look at it, and quote it every hour
in the day. I will never forget you, and never fail you."
Isn't it simple, and isn't it glorious?

There is one more word about the story. The last word
is that the man went on back home, after Jesus said: "Go
your way, now. You trust your boy to me, and I will take
care of you, and you will find out that I have not misled
you." The man went on back, and before he got back
home, even as he was going along the homeward road, his
servants came gladly to meet him, and when they met him
they said: "Master, the boy is well." And then the father
asked them when the change came, and they made an-

swer: "Yesterday at the seventh hour the fever left him."
So the father remembered that it was at that identical hour
in the which Jesus said to him: "Now that you have
trusted your boy to me, you may go back without any
anxiety, and you will find him all safe and well." The
father remembered that it was at that very hour, when he
turned his boy over to Christ and said: "I will trust you
with my boy." And then the father saw that it was true.
The father had the demonstration. There was the climax
of proof. There was the boy, living and well. And the
father, and the mother, and the boy, and the whole house
rejoiced, for they all found that Jesus did just what He
promised to do.

Let us give earnest heed as we apply this truth to our
own hearts. Isn't our trouble often that we want this last
part first? We want to see it all, and know it all, before
we will trust Christ and let Him later reveal to us His
mercy and blessing. Don't we want this last part first?
We want all this light, this knowledge, this assurance,
before we take this first plain step, and surrender, turn
over, commit, say "Yes" to Christ, when He says: "If
you will trust me, I will forgive and save." We want to
see it all, before we take this first great step of surrender
to Christ.

Oh, this first step must be taken, before we will ever
find out that Jesus surely keeps His word. If you had a
candle there in the house to be lighted, you would not
stand before the candle, with your match in your hand,
and say to the candle: "Burn now, so that we can see,"
before you struck the match. You would strike that match
and apply it to the candle, and then the light would be
kindled for all who are in the house. That is the way the
light comes. If you had a sickness, and the doctor should
be summoned and leave his medicines, with careful directions, you would not content yourself with saying: "Oh,
well, the medicine is in the house, and the doctor has told
me what to do with it, but I will pass it by; I will not take
it." You would not do like that at all, for when he came
back he would find you with the raging fever, and when

he questioned you, he would find out that you had not carried out his orders at all.

So when Jesus comes to you and says: "I will forgive you, I will save you, I will prepare you for heaven, I will fit you for earth, I will fit you for death, I will fit you for life, I will save you, I will write your name in God's own book of life above, if you will just surrender to me," you are not to say: "Well, I will wait and see the how about it." You are to say: "I will do that. I will take Him at His word. I will give up to Him. I will make that surrender." How simple it is, and how glorious it is!

The very essence of faith is taking Christ at His word. The very essence of faith is giving up to Christ. Do you say: "Lord, I cannot see through it?" Certainly, you cannot. I cannot. There is not a man in the world who can see how it is that one is born again. You cannot explain how one is born the first time, born of the flesh, and certainly, you cannot explain how one is born of the Spirit, that higher, more wonderful birth. But Jesus said: "That is my part. Mine it is to look after the birth. The mystery, the wonderful work—that is mine. Yours it is to turn your case over to me, that I may take you and save you my way. Will you turn that case over to me?"

Oh, soul, aren't you ready to say: "That is exactly what I will do?" It is as simple as daylight. Here it is. Christ does the saving, and does it all. But the sinner has to give up to Christ, and then when the sinner does that, Christ takes such sinner, forgives and guides and keeps such sinner for all the afterwhile. How simple and how glorious! Come, now. Haven't you waited long enough to take this eternally important step? He has spared you, this great Savior. He has been so gracious and so merciful. He has shown you such patience and forbearance. He has waited late and long for you, that He might do for you what needs to be done, which if left undone for you, He himself says: "Better for that person that he or she had never been born." Aren't you ready to-night to say: "I am ready that Christ shall save me His own way, without any dictation on my part?" Oh, haven't you waited long enough? God be thanked that He has been patient

with you, that He has waited, that He has borne and for-
borne toward you!

But now haven't you waited long enough? Somewhere
there is an end to that waiting. I heard that faithful, Bib-
lical preacher, George C. Needham, who held one of his
last meetings with our church in Dallas, a wonderful gospel preacher, tell of three brothers yonder in Scotland, who
got a boat and went out on one of the lakes of Scotland one
day, rowing in the little boat. But those lakes are often
swept by storms and winds that come down upon them
all unexpectedly, and when those three brothers were far
out yonder in the lake, a storm suddenly swept down on
the lake and turned over the boat, and the middle brother
was caught in the rigging and drowned outright, but the
oldest and youngest brothers somehow got out from under
the boat, and they swam towards a rock, hundreds of yards
out yonder, jutting up in the lake. That was their only
chance to be saved, and with extreme difficulty they made
their way toward that rock. At last the older brother
reached it, all worn out, and all exhausted in strength. He
just did reach it, and he looked back, and there, some yards
away, came the younger brother, barely able to move his
hands in those battling, climbing waves, his strength all
gone. This older boy called to him, with what little
strength he had left, trying to cheer him to hold out a little
farther, that he might reach the rock. But he came a little
farther and then went down. He could not make the rock.
His strength was gone. The people on the shore yonder
saw the distressing scene, and they got another boat and
came to this oldest boy, and they found him wild almost in his grief. And over and over again, he told the
story of how it all happened, of how quickly the boat
turned over, and how the middle brother drowned outright, and how he and the little brother got out and swam
the best they could, and how he reached the rock, but was
all given out, and how the little brother could not quite
reach it. And the great preacher said the boy would wind
up his story with the plaintive cry, over and over and over
again: "Oh, lads, little brother was nearly saved! Little
brother was nearly saved! Little brother was nearly

saved!" Sobbing his heart out, he would finish his story
every time with the plaintive cry: "Oh, I tell you, little
brother was nearly saved, nearly saved!"

God pity us, that is a picture of many who come to our
gospel services. They hear, they think, they desire, they
know, they feel, they are nearly saved. But nearly saved
is not enough! Almost is but to fail! Satan does not care
if people are serious, if they are interested, if they desire,
if they tremble, if their faces are white, and their hearts
beat faster from emotion concerning Christ's call to them;
Satan does not care, if they will just halt, if they will just
hesitate, if they will just wait.

Come now, haven't you, oh, man or woman; oh, husband or wife; oh, father or mother, young man or maiden,
boy or girl, haven't you waited long enough to make an
end of this waiting, and to say: "As for me, dark or bright,
whatever comes, God help me, I cast the die. I cross the
Rubicon. I cut the cables. I burn the bridges. I can do
nothing else. I surrender to Christ, that He may save
me His own way." I tell you, if you will, He will be
your Savior from that very minute. Aren't you willing,
and aren't you ready, for that great step to be taken on
your part?

I am going to ask every soul that has taken it to tell
us about it. Every soul that says: "Sir, I have heard this
simple message, and I am able to lay my hand on my heart
and say to you: 'I have already surrendered myself to
Christ, and have taken Christ to be my personal Savior.
I am able with uplifted hand to declare that I have made
that surrender, that I have made the choice of Jesus Christ
as my Savior.'" Every soul in this place that can say: "I
have done that," lift high the hand. It is a thrilling sight,
dear brothers. I greet you, and bid you Godspeed. We
are traveling to the better world, and a little later we will
strike hands in that better world, because of the saving
grace of Christ.

But now I ask: Aren't there those here who say: "I
could not lift my hand. I am in doubt and darkness about
it. But I do want to be saved, and I want you to pause

and all these hundreds and hundreds of Christians to pause, and pray one prayer for me, that I may not miss the way, that I may not be finally lost. I want you to pray one prayer for me, that I may be saved. I want that." Do you say: "I do want that, sir?" Every soul that says: "I am wrong with Christ, and a minute ago I could not lift my hand"—you did right not to if you could not. Sincerity, how vital that always is!—but do you say: "I lift my hand on your last call. I want to be saved by Christ. I want to be saved in Christ's own way and time. Pray a prayer for me that I may be saved, for I am wrong with God. I would lift my hand on that," then lift it, while I am looking now. I see your uplifted hands—they are many. Oh, my heart goes out to you all. In a moment we are going to pray. What are we going to pray for? We are going to pray that right now, these men and women and boys and girls saying: "We want to be saved Christ's way," may now settle it. We are going to pray that right now you may settle it, that right now the matter may be concluded—right now. Now, with every head bowed for a moment, let us pray.

THE PRAYER.

Blessed Savior, we bring these interested ones, all and each, the best we can, right now in our prayers, and commit them to thy mercy and grace. O blessed Savior, may the truth be clear to them right now, that they can never save themselves; that waiting, no matter how long, will not suffice; that no matter where they go nor what they do, that will not suffice. Give them to realize that Christ must save, and Christ alone, and that their waiting cannot improve, but will make worse their condition. Let them now say: "Lord, thou hast waited for me, but I will not ask thee to wait longer—not another week, nor another day, nor another hour, nor another service. I want to be saved, and I will give up to Christ right now, that He may save me His way. I will take Him through the darkness. I will come to Him, though unable to understand how He saves. I will be a little child, just as He tells me to be. Here, Lord, I give myself to thee—sins, doubts, and all, difficulties and temptations, weaknesses and fears, yesterday, to-day and to-morrow—I give myself to thee right now. I will say yes to thee now and forever." God help them by thy Spirit that this may be their decision, and made known before we go. For Jesus' precious sake. Amen.

We will sing this invitation song before we go:

Jesus is tenderly calling thee home—
Calling to-day, calling to-day.
Why from the sunshine of love wilt thou roam,
Farther and farther away?

Aren't you ready to say: "Sir, I am ready to announce my decision for Christ. Waiting cannot help me. Waiting might ruin me. I want it settled, and settled Christ's way, and His way is for me to yield myself to Him." Come, then, before all the people, and let me greet you as you make your public confession of Christ as your Savior.

(Numbers came forward, confessing Christ, while the song was being sung.)

We are going to offer a prayer of thanksgiving, in a moment, for these men and women and children who have come, but I implore you, before we pray, oh, Christian men and women, dedicate your best to this special work these three days remaining. I believe they are to be of the right hand of God. Dedicate your utmost to the incomparable quest of winning souls. The mother, the father, the wife, the husband, the friend, the neighbor, the acquaintance—oh, you ought to bring to the services hundreds and hundreds of people who are without Christ. And you will pray much I beseech you, that the preacher may bring such faithful, vital messages, that every soul that shall attend may be left without excuse, if such soul shall be finally lost. We will pray about the midday service to-morrow, and the midday service Saturday, and about the services that are to be had, God willing, on Friday night, and on Sunday. Let us dedicate our very lives to this work, that the people all about us may be turned unto the Lord.

THE CLOSING PRAYER.

And now, Lord, deep is our thanksgiving for the coming of these men and women and children to confess their acceptance of Christ as their personal Savior. The glory is all thine own.

May all these men and women and children who came, go now to live gloriously for Christ. Let them see the truth, clear as the light, that Christ does the saving, and does it all, and that any soul that surrenders to Him, henceforth has Christ for his Savior and Master. Let such souls, through the darkness, cling to Christ, no matter what comes.

Some did not come, and our heart ached with an agony about them. Lord, may they yet come to Christ to-night, before they close their eyes in sleep. O God, may these interested ones now say to Jesus: "We will end this battle, and this very night we will make our surrender to Christ," and may they come back to tell us to-morrow night, "We are going with you to God's gracious land." O God, have compassion on the lost all about us. We are thinking of many as we are coming to the close of the services—of men and women driven hard in life's daily battle; of business men preoccupied; toiling men, whose lot in life is hard; of men with burdens and sorest difficulties. O, for every such man and woman, Lord, toiling, and struggling, may there go such appeals from these men and women, in the hours just ahead, that all through this city, they shall know, by the hundreds and thousands, how much Christ's people care for their salvation. And then may the people in all ranks and conditions—the men who are poor, and the men with their money, supposing that that suffices, but which has in it awful peril, because it can make the soul to be filled with pride and self-sufficiency and forgetfulness of God—may they all be told this by lips of love and blessed appeal, which God shall direct in the hours just before us. May the spirit of prayer mightily rest on the hearts and heads and lives of this army of Christians. May there be many anointed of God to go here and there, to speak to son, or daughter, or husband, or wife, or mother, or father, or neighbor or acquaintance, and so to speak to God in prayer, that the Divine Spirit may give guidance, yea, give conviction to hundreds in these days before us, that they may be turned by grace divine unto the forgiving Savior.

And as we go now, may the blessing of Christ Jesus the Lord come like a balm to our every heart, and keep us in the right way. forever. Amen.

XX

NOON SERVICE, JUNE 22, 1917.

PRELIMINARY REMARKS.

In a moment I am to read a brief passage from the Scriptures, but before reading I would take time to follow up the earnest word said by the brother pastor, about our turning to the best possible account these two or three remaining days appointed for the special meeting. There are some occasions far more favorable than others for helping people religiously. Such an occasion is a series of meetings in which the way is made easy and natural for you to ask people to come with you to the public services; and then when you have gone that far, the way is easy and natural, more than it ordinarily is, for you to follow up your invitation with the right kind of conversation and questioning and testimony about personal religion. We must never get away from the immeasurably important truth that the personal element is indispensable in our witnessing and working for Christ. There are lives all about us that would be changed, if a conversation of a half hour or less, of the right sort were had with them. There are Christians in the darkness—they scarcely know why, or they may know why—who would be immediately changed for the better, if a conversation were had with them, by the right person, in the right way, at the right time. And there are people all about us, pre-occupied, and the things eternal have little place in their thoughts. Oh, if they could be spoken with, if they could be approached, if they could be appealed to, if they could be conversed with in the right way! I pray you, my fellow Christians, all of you and each of you, one by one, turn to the best account these days for helping the people. A meeting like this—indeed, every meeting—ought to be constructive; and what an inspiring thing it is, when scores and hundreds of Christians, coming to the midday service, and the vaster number to the evening service, go out through the day, and as best they can, speak for Christ personally to the people.

In this midday service, the preacher has desired earnestly each day to bring some simple but vital word, that would help us as we face the battle of daily life. He has desired to call us all back to the simplicities and vitalities of life. This morning, I am to speak to you on an old, but remarkably important theme, namely: "How May We Know Jesus Better?" That theme is suggested by the Scripture which I now read to you. You are ready to hear with reverence, as I read from the third chapter of the Epistle to the Philippians:

But what things were gain to me, those I counted loss for Christ. Yea, doubtless, and I count all things but loss for the excellency of the knowledge of Christ Jesus my Lord: for whom I have suffered the loss of all things, and do count them but refuse, that I may win Christ, and be found in Him, not having mine own righteousness, which is of the law, but that which is through the faith of Christ, the righteousness which is of God by faith: that I may know Him, and the power of His resurrection, and the fellowship of His sufferings, being made conformable unto His death; if by any means I might attain unto the resurrection of the dead. Not as though I had already attained, either were already perfect: but I follow after, if that I may apprehend that for which also I am apprehended of Christ Jesus.

HOW MAY WE KNOW JESUS BETTER?

Text: "That I may know Him."—Philippians 3:10.

One little sentence in the midst of those several sentences, points the message for us to-day: "That I may know Him."

Paul's deepest and most fervent longing evidently was to know Jesus better, just as it should be our deepest longing to know Jesus better every day we live, because the knowledge most of all desirable and necessary is the knowledge of God in Christ. Christ came down to the world to show us the Father. "He that hath seen me hath seen the Father." Jesus stood among men and said in effect to them: "I am God uncovered. When you see me, you see the Father—you see God." Now, the knowledge most of all desirable and necessary is the knowledge of God revealed in Christ Jesus the Savior. Such knowledge gives us a grip on the great spiritual realities, and we need to have such knowledge, even above all other knowledge.

How much, then, do we know about Jesus now? To begin with, how much does each man and woman, listening to me here know about Jesus now? Just what is your conception of Christ Jesus? Is Christ real to you, as some other person is real to you—real to you like mother, or father, or dearest earthly loved one? How real is Christ to you? We are never to lose sight of the fact that Christ is a person. He is not a principle—He is a person. He thinks, He lives, He commands, He feels. He is a person. The theory that God is a principle is fundamentally incorrect. God is not a principle at all. God announces principles. He teaches principles. A great person, He is behind them. Now, how real is Christ to us, to begin with? How much do we know about Him to-day? He is not some inspiring memory. He is not some vague dream. He is not some empty abstraction. He is a person, to be trusted and loved and followed forever—real as mother, real as teacher, real as physician, real as the most gracious, devoted earthly friend—a person. Christ is that to men. How real is He to us? How real is Christ to you? How much do you know about Him right now? How much does your inner nature know about Christ?

Some years ago, I was preaching to one of the universities of several hundred men, for several days, and the next to the last morning had come, when the senior class of thirty, with one exception, waited on me in a body. One of the men was not there, but the twenty-nine said: "We have come to ask how long you will be here?" I said: "This morning and in the morning, and then I must be away for my home." They said: "We have come to ask you to pray specially for one of our seniors. We are to be graduated in a few weeks. Our class of thirty men are all Christians, save this one man." And they were gener-

ous in their tributes to him. They said: "He has the
brightest mind in all the class, the keenest intellect in all
the group, but he is an unbeliever outright. He does not
accept what you are saying. He does not accept what we
profess. Oh," said they, "do your best for him. He insists
that he must have facts, if he ever is to become a Christian; he must have facts. He insists that he is a scientist
and must have facts." They said: "Do your best for him."
I went up the stairway to the chapel auditorium, and
changed my subject as I came up those steps. "This man
must have facts. Very well, I will give him a great fact,
and let him reckon with that." And so I came, a few minutes later, with the text: "He that believeth on the Son
of God hath the witness in himself." And I asked the
men: "What will you do with the fact of Christian experience? Once I did not know anything about Christ, and
once the less I heard of Him the better it suited me. But
He crossed my path in the preaching of His gospel, and
I was arrested. I was made serious. I prayed. I surrendered to Him, though it was as dark as midnight, and my
conscience knows that He has spoken peace to me. Now,
what will you do with that fact? What will you do with
the fact of Christian experience? Here is the fact. What
will you do with it?"

You remember that incident, do you not, of Dr. James
Simpson, the eminent scientist? He had been waited upon,
one day, by a group of fellow scientists, who would pay
the distinguished scientist their respects and honor, and
one spoke for the rest, telling him of the tribute in which
the world held him as a scientist, and then presently said
to him: "Sir James, if you should name your greatest discovery of all that you have ever made, what would that
discovery be?" And in one moment Sir James Simpson's
eyes were filled with tears, and he said: "My greatest discovery, gentlemen, is that Jesus Christ has forgiven my
sins and saved me." What will you do now with the fact
of Christian experience?

So those students followed me down to the president's
office, from day to day, where for two hours each day I
conversed privately with the students. I had not reached

the president's office more than a moment, until there was
a knock on the outer door, and I opened it, and there stood
the skeptic. I offered him a chair, and he said: "No, I
needn't sit down. I will be through in just a moment."
And then he was generous enough to say to me: "I believe
in you, or I would not be here at all. I think you are entirely candid and sincere, or I would not be here at all.
Now," he said, "you will forget that you are a preacher, and
forget that I am a senior to be graduated in a few weeks,
and answer a question I am going to put to you." "Very
well, young man; I will answer it if I can," I said, "and
I will be entirely frank. If I can, I will answer your question, and if I cannot, I will tell you so." "All right," he
said, "here is my question: Mr. Truett, is Jesus Christ
real to you, by which I mean, does your heart know, your
life know, your brain know, your inner self know, that He
helps you? Yes or no, is He real to you like that?" Now,
that was challenging me with a proposition very real and
candid and searching. It was the acid test. What would
you have said? Well, I will tell you what I said, if you
will not look on it as offensively personal. I laid my hand
on his shoulder, and I said: "Young man, if the truth is
in me, if I know what the truth is, if I am not utterly bedarkened and deceived about the truth and about life and
about all things, then I declare to you that Jesus is more
real in His help to me than is any other being in the world.
When every other being has failed me, He has not failed
me. When I have been on the storm-swept sea, and there
was no chart, nor guide, nor rudder, nor compass for my
little boat, and when the wild winds and waves beat over me
and drove that boat, I called to Him, and said, 'Thou alone
canst help.' And He answered back: 'I will help. Put your
trust in me and be unafraid.' The one thing, young man,
that my heart does know is that Jesus helps me." And
then he turned on his heel, his face serious, and he said:
"I will seek Him," and he left my room. The next morning
came on, and I stood to make the last address to the college
men, and I finished and said: "Now the cab waits at the
door for me. I must hurry to the train to get back to my
home, but before I go, has another man tried Jesus, just

honestly surrendered his case, doubts, darknesses, fears, sins, difficulties, questions—all of it? Has he surrendered his case to Christ? Does another man say: 'I have done that?' Before I go I wish he would walk down the aisle and take my hand." And the clever skeptic back yonder started toward me, and the men saw him, and they threw their hats to the ceiling, they were so moved, and then hundreds of them bowed at their pews and sobbed, for the carping skeptic was coming out of the darkness into the light. He just tried Christ. He just gave up to Christ.

Is Christ real to you? This morning I am to give you several suggestions about how we may make Him more real, and you will amplify them in your thought and heart as you go your ways. If we are to know Jesus better, then I come to say we must make much of His Book. God's first gift to the world is His Son Jesus Christ. His second best gift to the world is the Bible. The Bible reveals Jesus. Nature does not say a word about Jesus. Nature speaks the fact of the great God. The heavens declare His glory; the firmament showeth His handiwork; but nature nowhere says a word about His mercy and His forgiveness in Christ, the appointed Savior. The Bible tells about Jesus. If you and I are to know about Jesus, the one mediator between God and us, then we must come to the Bible and search. Oh, my friends, I pause a moment to make an appeal that we will treat right this Holy Book of God. It is appalling how little very many strong and clever people know about the Bible. Chinese Gordon said, when he went down into the Sudan, taking with him his splendid library, that it was not long until he found out that he did not really need his library at all. He said he needed really only two books— first, the Bible, and then, next, the Bible concordance, that would enable him to find quickly any passage in the Bible that he needed to find. We want more and more to mag- nify this Bible. Of old, God said: "My people are de- stroyed for lack of knowledge." We might say that to-day. If men are rooted and grounded in their knowledge of the Bible, they will go out against any sin, against any foe, against any difficulty, and they will overcome, for the Bible is a signboard pointing us to Christ.

And again, I say if we are to know Jesus better, then we need to have a time in our lives for meditation. I wonder now if meditation is not practically a lost art in our lives. Who of us stops now to go into the quiet place, where, all alone, we will just meditate on the things of supreme worth? This injunction that we shall have a place and habit in our daily life to be alone for some minutes for meditation on the deep, high things, is a matter of profoundest concern, in these days of stress and hurry and rush and extravagance. Oh, how important that every man and woman should find a quiet place in some nook to have daily meditation on the high things for the help of the soul! The psalmist said: "My meditation of Him shall be sweet." You remember how Ezekiel pictured those mystic creatures, with their mystic wings and mystic faces, and then the prophet went on to say: "When they stood, they let down their wings." And all along every one of us needs to let down the wings, and just wait on God. He himself says: "Wait on the Lord, and He shall strengthen thine heart. Wait, I say, on the Lord."

And I am coming to say next, if we are to know Jesus better, then we must magnify the habit daily of secret prayer. Mind you, I said, secret prayer. Now, isn't it just at that point that all of us are tempted sadly to fail? What if I pass the question to this crowded auditorium floor this morning, life by life, person by person, and pause there at your heart and ask: "How much do you pray in secret, day by day?" What would your answer be? Isn't it just at that point that most sadly we fail? The Bible says: "When thou prayest, enter into thy closet, and when thou hast shut thy door, pray to thy Father which is in secret; and thy Father which seeth in secret shall reward thee openly." I believe that Arnold of Rugby, that master teacher of boys, was entirely right when he said that, no matter what a man's or woman's difficulty, or what the sin, or what the doubt, or what the struggle, or what the temptation, or what the barrier, if such man or woman would go into the secret place, and there bare the soul honestly in secret prayer to God, such man or woman would be brought out of the darkness and be given victory over the trial. I believe he is right. It was when Moses was alone with God, that God gave him the sight of that bush that burned, but was not consumed. It was when Isaiah was alone with God, that God gave him that three-fold vision of God, and of himself, and of his fellow humanity, that completely changed the young prophet's life. It was when Jacob was alone with God, yonder at Jabbok on a lonely night, that God made that man over, made him a prince, so that ever afterward Jacob prevailed with men, because he had power with God. It was when Paul was alone with God, that he was caught up into the third heaven, and heard and saw what he could never tell. It was when John was alone with God, on the Isle of Patmos, that there were vouchsafed to him visions and revelations of the other world, some glimpses of which John gives us here in the book of Revelation. It was when Luther was alone with God, that he got visions of God and truth that he went out to speak, and so spoke them and wrote them, that he set tyrants to trembling and thrones to tottering, and brought in the mental and moral reformation of Germany and Europe and the world. It was when Bunyan was alone with God, that God gave him visions which he penned in a book—which book is an allegory unmatched, and forever, perhaps, to be matchless; a book probably next in importance to the Holy Word of God.

But I will come closer to you than to call your attention to these great worthies of whom I have spoken. Oh, it is when you and I, with our burden and battle, with our stress and difficulty, with our sin and temptation, make it a point to be alone with God, and bare ourselves before Him, telling Him: "I cannot let thee go except thou bless me"—it is then we are given victory and made princes in His sight.

May I speak a word about my mother, now in that yonder land these last few years, the best Christian I ever saw? May I speak a word about her faith? I was reared in a large family, far out on the farm, and I remember that when father and the older boys used to go to the farm, the least little fellow, about four, and myself, about six, too little to work, stayed behind, and many are the times I have seen my mother in the morning sobbing, and I have gone and said: "Mother, what makes you cry?" And she would say: "You are too little, my boy, to understand. Never mind. Don't worry about mother." And when the breakfast was over, and all the little things were done about the house in the morning, mother has said to the two little boys: "Now, you stay here while mother goes aside to be alone a little while." And she would go away with face suffused with tears, and she would come back in a little while, and every time she would come back singing, with a smile on her face fairer than the morning. And one morning I said to the little brother: "What do you guess happens to mother? She goes away crying, and she comes back singing. Let us see what it is." We followed along quietly behind her, and she went there into the orchard, near the little country home, and we saw her and heard her. She was down on her face before God. I can remember until yet the surpassing pathos of her prayers. She said: "Lord Jesus, I never can rear this houseful of boys like they ought to be reared, without thy help. I will make shipwreck with them, without thy help. I cannot guide them, I cannot counsel them, I cannot be the mother that a woman ought to be to her children, without God's help. I will cleave to thee. Teach me and help me, every hour." I heard her like that, and then she came back, singing, every morning. And when I grew older, and when manhood was reached, and when I learned in my heart what it is to know Jesus, I knew the secret into which my mother entered. She was the greatest Christian I ever saw. It is when you and I tread the path of secret prayer that we find out about Jesus, and are given to enter into the secret of His presence.

And, again, if you and I are to know Jesus better, we must watch with uncompromising watchfulness against sin. The only thing that will hide the face of God from us is sin. He says: "Your sins have separated between you and me." Sin is a veil through which Jesus cannot be seen. Sin is an insulator that cuts off the currents between God and us. I say it reverently, God cannot afford to answer some people when they pray, because they keep, hidden back in their hearts some wrong thing, some wedge of gold, some Babylonish garment, some evil thing. Recall what David said: "If I regard iniquity in my heart, the Lord will not hear me." If you and I are to know Jesus better and better, then we must put away every evil thing. We must refuse to let any kind of sin have a dominant place anywhere in our lives.

I go on to say that if we are to know Jesus better, then we are to make much of companionship with the right kind of Christians. How much there is in that! The longer I live, the more I am finding out the truth that life's companionships very largely make us or mar us in our earthly way. The Bible tells us: "He that walketh with wise men shall be wise," and it adds: "But the companion of fools shall be destroyed." It tells us: "Evil communications corrupt good manners." There came a time in my life when doubt, deep, dark and terrible, settled down on me, as if it would clutch my throat to my utter doom. I need not now recite the why. Doubt and darkness and trouble come from a thousand sources. I came to the place where all was dark as midnight, and a man several years my senior, both physically and religiously, seemed intuitively to know that I had come to a crisis in my spiritual life. And so one day he said to me: "If you have the time, I should like for us to go for a walk in the woods. I have something to say to you." We went for a two hours' walk in the woods, and it marked an epoch in my life. He told me how, years before, darkness and doubt had come to him, and his faith was well-nigh shattered, and then he told me what he did, and where he went, and he described my own case as he talked about his. He described my case better than I could describe it, and after that two hours' walk in the woods, wherein he did most of the talking, I came back, having passed an epoch in my life. Oh, tell somebody your Christian experience! And if you are in the darkness and must say: "I do not know whether I have one to tell," then go to somebody in whom you have confidence, and say to him or her: "What is Christ to you? Tell me what He is to you."

There was once an old shoemaker in my city, one of

the most victorious saints I ever knew; and often, when
darkness came to me, and when questions arose, I have
closed my study door and gone down to his shoe-shop and
said to him: "Tell me once again, I pray you, your Christian experience." And before he was through, sermons
flew through my mind like a covey of birds. He knew
God! He led me into the secret places, as he told me what
God had done for him.

There is another very practical word to be said. If we
are to know Jesus better, then we are to be busy for Him.
Will you heed that? Idleness explains a thousand doubts.
The idle Christian is always in trouble. Satan always
finds mischief for the idle hand. The idle brain is his
workshop. The biggest sociological problem in this country, in the entire social order, is the problem of idleness.
Out there in the realm of government, in the realm of business, the idler is the menacing problem. And when you
come to religion, idleness is a terrible menace. If you are
idle, and darkness has come to you, and you cannot see
your way religiously, just remember that your idleness
may explain it all. Even John the Baptist, who stood before Herod, the purple-robed ruler, and unquailingly called
Herod to time for his wickedness and sin—even that brave
spirit, when he was put in jail, and had a season of en-
forced inactivity, plaintively sent some of his men out
yonder, where Jesus was, to ask Jesus the question: "Art
thou He that should come, or do we look for another?"
John the Baptist's heart became faint and fearful when
he was inactive.

I am thinking now of a fine young fellow, a leader in
both the world of business and the social world, who came
for six Sunday nights in succession where I was preaching,
and on the sixth Sunday night, confessed Christ, and took
his place in the church. I never knew a more devoted,
more valiant young man for Christ for a year, and then
after a year, he began to drift. I missed him out of the
prayer-meeting—and every Christian ought to go to prayer-meeting—and I missed him out of the Sunday school—
and every Christian ought to go to the Sunday school—
and I missed him out of the Sunday service, and I said to

some of the young men: "What about him?" They said: "We fear he is drifting." I said: "Do your best to help him." One Sunday morning, a little after that, I saw him in the audience, and he was much moved under the service we had, and I dismissed the people and went back into my study, and immediately there was a knock on my door, and in came this young man, and he said: "When is the next business meeting of our church?" "Why," I said, "next Wednesday night." He said: "Have my name taken off the church roll next Wednesday night." I said: "Why? You must give a reason. That sort of thing must be done carefully and wisely. The Scriptures so teach. What reason shall we give when we say your name is to be expunged from the church roll?" And he said: "Oh, I think I am not a Christian. I guess I am not, and the sermon this morning went like an arrow through me. I cannot be inconsistent, and stay in the church if I am not a Christian." I said: "No, if a man is not a Christian, he ought not to be enrolled as a member in the church. It is a tragedy for an unsaved man to be a member in the church, just as it is a tragedy for a saved man not to be a church member." He said: "Well, I guess you had better have my name taken off." I said: "Listen a minute," and I reviewed those six Sunday nights when he came to the services, and then recalled that sixth Sunday night, when he came down the aisle confessing Christ, and then the next Sunday morning, when he took his place in the church, and that night, when with folded hands across his breast, he was buried with Christ in beautiful baptism, and then, as we left that baptismal stream, how he said to me, with his face moist with tears: "Oh, sir, I am going to live for Christ!" And how, for a year thereafter, he was as regular at the church house as was the preacher, and then something bewitched him and caused him to drift away. He was softly sobbing, as I reviewed all this. He slowly said: "I have heard you, but I guess you had better have my name taken off." I said: "Come back at seven o'clock, thirty minutes before the church service, this evening, and we will talk again about how to proceed; but won't you do me a favor this afternoon?"

He said: "Certainly; what is it?" I said: "Take my Bible, or yours, and go across the city to old man So-and-so's room, and read the Bible to him." "What? Read the Bible after what I have said to you?" "Certainly." "What shall I read?" "Read the twenty-third Psalm; read the eighth chapter of Romans; read the fourteenth chapter of John, and then if he has not had enough, read any of the Psalms, any of the one hundred and fifty, and come back at seven o'clock, and we will talk about your getting out of the church." He went his way with a serious face, and I went my way to pray for him much. And in the evening I was in my study, and five minutes before seven, there was a knock on the door, and in he came, laughing and crying, both at the same time, and he said: "Don't say a word to anybody about having my name taken from the church roll—not a word." I said: "What has happened?" "Oh," he said, "I went out to the old man's house, and I read the Bible to him, several chapters, and we laughed and cried, and he said to me, presently: 'Young man, won't you kneel down and pray for me, that I may be patient and trustful clear on to the end? I never get to hear anybody pray,' he said, 'but the pastor, and he is so busy he does not come often. Won't you pray for me?'" And the young man said: "I got down and prayed, and the old man shouted." And the young man said: "I think I shouted, too. Don't say a word to anybody about my leaving the church." You see the lesson: Get busy! Keep busy for Jesus!

One more word, and we will go. If we are to know Jesus better, let us pay the price to know Him. Everything worth while costs. These business men and these professional men pay the price for their success. Paul said: "I paid the price." "What did you pay, Paul?" "I have suffered the loss of all things for Christ, and I count them but refuse, that I may win Christ."

Men and women, no matter what your experience, your battles, your doubts, your sins, your difficulties—no matter what, in the church or out—put Christ first, and days of the right hand of God and of heaven on earth will come to you, and will grow brighter and happier and better, even unto the perfect and eternal day.

THE CLOSING PRAYER.

And now, as we go, Lord Jesus, let every man and woman here feel out after God with all honesty, that thy will may be revealed to us and followed by us. And let every man and woman in this crowded throng, this midday hour, speak from the heart this high decision: "Jesus shall now be my Savior and Master, by my choice, my quiet, intelligent and final choice. Other refuge there is none. Other helpers are all incompetent and insufficient. Here I am, a dying man or woman, fast passing through time into a land eternal, in which land I am forever to be conscious, for Christ there and with Him, or against Him and away from Him." O Spirit Divine, bind thou thus every man and woman here, to Jesus to-day and forever!

And now, as you go, may you go to follow Him until the day is done, and forever to do His will. For His great name's sake. Amen.

XXI

NIGHT SERVICE, JUNE 22, 1917.

PRELIMINARY REMARKS.

The regret in my heart is very deep, as was indicated last night, that I cannot at this time tarry beyond the coming Sunday night, in these special daily meetings. I beg you to know that I should gladly tarry for several weeks, as per the greatly appreciated invitation of the two cherished pastors, Drs. Smith and Edwards, and their noble churches, the Broadway and College Avenue, whose guest I am. I would gladly tarry for these weeks, if I could. The meetings in our cities are all too brief. We must come more and more to plan in all our cities for extended meetings, for this holiest and most important business of all—that of winning humanity to our Lord. These greatly honored pastors—and, if they and you will forgive me for saying it in their presence, I do not know two more faithful and trustworthy men of God within all my acquaintance of His servants—these two men and their noble congregations have been good enough to want me to come again for an extended visit, and at the earliest possible date I shall be most happy, God willing, to come for such visit. It would be right now, as I have said, but for an engagement next week in a distant state, that I cannot in conscience put aside.

How grateful I am for the fellowship and blessings that my own heart has experienced, these brief days of this visit! The memories of these days, with all this fellowship with these men of God and these two churches, and with other men and women of God who have come from the several churches throughout the city, shall come to me again and again, like some sweet dream of the morning. What a high and blessed thing is the fellowship of God's people! One of the evidences that I have that I am a Christian is the daily deepening interest my heart feels for every person in this world who accepts Christ as his personal Savior, and the longing in my heart that everybody else may receive Him as Savior and Lord before it is too late.

I beg to be indulged one other introductory word, and that is a word of deep personal appreciation, and, indeed, of deep indebtedness upon the part of us all, to The Record and Star-Telegram, these two great daily newspapers, that have so generously kept the meetings before the people, inside the city and far beyond. Letters many have come to us, during these days, from the city and far beyond, that these extended and splendidly written reports of the meetings have carried a gracious blessing to those who could not come here. We are all deeply indebted to those who have written the reports, and to the forces that have seen to their setting up, and from my deepest heart I breathe a fervent prayer to God that He will bless these papers yet more and more, and crown them with constantly increasing usefulness.

WHY ARE YOU NOT A CHRISTIAN?

Text: "And now, Lord, what wait I for? My hope is in thee."—Psa. 39:7.

As I come to speak this evening, there are two emotions in my heart, as there always are, when I approach the closing hours of some special meetings. The first emotion is the emotion of gratitude. How grateful, surely, we all are, for any and every blessing God has sent the people. To His name be every dust of the glory! It is all by Him, if any blessing has come, and we trust that many have been blessed. The mails to-day have told of blessings that we had not dreamed of at all, of citizens for whom you have prayed who mean to take their places with the people of God. How grateful we are for the blessings which God has sent! How grateful for the inspiring fellowship! How grateful we are for every Christian who has been renewed in spiritual strength, for every drifting Christian who has been arrested from such course and turned back to the right course, and for every soul that has been saved! And I pause just there for a sentence: Let the saved man and woman and child hasten to take their places in the church, with the people of God. And let the older, maturer Christians, who know about these babes in Christ, be certain now to speak the word of counsel and comfort to these timid Christians. I was so rejoiced to hear that quite a group thus took their place, when the opportunity was given them last Sunday morning. Oh, I trust that many will take their places the coming Sunday with the people of God, and on and on for weeks and months and years, may they so come because of these meetings.

There is another deep emotion in my heart as we approach the closing hour of the meetings. That is the emotion of distinct sorrow. Not all who come to a meeting are saved. I think I never saw a meeting come to its close where all the people who came, who were not Christians, were saved, and because of such fact sorrow pungent comes into one's heart. That is, indeed, a solemn Scripture where the refrain is given: "The harvest is past, the summer is ended, and we are not saved." And especially are those two last words painfully ominous and suggestive—"not saved," "not saved." That means not ready to die, and even so, it means not ready to live, for one who is not a Christian is not ready for any world, to meet it like it ought to be met—not ready for time, not ready for eternity, not ready for death or life, not ready really to meet any experience properly, if one is not in right relations with God.

I wonder why the one before me, who has held out against Christ's mercy and call, has done so. I should like to ask you a question, which question shall be the theme of this evening's message: Why are you not a Christian? If I should ask if all in this presence are Chris-

tians, probably nearly all would stand or lift their hands
to answer yes. Thank God! But not all would either lift
their hand or stand. There are in this large presence
men and women and boys and girls who are not Christians, and, therefore, not saved. Now I should like to ask
you the pointed question: Why are you not a Christian?
That is the theme, and it is suggested by this statement
in the thirty-ninth Psalm: "And now, Lord, what wait
I for? My hope is in thee."

Here was a man who evidently had been waiting to do
his full duty for quite awhile. He was meditating, when
he uttered this sentence, which is our text. He looked
around him and saw how brief the earthly life is, and then
how unsatisfying it is, and he commented on those two
arresting facts about the earthly life. He said the earthly
life was like an handbreadth, it was so brief, it went away
so quickly, it was so uncertain. And we see that illustrated
every day. How suddenly life is terminated! A prayer
was offered from my deepest heart to-day when I noticed
that one of your city to-day went away suddenly into the
unseen land, and my prayer was for all his loved ones, that
God's grace might be sufficient for them all, and that we
might remember that in such an hour as we think not,
the messenger of death may come for us. How brief life
is! That is what this man mused and meditated upon, and
then penned it here for us in this Psalm. How brief life
is! How transitory! How fast passing! How uncertain!
Let us wisely lay such fact to heart.

A little while ago a business man in one of our cities
got up early to read the Dallas News, as was his wont,
and as he was reading it, before he had yet pulled on his
shoes, he said to his wife, who had not yet risen: "Wife,
listen to this," and he read the account of a business friend
in another community, who had the day before, while pulling on his shoes, gasped and gone away into eternity, and
the man called his wife's attention, as he read, and said:
"I do not expect to go like that." And in a few moments
more, as she noticed him, he gasped, and though she summoned the physician, who was near by, life had fled when
he came. A judge stood up in one of our communities,

some time ago, to give his charge to the jury, in an important case, and the people saw him tremble, and then sink down, and in a moment more his life had fled. A noble preacher stood in one of our Texas pulpits, a little while ago, preaching on the text: "Watch, for in such an hour as ye think not, the Son of man cometh," and as he was speaking upon that solemn text, summoning the people to remember it, he gasped before his audience, and life left him as he was there in his pulpit. Human life, how illusory! How transient! How fast passing! How uncertain! This man said all that in our text.

And then he said the things of human life cannot satisfy the human spirit. Whatever human life may achieve, whatever it brings, whatever it is, whatever it gives, it cannot satisfy the human spirit. Jesus told us that with the most striking illustration that was ever given. He stated a question in profit and loss, never equalled. Here it is: "What shall it profit a man, if he shall gain the whole world, and lose his own soul?" It is the greatest question in profit and loss ever stated for a human being. "Go," said Jesus to the man, "and get the whole world, all that it has of wealth, all that it has of honor, all that it is and has of pleasure, go get the whole world, and let it all be yours—what shall it profit you if you get it at the loss of your soul?"

Supreme things are often lost by inattention. When I was speaking in an Eastern city a little while ago, in a mission, for some days, they told me of the going away of one of the city's mighty financiers. His name is a household word in this country. He sent for one of the ministers, and when the minister went into his room and sat beside him and took his hand, the minister said to him: "What would you say to me?" And he said: "Oh, man of God, sing to me, and then pray for me!" "What shall I sing?" inquired the minister. "Sing that old song:

> Come, ye sinners, poor and needy,
> Weak and wretched, sick and sore,
> Jesus ready stands to save you,
> Full of pity, love and power.

Sing me that." Mighty financier though he was, his money could not avail him in that testing hour.

There is a little plant that grows in a certain section of the world, which plant is called the Nardoo plant. The naturalist tells us that the plant is delicious to the taste. Men and women may eat it and delight in it. It is exceedingly palatable to the taste. And yet, though they may eat and eat and eat of that plant, and rejoice in it like they would rejoice in the eating of some delicious berry, it is utterly impotent to suffice for hunger, for they tell us that it possesses no nutriment at all for the blood, and they tell us that we can eat of it, and eat of it, and yet die from starvation, even while we enjoy the eating of that delicious plant. That is a parable and picture of human life. Go, if you will, and drink from every spring, go and sip the aroma from every flower, go and run the whole gamut of human experience, and still will it be true:

> This world can never give
> The bliss for which we sigh.
> 'Tis not the whole of life to live,
> Nor all of death to die.

Just because God hath set eternity in the human heart, nothing temporal, therefore, can satisfy and fortify the human spirit.

Now, this man of our text found all this out, and then he turned away from it all, saying, in the language of our text: "And now, Lord, what wait I for? My hope is in thee." And that suggests for us the personal theme that I am to press upon you these passing minutes: Why do you wait to be for the Lord? Why are you not a Christian? I wish I knew. If I knew why that man there, or that woman, or that child, was not a Christian, I should come right to that excuse, and seek to bring to bear the Word of God right at that point, to counsel you and help you.

Let me surmise the different things that keep people waiting and away from Christ. Let me give several conjectures, and if I do not give the right conjecture in your case, yet I pray you to face the truth, the principle that shall be discussed, and put to your heart the piercing question: Why am I not a Christian? Let me ask you, first, is it this: Do you say: "I am not a Christian because I do not need to be?" Is there one in all this vast concourse

of people to-night who would say: "I am not a Christian
because I do not need to be?" Is there one that would
make such claim as that? I do not think so. I think I
need not pause at that point. I think not one in all this
place would make such plea, in the face of the Bible, which
says that every rational being needs God, needs His guidance and forgiveness and help. This Book tells us that
no human being has moral resources within himself or
herself sufficient to live the life he or she ought to live,
and to meet the destiny out yonder that awaits us. And
then you would not fly in the face of Christ, the Light
of the world, who came among men and told us all: "You
must be born again—every rational human being—you
must be born again, born of the Spirit of God, born from
above, or you cannot even see the kingdom of God." I
do not believe, therefore, that I have a single man or
woman here to-night, who would say: "I scout the teaching of the Bible and the teaching of Jesus, and I say I do
not need to be a Christian at all." Oh, no, not one in this
presence will say that. And so I leave that to pass to
another conjecture.

Why are you not a Christian? Do you answer: "Sir,
I am not one because I cannot believe?" Now, let us
pause right there, and let me ask you, when you say you
cannot believe: What is it you cannot believe? Who is
it that you cannot believe? There are two pungent questions, that all rational men and women must confront.
Here they are: "What think ye of Christ?" That is the
first one. And then the other one is: "What shall I do
with Jesus, who is called Christ?" We are every one
called to think upon Christ. Who is He? Where did He
come from? What did He come for? What did He do
for men? What does He propose to do? What can He
do? "What think ye of Christ?" And then that other big
question—inescapable, inexorable, inevitable question:
"What shall I do with Christ?" Now, we must face those
questions. So I ask you, what is there about Christ that
troubles you? Here is a great personality that crosses
every one of your paths. You must vote for Him or vote
against Him. You must accept Him or reject Him. You

must crown Him morally in your heart, or you must morally crucify Him. You must be for Him or against Him. You must be His friend or foe. Now, which ought it to be? Which is sane and reasonable, as you face that inescapable alternative? And I beg you to remember, as you face it, that the wisest and best of earth have followed Christ. The most remarkable testimony that I have heard given to Christ Jesus in a long time was given by our nation's chief executive, Woodrow Wilson, to-night the first citizen in the whole civilized world. The greatest tribute that I have heard paid to simple faith in Christ, in years and years, I heard him give a little while ago, as he stood before a group of some two thousand of the nation's thoughtful men. "Oh, men, my brothers," the greatly gifted President said, in effect, "long ago I stayed my all on Christ, and I could not get on without Him and His Book, and I would not be willing to try." The wisest and the keenest and the strongest of earth have tried Jesus, and they have found out that He helps. They have found out that He saves. They have found out that He reenforces. And not only the great and strong and intellectual and keen-minded have thus tried Jesus and found Him true, but those modest ones who are near and dear to you and me. A little mother, who prays, never heard of outside of her village or community, maybe, but to you the sweetest and dearest life that earth ever had, tells her child, or the little wife tells her husband, how dear Christ is to those who receive Him as a personal Savior.

I was summoned to a dinner in a beautiful home some time ago, when the home was just opened, one of the most beautiful I have seen, and I said to the wife and mother in that home: "How happy you must be in such a home!" And she said: "Quite true, sir," and then she went on to say: "But, oh, sir, I would be gladly willing to live on bread and water, if only my husband would come with me and be for Christ, and walk beside me, and help me by his example and precept to bring the children in the heavenly way." Those that are nearest and dearest of all to you, come to you and tell you that Christ helps them, and we know it is true. So you will not be afraid

to venture your all on Christ. He is tested, experimental
ly; He is tried, experimentally, and we find Him true.

I have heard Booth Tucker give his testimony to the
power of God's grace. He was and is a mighty man of
God, as was his heroic father-in-law, General Booth, both
working with the people down in the trenches of life, with
the people who are down to hard pan. I have been glad
to stand beside them both, for the saving of the very poor
in one of our cities. I think nothing of that spirit that
seeks to make class distinctions, either in the realm of
church or of state. I think nothing of that cheap and
demagogic cry that would make such class distinctions.
It is a piece of cheap and wicked demagogism for which
right-thinking men will have no respect. The right-thinking man is as much concerned for the best welfare of the
man in the deepest depths of sin and poverty and squalor
and wretchedness, as he is for the President of our whole,
vast country. I heard Booth Tucker say that he preached
in Chicago, one day, and out from the throng a burdened
toiler came and said to him, before all the audience: "Booth
Tucker, you can talk like that about how Christ is dear
to you, and helps you; but if your wife was dead, as is
my wife, and you had some babies crying for their mother
who would never come back, you could not say what you
are saying." I was with Booth Tucker, as I have indicated to you, and just a few days after our separation, he
lost his beautiful and nobly-gifted wife in a railway wreck,
and the body was brought to Chicago, where Booth Tucker
had thus preached, and where the toiling man had stood
up and said: "You could not say that, if you were in my
condition." The body was brought to Chicago and carried
to the Salvation Army barracks. I pause to say that when
I think of such valiant workers, I want to stand with my
head uncovered, when I see how bravely they are toiling
to make better the world. And great old General Booth,
I always wanted to stand in his presence with my head
uncovered, because he so nobly served humanity. The
body of Booth Tucker's wife, as I have just said, was
brought to Chicago, and was carried to the Salvation Army
barracks, for the funeral service. That same toiling man

was present, who some days before had said what I have told you. And there was the casket in the chapel of the Salvation Army people of Chicago, and Booth Tucker at last stood up, after others had conducted the funeral service, and he stood there by the casket, and looked down into the face of the silent wife and mother, and said: "The other day when I was here, a man said I could not say Christ was sufficient, if my wife were dead, and my children were crying for their mother. If that man is here, I tell him that Christ is sufficient. My heart is all crushed. My heart is all bleeding. My heart is all broken. But there is a song in my heart, and Christ put it there, and if that man is here, I tell him that, though my wife is gone and my children are motherless, Christ speaks comfort to me to-day." That man was there, and down the aisle he came, and fell down beside the casket, and said: "Verily, if Christ can help us like that, I will surrender to Him," and he was saved.

Oh, my brother men, Jesus can be tested! If you ask me if I have tested Him, God help me, I tell you yes. Better than I know anything in the wide world do I know that Christ helps men, for when I was on life's wild sea, without chart or compass or guide or rudder, and no human voice could suffice me, and the storm drove hither and thither my little bark, Christ said: "Come to me, man, and give your case to me, and I will help you, and you shall know it." I found it was so. You can try Him and prove Him, for yourself. Oh, try Him to-day!

Why are you not a Christian? Do you say: "I am not a Christian because I have too much to give up?" Pray, tell me now, what have you to give up? Jesus, my Savior, and your offered Savior, does not want you to give up anything except that which is wrong, except that which hurts you, except that which poisons you, except that which, if you do not repent of it, shall kill you. Jesus wants you to give up only that which is wrong and blighting and deadly—just that. Suppose a man had two stores, and one of those stores was a tiny confectionery store, worth one hundred dollars, and the other store was a vast department store, worth a million dollars; and suppose the man devoted nearly all of his time and thought to that little one-hundred-dollar store, and gave practically no time nor thought to that million-dollar store. You would say: "Why, that is unspeakable." And yet, oh, soul, Jesus comes to you down here in this little space called time—thirty years, maybe, or twenty-five, or forty, or sixty, or mayhap seventy, but not many of us will live that long—very few of us will reach that period—Jesus comes to us, saying: "Don't put all your thought on that little tiny store. Give the great store the best attention. You are made to live forever. Out yonder, beyond time and the grave, is a conscious world forever. Build for that, as well as think wisely for this brief space here and now."

Why are you not a Christian? Do you say: "I am not a Christian because I am waiting until I get good enough to become one?" Where, pray, will you get your goodness? If you may get your goodness by your own doings, then Jesus need not have come, nor would He have come. Where, pray, will you get your, goodness? Jesus did not come to save good people. He himself tells us: "I came not to call the righteous, but sinners, to repentance." Thank God! If you are a sinner, you are eligible to be saved. They are now daily asking who is eligible for our country's arms. If you are a sinner, thank God, you are eligible to be saved, for Jesus came to seek and to save the lost. You cannot save yourself. You cannot work up your own goodness. You must be born again, and by the power of God, and so your waiting, pleading that you are waiting until you get good enough to come, is utterly specious and futile and ruinous.

Do you say: "Well, that is not it," as I ask you, Why are you not a Christian? But do you say: "I am waiting until I get strength to live the Christian life?" Then I will pass the question to you and ask you, Where will you get that strength? Jesus not only saves us, but He helps us after He does save us. Paul, that chief apostle, said: "I know whom I have believed, and am persuaded that He is able to keep that which I have committed unto Him against that day." Paul did not say that he himself was able to keep himself—never once. Paul said: "By the grace of God

I am what I am." He said: "By grace are ye saved,
through faith, and that not of yourselves—it is the gift of
God; not of works, lest any man should boast." Jesus
himself says: "You surrender to me and I will forgive and
save you. And then I will company with you. I will teach
you. I will guide you. I will fortify you. I will empower
you. I will strengthen and keep you." That is living the
Christian life. Jesus not only starts with us, but He com-
panies with us also as we go on the journey. Oh, I would
not risk my getting to heaven on the best five minutes or
five seconds that I ever lived in my own goodness and
strength. No, no. My hope is in a surer place than that.

> My hope is built on nothing less
> Than Jesus' blood and righteousness.
> I dare not trust the sweetest frame,
> But wholly lean on Jesus' name.
> On Christ the Solid Rock, I stand;
> All other ground is sinking sand.

I do not risk my salvation in the church, or in beautiful
baptism, or in the Lord's Supper, or in all the impressive
forms of religion. They all cannot save one soul. Christ
must save. Oh, you must give up to Him! Won't you do
that before it is too late?

I come to ask you again, Why are you not a Christian?
Do you answer me: "I am not a Christian because I look
around me and see professed Christians, and their lives are
faulty and ragged and defective, and I will therefore pass
it by?" What shall I say about that? Is it true that our
lives are ragged and defective and faulty? God forgive us,
yes. I do not know any perfect people. O man, we do
not plead ourselves. We plead Christ Jesus the Lord. He
is the world's hope, and He is its righteousness. And now,
come. When you have pleaded weakness in the Christians
round you, and faultiness and defects and raggedness, Jesus
looks at you, saying: "What has that got to do with your
soul, and what has that got to do with your personal
responsibility to me?" Jesus says to you: "Therefore, thou
art inexcusable, oh, man, whosoever thou art that judgest;
for wherein thou judgest another, thou condemnest thyself." You have made your case worse. Come away, I pray
you, from that faulty excuse.

Why are you not a Christian? Do you answer me: "Sir, I am not a Christian because I am waiting for the right kind of feeling?" Pray tell me, what do you know about the right kind of feeling in the matter of the Christian life? Can't you leave that with Christ? May I tell you that I prayed for feeling for many a long day, and at last, calm as I am right now, and calm as you are now, as you listen to the preacher to-night with such interest and deference, I said: "Lord, with or without feeling, come what may, I will surrender myself, for time and eternity, this very minute, to Christ." He took care of the feeling afterward. That is His part. Never one time does He say to you: "If you feel so and so, you shall be saved." Never once. But He says: "If you will believe on Christ, He will save you." He will save you whatever your feelings. He will save you in spite of your feelings. He will save you and give you the feelings you ought to have—the feelings He wants you to have. You are to trust Him, and He is to save you. Isn't it plain?

Why are you not a Christian? Do you say: "I have waited because I could not see through it, I could not understand it?" I pray you, come away from that, for you never can understand it—never. No man is wise enough to philosophize through the mystery of what it is to be born again. Why, you cannot even understand a great human life. A great human life has about him mystery, and the more you see him the more mysterious and wonderful he is. You cannot understand the mystery of a little, laughing baby's life. There is mystery in all life, clear above your comprehension. That strong man, Nicodemus, came to Jesus, and Jesus told him: "You must be born again." He said: "How can I be born again?" And Jesus said: "The how belongs to God. Yours it is to trust Christ." Jesus said: "The wind bloweth where it pleaseth, and thou hearest the sound thereof, but thou canst not tell whence it cometh, nor whither it goeth. So is every one that is born of the Spirit of God." Yours it is to trust, and His it is to save. There are mysteries in coming to Christ, but ten thousand times greater if we reject Him and go into the darkness. When

Frohman was going down with the Titanic he called it "the Great Adventure."

Why are you not a Christian? Do you say: "Well, I am waiting for somebody else to go first?" Oh, we are back again to daily, human, personal, responsible influence. Wife, art thou here this evening without Christ? If I were in your place, I would come, if necessary, through flame and flood. I would not wait for that strong man who holds back. Who knows but that thou must by thine own example win Him to Christ? I would come, oh, friend, I would come! Who knows but that sheltering behind you is somebody that will act when you act?

I was preaching in a distant city some time ago, and one night I made a call like this, at the close of the sermon: "I wish all the men and women and boys and girls who wish to be Christians, would walk down to these three front pews, while the people sing, and then when they have thus come forward, I have two or three things to say to them in two or three or four minutes, before we pray." Numbers came to those pews, quietly and thoughtfully. Our appeal should always be to men's judgment and conscience. Christ's religion does not need any other kind of an appeal. They came, and I noticed in the group, a girl of some fourteen or fifteen years, beautiful, and deeply serious. She kept looking back, oh, so pitifully she kept looking back. She had come away from the side of a man, who, as we learned later, was her father. She kept looking back, and I said: "I think now that we are ready in one moment to pray. I will wait just one moment, to see if somebody else won't come, before we pray, and sit on these pews with us, thereby saying: 'I want to be a Christian.'" And this girl could wait no longer, and she went back down the aisle and sat down beside him, where she left him some minutes ago. I waited. It was all rather striking. I waited to see the outcome, not knowing what it meant, but they told me later what it meant. She put her arms about her father's neck, and one sitting just behind them, heard her say: "Papa, you and I told mother we would meet her in the better world, when she left us last year, and I want to keep the promise. I want us to settle it, papa. I went forward that they might pray for me. I thought you would come. I want us to settle it to-night. Oh, papa, I want us to keep our promise to mother, but I could not stay down there without you. I have stayed with you since mother died, and we have been together. I have never left you except when I had to, papa. I cannot now go without you. I want to surrender to Christ to-night, but I cannot go without you, and I have come back to ask you if you won't go with me, and kneel down with me, and with me surrender to Christ?" And the strong, big, trembling man—and it turned out that he was one of the judges of one of the high courts of his state—said: "Little girl, papa will go with you. You are right." And together they came, and knelt together, and when the prayer was over, and I said: "Who has said yes to Christ?" he stretched out his hand and said: "I have." And the little girl said: "So have I, papa!" and she kissed him again and again. What if he had not come? Oh, soul, wait not for somebody else, because somebody else may be influenced by you!

Why are you not a Christian? I think you sum it up, some of you—ofttimes men sum it up and say: "Well, I am not a Christian, but I tell you, sir, I expect to be by and by. I intend to be to-morrow. I will be a little later." I suppose that is the excuse oftenest given by the human heart for not being on Christ's side. Men will grant their duty, and their need, and their danger, and men will confess their interest and their desire. Men will go on and declare their purpose some time to stop and surrender to Christ, but then they wait. They listen to a subtle voice: "A little later, by and by, to-morrow, not yet," and Satan's work is done, and the soul is enamored of the deceitful way and goes down to destruction and doom and loss.

That old-time ruler of Thebes, whose name was Archias, one night was going to a house of feasting and revelry, and one of his trusted servants intercepted him on the road, and thrust into his hands a note, and said to him: "Oh, Prince, do not go to that place—do not go." The servant said: "Serious matters await you, if you go. That note explains it. Read it. Do not go." And the prince said, as he thrust the note into his pocket: "Serious matters to-morrow, but none to-night. Feasting to-night, revelry to-night, music to-night, laughter to-night, a good time to-night. Serious matters to-morrow!" And he refused to read the note. Oh, if he had only read the note! The note, penned by the faithful servant, told him of a plot that very night to take his life, but because he ignored the warning he went right into the trap, and that night his life was taken away.

My fellow sinner—and you are such, for I am a sinner saved by grace—my fellow sinner, let not Satan cheat you and beguile you and trick you at that point, that you have time enough. When all is at stake, your soul at stake, your life at stake, your influence at stake, your happiness at stake, your usefulness at stake, your deep joy at stake, surely you have not time enough.

Now, this man of our text faced it, and turned away and said: "I have not time enough." And then what did he say? He said what I am coming to ask you to say. He said: "Lord, what do I keep up this waiting for?" And then he turned face about and said: "Lord, my hope from this hour shall forever be in thee." That is the prayer I pray for you. That is the exhortation I press upon you. "Lord, what do I wait for? I desist from it. My hope from this Friday night shall be in the Lord." Mark now his hope; mark where it was: "My hope shall be, oh, Lord, in thee." Oh, I pray you, my fellow-men, do not be beguiled at this vital point. Salvation is by a person, and that person is the Lord Jesus Christ. Salvation is not by a church, not by an ordinance, not by a sacrament, not by a ceremony, not by a creed, not even by the Bible. The Bible is just the signboard saying to us: "This is the way." Salvation is by Christ, and by none other. "Neither is there salvation in any other: for there is none other name under heaven given among men, whereby we must be saved." Jesus himself calls to us, saying: "I am the way, the truth and the life. No man cometh unto the Father but by me." Jesus calls to us, saying: "I am the door. By me if any man enter in, he shall be saved, but he that climbeth up some other way is a thief and a robber." Salvation is by

Christ, the person, and you are to just surrender to Him, that He may, by your choice, become your Savior.

Oh, I come to ask if you won't, like this man of our text, put away your waiting, and say: "I am coming right now to Him. Parent as I am, God help me, I am coming now, for my own sake and my family's." Business men, or toiling men, or professional men, whoever the man or woman or child may be, not a Christian, I am coming to press upon you the appeal: Won't you do as did this man in the text? Won't you say: "Lord, I stop my waiting; I am coming to thee?" What if you should not come? What if you should wait one day, one hour, one second, too long, too late, to come? What if you should refuse and defer one second too much to come? Oh, I am asking if you won't be done with your waiting now and come?

What arguments shall I marshal to help you? What motives shall I summon for you to consider? I pray you, think of your duty, and think of your need, and think of your danger, and think of your influence, and think of your happiness, and think of your usefulness. Great arguments, mighty motives, ought to have a large place in human thought and action, and by them all I am praying you to end your waiting. Many come up to this point and take all but this last step. They feel. They see. They hear. They know. They concede. They desire. They say: "Yes, that is right. A little later I will yield." They wait a little later. They come right up to heaven's gate, and they turn away unsaved.

Yonder in the Northwest a young couple went to build their fortune, and they went out several miles from the village and took up land, and there had their little cottage, and began their work. One morning the young husband went away to the village to get supplies for the little home. He was to return that evening, but after he had been gone some time, the snow began to fall, and it fell thick and fast and piled up deeper and deeper. The day died down to night, and he had not returned, and the little wife's heart was in her throat, so anxious was she; and all night long she stood there in the cabin door, and swung the lantern, if haply he came within its radius of light he might be pointed the way home. Several feet of snow had fallen, and the morning came. The night was past, and he had not come, and with a very agony of anxiety she started toward the village. Though the snow was some three or four feet deep, she started through it, and down yonder, just a few hundred yards from the little cottage, she stumbled on his body, the body of her own husband, frozen and cold. Back he had come, in sight of his own cabin—and was dead in sight of home!

Oh soul, that is a picture of what sometimes happens in gospel meetings. Men and women and children come and hear and feel and desire, but wait, through Satan's enticement. They come within sight of home and heaven and eternal life, and wait too long. End your waiting, I pray you, and come this night, and make your surrender to Christ, this very night and this very hour. He does the saving, but you are to consent, you are to decide. Your difficulties, your sins, your doubts, your temptations, do you say they are terrible? Make them a million times worse in fancy, than they really are, and yet I tell you that Christ will save you in one second, if you will honestly surrender your case to Him.

To-night will you make that surrender? These hundreds of Christian men and women want you to make that surrender to Christ, and they will join me in prayer for God to guide and help you. I will show you that they wish it. Every Christian in this presence who takes up the preacher's appeal, and would bind it on the hearts of all these that are wrong with God; and, further, every Christian that will join the preacher in a prayer for these that are waiting and staying away from God, in a prayer that they will stop their waiting and come in time; every Christian that says: "That is my wish. That is my heart. That shall be my prayer," will lift high the hand. Do you not see? I think it is a sight to stir the angels' hearts. That is sufficient. Come, now, tell me, every soul that says: "I want to be right with God, in God's own time and way." I will not ask you to lift your hand, for many did last night. I will ask you, if you are ready right now, to come to me and say: "My waiting is done." Let every head be bowed, while we pray God to guide us.

THE CLOSING PRAYER.

Great is our joy, O thou great Savior, that so many in this great press are friends of Christ and His followers. We would come now to thee with just one prayer. It is that every one who is improperly waiting, who is away from God, away from right, away from duty, away from safety, away from the right use of influence and the right expenditure of life, man, woman or child, may now end the waiting, and come to Christ; that the duty-neglecting Christian may say: "I have neglected duty long enough. I will renew my vows this night with Christ;" that the backslidden Christian may say: "I will renew my vows. I will come back to the Lord. I will come back before the people. I have wandered before them, and they may know about it, but whether they know or not, God knows it all, and I will come back, and renew my vows to-night with Him. To-night I will re-surrender my poor self to the forgiving Savior." Oh, we pray for such. And we pray for the men and for the women, the parents, the young men or women, the boys or girls, who are waiting, and the soul is more endangered every minute, and Satan gets in his work more terribly every minute. Oh, we pray that the one here waiting to-night shall say: "I stop now. Since Jesus saves, since He does it all, and since He bids me not wait until to-morrow, since He tells me, 'To-day is the day of salvation,' since He tells me if I will just commit my case to Him, no matter what the case is, no matter how bad, how perplexing, no matter how doubting, how fearing, how puzzled, how sinful, how tempted, if I will just turn my case over to Him, He, the great Soul Physician, will do for me what He knows needs to be done, I will trust Him now, I will make my surrender to Him now. I will end my waiting, Lord Jesus, and I will surrender to thee right now." God grant it by the power of His grace and Spirit. For Christ's sake. Amen.

The people will sing that simple song: "Jesus Is Calling." "Jesus is tenderly calling thee home, calling to-day, calling to-day." Sing that song, and while we sing it, let every one tarry these closing moments. Now, here is my hand, and with it goes my heart's Godspeed to you who wish to be right with God. I implore you to end your waiting. Does the backslidden Christian here, and the duty-neglecting Christian, say: "I have had enough of my waiting, and I will renew my vows with Christ right now, this Friday night." Does another say: "No, that is not my case. I am a disciple of Jesus secretly, and never made it known." Aren't you ready now to say: "To-night, I will stop my waiting, and be openly for Christ. I will to-night announce that I have already surrendered to the Savior." Does the man or woman or child say, "Not yet have you stated my case, but this is my case: To-night, I am ready, I am willing, that Christ shall be my Savior. To-night, I decide for Him. To-night, I cease my delay, to-night I end my waiting, to-night I surrender to Christ, that He may take me and do for me what He knows needs to be done." Come, take my hand. The chord is given us, and we will sing.

(The first and second stanzas were sung—while numbers came forward.)

Did you ever before see the sight we have just seen? I never saw it before, where a son brought his own mother to Christ. Never have I seen that sight before—and I have seen many confess Christ—where a young man came with his mother, and like a little child she tells us: "I will surrender to Christ, and I am going with you"—brought by her own son! Oh, you mothers who are not on Christ's side, end your waiting to-night, and come with the boy or without him. The probability is that you will have to bring the boy and the girl. Was there ever another next to the Lord so helpful to a human soul, as is a mother? Oh, ye mothers, wandering, waiting, in wrong positions, come to-night and settle it with your surrender to Christ. And ye fathers and brothers, men of affairs, men of toil and work, what you need above all else is Christ, and if you should have all else, you would yet be utterly poverty-stricken without Him. And the boys ought to come, and the girls, even others who are here to-night. God's breath from heaven is over you, as it was last night so sensibly. Oh, men and women and boys and girls, as they continue to sing, I pray you to say: "I am altogether persuaded to be for Christ." Jesus said to one who once came near Him: "Thou art not far from the kingdom of God"—not far from the kingdom of God, but that is not enough. You want to be in His kingdom. To be near is not enough. Almost is not enough. To be in sight is not enough. Hard by the gate is not enough. To be interested and serious and trembling, and desirous is not enough. Satan does not care if you tremble and are tearful and are serious, if only you will say: "I will wait." That is his masterpiece to destroy you. Do you say: "I will not linger and listen to him. I will not farther follow Satan. God help me, I will come to-night, and I will stop my waiting, and I will give up to Jesus Christ." Come then, and take my hand.

(The third and fourth stanzas were sung and others came forward.)

You may go in a few moments. I have a very earnest word to say to these Christians. It is this: Put your utmost of prayer and personal effort into these two waiting days, to the end that God may save multitudes about you.

Put your utmost into the noonday service to-morrow at the Chamber of Commerce auditorium, the mass meeting at three-thirty Sunday afternoon in the same place, and the meeting again here Sunday night. Oh, what need for prayer! You will pray much, I trust, by groups and alone. And then what need that you shall speak to the people who are without God, trying to help them. We have only one concern in these meetings, and that is to do the people good— eternal good.

And I have this earnest word again to say to these men and women who have decided for Jesus through these days and nights: Take your place promptly with God's people. Talk with some experienced Christian, if you are puzzled about any spiritual matter. Above all, talk with God, and set your heart to live that beautiful, obedient, Christian life, so glorious for us to live.

THE BENEDICTION.

And now, we go, with gratitude on our lips, welling up from our hearts, O God, for thy manifest blessing upon the people here. How we bless thee for the influence of thy Spirit upon the people, and for the decisions of these who come, saying: "Our waiting stops. Our surrender is given to Christ Jesus." O, may they all go to take their places promptly in Christ's army, to be His soldiers, living the Christian life in the noblest way possible. May they be cheered and counseled from thyself and from their fellow Christians, even according to their need. O Lord Jesus, send out with thine own passion in their hearts, the whole multitude of Christians, to speak to the children and to sons and daughters, to speak to friends, to loved ones, to neighbors, to all the people, passing nobody by, to speak the right word, the God-directed word, about personal religion, and to speak it in the hours just before us. May we wait upon God as never before, and call down by prayer and worthy effort God's gracious mercies upon this fair city!

And as the people go now, may the blessing of the triune God be granted to all and each, to abide with you forever. Amen.

XXII

NOON SERVICE, JUNE 23, 1917.

PRELIMINARY REMARKS.

For just a moment, I would follow up the announcement made concerning the men's meeting in this auditorium at 3:30 o'clock, Sunday afternoon. Concerning it, I would make these two or three suggestions: Let every Christian man take this occasion to speak to his neighbor and friend and acquaintance, wherever he is in the community, and ask such man to come with him to the services. Oh, how the world waits for personal attention. There can be no substitutes for personal attention. The world is dying from the lack of that personal touch. These Christian men will bethink themselves, and call to mind now and through the day, certain men throughout the city who, they have reason to think, are not Christians, because they are not aligned publicly with God's people. These all should be approached in the right way. Not one should be passed by. You think about them now. There are men in the stores, in the banks, in the shops, in the mills, and in the factories, everywhere. Take this occasion to help them. My fellow-men, if the religion of Jesus Christ be worth a button, it is worth dying for, and surely it is worth living for. You will now see about helping your brother men to the last limit of your power. And then these women, who will not meet with us in that afternoon meeting for men, will singly, or in little groups, I trust, see how by prayer they can help the meeting. Is there any other way

whereby we may more powerfully help the world than
by prayer? What a suggestive expression that is in the
Bible: "Ye also helping together by prayer!" What a
marvelous force is prayer! Now, these women can help
in that way, yonder in their homes, and all of us can help
as we get ready for such service.

Very deeply has my heart been touched from day to
day, in these brief noonday services, that large throngs
of men and women have been minded to come at such
hour, for such services. And as I have seen you come in,
and have searched your faces, and have read therein the
lines of burden and struggle and questioning and wistful
yearning, as best I could, I have cast myself upon God,
and besought Him to help me to help you. That longing
is in my heart this Saturday noon, as you come to this
last midday service.

Life is so stressful, so crowded with work and battle
and burden that we need all along to fortify ourselves with
the promises from God's Book. One does not even know
how to pray like he ought, if he cannot take these promises, and fill his mouth with them, and plead them before
God, saying, as did one of old: "Do as thou hast said."
These promises are designed to inspirit us, and rest us,
and fortify us. We do not make enough of these promises
from God's Book. They fit every condition in human
life. If we will only find it, there is no condition that is not
met by a promise out of God's Book, and these promises
give us a grip on spiritual realities. I summon you to-day,
my busy men and women, to search out these promises
from God's Book constantly, and appropriate them, and
make them your own, and plead them before Him. One
promise from God's Book has, times without count, anchored a human soul and kept it going in the right way.

A PROMISE FOR EVERY DAY.

Text: "As thy days, so shall thy strength be."—Deut. 33:25.

I wonder if there is any other promise in the Bible that
has more frequently proved itself a balm to men and
women than this promise that now I read to you, as the
text for to-day: "As thy days, so shall thy strength be."

This morning, for a little while, let us ponder that

promise. How heartening it is, in view of our weakness! Over against our weakness, there in that promise is the promise of strength. "As thy days, so shall thy strength be." How heartening that promise is, in the face of our weakness! And our weakness will be discovered to us, in any one of many directions that we may take. Take our own duty, whatever it is—and who has not cried out time and again, as he faced his duty and grappled with it—be he preacher, or parent, or professional man, or other toiler, whoever he is—who has not cried out, saying, "Who is sufficient for these things? How can I get through this task?" Now, over against our sense of weakness and weariness and faintness, here is this promise of strength.

This promise comes to hearten us as we look at the progress that we are making in the better life. Whenever we turn the glasses within, and search ourselves thoroughly, how pained we always are at the meager progress that we are making in the better life. We look around us, and see certain personalities who are growing and expanding and triumphing in a remarkable way in the Christian life, as it seems to us, and then we look at ourselves and behold how little the progress, how meager the growth, how few the attainments that we have made and are making in the Christian life.

But especially does this promise come to hearten us and re-enforce us, when we look at our besetting sin or sins in life's daily battle. Every man has his besetment, and every woman hers. The Bible speaks of the sin which "doth so easily beset us." Every one has his besetment, to enslave him, to handicap him, to hinder him. Now, a promise like this is of great worth to us, as we grapple with our besetment, whatever it is. With one person it is one thing, and with another it is another thing, but every one has his besetment, every one his handicap, his weakness, and we need strength to set over against it, and here it is promised us in this heartening promise. One man's besetment is the tendency all along in human life to be discouraged. Oh, what a pitiful thing in human life to feel keenly the pressure and the weight of depressing discouragement! Every man should set himself against

it, and every man should be an encourager. A discourager
hurts human life. Every man is to be an encourager,
positive and constructive in his daily battle and message.

And then here is another, whose culpable weakness, it
may be, is envy. Oh, what a terrible besetment that is!
The Bible asks the question: "Who can stand before
envy?" It is as rottenness in one's bones. Envy is incip-
ient murder. Envy eats up every noble thing. If a man
finds envy anywhere in his life, he should pluck it out
and fling it away, as he would fling away the deadly cobra,
seeking to coil about his heart.

Another man's handicap is the temptation to uncharita-
bleness. What a serious handicap that is! In His fundamentally revolutionary Sermon on the Mount, Jesus uses
the searching words: "Judge not, that ye be not judged.
For with what judgment ye judge, ye shall be judged; and
with what measure ye mete, it shall be measured to you
again." And then He asks a biting question: "Why beholdest thou the mote that is in thy brother's eye"—a
mote is a tiny splinter — "Why beholdest thou the tiny
little splinter in thy brother's eye, but considerest not the
beam"—that is, the big log—"considerest not the big log
that is in thine own eye? Thou hypocrite," said Jesus,
"first cast out the beam"—the big log—"out of thine own
eye; and then shalt thou see clearly to cast out the mote"—
the splinter—"out of thy brother's eye." Oh, if you have
the tendency to harshness, to censoriousness, to uncharita-
bleness, put it utterly away, it is so disastrous in its blinding and blighting effect on life!

But does some one say: "No, that is not my trouble?"
Does he or she say: "My trouble is the trouble of anxiety—eating, consuming, apprehensive, corroding anxiety?"
I suppose that comes to us all more or less—the trouble
of anxiety. So Jesus speaks in His Sermon on the Mount:
"Be not anxious about what you shall eat, or what you
shall drink, or what you shall wear." Be not anxious!
Jesus there teaches us to put anxiety away, and He gives
us the reasons why we should put it away, why we should
refuse to be enslaved and dispirited by corroding, consuming anxiety. He tells us, in the first place, that anxiety is

utterly needless. "Which of you by being anxious can add one cubit to his stature?" Anxiety won't help us at all, says Jesus. And He goes on and tells us that God cares for us, and therefore we are to refuse to be swept with anxiety. "If He clothes the grass of the field, which to-day is, and to-morrow is cast into the oven, shall He not much more clothe you, oh, ye of little faith?" If He feeds the birds, if He paints the lilies, will He not care for you? And so He bids us, by His own fatherly care, not to let anxiety eat like a destroying microbe into our life. And then He goes on to tell us that such anxiety is heathenish. "After all these things"—something to eat, and something to wear, the temporalities—"after all these things," says Jesus, "do the Gentiles seek," and you are to do better than they. And then He goes on to tell us that anxiety only adds to what is coming to-morrow. "Sufficient unto the day is the evil thereof." For all these reasons He bids us to put anxiety utterly out of our lives. Well did the immortal B. H. Carroll, our incomparable Texas preacher, say that there are two things that nobody should worry about. First, he said we should not worry about what we can help. Let us help it, if it can be helped. And next, we should not worry about what we cannot help. If we cannot help it, worry will not improve it at all. Those two things, what we can help and what we cannot help, cover the whole case. Now, if we can help it, let us help it, and if we cannot help it, let us cast it all on God, and say: "Lord, lead thou me on, and I will follow where thou leadest," and leave it just there.

Let me ask you to look a little more closely at this gracious promise, with which I would fain fortify your heart and mine this day. "As thy days, so shall be thy strength." Whose is the promise? It is the promise, in essence, which God makes to His friends, times without number, here in this Holy Book, by direct statement, and by implication. That is the unending promise of God all through His Book. Now, since that is God's promise, His pledge, that pledge is well-grounded. There are promises human. They are often frail; they often come short; they often break. But this is God's promise, and when we

know it is God's promise we can rest upon it with all
the tranquility and peace with which a child lies back upon
its mother's heart. Yes, it is God's promise. He comes
to us, saying: "You cling to me, and follow as I point
the way, and your strength shall be meted out to you.
Whatever your doubt or duty or difficulty, whatever your
sin or sorrow or suffering, so shall be your strength, if
you will only cling to me."

But I beg you to notice that there is a limitation in
that promise. Many of God's promises have limitations,
and all this is to be looked at carefully. This promise
here has a limitation. Notice it: "As thy days, so shall
be thy strength." "As thy days"—you see the limitation.
"As thy days, so shall be thy strength." Nowhere does
God say: "As thy desires," because many a time our desires are improper. Many a time our desires are selfish.
Many a time, if our desires were granted us, we would be
far worse off. There is such a thing as withheld answers
to prayers, just because God loves us too much to send
an answer to some prayers we offer. If your little child
comes into the room in the morning, before the tasks of
the day begin, perhaps as the father is at the mirror shav-
ing, and the little thing reaches up and clutches for the
razor, and insists that the father shall give it the razor,
the father holds it back and will not let the child have
that deadly thing in its little hands. The father knows that
the child will harm itself with that instrument, and he
loves the child too well to grant the child its desire. And
many a time you and I cry in our hearts for something
which we so much wish, and God sometimes withholds the
answer, for if we got the thing that we pant for and yearn
for, it would be a razor with which we would cut ourselves,
and so God knows best.

That is a remarkable picture of Paul, with his thorn in
the flesh. No one knows what Paul's thorn in the flesh was,
but it was something very serious. Paul was not a cry-baby.
If ever there was a manly preacher, who left his impress
in the sands of earth, it was the Apostle Paul. Sincere
was he as the sunlight; genuine to the very depths of his
heart, as every man of God ought ever to be. The funda-

mental virtue in life is truth and integrity and sincerity. If a man be not sincere, his life is a ghastly lie. This man Paul was the incarnation of sincerity and integrity and truth. But he said: "There was given me a thorn in the flesh, the messenger of Satan, sent to buffet me." He said: "I imitated my Lord in the garden, who poured out His prayer to His Father three times. So did I pour out my prayer," said Paul, "beseeching the Lord thrice that He would take that thorn out of my flesh." And the Lord answered him: "I will do nothing of the sort, Paul. I am going to leave that thorn right there in your life." Mark you, it was a "messenger of Satan, sent to buffet him." Oh, how it goaded him, and harassed him, and tortured him, and burned him! But God left it there, even though Paul prayed three times that God would take it away. And wouldn't you have rejoiced to have heard Paul pray? Evidently Paul was at his best when he was on his knees. Wouldn't you have been glad to have heard Paul pray that prayer to God three times: "Take this thorn away?" God did not take it away, but He gave His gracious re-enforcement: "Paul, my grace is sufficient for thee." And after that, Paul went his way singing: "Most gladly, therefore, will I rather glory in my infirmity, for when I am weak, then I am strong. The power of Christ," said Paul, "rests upon me because of this thorn, as I never would have had it if the thorn had not come." Now, doesn't that explain very much? God comes with His fortifying power to help his child, whatever the need, whatever the day.

Let us look into this promise a moment further: "As thy days, so shall be thy strength." It does not say: "As thy fears." Wasn't it Spurgeon who said that everybody has a trouble factory at his house, and if the trouble does not come along easily and quickly, we put the factory to work to see that it comes? Oh, what fearful folk we are! Everywhere God's message to us is: "Fear not." One of the most wonderful things said by Jesus is in the last book of the Holy Bible. It is His ringing word: "Fear not." "Fear not to live," said Jesus, "for I am alive." "Fear not to die," said Jesus, "for I died. I have explored every chamber of the grave, and you need not be afraid."

"And then you need not be afraid of what is coming after
death," said Jesus, "for I hold in my hands the keys of
death and of the invisible world." "Fear not," Jesus said,
"because I am alive, you need not to be afraid to live,
whatever comes to you. And you need not be afraid to
die, no matter where nor when. And you need not be
afraid of what is coming after death, for I have the keys
of death and the invisible world in my hands. You trust
me and be without fear." That is His wonderful word.
Let us hide it in our every heart.

In a certain pastorate, there was one woman who had
a good deal of property—only one. The rest were very
poor. This woman was far along in years, indeed, around
seventy, I should say, and all her children were married
and gone; and yet every time the young pastor went to
see her, how fearful she was lest her bank stock should
somehow be lost, lest her property somehow should take
wings and fly away, or be burned up; lest she should at
last die in the poor house. She said that to the young
preacher, again and again, until at last, he turned and
said to her, as tenderly and faithfully as he could: "What
does it really matter, dear sister, at last, if you trust your
all to Christ, if you should die in the poorhouse? God
will send His chariot to carry you home, whether you are
in a hovel or a mansion, if you really trust Him as your
Savior. Put your fears away."

I am thinking now of an old farmer, and his case es-
sentially describes us all, I judge. He had to make a train
at a certain hour in the early morning. He lived some
three or four miles out there in the country away from
the railway station. And so he set his alarm clock to
rouse him, that he might reach the station at a certain
hour; and then, wonder of wonders, he sat up and watched
the alarm clock, to see if it went off at the time he set it!
Now, we smile at that, but isn't it true that we are smiling
at ourselves? Oh, how our fears harass us, and corrode
us, and appall us and enslave us, and dispirit us! The great
promise to-day would teach us to put our fears away, once
and forever.

Let us look at this promise yet a moment further. What
is it? "As thy days"—not as thy weeks, not as thy months,
not as thy years, not as thy seasons—"as thy days." God
comes to us saying: "Live one day at a time. Cling to
me, and do my will, and stand faithfuly at your post,
one day at a time, and all shall be well." You say: "We
want to see long stretches at once." You say: "We want
to see years, with all their hidden secrets and undisclosed
meanings, in one little day." But that is not God's way.
You say: "We demand that the long future shall tell us
its secrets," and it refuses to do it. Jesus comes, saying:
"Take it one day at a time. And from morning until noontide, and from noontide until the nightfall, and when earth
is wrapped in the shadows of the night, just one day at a
time, take it, and cling ever to me, and even the seeming
defeats of life shall be turned into triumphs."

Note well the limitation to the promise. It says: "As
thy days"—you see how comprehensive that is; that includes all the days, whatever they are, however they
come—"so shall be thy strength." Some days are dark,
and other days are bright. Some days, we feel more and
drink deeper of the awful draught of human pain and experience and wounding and surprise and wonderment, than
in thirty whole years beside. Ah, me! Some of us know
about it. Some of us know what it is, in one short day,
to have had more pain and battle and wonderment and
agony and surprise—in one short day when the heavens
were all darkened, when neither sun, nor moon, nor star
would shine at all—some of us have known more of suffering in one dark day like that than in thirty years beside.
But this promise covers a day like that. Job had his black
Friday, when everything was swept from him—servants
and property and children and health and friends—and
even his own wife—God save the mark!—said to her husband: "Curse God and die!" And Job simply said: "Let
come on me what will, though He slay me, yet will I trust
in Him." And out of the deepest depths he came again to
higher heights than ever before. That is God's promise.

Some days are little, and some days are large, and in
all those days, commonplace and ordinary and routine

days, Jesus says: "I will be with you." And then when
come life's testing days—days big with meaning, with
terror, with pain, with duty, with trial—Jesus stands there
to fortify us as we go on clinging to Him.

And then there comes a last earthly day—the day of
death. Somebody asked Dwight L. Moody if he had dying
grace, and he said: "Why, no. I have living grace, but
when I come to die I shall have dying grace." And when
they carried him home from a meeting he was conducting
in Kansas City, where a fatal sickness had seized him, there
propped up on his pillows, with his loved ones around him,
he looked at them, and then looked up into the open heavens, and said: "The world is receding. Heaven is opening.
God is calling me, and I must be away." He had dying
grace when death came.

I recall very vividly the recent going away of the wife
of one of our most honored Texas judges. She had said
to me again and again, that she greatly feared she was
not a Christian, and her fear came because all her lifetime
she was in bondage through fear of death. She never went
to a funeral, or into a death chamber, if she could avoid
it. She had that unspeakable fear of death which is described in that Scripture which says: "Who through
fear of death were all their lifetime subject to bondage."
I said to her again and again: "Mrs. So-and-so, if you
are trusting Christ"—and she would say: "If I am trusting
Him? Though He slay me, yet will I trust Him." And
then I said: "If you are trusting Him, when the day comes
for you to go, His grace will be sufficient, and if you are
conscious that day, you will know that it is sufficient."
And the day did come a little while ago, and the nurse
and the doctor were there, and she turned her lustrous eyes
to the doctor, and said: "Doctor, what is this?" And he
did not reply. He was a very dear friend of the family.
And she said again: "Tell me frankly, doctor, is this
death?" He said: "Yes, Mrs. So-and-so, it is death." And
then she turned to her husband, and she said: "Oh, dear
husband, you know this is the hour that for thirty years
I have dreaded. This is the hour of all hours I have
shrunk from." And then she said: "Husband, don't you

see that face? Don't you hear that music? Christ is here.
I have never known such rapture of light and peace and
joy." And in a very flood of celestial glory the timid wife
went out into the night, and through the night into the
land Elysian. She found that God's grace was sufficient.

Will you take this promise to-day and make it yours?
Will you take this promise and incarnate it in your life?
Oh, if you will cling to Jesus as your Savior and the Master of your life, if you will let Him come into your life
and save you His own way—and He will never save you
any other way but His way—and then let Him guide you
His way, and let His will be the law of your life, and let
His program be fully accepted by you as your program,
you will turn the battle back from the gate, no matter
what it is, and you will have days of heaven upon the
earth, no matter what else you have. He will verify to
you this promise through all the days, and He will love,
and He will guide, and hold, and help, and lead you, till
the day is done.

There is just one concern for every one of us to have,
and that concern is to be faithful to Jesus Christ. There
is one thing I want to hear from Him at last, when I shall
see Him face to face—one thing I long to hear—and that
is that blessed plaudit: "Well done, good and faithful
servant." His challenging word is: "Be thou faithful
unto death." He does not say "until death." He does
not mean that. He says: "Be thou faithful unto death"—
faithful to the dying point. Die any time, and die anywhere, before you will be unfaithful. The one supreme
canon of human conduct is: "Is this right? Then I will
do the right, though the heavens fall." "Be thou faithful
unto death, and I will give thee a crown of life."

Out of my boyhood there comes a memory—you will
allow me to speak of it—one of the tenderest memories of
all my life. Many have been the days that, far back in the
mountains, hard by the little country schoolhouse, I have
sat beside another boy, 14, 15 or 16 years of age, and we
have builded our air castles, as boys will, and as they
ought to do. We dreamed our dreams. He was going to
be a victorious business man, and delight the world with

his philanthropy and service, and he has already made good. And I was going in another direction. I was going to be a lawyer, and give my life to that noble calling. The flying years came on, with their many changes and deeper questions. This young fellow came to the great West earlier than I, and afterward, God met me one day in a quiet country church house, and from that hour I have traveled another road. The years have passed since we used to have those dreams together, beside the modest, country school house. A little while ago I was this big man's guest, in his own fair home. His community had arranged a notable public occasion, and had me as their invited guest, to speak to them. I was a guest, of course, in Jim's fair home while I was there. And after the address, and when we had had our meal, and after the hours had galloped away like minutes, I said: "Now, Jim, I must make ready to go to the train." He said: "Well, we will walk, if you don't mind it, that we may talk like we used to talk in the far-off hills." And out of the years we talked, and talked, and then he said: "Would you like for me to tell you the sweetest memory out of all my life?" Of course, I wanted to hear it, and he reminded me that his father was an invalid for years, and that he who was conversing with me was the only boy, in a houseful of sisters, and that the burdens of the family fell on him, while sometimes he would chafe under the burdens, they were so trying and so heavy. One day the invalid father sat on the porch in his deep chair, as was his wont, and Jim said to him: "Father, couldn't you attend to certain little chores at the barn to-day?" He answered: "Why, certainly, son." Jim said: "I will be until after dark, plowing in the lower field, and if you can attend to those little chores, it will help me." The father said: "Certainly, my boy, I will be so glad to do it." Jim came in after nightfall, and came to the porch, where sat his father, and they commenced talking, when Jim remembered and asked his father: "Did you look after the little chores at the barn?" And, with a pitiful sigh, the father said: "My boy, I am ashamed to tell you, I forgot all about it." And then Jim said that the hot words of impatience, for he was tired, were ready to fly from his lips, but he swallowed them back—God forgive you and me, when we do not swallow them back!—and Jim said: "Never mind, father; I can fix it in a few minutes, and then I will come back and tell you some splendid news about the lower farm. I will soon fix it. Don't you worry, father." And the old man said, with surpassing pathos in his voice: "Come back now, Jim. Come back now—right now." Jim came back, and the old man said: "Come where I can feel you. I can barely see you in the day time, and cannot see you at all after night." And Jim came nearer, and the father put his hands upon Jim's head, and then the old man sobbed for a minute or two, unable to speak. And when he could speak at last, he said: "Oh, my boy, God bless you, just because you are always so faithful to duty! You will never know what a comfort you are to me, you are so faithful, my son, to duty." Jim could not speak after that; of course not. What boy could speak after a speech like that from his father? And Jim turned away, and attended to the chores, and came back singing a few minutes later. A boy who lives like that has a right to sing. And as he approached the high porch, where his father sat in his deep chair, he began talking. "Father," he said, but there was no response. And again he said: "Father," but there was no answer. And he was beside his father immediately, touching his pulse, but it was still, and the hand of the son was thrust above the old man's heart, but it had ceased to beat. Out of the weariness and pain of life, the tired old man had gone to that land where there shall be no more death, neither sorrow, nor crying; neither shall there be any more pain. And then this great citizen of the West, one of the worthiest the great West has ever had, and one of the most useful, said to me, with a sob: "Oh, sir, the sweetest memory of all is father's word, 'God bless you, my boy! You are such a comfort to me, because you are always so faithful to duty.'" You want to hear that at last, and so do I, when we stand face to face before Him whose we are and whom we live to serve.

Let us cling utterly and only and always to Christ.

Let us trust Him till the day is done, and then go to be with Him and to be like Him forever.

THE CLOSING PRAYER.

And now, as the people go, O Lord Jesus, speak thou the word in season to our every heart. From to-day, let us go to live the life which is life indeed. Let parents here set themselves, with a devotion that sin and Satan cannot break, to put Christ first forever, whatever His way and wherever He leads, and they shall walk in a path crowned with the days of heaven upon the earth. May thy mercy come upon all the people of this vast expanding city, charged as it is with such responsibilities, and freighted as it is with such destinies. O, touch thou this whole city with the touch of God to-day. And to-morrow, when the people meet in their every place of worship, may they worship thee in the beauty of holiness, with the favor of God upon every preacher, and upon every church, and even upon those who may not go to church and may have no care for the things of God and their own souls. Save the people, O God, and they shall be saved, and the glory shall all be thine.

And as you go now, may the blessing of the triune God be granted to each and all, to abide with you forever. Amen.

XXIII

SERVICE FOR MEN, SUNDAY AFTERNOON, JUNE 24, 1917.

PRELIMINARY REMARKS.

Very gladly, my brother men and gentlemen, do I welcome the privilege of speaking at this hour to the men of this goodly city. I know about men's battles, their temptations, their questions, their heart hungers, and I find in my own heart a longing inexpressible to help them. That is the feeling now in my heart, as I look you in the face, and stretch out to you a brother's hand, and offer you a brother's heart. I have counted it a very rare privilege for these past few days to be the guest of the two honored pastors who sit behind me, Dr. Smith and Dr. Edwards, and to be refreshed by fellowship with them—men modest and valiant and true; men whose ministry is so nobly constructive, and men whose words and examples point always toward the morning. I have counted it a rare privilege to be their guest, and the guest of their two noble congregations. And, more, I have counted it a very refreshing privilege to meet many of God's men of other congregations than these two, to meet many of the noble ministers of these various flocks, and their people, whose courtesies to the visiting preacher have been so constant and gracious. And still more, I have counted it a privilege to meet face to face, and to know at close range, many of your citizens who are not yet church men at all, but who are giving their splendid, capable energy to aid in bringing in a larger and better civilization for the world. These men, I pray, may soon come with us to the side and service of Christ.

I covet every man of you for Christ. I have a passionate longing for the spiritual welfare of this whole great state of ours, and though I live in one of its cities, and have for a long time therein lived, I have the most earnest interest in all our cities and in all our people. I have said, from one coast of America to the other, that nowhere in all this world, in my humble judgment, was there a greater-hearted, cleaner-minded, more forward-looking type of men than we have here in this vast, renascent, responsive state. The men of this state incarnate as do no other men I know, that little poem:

WHERE DOES THE WEST BEGIN?

Out where the handclasp is a little bit stronger,
Out where the smile lasts a trifle longer—
That's where the West begins.
Out where the sun shines a trifle brighter,
Where the snows that fall are a trifle whiter,
And the bonds of home are a wee bit tighter—
That's where the West begins.

Out where the sky is a trifle bluer,
Where friendships formed are somewhat truer—
That's where the West begins.
Out where a fresher breeze is blowing,
Where there's laughter in every stream that's flowing,
Where there is more of reaping and less of sowing—
That's where the West begins.

Out where the world is in the making,
Where fewer hearts with despair are breaking—
That's where the West begins.
Where there's more of singing and less of sighing,
Where there's more of giving and less of buying,
And a man makes friends without half trying—
That's where the West begins.

Oh, how I covet this great West, every man in it, for Christ, my Savior and Lord!

THE ONE SUFFICIENT REFUGE.

Text: "Refuge failed me. * * * I cried unto thee, O Lord, I said, Thou art my refuge."—Psa. 142: 4, 5.

What shall I say to you, my brothers, as I come for an afternoon service, for a little while just with the men? I would say to you that all is well, whatever comes, whether in life or death, or in God's great beyond, forever, if it is well with the soul. And I would say that nothing is well, nothing really and abidingly succeeds, if it is not well with a man's soul. In the old world there

is a painting, which has been copied, and the copy hangs
in every noble art gallery in the world—a painting of a
storm, before which terrible storm, men and beasts are
fleeing, if haply they may find a refuge. That is a picture
of every rational human life. This, then, is the text upon
which I would speak to you: "Refuge failed me" (or as
the marginal reading has it, "fled away from me"), "then
I cried unto the Lord, and said, 'Thou art my refuge.'"

. A refuge means protection against danger. It means
a source of safety. I wonder, as I search this audience
now, and glance at every face before me, if you have a
refuge, each one of you, for your soul, and what is that
refuge, and does that refuge suffice you, and is that refuge
safe, and will that refuge meet all the tests?

You will agree with me, I doubt not, that the fundamental need of every man is a refuge for his soul. That
need takes precedence of every other need, and that need
is fundamental. That every man needs a refuge for his
soul will be indicated by a glance in any one of many
directions. For one thing, a man needs a refuge against
the accusing cry of his own conscience. Oh, what pain
there is, at times, in the human conscience! 'Tis the
acutest and most terrible pain of all, and every man needs
a refuge against the accusing cry of his own conscience.
Conscience may be dulled; conscience may be seared;
conscience may be mistaught; and yet conscience will have
its hours when it will make its serious and terrible cry.

I talked a little while ago with a man well reared. His
position has been lofty, but he has missed the right road
terribly, and has fallen more terribly. He said to me
after our interview, and as we were separating: "Oh,
man, God Almighty alone knows how I have suffered in
my conscience!" Every man needs a refuge from the accusing cry of his own conscience, for every man must
live with himself.

When we turn to the Bible, it makes that insistence,
by precept and by illustration, after the most impressive
fashion. Take the case of John the Baptist, that intrepid
preacher who stood before purple-robed Herod and spoke
to him concerning righteousness and temperance and the

judgment to come, and at last paid for it with his life. You remember the outcome of it to that man Herod. Herod had John killed, and you remember the later outcome. Months afterward, as Herod with his courtiers feasted, suddenly the topic of conversation with him and his men changed, and they began to speculate as to who that wonderful man was out yonder in the country, who was so speaking that the very cities were emptied of their people, to go out by the riverside to hear what He said. And Herod rose up, trembling like an aspen leaf, and blurted out his cry: "I suspect you are talking about John the Baptist, whom I beheaded months ago, but who has risen from the dead." Conscience was not dead!

You recall the tragic case of Judas, who sold Jesus for thirty pieces of silver—about fifteen dollars of our money—and then came back a few hours later, and threw down the thirty pieces of silver to the men with whom he traded, and said: "Let's rue the bargain. I have betrayed the innocent blood. Take this money back. It burns my brain. It burns my pockets. It burns my hand. It burns my conscience." And the men with whom he traded, mocked him and scorned him, and then, goaded by conscience, Judas went out and took his own life. Oh, my brother men, there is no pain so terrible as the accusing cry of the human conscience!

Take human life, temporal and secular, and it is crowded with illustrations bearing upon this same point. I recall that realistic story of a man in another land, years ago, a judge, who had there in his court a young man charged with murdering his master, and who, to conceal his crime, had burned down the house over the master's head. The trial was stubbornly fought, and was at last drawing to a conclusion, and the judge had to give his charge in the matter. He stood up to give the charge, and they saw his exceeding agitation, and then he sat down without speaking. And then, with still deeper agitation, he left the judge's bench, and went down into the prisoner's dock, and sat down beside the prisoner, and put his face in his hands and groaned aloud. There was a sensation, of course, in the court room. Lawyers on either side looked aghast at one another and wondered what it all meant. And presently, when they got up and went to him, and said: "What on earth is it, Judge?" with choking difficulty he said to them: "I have tried my own case. Thirty years ago I murdered my master, and to hide my crime I burned down the house over his head, and if any person ever suspected me, I do not know it. I cannot go on with this trial. I have tried my own case. I cannot continue further with this case." Thirty years had elapsed, but conscience had made its cry.

The writings of the great dramatists, Shakespeare and George Eliot and Victor Hugo, and men and women of their class, are going to live, while ten thousand piles of trashy literature die, because they have recognized the vitality of the human conscience. Take Macbeth; see the effort made there to get the blood off the hands, and hear the pitiful cry as the hands are lifted up, with the exclamation: "Oh, the blood, the blood! Though I lave here in this basin, I cannot get it off!"

Take the story by George Eliot, where she tells of the fatal going astray of a young girl. Earth's saddest sight is that. Let angels veil their faces, and let crepe be put on the door of heaven, when a young girl thus falls into shame. George Eliot tells it in her own inimitable fashion, and then she describes the young girl putting to death the little child to which she had given birth, seeking thus to hide the shame and crime. She slew the little child out there in the hedge, and later she was apprehended and brought to justice and judgment, and kindly women got around the wretched and fallen girl, and sought to counsel and help her. She listened to them — listened as if in a trance — and when they would finish saying to her every kindly and helpful thing they could think to say, she would answer them with the wailing chant: "Yes, yes, I hear all that you say, but will I always hear the cry of the little child that I put to death in the hedge?" What is the great dramatist saying? She is saying that conscience lives, and that men must reckon with conscience. Now, every man needs a refuge from the accusing cry of his own conscience.

Nor is that all. Every man needs a refuge from the slumbering power of sin in his own life. I grieve for any man who boasts of his strength. No man knows how weak he is, and every man needs a refuge against the slumbering power of sin in his own life. Many of the finest, most splendid, most gifted, most generous, most lovable men, go down to doom and death because of the slumbering power of sin in their own lives.

Every man needs a refuge when he comes to that last hour that awaits us every one, to that grim sarcasm of human life called death. Every man needs a refuge when he comes to that hour—an hour we cannot escape, an hour we cannot evade or miss. Oh, there are times when we wonder if there is not some way past it!

I told a group the other day of the recent funeral of a mother in my city, who left a houseful of children, and the oldest girl mothered all those younger children. It was pitiful, and it was wonderful, how she mothered those little girls and boys, who cried in vain for the mother, the child's best friend, who would never come back. And when we got to the cemetery, and they lowered the body into the grave, the children seemed wild with grief; and the oldest girl went up and down the line, saying to this one and that one: "Do not cry. Maybe it is not so. Maybe it is all a dream. Maybe we are at home in bed. Maybe we will wake up in the morning and mother will be with us and kiss us, like she always did. Maybe it is not so. Maybe it is all a dream!" Oh, how we would get away from death! How we wish we might! Every man needs a refuge against death.

And every man needs a refuge out yonder beyond death, where the issues of conduct and character are going to come into judgment before Christ. Every man needs a refuge when he comes to that day of days, called the judgment day of God. Now, that there is such a day is insisted upon even by human reason. Human reason makes its cry that somewhere there ought to be a place for explanation, for revelation. Somewhere there ought to be a place where the tangled threads shall be disentangled, where the irregularities shall be straightened out, where the mys-

teries shall be interpreted and explained. Every man
needs a refuge at that great day. When we turn to the
Word of God, the Holy Book, the guide-book for men, it
is clear as the light about the reality of a judgment day.
Listen to it: "God hath appointed a day in the which
He will judge the world in righteousness by Jesus Christ."
Listen to it: "We must all appear before the judgment
seat of Christ." Listen to it: "We must every one give
account of himself to God." Surely, my brother men, when
we stand at that great assize, at that day of judgment,
every man of us will need a refuge.

Every man has a refuge of some sort. There went
through this country some years ago an almost matchless
orator, who was also an aggressive opponent of the Christian religion. I need not speak his name. No man should
carelessly speak the name of either the living or the dead.
This brilliant orator, an infidel, went up and down the land,
caricaturing Christians and their faith, but he had his refuge. He began one of his most caustic addresses with the
remark: "So-and-so and so-and-so is my religion." He
had his refuge. Every man, my brother men, has a refuge
of some sort for himself, something that he falls back on,
something that he hopes in, something in which he trusts.
Alas, alas, my brothers, full many a time the peril is that
the man's refuge is untrustworthy, that it is vain, that it
is false! The Bible warns us at that point. The Bible
tells us that we can cry peace, peace, when there is no
peace. Jesus himself tells us: "Not every one that saith
unto me, Lord, Lord, shall enter into the kingdom of
heaven, but he that doeth the will of my Father who is
in heaven." Jesus tells us that, and then He goes on to
tell us a sentence that is enough to make every man of
us pause and search our hearts and shudder. Listen to it.
Jesus says: "Many will say unto me in that day" — the
day of judgment — "Lord, Lord, have we not prophesied
in thy name?" Were we not preachers? "Have we not
prophesied in thy name, and in thy name cast out devils,
and in thy name done many wonderful works? And then
will I profess unto them" — Jesus is speaking — "I never
knew you. Depart from me, ye that work iniquity." Oh,

how serious is this matter of our meeting that final test like we ought to meet it, and of our having a refuge sufficient in that hour of hours!

And now, gentlemen, it is an all-important matter that we be able to detect the false refuges behind which Satan would have us hide, and lure us, to deceive us and destroy us. May we detect these false refuges for the soul? We may. There are certain inexorable tests whereby we may detect the false refuge for the soul. What are these tests? For the moment, I will lay aside the Word of God, the guide-book, the divine revelation for human conduct and character and opinion, and I will come to certain other inexorable human tests that we must grapple with. If our refuge for our soul be trustworthy, if it be reliable, if it be dependable, if it will suffice us, then such refuge will meet every test, no matter what the test may be. If the refuge for a man's soul will do to trust, then I say that such refuge will meet these four tests. Look at these tests.

First of all, it will satisfy the conscience. I have already indicated what an exacting test the conscience makes. It must satisfy the man's conscience, if a man's religious refuge, whatever it is, be trustworthy and reliable. Nor is that all. If a man's refuge for his soul be trustworthy, then it must make his life better. Mark that. A tree is known by its fruits, and if a man's religious refuge does not make his life better, then such refuge is vain and false. Life must be made better if one's religious refuge be dependable. And, again, if a man's religious refuge be dependable, it will fortify such man and uphold him in the solemn hour when he comes to die, when all the masks are off, when all the guises and disguises must be laid aside, when his feet dip into the stream separating time and eternity. If a man's refuge for his soul be trustworthy, it must be one that will suffice him when his feet touch the river of death, and the mists from that river come up into his face.

Moreover, if a man's refuge for his soul will do to tie to, will do to rely upon, then such refuge must completely fortify a man out vonder at the judgment, when he makes personal answer to Christ, as every man of us must make such answer.

What are some of the false refuges? I will tell you four. There are many more, but I will briefly tell you four, and these four are representative—four false refuges that lure men to deception and darkness and death. I dealt with four men recently, in another place, and they gave these four different false refuges, behind which men are lured, and by which men are deceived and lost. The first one said: "I am trusting in my own goodness. Therefore, I am good enough in myself without God's help at all." His refuge for himself, for his soul, was his own goodness. Do you think that refuge is sufficient? Will that refuge meet the tests? Mind you, we are considering four great tests, not naming the fifth, which is the Book of God, which I leave aside for the present. There are four inexorable tests for these refuges for our souls. Now, will this false refuge I have just named, the man's own personal goodness, as his dependence for safety and salvation, meet these four tests I have just named? First, will it satisfy his own conscience? Is your conscience satisfied, and is mine, for us to say: "I am good enough without God's help at all?" Is our conscience satisfied to say: "No matter what this Bible teaches, and no matter what Jesus taught, no matter though He died, I am good enough?" Does that satisfy your conscience and mine? It does not satisfy mine.

I pass you to the next test. Does it make your life better to say: "I am trusting to my own goodness, and I will discard Christ and His religion, and all that?" Does that make your life better? And, mind you, if a man's refuge for his soul does not make his life better, he is missing the road. But I pass you to the next test. Will it suffice you in the solemn hour when you shall be dying upon your couch, and let us fancy that I shall be beside you, and take your hand, and say: "My friend, do you know that this is the last hour?" Will you answer me: "Yes, I know it well. The doctor has told me, and I am conscious that he speaks correctly." And I shall ask you: "What is your hope?" Do you think you will be able to

look me smilingly in the face, and say to me: "Why, man,
I am good enough! You need not pray, nor take the Bible,
nor talk of Christ. I am good enough?" Do you think
that will make the pillow soft when a man comes to die,
to wave Christ's religion away with his hand, and say: "I
am good enough without it?"

I pass you to the other great test, out beyond death.
When you shall answer to Jesus, as He sits upon His
judgment throne, as every man of us must personally there
answer by and by, do you think it will suffice you to say
to Him: "I am here, but I am good enough without you,
or your gospel, or your blood, or your grace?" Do you
suppose that any sinner of all the earth will at last make
such a presumptuous plea as that at the judgment bar
of Christ? No man will say it. That is not your refuge,
is it?

Then, here was the second man's false refuge. It was
just the opposite of this first man's refuge. The second
man said: "Oh, well, I am not very good; I am quite
frail, and know it, and grant it, but I am as good as a great
many around me, in the churches and out of them, and
therefore I will just let it go at that." His refuge was this:
Not his own goodness, but the fact of other people's
badness. Come, gentlemen, will that meet these four great
tests I have named? Does it satisfy a man's conscience
to say: "I will put these challenging claims of Christ
away, because a great many other men have done the same
thing?" Should it satisfy a man's conscience, and can it,
to say: "I will not pay my debts to the doctor or the
grocery man or the merchant or the bank, because a good
many other people evade theirs, and won't pay theirs?"
Does it satisfy to say: "I will ignore Jesus and put Him
away, because a great many other people are doing the
same thing?"

But I pass you to the next test. Does it make your
life better to say: "I am as good as a great many other
people, and I am going to let it go at that, and pass it
all by?"

And then I pass you to the next great test. Does it
satisfy you, and will it, when you come to the solemn

hour of death, to say: "I am dying without Christ and His religion and His comfort and strength, because other men have essayed to go the same dark way, and I am going just as they have gone?"

And then that other test that awaits you beyond death and the grave, when you shall answer at the judgment seat of Christ, will it suffice you then to say to Christ: "I rejected you, Lord Jesus, and put you away, and would not have you, because a great many other men did the same thing?" That refuge is not yours, is it?

The third man stated this as his refuge: "I do not believe any of it. I am an outright and downright disbeliever. I reject it all." Now, come, is that the refuge of any man here—unbelief? No matter what its form, infidelity; atheism, agnosticism, materialism, no matter what its form—unbelief—does that meet the tests? Let us see. Does it satisfy your conscience to say: "I reject the Bible and reject Jesus both, as untrustworthy, in the face of all that the Bible has done, and in the face of Christ's influence over men, great and small, big and little. I reject it all as untrustworthy?" Does that satisfy your conscience? Then I pass you to the next test. Does it make your life better to say: "Unbelief is the refuge for my soul?" Does it help your life to be better? And to the next test I bring you quickly, to the time when you shall depart from time into death. Are you able to contemplate that hour with complacency and felicity, saying: "I reject Christ and the Bible, and all that they offer to man, because I do not believe any of it?" And then I pass you out to the final test, when you shall answer personally to Christ himself at His judgment bar. How will you answer to Him, as each man of us must personally answer by and by? When you answer there to Him, saying: "My theory, my pilot, my defense, my refuge was unbelief. I rejected all the claims and teachings of Christ, because of unbelief"— do you think that will suffice you? When you stand before Him, He will say to you what He says to you now, while you are in life, in the flesh, this side of the grave, here in earth's battle: "Whatever your unbelief, you may know the truth about Christ's religion." Do I speak to

some man in this audience who is a doubter? Oh, I stretch
out to him a friendly hand! I know something of the
darkness and withering power of doubt. Do I speak to
some man who doubts? Let me pray him not to trifle
with his doubts. Somebody has well said that doubt is
the agony of some earnest soul, or it is the trifling of some
superficial fool. If I speak to some man who doubts, let
me pray him to probe his doubts clear to the bottom, and
make his doubts give him re-enforcement, or throw them
every one away. Jesus comes to you, saying: "No matter what your doubt, no matter what your unbelief, no
matter what your question, no matter what your skepticism, if you will just be candid and honest, I will bring
you into the light, and you shall be the judge." Listen
to His clear challenge, which now I quote to you. What
a challenge it is! Listen to it: "If any man"—that is as
broad as the world, as comprehensive as humanity—"if
any man willeth to do the will of God," says Jesus, "he
shall know of the teaching, whether it is of God."

Oh, my brother, if any man will come to God like this:
"Oh, God, if there be one, on the premise, on the hypothe-
sis that there is one—I don't know—I want light. If thou
hast any interest in my getting it, and if thou wilt give
light, no matter how it comes, I will follow it, no matter
where it leads," any skeptic on the earth will be brought
to God, if he will follow the light like that.

Some time ago, two of the world's most prominent
skeptics were Gilbert West and Lord Littleton, and they
were two of the most brilliant intellects of their own or
any age. They made fun of Christianity, whenever they
met. By and by, they said: "There are two things we
must explode, and then we will have the Christian religion
all tumbled into the ditch, and nothing will be left." And
these were the two things they said they would have to
explode: They said they would have to explain away the
doctrine that Jesus Christ rose from the dead on the third
day, as the Scriptures teach, and they would have to explain that wonderful man, the Apostle Paul, whose influence was so powerful in the world eighteen centuries even
after he had died. Gilbert West said: "I will explode the

resurrection of Christ and blow it all up," and Lord Littleton said: "I will explain Paul." They went their way, and after weeks and weeks, by appointment they came together again, and Littleton said: "West, what have you to say?" Gilbert West replied: "Oh, Littleton, I have something wonderful to tell you. When I came to explode the doctrine that Jesus of Nazareth rose from the dead on the third day, I had to be candid, I had to be sincere, I had to be honest, I had to search for my evidence. You may laugh at me, Littleton, if you will, but when I looked into it honestly, my mind and my deepest soul were convinced that Jesus did rise from the dead, and I prayed to Him, and He saved me, and I am His friend." And then Lord Littleton answered: "Thank God, West! I have something just as wonderful to tell you. When I came to explain that man Paul, and get rid of him, I, too, had to be thorough and candid. I had to search. I had to be true. And you will rejoice with me, West, when I tell you that after I had searched and studied about Paul, by and by I found myself down on my knees, just as Paul got down on his knees on that Damascus road, and my cry was his: 'Lord, what wilt thou have me to do?' And I am a Christian, also, West." And these two outstanding skeptics became two of the world's most noted Christians, and have written two of the noblest apologies of the Christian religion that have ever been penned.

Gentlemen, the Christian religion submits to the scientific method always, and that is the method of personal experience. My brother men, you will not think I am boasting — I speak it to the praise of my Savior: One thing I know, whereas I was blind, now I see. Once I went my way reading law, wanting to give my life to that high calling. One of earth's noblest callings it is. And the Master crossed my path, and I was reminded of my sins, and I went to Him and said: "Have mercy on me," and He did. That is the thing, gentlemen, that I know better than I know anything else in the world. Oh, men, unbelief can find the way out! Obedience is the solvent of every doubt in the world. If a man will turn to Jesus and say: "Show me the way, and I will walk in it,

wherever it leads, and whatever it costs," he will be
brought in the right way safely home at last.

And now the fourth man, the last man, said: "Well,
here is my refuge. I do not expect any man to be lost.
I expect every man to be saved in God's fair heaven above,
not one of them missing, no matter what his crimes, no
matter what his sins, no matter what the wretchedness
of his conduct and character." That was his refuge —
universal salvation. Now, will that meet the tests? I
waive the Bible, for the present. The Bible speaks plainly
on all these points, but I waive that for the moment, and
I come to other grounds for the present moment. Will
that meet the tests, that no matter how a man lives and
sows and dies, yet all is well out there beyond? First,
does it satisfy a man's conscience to say that vice and
virtue shall have the same reward? Is a man's conscience
at rest to say that this good man, who serves God and
follows Him, shall have no more, and nothing different,
from the man who does not serve Him, and wastes his
life? Is the man's conscience at rest to say that they shall
have the same harvest? I pass to the next test. Does it
make a man's life better here and now to say: "No matter how a man lives, all will be well a little later, beyond
the sunset and the night?" I pass you to the third test.
Is a man made ready for the solemn hour of death who
says: "I can sow to the flesh, and give absolute license
to the sins of my life, and no matter, for all is well for
me?" Do you think that will qualify a man to die in
peace, when the hour comes for him to go? And then
beyond death, do you think a man can stand up yonder,
before the face of Jesus, who said: "I came to the earth
to die for sinners, that they might not die and shall not
die, if they will repent of sin and turn to me"—do you
think a man will be fortified in the judgment at last to
say to Jesus: "I am here because I said, I taught, and I
believed that no matter how a man sowed, the harvest
would come out all right?"

Oh, gentlemen, you will not take that theory, either.
A man does violence to all law and to all philosophy, unless he knows that as a man sows, so must he reap. If a

man sows wheat, he will reap wheat. A man will not sow
one thing and reap another. If one man comes humbly,
despite all his weaknesses, and gives his case to Christ,
Christ will be his friend and helper. If a second man
'says: "None of it for me; I will put it away," the two
men cannot have the same result. They cannot have the
same harvest. And your own conscience, your own judgment, and all law, and all philosophy, rise up with the cry
that as men sow, so shall they reap.

There is a law of physical gravity in the physical world,
but it is no more real than the law of moral gravity in
the moral world. Every man, gentlemen, when he comes
to die, "shall go to his own place." If he continues in the
wrong road here, the wrong road there will be his portion.
If he chooses the right road here, the right, there, will be
his portion.

Now, this man who speaks our text, tried the false
refuges, and this is his cry when he tried them: "Refuge
failed me. Refuge fled away from me. Refuge broke
down. Refuge could not suffice me. The bridge went
down. The physician could not help."

What are we to do? Nowhere, gentlemen, in all this
vast world, is there a human refuge ample for a human
soul. Nowhere, human and earthly, is there a refuge sufficient for the human soul. What shall we do about it?
Is there any door of hope in the valley of Achor? Is there
any gate through which a man may pass, and have deliverance and safety?

> Oh, where shall rest be found,
>   Rest for a weary soul?
> 'Twere vain the ocean's depths to sound,
>   Or pierce to either pole.
>
> Beyond this vale of tears
>   There is a life above,
> Unmeasured by the flight of years,
>   And all that life is love.
>
> There is a death whose pang
>   Outlasts this fleeting breath.
> Oh, what eternal horrors hang
>   Around man's second death!
>
> Lord God of truth and grace,
>   Teach us that death to shun,
> Lest we be banished from thy face
>   And evermore undone.

Come, my brother men, is there any refuge sufficient
for you and for me? Is there any balm in Gilead ample

for us? Is there any physician anywhere that can take
me and take care of me, a sinful, eternity-bound man? Is
there any door of hope in the valley of Achor for you and
for me? Thank God, there is! There is a refuge sufficient
for us, and here it is, and I bring you to it. This man
said: "Refuge failed me, fled away from me, broke down,
could not suffice me." Now listen to him: "Then I turned
to the Lord, and I said to the Lord, Thou shalt be my
refuge."

Oh, he is on terra firma now! He is on sure founda-
tions now. I turned away from these refuges that misled
me, false and illusory and deceiving and insufficient, and
I turned to the Lord, and I said: "Lord, I will surrender
to you, that you may be my refuge forever." Gentlemen,
the Lord meets all the tests. Of course, He meets the
test of the Bible, for He gave the Bible to us, and is in-
separably linked with it, but He meets all these other
tests. Every test you can think of for a human soul, no
matter how bedarkened and sinful, the Lord Jesus Christ
meets it.

I will show you that He meets these four inexorable
tests that I have just described. First, the Lord Jesus
satisfies the human conscience. We sowed to the flesh.
We went to the bad. We sinned. We went the wrong
road. Every man of us has come short of God's glory.
Not a perfect man is there in all this group, or in all the
world, and our consciences know it. Jesus comes to us,
saying: "You submit your case to me. I died, the just,
for you, the unjust. If you will submit your case to me,
if you will give up to me, if you will be for me, if you will
say yes to me, and mean it; if you will surrender to me,
I will take care of your conscience." And though we have
sinned and come short of God's glory, we can be at peace,
because Jesus, to whom we yield, speaks peace to our conscience. Paul would have gone with a ball and chain
about him, but for the fact that he gave up to Jesus, and
Jesus said: "My blood forgives and sets you free. Let
Satan clamor and let him accuse. I do the saving, and I
will take care of you."

Jesus meets the next test. He helps a man to live. I
would be found a false witness to-day, if I did not declare
to you men that He is helping our Christian men to live.
I can prove it by these hundreds of men before me. A
big fellow lost his property the other day, and he was a
pauper, whereas twenty-four hours before he was counted
a rich man. I went to him and said: "What have you
now to say?" He bowed his head and said: "Wife and
I did not sleep last night, but, oh, sir, we have Christ left,
and why should we grumble? Christ is our Savior." I
saw a toiling carpenter the other day put away his wife's
body in the grave, and she left six children, and they cried
from morning till night, after the mother that could not
come back. What so wrings the heart as the cry of a
bairn for its mother, who will never come back to the
child? I laid my arm in this carpenter's hand, and we
went away into the other room, and the babies gathered
around us, and when I had quieted them the best I could,
I said: "I am going to pray that God will help us." And
I prayed, and when I had finished, he turned to the children and said: "Children, we are going to be brave and
strong. Papa has peace in his heart. Jesus is going to
help us; papa is trusting Jesus, and you children are going
to follow papa as he trusts Christ and serves Him." And
the oldest little boy said: "Papa, I am going to trust Him
now." And then it seemed that the night was turned into
day, and the shadow of death was turned into morning.
Oh, men, Christ fortifies us when the black Friday comes!

And He will help us to die. You recall the recent letter from one of the chaplains on the far field of battle, telling how one of the fine Christian boys died there a few
weeks ago. He was torn by shot and shell, his head
frightfully torn, and yet for hours he was conscious, but
he grew steadily worse, as he lay there dying on his cot.
Presently his mind wandered, and he imagined that the
chaplain, who was comforting him, was his mother, and
the dying boy said so tenderly: "Mother, put your dear,
soft hands under my head. It hurts me so, and your soft
hands will make it better." The chaplain did just like the
mother would have done, the best he could, and then the

dying boy said: "Mother, bend over me. You taught me the way to live, and I am ready to die. Bend over me and kiss me once more, mother, and then I will pray my last prayer and leave all to Christ, for I am not afraid to die." And the chaplain did just what you or I would have done. He bent over the boy and kissed him as nearly like a mother as he could. And the boy faintly said: "Thank you, mother. Now let me tell Jesus as I am dying that I will just lean on Him, for I leaned on Him back yonder, months and years ago, and now I am not afraid." Yes, my brother men, Jesus helps us to die.

There is more yet to be said. He is going to help us yonder at the judgment. Let us imagine that this audience of men is now assembled at the judgment bar of God. What are you going to plead there? What am I going to plead? I will tell you what I shall say when I get there: "Lord, I am not good in myself. I did not plead myself, Lord Jesus, on earth. In Fort Worth I said: 'Other refuge have I none, hangs my helpless soul on thee.' Lord Jesus, on earth I said that I trusted my case wholly to thee, and here at the judgment thou art my refuge." And I shall pass to Christ's right hand, and all will be well forever.

Come, my brother men, I would take the hand of every one of you, and look up into your faces and say: "My brothers, come now to Christ, before we leave this building." Oh, my brother men, do you say to me: "Sir, I can lay my hand on my heart and tell you that Christ is now my refuge; that fact is settled?" Every man here that says: "I can lay my hand on my heart and truthfully say to you and to these comrades about me that I am relying on Christ as my refuge, I have already received Him for my Savior," will please lift his right hand, this moment. I see you. That is a sight to move us profoundly.

But before I let you go, I come to ask: Are there men here who personally say: "I am wrong with God?" It may be that you are in some church, or never were in a church, a professor of religion, or never a professor of religion, but now you say: "I am wrong with God. To-day I tell you, and these men about me, that I want Christ

for my refuge. I want it to be well with my soul here
and hereafter. I want Christ to be my refuge in His own
way and time." Every man here who says: "I want
Christ for my refuge, for I am wrong with God," will
please tell us so, just now. I want you to be candid, like
these Christians were, and tell us so. I will now look
slowly over this audience, from the right to the left, to
see the uplifted hand of the man who says: "I lift my
hand to tell you I want you to pray for me, for I want
Christ for my refuge, before it is too late. I am wrong
with Him, but I want you to pray for me, that I may be
right with God, in His own time and way."

(In tense silence many men lifted their hands.)

My heart is deeply moved, my brother men, that so
many of you candidly tell us of your desire to be right
with God. Settle the matter to-day. Oh, the grandeur of
decision! Interested men, purposeful men, living men,
dying men, eternity-bound men, needy men, sinful and sinning men, my brother men, knowing what I know, if I
were in your place, I would end the battle to-day and stop
my delay. This day I would take the supreme step and
say: "I surrender my life to Christ." Remember that
waiting does not do any good. Waiting cannot help. Waiting is the very thing that Satan wants you to do. Say
it: "I surrender my life to Christ. I am a duty-neglecting,
wandering, backslidden Christian. Something turned me
away. Something set me drifting." No matter what it
was, nor when, you find yourself now drifting, and neglecting duty, but your conscience is alert this hour, and
you say: "I do not want to keep this evil course. I do
not want to continue in this wrong and hurtful way. To-
day I want to take a great step forward and upward and
surrender my life to Christ." Do you say: "That is my
case?" Then I pray you, just surrender yourself, your all,
this hour, to Christ. I am going to ask if every interested
man here will not settle the matter to-day. Here are
scores of men who tell us: "We are wrong with God, but
wish to be right." Some of them are duty-neglecting,
backslidden Christians. Many others have never been for
Christ at all. I am going to ask all these, my brother

men—you will now act just as you think you ought, and you are not to feel at all embarrassed by the proposition I am going to make. I would have you follow your own judgment and conscience, as I ask you, if every interested man in this room is not willing to stand before us all to-day and say: "God help me, because it is my duty, because it is my need, because of my danger, because of happiness, because of influence, because of time, because of eternity, because of life and death and the judgment and the issues of eternity, I am both willing and ready to-day and now to stand to say, I do now surrender my life to Christ, that He, in His own way, may forgive me and be my refuge and strength forever." Every man in this room who can stand on that proposition will do so now.

(The vast audience was profoundly moved, as many men rose to their feet.)

Just a moment do I wait, for nearly all the men are on their feet. My brother, I call to you yet again for just a moment, not to embarrass you—God forbid!—but to help you. I would come and kneel at your feet if that would help you, and if that were proper. I want to ask you if there are not other men who can stand in this decisive hour? My appeal is to your judgment and conscience. I have no respect for any other kind of appeal in my Master's name. Does still another man rise to his feet to say: "I will surrender?" There stands another. Does yet another stand, saying: "I am ready to-day to make my surrender to Christ, and leave the case with Him?" I search the balcony. I wait a moment. Does another in the balcony stand, saying: "That is my case?" I see you, my brother. Does another? There stands another man. Does another man stand, saying: "That is my case?" God be praised!

THE CLOSING PRAYER.

And now, Lord, before we go our ways, O, we pray thee that this army of men who have heretofore followed Christ may be better Christians from to-day than ever—far better. But here are numbers and numbers who stand with us to-day to say that from this day they will follow Christ. O God, forgive and guide, and keep them all. They may be, some of them—thou knowest—duty-neglecting Christians, lapsed church members. This or that or something else has turned them from the right path. They have gone away from thee and the darkness came, and doubts came. They have drifted from thee, and have gone away as they should not have done. But to-day they wish to be right with thee, and return to thee, and to do their duty. Grant that from this hour they may go and do and say and be in thy sight just as thou wouldst have at their hands.

And then, here are men who to-day stand with us to say: "To-day we take our places with Christ's people. To-day we surrender to Christ. To-day we see the truth of the glorious gospel of Christ, that salvation is by grace, that it cannot be by what we will do, or by what any human instrumentality shall do for us, but Christ alone can save, He alone must be our refuge, and to-day we surrender to Christ. From to-day we will follow Him." Lord, from to-day, may they humbly follow Christ forever.

And then there are some who are not ready yet to follow thee. Lord, we breathe our most fervent prayer for them. Speak to their minds, speak to their judgments. Speak to their wills, the initial springs of human action. Speak to their consciences. Oh, bring to bear upon them such mighty motives as move serious men to make mighty decisions. Oh, grant that these men, all and each, who do not find themselves ready to take the great step right now, grant that the hours may be just a few, that even this very day, before they sleep, that every man will be gladly ready to say from his heart: "To-day is my crisis day, my epochal day. To-day I make the surrender of my life to Christ, consenting that He may be my refuge to-day and to-morrow and forever."

Oh, bless with God's own gracious blessing this vast group of men, and their brother men throughout Fort Worth, every man in the city, in every place, however high, however low. Bless all and each, and through these men may the kingdom of God be brought in in Fort Worth, and in the great West and around the world.

And as you go now, may the blessing of God, bright like the light when the morning dawneth, and gracious as the dew when the eventide cometh, be granted you all and each, to abide with you forever. Amen.

XXIV

NIGHT SERVICE, JUNE 24, 1917.

PRELIMINARY REMARKS.

This vast press of people will co-operate, I am glad to believe, to the utmost of your power, to turn this last service to the best profit. And since it is the last service of these brief meetings, I should like to be indulged to make two or three general remarks. The first is an expression of very keen regret that I cannot at this time, midsummer though it is, tarry for several weeks in daily special meetings, with these two beloved pastors and their noble congregations, whose guest I have been these several days. Duty that I cannot in conscience put aside makes it impossible for me to tarry longer than this evening service. I shall cherish the very gracious invitations pressed upon me to come again for an extended meeting, and shall most gladly avail myself of that invitation at the earliest time that duty will allow. Meetings in a modern city like this should be continued for weeks and weeks, that the attention of the pressing throngs of people may be awakened and called to the highest things.

I would also be indulged in the expression of profoundest gratitude again to the two churches and their pastors, who have been so considerate of the visiting preacher, and to the many others outside of these two congregations, who have been so courteous and beautiful in their co-operation. How it has touched all our hearts that the great daily papers of Fort Worth have, without stint, given themselves to setting forth the great things of religion during these passing days. God bless them, I pray, and crown them with constantly increasing usefulness!

I would earnestly add this further word: Though the public meetings close this evening, yet I pray, and am very glad to believe, that the work and influence of these meetings shall go graciously and powerfully on, in lives all about you, with the days and weeks and months and years before you. The most earnest word that I can speak would I speak to these mature and older Christians. Take this occasion, as parents, and as teachers, and as neighbors, and as friends and acquaintances, to help the people all about you in the higher and better way. There are many during these days who have become Christians, through God's grace. They need to take their places with the people of God in His church. You are to counsel, cheer and help them now. I beg you to remember it. It is a tragedy for a Christian not to be in the church with the people of God. All about you there are timid, untaught, young Christians, young people who have recently made their decision for Christ. Very glad, indeed, was I to hear that numbers, a week ago to-day, took their places in the churches, and still others again this morning. So I pray that it may continue to be in the immediate future, after a noble fashion. Help the young Christian now, timid and shrinking, and greatly in need of counsel. Help that Christian, who, for one cause or another, has been bewitched away from the right path. Something came to trouble him. Something came to turn his feet away from the right road. Something came, maybe, to make his heart bitter. Something came to raise questions that have perplexed and hurt the heart. Oh, now, I pray you, my fellow Christians, help that Christian!

And then, there are all about you undecided men and women, and young people, who have come near the kingdom these days. That expression of Christ, I have no doubt, applies to many of them: "Notwithstanding, be sure of this, that the kingdom of God has come nigh unto you." These hesitating ones need your best help—the boy, the girl, the young man or woman, the father, the mother, the citizen, the neighbor, all about you. The right word needs to be said now, and said in the right temper, that these may see how sane it is, how wise it is, how glorious it is, to be friends and followers of Christ.

THE PASSING OF RELIGIOUS OPPORTUNITY.

Text: "And when He was come near, He beheld the city, and wept over it, saying, If thou hadst known, even thou, at least in this thy day, the things which belong unto thy peace! but now they are hid from thine eyes."—Luke 19: 41, 42.

And now, as I come to the message of this evening, and look over this vast throng, I find my heart touched with the most compassionate interest for the people. There is nothing in the world that so appeals to me as a human face. And what a vast press of faces look up into my face in this gathering of thousands of people. Oh, how I covet you every one for Christ Jesus! What tragedy is comparable to the tragedy of a wasted life! Jesus not only would save the soul, bringing you home to heaven at last— Jesus would save your life here and now, in the flesh, in the earth, and have you positionized properly now. I lift up my voice to beg you, for your own sake, oh, soul, not yet openly positionized for Christ, and then for the sake of lives you shall daily touch, to give heed and face faithfully this biggest question of all—your own right relation to Christ Jesus. I would speak this evening on this ex-ceedingly solemn theme: "The Passing of Religious Op-portunity." It is suggested by this solemn text, from the nineteenth chapter of Luke: "And when He was come near, He beheld the city"—the city of Jerusalem—"and wept over it, saying, If thou hadst known"—or if thou hadst recognized — "the things which belong unto thy peace! but now they are hid from thine eyes."

The text suggests the solemn word that I am to leave with you—the passing of religious opportunity. Tears are always touching—genuine and sincere tears. You are of a strange make-up if you should see the genuine tears of a little child, and not be moved by that sight. And how moving is the sight of the tears of a strong man, no matter what the emotion that grips the heart! Here in our text we have a picture of the Savior, our Divine Lord, sobbing out His great heart, as He looks over the city, His own country's fair city, the city of Jerusalem. There must have been a compelling reason why Jesus thus wept, as He looked over the city. There was such a reason, and the text, with its context, faithfully indicates what that reason was. The reason was that many of the people in that city of Jerusalem had allowed their religious opportunity to go by unimproved. They had neglected it. The things of light and leading and love from God had all been over-looked. Jesus had taught and had called, but they had gone on unheeding, and so His compassionate heart over-flowed through His eyes, and we have here the picture of Him sobbing over the fact of the passing of religious opportunity. Isn't that a fearful possibility in a human life, that religious opportunity, gracious and precious, may come and may go by, and may be returnless forevermore? Satan does not care if men and women come to the house of God, and to public services such as these, and are at-tentive and serious and deeply moved, if only they will let the religious opportunity pass, and be unimproved. Oh, dreadful possibility, that religious opportunity may come and pass by, and the highest things of the soul be lost and forfeited forever!

Jesus, who visited the earth once in the flesh, visits men and women yet, not in His flesh, as of old, but in the person and by the power of His own Divine Spirit. He himself told us that when He went away He would send that Spirit, to teach of the things that He said and says, and show them to the children of men. Jesus says: "It is expedient for you that I go away; for if I go not away, the Comforter will not come unto you; but if I depart, I will send Him unto you. And when He is come, He will reprove the world of sin, and of righteousness, and of judgment." The great work of God the Holy Spirit in the world is to comfort and counsel God's people, and to bring to bear conviction upon the human judgment and conscience, that by such light and conviction sinners may be turned into the upper and better way.

Mark you this, my men and women! Every inclination that the soul has to come to God, every longing in your spirit to be right with God, and to be forgiven of Him, and to be saved by Him, is the direct drawing, the direct work, of God's good Spirit on the human heart. The desire to be right with God does not come from the human flesh. The desire to be right with God, to have one's sins forgiven, to be saved, is the direct drawing of the good Spirit of God himself. And remember this, I pray you, that no rational soul shall ever come to God unless the Divine Spirit shall draw him, shall counsel him, shall convict him of need, and shall himself work that desire to come in the human heart. Jesus yet visits men in the person and power of His Spirit. How does He visit them? He comes in early life probably to most people, with the call of heaven, the call of grace, the call of salvation. One of the serious questions for parents and teachers is, How early do our children reach the age of personal accountability, and when do they reach the line of accountability, so that they must personally pass on these questions of right and wrong, of God's light and counsel? Where and when do they reach that line? Blessed is the teaching that our little ones, dying before they reach that line of personal accountability to God, are taken to His home above, through the riches of His own mercy and grace. We are not anxious about our little ones who die before they can personally pass on these big questions of repentance and faith and coming to God. All is well with them. Ye parents, be not disturbed at that point. Our concern is, How old are children when they reach the line of personal accountability, where, if they die unrepentant and unbelieving, they shall die like the adult who dies unrepentant and unbelieving? Very early in life, evidently, God's Spirit comes to many of our children, counseling and calling them in the better and upper way.

And then very many are the ways which God employs to counsel and call men and women into the upward way. One of God's mightiest ways is to call the people by the right kind of preaching. There can be no substitutes for the right kind of preaching. The Bible tells us so. "Faith cometh by hearing, and hearing by the Word of God. How shall the people hear without a preacher?" The Bible tells us that "it pleased God by the foolishness of preaching to save them that believe." He did not say "by foolish preaching." There is untold harm done by foolish preaching. He said: "It pleased God by the foolishness of preaching"—by as simple a thing as preaching, by the method of preaching, by a man saved by grace as I am saved, and as these honored men about me are saved, and called by God's Spirit thus to witness for Christ. It pleased God by as simple a thing as this, for a man saved by God's grace and set apart by His Spirit to be a preacher, to stand up and call to his fellow-men: "Ho, every one that thirsteth, come ye to the waters, and he that hath no money; come ye, buy and eat; yea, come, buy wine and milk without money and without price." How marvelous is God's way of turning men and women into the upward way, by preaching!

But preaching is not His only method. God has many methods to call the people into the upward way! How great is the message and the blessing of the right kind of a teacher, and the right kind of a writer! How much God employs such to bless the world! And how marvelous is God's employment of the modest mother, shrinking and timid, but who puts the serious things of God and His truth into the deepest hearts of her little ones who rest on her breast, and who kneel beside her, as she teaches them to lisp the name of Jesus! How marvelous that instrumentality, the instrumentality of the parent, to bring people in the right way! How marvelous the instrumentality of the friend, who goes out in the right spirit and seeks to turn his friend into the upward way! How God blesses a simple thing like that! How marvelous are God's providences, some of them white-robed, and some of them veiled in black, to turn us and bestir us, and give us to think, and, thinking, to turn to the upward way! And above all and through all, how wonderful is the work of Christ's great witness in the world, namely, the Holy Spirit, as this Holy Spirit takes of the things of Christ, and brings them to bear on men's minds, and consciences. Many are God's messengers for the calling of the people unto himself.

Now, our text points for us, to-night, the exceedingly

solemn truth that the visits of God, in the person of the Divine Spirit, may be resisted. In the case of these men and women of old, in the city of Jerusalem, where Jesus lived and loved, where He preached and prayed, where He wept and died, there many resisted His heavenly influences, and put them all away, and went the downward way. So we are confronted to-night with that awful possibility in human life, that a rational, responsible, human being can say yes or say no to the call of God. The highest dignity of human life is that human life must choose whether you will be for God or against Him. Along with that highest dignity of human life, in which you are allowed to say yes or no to God, and consequent upon it at the same time is the very gravest danger. While you and I may say yes or say no to Jesus, the awful peril is that, though He brings to bear in His own multiform and wonderful way His light and love, His counsel and goodness, summoning us to come the right road—the fearful possibility is that we will rise up and resist it all, and miss the upward way. One thing is sure: God the loving Father is never at fault that a sinner is lost. Listen to His solemn appeal: "As I live"—and He swears by himself, for He can swear by no higher—"as I live, saith the Lord God, I have no pleasure in the death of the wicked; but that the wicked turn from his way and live." And then God himself exhorts: "Turn ye! Turn ye! Why will ye die?"

It is, indeed, inflexibly certain that Jesus is never at fault that a sinner is lost. See Him here in our text, as He stands weeping over the city of Jerusalem, in which were many people who had turned aside His counsel and missed the road to heaven, and listen to Him as He says: "Oh, Jerusalem, Jerusalem, how often would I have gathered thy children together, as a hen doth gather her brood under her wings, and ye would not! Behold, your house is left unto you desolate." Jesus is never at fault that a soul rational and responsible misses the way of light and life and salvation.

But our text brings us on to a still more serious truth, and that truth is that there is an end to God's visits to rational, accountable human beings. When does such end come? I shall make answer to that in two remarks. Mark it, I pray you, oh, my fellow-men and my gentle sisters, listening so deferentially to what the minister says—mark it well. If you should go down into your grave, unrepentant and unbelieving, the battle for your soul is forever lost. Destiny eternal is settled this side of death. "As the tree falls, so shall it lie." Jesus finally turned upon some men who carped and caviled at His words, and said: "Ye shall die in your sins." That will be the outcome of it all. And then He added: "Whither I go, ye cannot come." Destiny for the soul is determined this side the grave. Christ's words have no meaning, if that is not correct, and the man is a trifler, a trickster with words, if he should essay to offer a rational human soul hope beyond the grave, if such man shall die in his sins. This side the grave is determined the big question of whether heaven is to be your home, or whether it is to be the dark world of waste and night, the name of which is hell. Your destiny for the one or the other place will be decided before you reach death and are laid in the grave. Oh, how serious is that! And since death comes with unexpectedness, times without count, and since there are ten thousand gates to death, and since the easiest thing in all the world is just to die, and since the coming of death is more uncertain than the morning cloud, and since death is transitory and illusory, and the time of its coming is known only to God, how speedily should every rational human being say: "While I have my wits about me, while my mind is clear, while duty comes knocking at the door of my heart, while need is urgent, while danger is consciously imminent and apparent, now I will decide the biggest question of all, calmly and gloriously, by making my surrender to Christ."

I was preaching in a distant community some months ago, to a throng of thousands, like these thousands here to-night, and one man was seen to be greatly interested, and an earnest Christian standing near him went over to him, and ventured to whisper a word to him, while the last song was being sung. Men and women and children came down the aisles, saying: "The battle is decided. We will surrender to Christ." This Christian man said to the interested man: "You are interested and serious now; you should now end all delay, and publicly make known your surrender to Christ." He said: "No, I will see that man to-morrow. I will talk with him to-morrow. I will find him at his room in the hotel to-morrow, and I will have it out with him. I will not settle it to-night." But when the morning came, in one sharp stroke, with a strange turning that often comes to human life, he was plunged into unconsciousness, and before noonday went away into eternity. Oh, rational, responsible human beings, I summon you, I charge you, I pray you, settle first things first, the supreme things, the one supreme thing, in the day of your health, with your wits about you, calmly, quietly, thoughtfully, grandly, settle this supreme matter while you may.

There is the other answer to be given to the fact that there is an end to God's visits to men. Jesus was looking over a city which He had sought to help, but many had failed of His help, and Jesus was sobbing out His heart, as in effect He said: "Light is gone and opportunity has passed." They were yet alive, and were yet in health. They went about their tasks. But Jesus said: "Religious opportunity, that came, and was clear and strong, has been refused, and now it passes." Opportunity of any sort pauses at one's door, but if that opportunity be not taken hold of, it passes and is returnless. "The mill will never grind again with water that has passed." These men and women had heard and had seen and had felt and had known, and they put away the great claims and counsels of Jesus; which leads me to say that my judgment is fixed deeply from an experience of twenty-odd years in dealing with men and in studying the Word of God, that there is no peril comparable to the peril of resisting religious light and opportunity when they come to the human soul.

And when opportunity passes, how fearful is the fate of such soul! And when it does pass, how is that fearful tragedy brought about? The trouble about dealing lightly with religious opportunity and religious light and religious privilege is that men and women in thus dealing lightly, sin against knowledge. If the religion of Jesus Christ be worth a straw, it is worth more than the material world. One soul outranks in value the material universe. Now, to deal lightly with the call of Jesus and the death of Jesus for such soul, is to sin after a most terrible fashion. Men hear and feel and intend and know, and yet put religious calls away, and consequently go the downward way.

Nor is that all. Men who resist God's call and counsel, sin presumptuously. When they are spoken with candidly and faithfully about the great claims of Christ, they make answer: "Yes, I grant it all, but I will risk it. I will presume. I will wait. I will defer. I will delay." And they loiter on until the little boat takes the fateful plunge over the rapids, and opportunity is forfeited forever.

Moreover, when men thus sin against light, they sin with the will. The human will is the initial spring of action. Men hear and know and feel and intend and desire, and yet they delay. They sin against the will, and that involves premeditation and decision. Men hear Christ's call, and their judgments and consciences and moral natures say yes. But they go on and say: "Not yet. I will not have Christ to reign over me yet." They go on and say, like one of old said: "Go thy way for this time. When I have a convenient season I will call for thee." And in that way light darkens, and convictions fade, and religious opportunity passes.

Still again, when men sin against God's clear call to repentance and faith, they sin against God's Spirit, who takes of these great truths and binds them on men's judgments and consciences. When men rise up and say: "Though I know it is right, and though I feel its weight and power, yet I will put it all away," men are sinning against God's great messenger, even God's Holy Spirit, who is wooing and counseling and convicting and drawing, that the people may come to Christ and be saved. And this Divine Spirit, in His wooing power, is God's first, last and supreme messenger to turn the world to Christ Jesus. If men sin against God the loving Father, as they do, there is Jesus, the offered Savior, who is men's proffered

helper, if they will only have Him. If men put Jesus away,
the Holy Spirit patiently calls and counsels and woos, and
they feel it and know it, that God is striving with them.
If men put this Holy Spirit away and say: "I put light
and duty and God's call out of my thoughts," by such definite resolve and effort, they are sinning against God's last
great court, His Holy Spirit, who would turn sinful men
and women toward the Father's house of light and love
and life. And just there is the peril of all perils. Oh,
there is no peril like the peril of the human soul which
feels and says: "I ought to follow Christ, but I will not
now!" There is no peril so serious as that.

Years ago I was preaching in one of our cities on that
solemn text: "Ye do always resist the Holy Spirit," and
I was making the point that a man may so resist light
and counsel from God, that light will at last turn to darkness; that a man may so trifle with conviction of a course
that he ought to take, until the conviction gets fainter and
feebler, and at last he seems to have no conviction at all.
I was making the point that somewhere in its fight against
God, the human soul may put away these highest matters,
until at last they seem to have no weight, no meaning, no
appeal at all. And no sooner had I said that, than a man
in the audience, perhaps forty-five years of age, with the
gray beginning to tinge his hair, stood in the audience and
said: "Preacher man, you are describing my case." I said:
"Not consciously; I do not even know you; I am discussing
the Word of God." "Very well," he said, "but that is my
case; you are describing my case, and if you do not mind,"
he said, "I will tell you a little about it." I said: "I will be
pleased to let you tell us. Maybe we can help you. I want
to, if I can." He said: "Years ago, when I was a young
man, I had often heard and felt, concerning religion; I had
often been counseled and called, I had often trembled and
resolved, but I kept putting the matter off. I kept saying:
'To-morrow.' I kept saying: 'By and by.' And at last,
there came a powerful appeal from God's man one day,
where all of my mind and conscience and heart and will
were aroused beyond words, and I felt: 'This is the supreme crisis. This is the hour epochal for my soul.' Other

men went down the aisles to make known their surrender
to Christ, but I held out against it all, and by and by I
summoned myself and said, down in my soul: 'I will not
follow God until it suits me. It does not suit me at all
just now, and I will put it off,' though I trembled through
it all, like the aspen leaf." And then he looked at me
sadly a moment or two and said: "Preacher man, that
day I went over the line. That day I passed the day of
grace. That day my soul died, and your teaching as to
the peril there is in resisting God's Spirit applies, sir, to
my own poor case." Quickly did I adjourn the service,
and then I sought him out, and for two long hours I
brought to bear, as best I could, the glorious invitations
of Jesus to sinful men, no matter what their sin or doubt
or fear or difficulty. For two hours, I brought to bear
these promises and calls of Jesus on this man, and yet he
heard me through it all, and said: "Sir, I have had no
response at all for years. I have crossed the line, and I
know that I have crossed it."

I cannot discuss the philosophy, the psychology, the
deep meaning of this case. I do not know it. I am simply
making the point that somewhere the human soul may
resist God and His love and light and heavenly leading,
so late, so far, so long, that light turns into darkness, and
convictions fade, and the highest things are missed and
lost. There comes again the old-time hymn, emphasizing
this same point of the danger of putting away religious
light, religious calls for the human soul, the danger of
putting them off until to-morrow. Let us ponder again
the solemn lines:

> There is a time, I know not when,
>   A place, I know not where,
> Which marks the destiny of men
>   To heaven or despair.
>
> There is a line by us not seen,
>   Which crosses every path;
> The hidden boundary between
>   God's patience and His wrath.
>
> To cross that limit is to die,
>   To die, as if by stealth.
> It may not pale the beaming eye,
>   Nor quench the glowing health.
>
> The conscience may be still at ease,
>   The spirits light and gay.

That which is pleasing still may please,
And care be thrust away.

But on that forehead God hath set
Indelibly a mark,
By man unseen, for man as yet
Is blind and in the dark.

And still the doomed man's path below
May bloom like Eden bloomed.
He did not, does not, will not know,
Nor feel that he is doomed.

He feels, he sees, that all is well,
His every fear is calmed.
He lives, he dies, he wakes in hell,
Not only doomed, but damned.

Oh, where is that mysterious bourn,
By which each path is crossed,
Beyond which God himself hath sworn
That he who goes is lost?

How long may men go on in sin,
How long will God forbear?
Where does hope end, and where begin
The confines of despair?

One answer from those skies is sent.
"Ye who from God depart,
While it is called to-day, repent,
And harden not your heart."

My fellow-men, if there be interest, if there be an awakening, if there be concern, if there be a wish, however faint, if there be a longing, however feeble and fluttering, it makes its cry in your heart, if it be there, to be right with God, to have your sins forgiven, to be saved, if I were in your place I would to-night make my surrender to Christ, if I had to go through fire and through flame to make that surrender; for if a man passes his day of grace, and when the battle for the soul is finally lost, then spiritual things, this text tells us, are hidden from the eyes of such soul and life. Jesus said: "Oh, men of Jerusalem, who have let your religious opportunity be forfeited and lost, now these religious truths and matters are hidden from your eyes." Hidden! No light now!

Have you ever been through Mammoth Cave, that wonderful, subterranean cavern yonder in Kentucky? If you have been through there, the guide has shown you fish in those subterranean waters whose eyes look like other eyes in other fish, and yet the guide goes on to tell you that these fish have been so long in the darkness of those underground waters that they cannot see at all. One awful truth stands out from the teaching of this text and many

other teachings of Jesus elsewhere in the Bible — that a
man can put away religious light so long, so late, so far,
so terribly, that at last he may not see at all.

As men fight the call and counsels and pleadings of
God for their souls, they come to the place where feeling
grows less and less with every appeal that is made. Less
and less does the heart respond, if truth is heard and felt
and granted, and yet set aside and put away. It is an
awful sentence, there in the Bible, about the conscience
being seared as with a hot iron, so that at last the human
soul reaches the place, in its conscience, where it is past
feeling. If the doctor is summoned to his patient, and
the family and the patient explain to the doctor when he
comes that the patient has no feeling in part of the body,
that part of the body being utterly unresponsive, the doctor shakes his head ominously, for that sign—no feeling—
is the precursor of serious trouble. I have been many a
time with the great-hearted cattlemen in the West—glorious, mighty men! For years I have rejoiced to be with
them in their camp-meetings, and many of them have I
seen as they yielded their lives to Jesus. No true, nobler
men have I ever met in the world than these. I have been
out there and have seen them, after the meetings and before, as they would have the cattle rounded up for brand-
ing, and I have seen them put the hot branding-iron on the
cattle, and I have heard the cattle moan and low and have
seen them flinch under that hot branding-iron. And then
the cattle are released, when the hot iron has burned the
brand, and you may go back a few weeks later, and take
that same branded place, and pick such branded place with
knife or pin, and yet the beast cares little for it now. That
branded place is now past feeling. Oh, the peril that the
human soul shall be desensitized, if a man hears and knows
and feels the call of God, but says: "I will put it all away
until some indefinite future."

It follows, my fellow-men, that the most serious thing
in this world is the resistance of the religious light that
comes to you. The most serious thing in the world is the
putting away of light and feeling when God's gospel is
preached, and the soul is sought after, and the soul hears

and trembles and feels, and yet puts it all away. That is
the most serious and presumptuous risk ever taken by
the human soul. I am coming to say a most serious closing
word, namely: There comes a last visit from God for the
human soul. When is that visit? Certainly, no man is
wise enough to know. But there comes a last visit from
God, seeking for a rational human soul. When is that
visit? Will it be this year? Will it be this month? Will
it be this week? Will God's last visit for an intelligent,
an awakened, responsive soul to come to Him, be to-night?
God alone knows. No man can tell. But when we consider
the possibilities of such startling fact, then we may well
long for our every face to be in the dust of prayer to God,
that no rational human soul in this place to-night shall be
willing to go on, when everything is at stake, and put God's
call away into some vague, indefinite hour of the indeter-
minate future!

Oh, man or woman or child, in this vast assemblage
to-night, wrong with God, I summon you, if you have any
degree of desire to be saved, I summon you, act on that desire, act on that light, and make your surrender to Christ.
Mark it! Mark it! The great issue confronts you, and
what is that issue? You have to make a choice between
Jesus and Satan. One or the other is the master of every
rational human soul. Which shall your choice be? You
must make a choice between two lives—a life on the right
side, or a life on the wrong side. Which should be your
choice? You must make a choice between two deaths—
the death of peace and triumph, because of Jesus, or the
death of waste and fearful terror, because you have put
Jesus away. Which death would you die? You must make
a choice between one of two positions, when you stand at
the judgment bar of Christ. One of two positions there
shall be yours. He will have us to pass to His right hand,
because we trusted Him here, or we will turn away to His
left hand, because we let the day of opportunity go by unimproved. Which shall your choice be? It is a choice
between one of two worlds after this world. Out yonder
is the world of love and life and peace and hope and knowledge and holiness and ever-increasing blessedness, the

name of which is heaven; and out yonder is the world of sin and waste and failure and defeat and remorse, the name of which is hell. We must here, with our wits about us, make our choice. Oh, soul, since there is so much at stake—your soul, your life, your all—ought not this most important of all matters, this Sunday night, to have your wisest choice?

And, remember, whatever may be your difficulties, Jesus is master of any case. Do you tell me: "Sir, my difficulties are terrible, beyond human speech?" I do not mind that. I am not given pause by that. Though your sins be as scarlet, if you will surrender to Christ, He will save you. Though your doubts are like the stars for number, if you will surrender to Christ, He will save you. Though your temptations are fiery with the hot breath from the pit below, if you will surrender to Christ, He will save you. Though you tell me: "Sir, I cannot see through it, I cannot understand it, I cannot reason it out, yet, sir, I want to be saved," I answer you back in a moment, that if you will surrender to Christ, saying: "Lord Jesus, I cannot see through it. I am frail, I am weak, I am unworthy, I am sinful, I am tempted and temptable, yet I will wholly give up to Christ, who died for sinners," Christ will take you and save you this very hour.

What do you say, then, about the incomparable issue? Oh, the hundreds and hundreds and hundreds of Christian men and women here, who want to join the preacher in prayer for those that are not right with God, that such may hasten to be right with God, without further risk or presumption, to be right with God—the vast army of Christians that want to join the preacher in prayer for you! I will show you that they do. Every one here, who has made definite surrender of himself to Jesus to be his Savior, and now takes up the preacher's sermon, and would pass it on to all the people who have not decided for Christ, and who also would unite with the preacher in the prayer to God that He may now be merciful to the people, every Christian that says: "That is my case, sir," lift your hand high, that the people may see you thus witness for Christ

I thank you! I believe the angels look upon it, moved in spirit, as they see it.

I have a moment more to detain you before we sing our closing hymn and go our way. I am here to ask—in this last moment, when I would give my heart's blood to help you, and God knows I speak the truth—I would give my heart's blood to help you, and am giving it right now—in this last moment, I am coming to ask every man, woman and child, a professor of religion once, a church member once, and maybe yet, but all wrong with God, and sadly drifting and backslidden, and neglecting duty, and also to ask every person not in the church, not decided, not forgiven, not saved, not a Christian, every person here who says: "I am wrong with God, and I know it; but, sir, I tell you truly that I want to be right with God before it is too late; I want to be right with God before my soul's opportunity goes by and is lost, and I want you who pray to pray that I may be right with God before it is too late;" every soul that says, "That is my desire," will now lift your hand, and we will offer our most fervent prayer for you. Oh, it is an appealing sight to see so many hands!

My brother men and gentle women, and boys and girls, settle the great matter right now, I pray you, and settle it right by being for Christ forever. I am not willing to part from you, never to meet you all again until we meet at the judgment bar of God—I am not willing to part from you without pleading, yea, beseeching that here and now every soul that says: "I have sadly drifted as a Christian; my life is marred and miserable from backslidings, but I will renew my vows to-night with God; I will come back and surrender afresh to Christ"—I am not willing to go without asking you to come and take my hand, in this public pledge of your honest surrender to Jesus.

Nor am I willing to let these men and women and children go, who are not saved, not ready to die, not ready to live, not ready for any world—I am not ready to let you go, without begging that right now you will stop and say: "I will this hour make my surrender to Christ. Here, with my heart's highest resolve, in Fort Worth, I publicly register my verdict. It is yes for Christ. Lord Jesus, to-night, through the darkness, and with all my limitations, and sins, and doubts, and hesitation, I will surrender my case to Christ. I will now register my verdict." If that is your heart's decision, come and take my hand. Oh, God of all grace, give the people to act like they ought, and as they will wish they had, when they stand before Christ at last! For His great name's sake!

They are going to sing that simple song, "Jesus is tenderly calling thee home, calling to-day, calling to-day," and the great press of people will stand in a minute, as quietly as you can stand, until we finish this singing, without any one leaving, unless you must, so that we may help in these last moments, every interested person here, to the limit of our power to help. And I am asking anew, as we sing this simple gospel song: Where is the backslidden Christian, who says: "I will register publicly my verdict; I am going to renew my vows right now with Christ, and surrender myself afresh to Him?" And where is the man, or the woman, the boy or the girl, that answers: "No; that is not my case. I never have given my verdict, never have made my surrender, but I will make it right now?" It is difficult for you to come, but I am going to ask you to do a difficult thing, and that is, to come, as difficult as it is, through this vast press of people. I am asking you to come and take my hand, and then pass back to your pew, as they sing these stanzas. Everybody will rise to sing. You will begin with that stanza, "Jesus is pleading." Isn't that true? You have heard Him to-day. "To-day, if ye will hear His voice, harden not your heart." You have heard Him. You said so, with your uplifted hand, a moment ago. Satan does not care that you now are interested, if you will only delay. He does not care, if you will just postpone your decision until some other time.

(The first and second stanzas were sung, while numbers came forward.)

Yonder, to the great Northwest, a young civil engineer went to construct a bridge across a mountain chasm, and after weeks and months, with his group of helpers, he had almost finished the bridge at the close of a certain day.

He said to his men: "Come back men, after supper, and we will finish it in about an hour, and I will pay you a day's wages for the extra hour." "No," they said, "we have made other arrangements." He said: "Come back, and I will give you two days' wages." They said: "No; but why do you urge it?" He said: "If a great storm should come down to-night on the mountains, it would sweep this unfinished bridge away. We have not quite secured the bridge." But they went their way, saying: "It won't rain in months." But the clouds were filled with rain that very night and emptied their floods upon the mountains, and the floods came down, resistless in their power, and swept the unfinished bridge utterly away. Oh, men and women, that is a parable and picture of the soul that knows and wishes, and yet presumes and delays and waits.

As I was leaving Washington City, some time ago, I stood in one of the depots there, and saw a strange mark on the wall, and I asked a policeman what it meant, and he said at once: "You are a stranger?" "Yes." "That is the death mark for President Garfield, who was standing right here when he received the bullet from the man who took his life, and this singular mark is put here on the wall to indicate the place where he met his death." Oh, to-night, I wonder if, standing there, or there, or sitting here, or somewhere under the sound of my voice — I wonder if some soul, hearing and feeling and interested, says: "Not to-day; by and by; not yet," and shall go away, and this shall be the place and the time of the death mark for your human spirit. God forbid, and I pray it from my deepest heart!

Does the man and woman say, and the child: "I am ready to burn the bridges, to cast the die, to cross the Rubicon. I am ready to cut the cables. I am ready to-night to register publicly my surrender to Christ?" Come then, as they sing earnestly this third stanza now.

(The third stanza was sung, and numbers came forward.)

These men and women who have come have done as they ought, when they pressed forward here, with the aisles thronged, even from the outskirts of the great press, and some from beyond the tent. Great sight, these numbers that have come. But not all have come. Listen!

> Why do you wait, dear brother,
> Oh, why do you tarry so long?
> Your Savior is waiting to give you
> A place in His sanctified throng.

Listen again:

> What do you hope, dear brother (or sister),
> To gain by a further delay?
> There's no one to save you but Jesus,
> There's no other way but His way.

Listen yet once again:

> Do you not feel, dear brother,
> His Spirit now striving within?
> Oh, why not accept His salvation
> And throw off thy burden of sin?

Oh, my friends, a multitude have come—strong men, gentle women, and two or three of these blessed children— a multitude! Have all the men come who ought to come? And the women? Have all the boys and girls come who ought to come? Do others say: "I am coming. I shall not simply stop with 'almost;' I will be altogether persuaded. I will act up to the light I have, to the last limit of all I know to-night? Jesus tells me, whatever my case is, my need, my doubt, my sin, my wandering, my waste, my difficulty, my temptation, if I will surrender to Him honestly, He will forgive me and save me. I will make that surrender."

(The last stanza was sung, during which still others came forward.)

You see, my Christian friends, all these people who have come forward, and you saw those who came in the Chamber of Commerce auditorium to-day, and the others who came from day to day. I beseech you to do your duty by them all. And you who have come to Christ to-night, numbers and numbers of you, go now and live for Christ. Take your place with Christ's people promptly, and be faithful members in His church. And you who have not yet come to Christ, but are almost persuaded, oh, before you give yourselves to sleep to-night, I beseech you to make the surrender of yourselves for time and eternity to the great good Savior!

Yonder on the battlefield at Gettysburg, when the awful conflict had passed, an army surgeon came back, looking for the wounded and suffering, if haply he might help them, and he saw the dead on every side. As he rode along he saw a poor fellow lying in a trench. The surgeon reined up his horse, but thought: "I need not dismount; this poor fellow is gone." And then he saw a smile play about the man's face as he lay there in the trench. The surgeon then dismounted and got down in the trench beside the dying man, and every minute or two, he said that smile would play about the dying soldier's face, and he would whisper one little word. The word was, "Here!" Presently, the army surgeon shook the man and rallied him back from the gates of death for a minute, and said: "Comrade, what do you mean by saying, 'Here?'" And the dying fellow answered: "Oh, Doctor, they are calling the roll up in heaven, and I was just answering to my name, 'Here!'"

Oh, men and women and children, with my last sentence, I beseech you, as this call comes to-night from the great Savior to you, answer Him, and say: "Lord Jesus, I decide, and receive thee as my personal Savior and Master, and by thy grace I am going from this Sunday night with thee, forever!"

THE CLOSING PRAYER.

And now, as the people go, we give God our devoutest thanks for His grace and favor upon us this hour, and on the afternoon hour, and on these recent blessed days. For all the mercies and blessings of these glorious days, we give God all the praise. Every dust of the glory shall be His. Many have found Christ these days, and have confessed Him. To God be all the praise! Others, we hope, are already trusting Him in secret, and, if so, may they speedily confess Him! May all those who have found Him be led of thee to take their places in thy church, with God's own people, to live as they ought for Him, from this June month, even until God calls them to the Father's house above. And, oh, may Christians drifting, whatever the cause, and lapsed church members, whatever the cause, be rallied now all through this vast expanding city, to Christ's cause and church and holy service. Oh, may there be a gracious visitation from Jesus to every house in all this city. May Jesus this very Sunday night visit every house, from the fairest mansion to the humblest hovel in all the city. Yea, may Jesus knock at the door of every heart in the city, bringing the breath of God's goodness and mercy to every life. And may we all be true to Him at the post where He would have us live and labor, even until the earthly day is done, and then may we go to be like Him, and to be with Him, in the Father's house above, forevermore.

And now, as the people go, may the blessing of the triune God, even of Father, Son and Holy Spirit, be granted you all and each, to bless you, and guide you, and keep you in the right way, to-day and to-morrow, and throughout God's vast beyond, forever. We pray it all in Jesus' name. Amen.